SAGE was founded in 1965 by Sara Miller McCune to support the dissemination of usable knowledge by publishing innovative and high-quality research and teaching content. Today, we publish over 900 journals, including those of more than 400 learned societies, more than 800 new books per year, and a growing range of library products including archives, data, case studies, reports, and video. SAGE remains majority-owned by our founder, and after Sara's lifetime will become owned by a charitrust that secures our continued independence.

Los Angeles | London | New Delhi | Singapore | Washington DC | Melbourne

Advance Praise

We live in exciting times. Technological advances force us to question long-held beliefs in many areas of life. This is true in the area of marketing as well.

There is no doubt that marketing has undergone a huge transformation in recent times because of the shift to digital. Today, companies must co-opt digital methods in their marketing campaigns.

But how to use digital methods poses huge challenges. For one thing, newspapers and television no longer hold audiences captive for advertising. In online interactions, the terms of engagement are not dictated by mass media but by the consumer. Nor do the earlier rules of marketing apply; today, advertising content can become viral but may contribute nothing to top-line growth. Hence, many online businesses remain 'brands without profits' as this book points out.

Today, the Internet is not just a means to reach consumers, but it has also evolved into a method of engaging and delighting them. Companies that take the position of deploying digital technology across the value chain stand to survive in the long run.

This book is a departure from most other books on the subject, which take the view that digital marketing is limited to getting views, likes or shares of content posted by companies. It takes a refreshing look at marketing in the digital era and suggests that advertisers need to go beyond vanity metrics. In that sense, it represents a major contribution to modern marketing thinking.

At Jagran Lakecity University, Bhopal, we encourage intellectual pursuits and are happy that our faculty members are contributing to research and publications. The numerous case studies in the book and the examples cited are not only interesting but also contribute to the learning of students who wish to make a career in marketing.

The book fulfils a long-standing need of marketing students and professionals to study digital marketing in terms of not just the message but also the fast-changing technological environment. I hope that it inspires readers to study the subject from the point of view of growth and profits, going beyond the reach that the Internet offers.

—**Abhishek Mohan Gupta**
Pro-chancellor, Jagran Lakecity University, Bhopal, India

It gives me great pleasure to write this word of praise for Professor Dinesh Kumar's new book *Marketing in the Digital Age*. I have known him as a colleague at the Birla Institute of Management Technology (BIMTECH), Greater Noida, and always found him passionately interested in all aspects of marketing. This interest has, earlier, translated itself into several books written by him covering marketing channels, consumer behaviour and rural marketing. His current work demystifies many of the myths surrounding digital marketing—the newest kid in the marketing block—and also its scope, limitations and the place it occupies in the modern marketer's repertoire. It goes beyond the generally accepted definition of digital marketing that focuses on merely spreading the message using digital tools. It describes how digital methods can enhance marketing and goes beyond vanity metrics of 'likes' and 'shares'.

Lucidly written, I have no hesitation in recommending it as a textbook on digital marketing for Indian business schools. Drawing on cutting-edge research from the best journals, the book is liberally littered with contemporary case studies as prefaces and endings to the different chapters, thus ensuring that the student would have ample input to thoroughly understand and digest the contents contained therein and place them in a real-world context.

The different chapters in the book look at the concepts of marketing, which are traditionally covered in marketing textbooks through a digital marketing lens and outline and suggest ways and means of integrating the digital aspect into the whole gamut of a company's marketing armoury. They culminate with the development of digital marketing strategy and a peep into the future of this fast-developing field.

I wish the author all the success and congratulate him on this much-needed new addition to the world of marketing literature.

—**Dhruva Chak**
Professor of Marketing and Chairperson, Centre for Faculty Development,
BIMTECH, Greater Noida, Former Head of the Marketing and Business
Communication Areas at BIMTECH; Former Head, Gati

For Karan, Evelyn and Alisha

Marketing in the Digital Age

Marketing in the Digital Age

Dinesh Kumar

Faculty, Jagran Lakecity University, Bhopal, India

Los Angeles | London | New Delhi
Singapore | Washington DC | Melbourne

First published in 2021 by

SAGE Publications India Pvt Ltd
B1/I-1 Mohan Cooperative Industrial Area
Mathura Road, New Delhi 110 044, India
www.sagepub.in

SAGE Publications Inc
2455 Teller Road
Thousand Oaks, California 91320, USA

SAGE Publications Ltd
1 Oliver's Yard, 55 City Road
London EC1Y 1SP, United Kingdom

SAGE Publications Asia-Pacific Pte Ltd
18 Cross Street #10-10/11/12
China Square Central
Singapore 048423

Published by Vivek Mehra for SAGE Publications India Pvt. Ltd. Typeset in 11/13 pt Goudy by Zaza Eunice, Hosur, Tamil Nadu, India.

Library of Congress Cataloging-in-Publication Data

Names: Kumar, Dinesh (Professor of marketing), author.
Title: Marketing in the digital age/Dinesh Kumar.
Description: New Delhi, India; Thousand Oaks, California: SAGE Texts,
  [2021] | Includes bibliographical references and index.
Identifiers: LCCN 2021007134 | ISBN 9789353887681 (paperback) | ISBN
  9789353887698 (epub) | ISBN 9789353887704 (ebook)
Subjects: LCSH: Internet marketing. | Marketing.
Classification: LCC HF5415.1265 .K86 2021 | DDC 658.8/72—dc23
LC record available at https://lccn.loc.gov/2021007134

ISBN: 978-93-5388-768-1 (PB)

SAGE Team: Amit Kumar, Indrani Dutta, Shruti Gupta, Aishna Bhatt and Rajinder Kaur

Detailed Contents

List of Figures

List of Tables

List of Abbreviations

3Ps	Property, path and purpose
4Ps	Product, place, promotion and price
AI	Artificial intelligence
AIDA	Awareness, interest, desire and action
AOC	Always-on consumer
AR	Augmented reality
ATL marketing	Above-the-line marketing
B2B	Business to business
B2C	Business to consumer
BIMTECH	Birla Institute of Management Technology
BTL marketing	Below-the-line marketing
C2C	Consumer to consumer
CDJ	Consumer decision journey
CEV	Customer engagement value
CIE	Customer influence effect
CIV	Customer influence value
CKV	Customer knowledge value
CLV	Customer lifetime value
COD	Cash on delivery
CPL	Cost per lead
CRM	Customer relationship management
CRV	Customer referral value
CSAT	Customer satisfaction
CX	Customer experience
DART	Dialogue, access, risk assessment and transparency
DAT	Digital Acceleration Team
E-CRM	Electronic customer relationship management
ERP	Enterprise resource planning
FMOT	First moment of truth

HR	Human resources
HUL	Hindustan Unilever Limited
IMC	Integrated marketing communication
IoT	Internet of things
IT	Information technology
JIT	Just in time
KKT	Kan Khajura Tesan
KPI	Key performance indicator
LSI	Latent semantic indexing
MOT	Moments of truth
MQL	Marketing qualified lead
OCSE	Online customer service experience
OVP	Online value proposition
P&G	Procter & Gamble
PDAs	Personal digital assistants
PESO	Paid, earned, shared and owned
PPC	Pay-per-click
PR	Public relations
ROI	Return on investment
SAVE	Solution, access, value and education
SCRM	Social customer relationship management
SEO	Search engine optimization
SI	Stickiness index
SMOT	Second moment of truth
SQO	Sales qualified opportunity
TMOT	Third moment of truth
TTL marketing	Through-the-line marketing
TV	Television
UX	User experience
VOC	Voice of the customer
WOM	Word of mouth
ZMOT	Zero moment of truth

Foreword

When I studied for my marketing qualifications in the 1980s, digital marketing did not exist. Even by the mid-1990s, when I was the marketing and public relations manager for a headwear manufacturer, we had one desk computer for 15 of us; we used fax machines to communicate with suppliers and clients; and my secretary was struggling to use a word processor rather than a manual typewriter. I bought my first mobile phone in 1993, costing me £15 for 15 minutes of phone calls a month. It had no text or Internet options. Businesses were beginning to use email, but it was not used significantly for personal use. The World Wide Web opened to the public in August 1991—less than 30 years ago. Text messaging started to become commonplace in the late 1990s when people could start to text across the various phone networks. It was only as we moved into the 21st century that social media began to expand.

And how things have changed over the past 20 years!

Digital technology has impacted nearly every aspect of our lives. Communications have never been so rapid and 24/7. As a result, the world has become smaller, and consumers can and do buy from retailers from across the globe. This week alone, from my sitting room in England, I have purchased flowers for my aunt in the USA, ordered items from China, provided services to a client in Nepal and received a gift from a local supplier, which was ordered by a friend in America. Buyers are better informed of options and can easily compare prices of suppliers. The decision-making process has become faster, as has the diffusion of innovation. Product life cycles are often much shorter. This has implications not just for marketing but also for manufacturing and logistics. Additionally, we now have many more tools available to us as marketers. We have data analytics that I could only dream of 30 years ago. Most marketing courses incorporate significant elements of digital marketing. Like data analytics, customer experience and web design have become major elements of marketing; it is not surprising that many people coming into marketing now have information technology and computing skills rather than business and marketing. Dr Kumar's book will be of use to these technical specialists who require an understanding of marketing just as much as it will support students studying digital marketing.

I have 25 years' experience in higher education, most recently as a dean of a UK business school and principal of a higher education college in London. Currently, I am the vice chair of the Chartered Institute of Marketing. I am passionate about ensuring that the marketing curriculum is fit for purpose and keeps up with the needs of employers. I am always seeking textbooks that marry theory and practice. *Marketing in the Digital Age* achieves this through the extensive use of case studies within each chapter.

I have had a longstanding relationship with Jagran Lakecity University, Bhopal, for many years, having taught there several times when I was an associate dean at Leeds Beckett University in England. I recently had the privilege of meeting Dr Dinesh Kumar when I contributed to the International Igniting Minds Lecture series at the university in October 2020. It is clear that Dr Kumar is extremely knowledgeable and passionate about digital marketing and ensuring that students can apply theory to practice.

There should be no division between digital marketing and traditional marketing. Each should embrace the other. Yet, many existing digital marketing textbooks focus on social media with little or no appreciation of marketing strategy and key marketing principles such as new product development or pricing strategies. Digital marketers do, themselves, no favours with this myopic viewpoint. Dr Kumar successfully articulates how the mainstays of traditional marketing, like the marketing mix, can be reinterpreted from a digital perspective to enhance an organization's marketing initiatives. Right from the start, Dr Kumar makes it clear that digital marketing is not just about social media which is just one element of the marketing communications mix (and which itself is one element of the marketing mix). This book describes how traditional methods are evolving to remain relevant in the digital era.

Dr Kumar comprehensively addresses the main elements of digital marketing within this book from strategy and branding to the digital marketing tools and techniques. He considers how businesses can add value through the use of a virtual value chain and also discusses the ethical issue surrounding the collection, storage and use of data. This data enables businesses to understand, segment, target and engage with customers in a way that was not possible 20 years ago. As marketers, we need to be fully aware that data collection, the use of AI and location-based technology, with powerful tools, create new and complex ethical issues that we need to address, in particular, in relation to privacy. My own research has shown that many consumers are prepared to give away their privacy in exchange for short-term convenience and rewards. We need to not only educate the consumer regarding ethical issues but also adhere to ethical standards in our handling of such personal and personalized data. One of the unique attributes of digital marketing is its ability to be measured in an almost real-time environment, enabling tweaks to be made to the execution of the strategy without significant cost. While I am always excited by the amount of rich customer data we can gather and analyse, what really excites me is the power and potential of co-creation and online communities.

I am writing this foreword from the UK on the eve of coming out of a second lockdown due to COVID-19. The pandemic has accelerated changes in consumer behaviour that were happening anyway; we live in an ever-increasing digital world that we have all had to adapt to over the last year. In the past week, two major clothing retail chains in the UK have gone into liquidation, in part, for not embracing digital commerce sufficiently. As bricks-and-mortar retails suffer, online sales have rocketed, and it is those businesses that have embraced digital that are succeeding. Digital is here to stay. It is not a gimmick or an add-on to any business proposition but a core element of any business strategy. Whether you are a student or in business, I recommend Dr Kumar's book to you.

—**June Dennis**
BSc (Honours), MBA (Distance), Post Graduate Diploma in Management,
Fellow of the Chartered Institute of Marketing, Fellow of the Higher Education
Academy, Chartered Marketer, Managing Consultant, Mountain Top Perspective,
Vice Chair, Chartered Institute of Marketing, UK

Preface

The marketing manager of a company was describing his latest online campaign to me.

'We've had a million views,' he told me, 'It has been very successful.'

'How many conversions to buying customers or how much money did the company make?' I asked.

Answers to such questions are difficult to get. This is because, today, many companies are more focused on advertising on the Internet rather than using it for marketing, which brings me to the question: 'Is the purpose of marketing to post videos that become popular or is it for the revenue growth?'

This textbook is a result of raising this question with marketing practitioners and students. While they answer in favour of revenues, many start-ups and even large companies are focused on the popularity of the message. It is hardly a wonder that many popular online brands do not make money at all, while others just fade away.

When it comes to marketing in the modern era, digital methods dominate popular thought. It is commonly believed that all marketing will shift online because most customers are there. This belief hides many realities.

I remember reading an analysis 20 years back by a consultancy firm which said that marketing and advertising would move online, and that mass media would die away in a few years. Many writers had predicted the demise of television and newspapers. It certainly seemed plausible, but it has not turned out like that—even today, Internet advertising remains at about 20 per cent of the total advertising spend in the country (Chapter 1). Although mass media has declined, television, newspapers and outdoors are still used for advertising, even by the Internet-only companies. A major share of advertising still goes into traditional marketing channels.

At the same time, according to digital media experts, marketing today consists of posting content and messages that can be delivered to millions of mobile devices. Platforms such as Facebook and Instagram have millions of users and are projected as a captive audience keen to receive advertising messages. Marketing, therefore, can be done today by sitting in front of a laptop, clicking on boxes to select attributes of the target audience and posting content on such platforms. If only things were that simple.

The fact remains that while online presence works for celebrities and entertainers, brands have to work very hard to get the attention of viewers. A message cleverly crafted and posted online may gather many likes and views but may fail to contribute anything to marketing objectives. For one thing, click-through rates and conversion rates remain dismally low. This leads to the second truth of marketing; that is, the cost of online customer acquisition, when calculated over the sales funnel, is extremely high even though the rates look very little at first. In any case, looking at digital marketing through the narrow lens of delivering, advertising messages ignore the enormous capabilities that the new technology brings to marketing. Today, customer experience can be transformed across the value chain by digital technology (Chapter 2).

Yet, most efforts at digital marketing are still limited to 'advertising delivered through digital channels'. Digital marketing courses teach how to get the message to personal devices and get a high rank in search engines. New methods are used to push messages under people's noses as they use their mobile devices. Ads pop up and stay on screens to make sure they are seen, bypassing ad blockers.

For the most part, they remain irritating interruptions. Users learn to bypass ads or ignore them altogether. Mere online presence is not enough, and business models tend to ignore the very high cost-driving traffic converting into revenue, as this book shows.

Further, the digital divide makes it difficult to reach audiences. If we add an Internet penetration rate in India of 50 per cent in 2020, any online strategy, even today, ignores half of the country's population. Online brand building has indeed become a challenge (Chapter 7).

Digital marketing moves from one fad to another. While earlier it converted thought of the Internet as a media channel or information provider, today it is seen as an engagement channel using the power of social media. This leads to an emerging viewpoint that Buehler articulates in his book, *The Digital Delusion*: Is the efficacy of digital methods overrated, pushed by the Internet giants who stand to gain from it? Have companies been deluded into thinking that the online world is the next gold rush?

Using social media means stepping in a minefield. Harmless ads become the target of trolls, and hashtags quickly appear to boycott one company or another (Chapter 10). Companies are worried that their ads will appear next to hateful or polarizing content. This just shows that digital marketing is not just about posting brand content that people will like.

This book cuts through the clutter. It shows that marketing in the digital era is much more than the mere spreading of the message. Digital technologies can do so much more when they are used to enhance. It takes the view that companies should use it as a powerful technology that can transform business models and value chains. The true power of the Internet lies in using technology to transform companies, as this book amply illustrates.

ABOUT THE BOOK

While writing this book, I kept in mind a number of things. Readers will notice that the book meets the requirements of course syllabi of most institutes teaching the subject. Concepts are explained with the help of numerous examples.

Many teachers have expressed the need for a book that contains activities so as to engage students in their classes. Keeping this in view, each chapter includes exhibits with 'marketing insights', which can be a great source of discussions in the class. Students can give their own opinion on questions raised after each insight. Each chapter has several case studies, including an opening and closing case study. Cases of well-known companies have been included so that students can relate to them. The cases are written in a crisp and explanatory style and lead to important questions. The questions in the opening case study provide a direction to the reader to focus on certain aspects while reading the chapter, while the questions in the closing case study help revise the concepts.

Each chapter also has short and long questions, along with projects that the students can take up. These can be used by the instructor to involve them in interesting activities. The book can be used in a participatory manner that encourages a two-way communication in the classroom.

Some of the important features of the book are highlighted here:

- **Easy-to-read style:** The book has been written in an easy-to-read style to keep students interested. Several exercises and discussion points can make learning a highly interactive learning process.
- **Syllabi requirements:** The chapters meet the syllabi requirements of most business schools. They aim to build an understanding of key issues and concepts.
- **Real-life cases:** Students learn more from real-life cases rather than hypothetical ones. The book contains interesting cases throughout. Each chapter has an opening and closing case, apart from exhibits of marketing insights. Students can relate to the companies discussed and check out the latest developments in them.
- **Critical approach:** The book takes a critical approach to concepts and theories. It draws from real-life applications of marketing. This approach helps students learn for themselves by engaging in discussion and sharing of views.
- **Research from the best journals:** Research from the best journals has been used to write this book. Readers can refer to the research for further insights.

Marketing in the Digital Age is a result of questioning how marketing and selling can be transformed by new technologies. I hope that it helps students understand the importance of a digital strategy (Chapter 8). Marketing professionals also have to understand changing consumer behaviour and customer relationship management (Chapters 3 and 4).

ACKNOWLEDGEMENTS

Writing this book has been a rewarding experience. I would like to thank the people who have been a constant support to me. I would like to thank Shri Hari Mohan Gupta, Chancellor, Jagran Lakecity University, who has been a constant source of inspiration. I would also like to thank Shri Abhishek Mohan Gupta, Pro-Chancellor, Jagran Lakecity University, for his unflinching support.

My family has been lifelong support in my endeavours, and I would like to thank Dr Punam Gupta, my wife, for always being helpful. I would also like to thank my son, Dr Karan Gupta, and his wife, Evelyn, for helping me with insights from across the globe.

Any effort is enhanced by insights from its users. I eagerly look forward to receiving your valuable comments and suggestions for further improvement to the book. My email is mmindchd@gmail.com, and I look forward to hearing from you.

About the Author

Dinesh Kumar (PhD) is an Associate Professor at Jagran Lakecity University, Bhopal. He has corporate experience of over 15 years, after which he switched to teaching in 1995. He has taught at leading business schools in India, including BIMTECH; FORE School of Management; Amity Global Business School, Mohali; and University Business School, Panjab University, Chandigarh. He has travelled widely and has written extensively on sustainable development, environment and social marketing. He is the author of four major books on marketing, including *Marketing Channels* (2012), *Consumer Behaviour* (2015), *The Connected Consumer* (2015) and *Rural Marketing* (2017), which was published by SAGE.

CHAPTER 1

Traditional Digital Marketing

Learning Objectives

Digital marketing has changed the way business is done. It has impacted marketing in a very big way. This book lays the foundation of the new marketing, which rests on the integration of online and traditional channels.

After reading this chapter, you will be able to learn about the following:

☐ Importance of aligning digital with marketing objectives

☐ Evolution of digital marketing and how it has impacted marketing thought

☐ Internet marketing mix: Product, place, promotion and price (4Ps) to solution, access, value and education (SAVE)

☐ Nature of the new media: Paid, earned, shared and owned media (PESO)

OPENING CASE

USING DIGITAL TECHNIQUES: REACHING UNREACHABLE CONSUMERS

Many managers and companies have the mistaken belief that digital marketing consists of reaching and engaging customers through social media, online ads and content. This book takes the view that digital technologies have much greater power than that. This case study describes some extremely creative approaches to reach their customers.

The real efficacy of digital methods is in expanding the customer base, and India has a very large population of underserved customers. These customers live in small towns and villages, consisting of two-thirds of the population or more than 900 million people. Many of these villages are out of coverage areas of traditional media and are called 'media dark'. Technology has been used to reach these consumers, and in the process, the companies have expanded the reach and scope of digital methods.

(Continued)

(Continued)

Colgate's Use of Location-based Technology

Colgate decided to use the Maha Kumbh Mela to reach rural customers and to tell them about the importance of oral hygiene and benefits of using toothpaste. The company, thus, expanded its market and increased toothpaste penetration in rural India.

It did so using mobile and location-based technologies. The company tied up with the telecom company Airtel, which generated an automated call to the cell phone the moment any visitor entered within 3 km–5 km radius of the Maha Kumbh Mela area. Airtel customers or those roaming on the Airtel network could, thus, be targeted the moment they entered the virtual circle around the mela area. The call consisted of a message from the immediately identifiable voice of Ameen Sayani, the legendary Indian radio personality. Users were told to visit the Colgate stall and collect free samples and win prizes. It was the first campaign of its kind in India.

The campaign was highly effective; foot traffic to the Colgate booth reportedly increased by over 300 per cent as compared to the pre-promotion period. The campaign covered over 700,000 visitors. It showed that digital marketing methods go much beyond using the Internet to reach customers. Reaching underserved customers in rural India shows that technologies can be used in many different and innovative ways.

Hindustan Unilever Limited's (HUL) Entertainment on Demand

Another innovative use of technology to reach customers was shown by the consumer goods company, HUL. The company developed its own communication channel to reach difficult-to-reach consumers in rural areas. Using completely out-of-the-box thinking, the company developed a free radio-on-demand service called the Kan Khajura Tesan (KKT). The name derives from a rustic phrase meaning 'worm in the ear'.

This is how it works: A mobile phone user gives a missed call to the number 180030000123 to immediately get a return call that plays a mix of entertainment and advertisements for 15 minutes. The tagline of the station is 'Missed call lagao, muft manoranjan pao' (give a missed call, get free entertainment). The free and on-demand entertainment mobile radio channel is the first such initiative in India. Launched in October 2013 in Bihar and Jharkhand, the service was expanded in 2014 across many states in India and can be accessed from anywhere.

The channel has become very popular in a short period of time. It is already the largest radio station in Bihar in terms of subscribers and shows the phenomenal reach of digital methods. Since FM stations do not cover many villages, it has found acceptability in villages where other media channels do not exist. In villages across India, people regularly listen to movie songs, dialogues, radio jockey talk, jokes and other entertainment on their mobile phones, reports *The Economic Times* (2014).

The advantage is that the company collects user data through this channel and is able to generate user profiles which are used to plan customized strategies for its brands. The usage of the channel is tracked through a live dashboard, which shows data about users and their location. The dashboard shows the number of ad impressions for its various brands. The phone number for the channel can be found on product packs and communicated through banners outside stores (Figure 1.1).

FIGURE 1.1 *The Ad for KKT*

Source: https://brandequity.economictimes.indiatimes.com/news/marketing/hul-opens-up-kan-khajura-tesan-to-advertisers/47824652 (accessed on 21 January 2021).

KKT has more than 35 million subscribers and interacts with about 0.1 million consumers every day. These initiatives show that digital marketing is not limited to the Internet or social media but goes much beyond that. More importantly, it shows that digital marketing must be used as part of meeting larger marketing objectives, which is the theme of this book.

While reading this chapter, try to answer the following questions:

1. How can marketing benefit by using digital methods?
2. Is there a difference between traditional and digital marketing? Are they distinct? How can these differences be used for marketing?
3. How has digital marketing evolved over the years?
4. How has consumer decision-making changed over the years?

Sources

Gangal, A. 2014. 'Kan Khajura Tesan: The Full Story.' afaqs. Available at: http://www.afaqs.com/news/story/41226_Kan-Khajura-Tesan-The-Full-Story (accessed on 21 January 2021).
http://www.kankhajuratesan.com/ (accessed on 21 January 2021).
HUL website: https://www.hul.co.in/news/news-and-features/2014/kan-khajura-tesan-sets-world-record.html (accessed on 21 January 2021).
Irani, D. 2015. 'HUL Plans to Let Other Firms Use Its Mobile Marketing Channel Kan Khajura Tesan.' *The Economic Times.* Available at: https://economictimes.indiatimes.com/industry/cons-products/fmcg/hul-plans-to-let-other-firms-use-its-mobile-marketing-channel-kan-khajura-tesan/articleshow/47823037.cms?from=mdr (accessed on 21 January 2021).

(Continued)

(Continued)

Kumar, D., and P. Gupta. 2017. *Rural Marketing: Challenges and Opportunities.* New Delhi: SAGE Publications.

Malviya, S. 2014. 'Hindustan Unilever Runs Bihar's Most Popular Radio on Mobile Phones.' *The Economic Times.* Available at: https://economictimes.indiatimes.com/industry/media/entertainment/hindustan-unilever-runs-bihars-most-popular-radio-on-mobile-phones/articleshow/31361073.cms (accessed on 21 January 2021).

■ INTRODUCTION

Digital methods help marketing in a variety of ways. Digital technologies are deployed widely across industries and across functions to create value for the customer. Many companies have indeed used such methods very effectively. The number of transactions on the Internet and their volumes have increased manifold over the years. With the spread of the coronavirus, digital marketing will only expand further. Demands for contactless retail and safe buying options will further fuel digital innovations in the way business is done in the future.

Digital marketing, however, suffers from the hype that is created around it. Thousands of consultants have been telling us that traditional marketing is dead (Lee 2012). Digital marketing courses abound on the Internet. The hype is fuelled by Internet giants who stand to gain from the digital shift. However, the expectations have turned into a bubble several times (Chapter 5). When the bubble bursts—as it has several times—there is widespread disappointment and sorrow as dreams crash. Companies make huge investments following digital fads—like early investments in customer relationship management (CRM) software—but have to silently write off those investments after a few years.

Indeed, although people generally believe that digital marketing will dominate in the future, many companies still struggle to find the ways that digital marketing can go beyond generating likes and shares of digital content. New companies and apps depend on venture capital to sustain themselves and flounder when the capital dries up. Others have spent huge amounts in gathering users by offering free or subsidized services that they lost view of revenues and profits (see case study 'Brands without Profits' in Chapter 2). Those who point to the success of Amazon forget that the company could not make a profit for 10 years before it turned the corner.

This book describes the role of marketing and how digital technologies transform it. Understanding technology and making innovative use of it is the need of the hour, as illustrated in the Opening Case of this chapter. A successful competitive strategy still depends on economic concepts of customer needs, economic value and revenue generation, which remain central to any business. Managers, hence, need to go beyond digital media reach and invest in information assets that deliver value (Chapter 2).

This book stresses the need for building sound business models that create and deliver value. So instead of adding digital channels to traditional businesses or adding a physical channel to a digital business, companies have to look for opportunities to add value by the integration of new technologies while keeping marketing objectives firmly in focus. Krispy Kreme's Hot Light is an example of turning a physical advantage into an app to help customers getting freshly baked, hot doughnuts (see Marketing Insight 1.1).

MARKETING INSIGHT 1.1 *Krispy Kreme's Hot Light*

This book argues that companies that use digital capabilities creatively can add value to customer offerings and thereby gain competitive advantage. Businesses have to go beyond web and social media interactions to delight customers. This mini case study shows how Krispy Kreme, the doughnut maker, used technology to provide hot and fresh doughnuts to its customers.

Consumers know that freshly baked doughnuts taste far better than stored ones. But stores have different times of baking their products, depending on when the stocks run out. Krispy Kreme devised a way to inform them when the doughnuts were being made; it has a neon red sign outside its stores that lights up when a fresh batch of doughnuts is coming out of its stores' ovens. Nearby customers could, thus, rush to the store and treat themselves to fresh, hot doughnuts.

As mobile phones became ubiquitous, the company decided to transform this experience digitally. It designed its 'Hot Light' app which informs customers of freshly baked buns in a nearby store. As a fresh batch of doughnuts rolls out at a Krispy Kreme store, the light is triggered outside the store as well as on the app, informing customers that they can treat themselves to hot doughnuts.

The Hot Light app has been extremely popular. It generates a 'Hot Now' symbol on the phone and informs people wherever they are—in offices or homes—to go and collect hot doughnuts. Launched in 2012, it uses geo-navigation to connect the users' mobile phones to the nearest store, to activate the light and to send push notifications and information about special promotions in the area.

The app no doubt helps customers get fresh doughnuts, but it also helps the store to clear out stocks fast. Since the products have limited shelf life, this helps in increase in efficiency and also in the company gaining a competitive advantage over other bakers.

Do you know of other businesses that have transformed their physical advantage to digital advantage?

Sources

Bratskeir, K. 2015. 'Krispy Kreme's Hot Light App Tells You When Donuts Are Fresh Out of the Oven.' *Huffington Post*. Available at: https://www.huffpost.com/entry/krispy-kreme-hot-light-app-fresh-hot-nice_n_7276544?guccounter=1&guce_referrer=aHR0cHM6Ly93d3cuZ29vZ2xlLmNvbS8&guce_referrer_sig=AQAAAKefFPwWv9vSeSQqoRVBew YnYDEd9j5nLFgVhPiElp5-jpjc7SBcBauSz4hTmW9S6b4P-MWrgGH3glt19soRiulj8P V3eysVDJTuF6d08l4egK7BK9iRg814SBHUXKJ_TFYZ08fHvDSaKkHUh-jPf9u1ZHgAyZiOvYrabEsulv1p (accessed on 21 January 2021).

Laliberte, M. 2019. 'The Secret to Getting the Freshest Krispy Kreme Doughnuts.' *Reader's Digest*. Available at: https://www.rd.com/article/fresh-krispy-kreme-doughnuts/ (accessed on 21 January 2021).

UNDERSTANDING DIGITAL MARKETING

There is a need today to take a marketing view of the digital space. This book shows that digital methods can indeed help marketing in achieving its objectives, provided that companies understand the nature of digital methods and devise ways to use them innovatively. It will explore how marketing has changed in the digital era and describe marketing strategies to deal with changing consumer behaviour. It will answer the question of whether digital marketing will transform traditional marketing or whether integration with traditional methods is a more feasible option.

Unfortunately, the skills required for using digital technologies are lacking in many companies. Royle and Laing (2014) write that managers in companies lack specific technical skills, best practice guidance on evaluation metrics and intelligent future-proofing for dynamic technological change. Managers have a key skill gap of 'integrating digital marketing approaches with established marketing practice', they write. Part of the reason is the way that digital marketing is understood; many companies think of it as a separate activity from other marketing methods. It has the aim of garnering followers or likes for online content. Hence, digital marketing remains a distinct department of many organizations and is guided by 'vanity metrics'—numbers that give the impression of huge fan following—but they hardly translate into revenues or profits.

Another problem is the way digital marketing is defined. It is commonly understood as 'the use of digital technologies to create integrated, targeted and measurable communications which help to acquire and retain customers while building deeper relationships with them' (Wymbs 2011). But acquiring customers is not the same as making profits, as a host of companies such as Paytm and Airbnb have discovered. A better definition would be one that links digital marketing to meeting traditional business objectives.

We, therefore, define digital marketing as 'the use of digital technologies by companies to meet business objectives of revenue growth and profits'. It includes marketing on the Internet through mobile phones, display advertising and any other digital device. It encompasses creating digital value (Chapter 2) and the formulation of digital strategy (Chapter 8).

Digital technologies have many advantages which can, well, be used in marketing. A practical word of wisdom is spoken by Philip Kotler (2014). He says, 'It would be foolish for any company to go overboard on digital media… [it] can experiment with the amount of digital media that is optimal but it is unlikely that companies will only use digital marketing.' Interestingly, Michael Porter (2001) had foreseen this and advised caution. 'Many Internet businesses active on the Internet are artificial businesses competing by artificial means and propped up by capital,' he wrote in his article, 'Strategy and the Internet'. 'But as market forces play out, the old rules regain their currency.'

The same sentiment is echoed by other writers. Shapiro and Varian (1999) write in their book, *Information Rules*, 'Ignore basic economic principles at your own risk. Technology changes. Economic laws do not.'

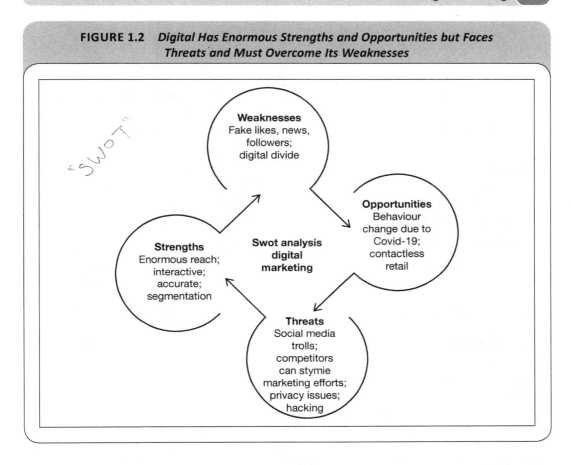

FIGURE 1.2 *Digital Has Enormous Strengths and Opportunities but Faces Threats and Must Overcome Its Weaknesses*

This book has been written from the point of view of using digital methods in marketing. It explores the many ways with which companies become 'digital masters' (Chapter 8). Companies have discovered new ways of doing business or targeting new segments by the use of digital technologies. Starting with describing the web's unique capabilities, this book takes you into a journey of marketing in the digital era by using its strengths and opportunities, while at the same time avoiding weaknesses and the looming threats (Figure 1.2).

■ EVOLUTION OF DIGITAL MARKETING

Digital marketing includes marketing on the Internet through mobile phones, electronic display advertising and deploying technologies in many creative ways. It started in the 1990s when companies started advertising on the Internet. The first e-commerce transaction is estimated to have taken place in 1994. Companies have used websites, banner ads, emails, search engines and social media marketing over the years. When we

TABLE 1.1   *From Media to Technology: How Digital Marketing Has Evolved*

Digital Marketing Approach	Objective
Internet as media	Generating traffic for a site or product; using ads and click-throughs
Internet as information provider	Generating content to influence people
Internet as a communication channel	Engaging people in a two-way communication
Internet as social media	Gathering likes and views; getting venture capital based on the number of users
Internet as an engagement platform	Building brand communities
Internet as a selling medium	Attracting a large number of online buyers
Internet as technology	Transforming marketing by data analytics and new technologies

see how digital marketing methods have evolved, we can see the mistakes made by earlier converts.

The evolution of digital marketing from its earliest days shows that companies have struggled to get their digital act right by following different approaches (Table 1.1). Early attempts of digital marketing focused on using the Internet as a media channel and information provider. It was assumed that having an Internet presence was enough, and that search engines would take users to the company's site. That is what Google Ads do: When a person searches for a product, the search engine shows some sites at the top of the list of searches. Search engine optimization (SEO) is based on using words in the content that search engine algorithms track so that the sites containing those words are featured on top of the search list. This worked, but for companies looking for volumes, it was a slow process, and they had to rely on the mass media as well.

Slowly, companies realized that the Internet was not just another media channel. Going by the slogan 'content is king,' online content was created with the hope that people would see the article or video and get influenced by the brands that sponsored it. What happened was that people loved the videos and the pictures and shared them but not the brand or the company's name. India's first transgender or lesbian ads, for instance, generated a lot of buzz when they were put out on YouTube, but today people will be hard-pressed to remember the brands that created them, leave alone buying them.

When social media started becoming popular, companies believed they could advertise and sell to people who had taken to it in a big way. But they soon realized that people went to social media to engage with each other, not to listen to advertisers. For some years, the online media strategy consisted of placing links and banner ads on popular sites or starting pages on social networking sites, hoping to drive traffic. Some companies started their e-commerce pages on Facebook, called F-commerce, but later opted out of it (see the Closing Case). Piskorski (2011) explains that companies merely imported their digital strategies into the social space, forgetting that commercial messages intruded into the personal space of users. People turn away from such actions because their objective is to connect with people, not with companies.

This is not to say that these strategies were complete failures. Some businesses found social media to be an apt advertising tool. A person making cakes or candles could spread the message on social media and could get some orders from friends. But the challenge for a big business in digital marketing has always been to convert online visitors to paying customers. Apart from some successes, many companies could not get their act together. Some industries committed suicide by offering their entire services online, driving customers away (see Marketing Insight 1.2).

MARKETING INSIGHT 1.2   *Internet Euphoria and Industry Suicide*

The growth of the Internet has resulted in euphoria about its capabilities. Companies were ecstatic and wanted to get a share of the online pie. They established online presence in any way they could. Little did they realize that their actions would lead to industry suicide and that they would be gobbled up by Internet giants or become irrelevant.

Newspapers, for instance, went online and uploaded all their content on their sites hoping to get a wide readership. Many of them even put their entire daily editions online as 'e-papers'. But by putting their entire content online, they gave it away to search engines for free. Users started getting all their daily news through search engines; there was no reason left for them to either buy a newspaper or visit news sites.

The newspaper industry gave it all away on the Internet and thus committed collective suicide. With revenues drying up, many publications struggled and even shut down. Newspaper sites now carry appeals for donations to 'keep quality journalism alive'. Paywalls were set up by newspapers belatedly; while a few succeeded, others found that users were not interested in paying for what was freely available on the Internet. It was only after prolonged legal battles in France and Australia that Google relented in 2020 and said that it would launch 'a licensing programme to pay publishers for high-quality content for a new news experience'. It remains to be seen whether this would make an impact on the health of news organizations.

Banks also committed a similar mistake. They invested in providing online banking to customers, which was so convenient that they could accomplish all their tasks without ever going to a bank branch. By doing so, the banks gave away their major revenue stream—of selling financial products to walk-in customers. They started selling credit cards, mutual funds and insurance policies through telecalling but with dismal conversion rates. Instead of building a bricks-and-clicks business, the banking industry had followed the 'me-too' approach and built capabilities that kept customers away. It is hardly a wonder that banks now impose heavy charges on customers but have seen their profits wither away. In India, several bank failures and many other floundering ones show that the industry cannot survive on the loan business alone. Today, banks face competition from e-wallets and similar apps which offer cheap or free online banking services and are no different from traditional banks which are set up with huge investments.

(Continued)

(Continued)

> That is why it is important to understand the web's unique capabilities before jumping in on the online bandwagon blindly. While it is important to provide facilities to customers, businesses must maintain the marketing advantage of cultivating paying customers or at least keep in touch with them to up-sell and cross-sell. Maintaining competitive advantage in the age of transparency is also a challenge.
>
> *How can companies use Internet capabilities but still protect their competitive advantage?*

Success in marketing lies in using technology in its various forms to help consumers solve their problems. An example is that of facial recognition technology: It is now being used in marketing to recognize customers and track them. Once we start thinking of the Internet as technology, other ways of doing business emerge, such as 3D printing, enterprise resource planning (ERP), animated displays, anytime shopping and many others.

ONLINE MARKETING SPENDS

Knowing that their customers are online, businesses have increased their online spends over the years. They have tried various methods—online advertising, content marketing, social media interventions—but have had mixed results. Technical experts found ways to place ads as pop-ups as people opened websites during YouTube videos and in mobile apps. Users are quick to get rid of them and find them as irritants as they interrupt their online activity.

Companies also learnt that people like to share content if it is interesting, but such promotions do not result in either brand building or improved customer loyalty. For example, customers would be happy to see a funny video online and share it but scarcely remember the brand afterwards. Online ads also do not work the way they were intended to: Companies achieved high click-through rates but few conversions, thereby increasing their customer acquisition costs. In case users did not like online ads, they were quick to install ad-blocking apps. Emails are directed to spam folders where they die away. SEO may guide users to a particular site, but if it is not helpful to them, they will simply go away.

'In the era of Facebook and YouTube, brand building has become a vexing challenge,' writes Holt (2016). 'Viral, buzz, memes, stickiness, and form factor became the lingua franca of branding. But despite all the hoopla, such efforts have had very little payoff.'

That is the reason that digital advertising spends have not grown as much as they were expected to. As the Internet grew, it was expected that print and television (TV) advertising would decline and even die off completely and that all advertising would shift online. Figures show that Internet advertising still lags behind traditional channels or TV and print (Figure 1.3). The 2018 figures show that Internet advertising is still a little over 20 per cent of the total advertising spend of ₹759,560 million. Although this may increase, certain trends may well limit online advertising in the future.

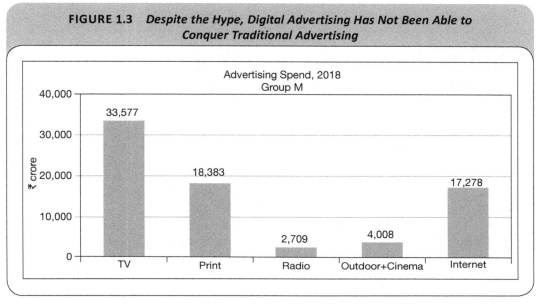

FIGURE 1.3   *Despite the Hype, Digital Advertising Has Not Been Able to Conquer Traditional Advertising*

Source: GroupM (2019).

In 2017, it was reported that consumer goods giant Procter & Gamble (P&G) was cutting $140 million in digital spending (see Chapter 6). In 2020, many companies decided to boycott social media advertising as a backlash against racist and violent posts (Chapter 10). Such trends, along with rising privacy concerns and reports of data misuse, may well see the evolution of other methods in the coming years. So far, the earlier forecasts about the death of traditional marketing and advertising have not come true. Considering that digital marketing started in the 1990s, its volume growth over the years has been quite modest.

Even today, traditional media holds a strong position in ad spends, and though digital spends are growing, advertisers still depend on traditional media and marketing methods. Success will be realized by those players who can combine traditional elements of garnering customers with online methods of search and engagement. To understand how this can be done, we must first understand the methods of both traditional and digital marketing.

■ TRADITIONAL AND DIGITAL MARKETING

In an omnichannel approach, companies have to build on synergies of both traditional and modern methods. Early players focused on generating traffic to their web pages, and they succeeded too, but this did not translate into customers. Later, buzz marketing became fashionable. So companies made endearing ads and placed them on YouTube or

MARKETING INSIGHT 1.3 *Shah Rukh Khan's* Fan: *An Online Campaign*

The Internet is an ideal platform for marketing forthcoming movies. It is assumed that if people get talking about one and a buzz is generated, they would be motivated to see it in a theatre. Yash Raj Films took the digital route to promote its film, *Fan*. It used videos as a primary digital marketing strategy, along with a bunch of interesting social media engagements around the movie. The movie starred Shah Rukh Khan, a superstar, who has a huge fan following and a number of hits to his credit.

Yash Raj Films used a series of fan stories in videos titled 'Tu Nahin Samjhega' published on YouTube, which integrated with the theme of the movie—the love–hate relationship between a superstar and his fan, also played by Mr Khan. This was part of the digital marketing strategy of Yash Raj Films for the promotions of the film. The movie was released on 15 April 2016.

The videos tried to build an emotional connect with viewers through a marketing campaign connecting real-life fans of Shah Rukh Khan. The movie was billed as a tribute to the fans who go to great extent to express their love for the superstar. Among the videos that were posted on YouTube was that of Muhammad, who used to fly from the Maldives to India or Sri Lanka to see Mr Khan's movies on their first day first show. He met his favourite superstar after 20 years. Another fan that was featured was Vishal Singh from Lucknow who changed his name to Vishahrukh Khan. He has a museum dedicated to Mr Khan at his home, and the video showed people visiting his house and meeting his family, who are also dedicated fans of the star.

The teaser for the movie fetched more than six million views. This was followed with a tie-up with an online shopping portal, Yepme, with the launch of #iamfan contest in which 100 lucky fans of @iamsrk could feature on its logo. Along with this, the social media accounts of the movie created and sustained the buzz around the movie with various trivia and the #iamfan contest. The movie has an anthem song, which was also featured on social media.

The next move was to bring back the memories of the days when fans used to write letters to their stars. The social media channels asked fans to write letters for Shah Rukh Khan, which would be read by him. Mr Khan read the letters, and he also performed requests made by his fans.

As the release date came near, the social media team focused on building the buzz around its first day first show. #FirstDayFan was launched on social media to keep the tempo high near its release date. A contest was announced for fans who saw the very first show of the movie.

Did the social media strategy result in people flocking to theatres to see the film? *The Indian Express* (2016) writes that the box office collections of the movie started witnessing a decline in the second week itself. Although the film opened to good reviews and also saw a good opening on 15 April 2016, the collections started falling very quickly. The first-week collection was ₹715 million, but the second-weekend collections saw a steep dip with just ₹77.5 million. Surprisingly, the movie failed to collect box-office revenue of ₹1,000 million, which was the benchmark of a superstar hit. His earlier releases had achieved this figure without a huge online spend. The verdict was that the movie lacked conviction and belief and was not realistic or convincing.

This brings us to the questions: Did the social media interventions work? Would the promoters have been better off if they had not spent on a digital strategy but depended on traditional promotions only? While one can argue that the quality of the product is important to push sales, it would be important to find out whether digital engagements resulted in bringing people to the theatres, people who otherwise would not have seen a movie starring a superstar. Such figures are not available. It is easy to conjecture that the box-office figures show that a certain section of the audience would go to their favourite superstar in a movie, with or without digital engagement. Moreover, the social media engagement was with fans who already knew the superstar, so it is doubtful that any new viewers were obtained by this intervention.

Can online methods really result in paying customers for movies? How?

Sources

Express Web Desk. 2016. 'Fan Box Office Collections: Shah Rukh Khan's Film Earns ₹82.95 Cr.' *The Indian Express*, 30 April. Available at: http://indianexpress.com/article/entertainment/bollywood/fan-box-office-collections-shah-rukh-khan-movie-great-start-2755019/ (accessed on 21 January 2021).

Naidu, P. 2016, 15 April. 'Inside the Jabra Digital Marketing Promotions of SRK's Latest Movie FAN.' Available at: http://lighthouseinsights.in/fan-movie-digital-marketing.html/ (accessed on 21 January 2021).

Facebook. Some of them became very popular indeed and spread virally, but again the views hardly translated into paying customers. It is one thing to get people to 'like' something but quite another to convert them into paying customers.

To build synergies, it is necessary to understand the differences between traditional and digital marketing (see Table 1.2). Traditionally, marketing activities have included advertising, communications, distribution and sales. Companies have used ads to communicate with consumers, hoping that these would make people go to stores and buy the products advertised. It has worked for many years and still does. Companies such as P&G, Unilever and Coca-Cola have created some of the most memorable advertising in history and, along with it, some great brands. Ads work all the time through newspapers and TV, hoardings, product placements, sponsored events, pamphlets and flyers. The development of mass media gave producers a way to get right into people's homes and communicate to millions of people at the same time.

Some of the ads indeed entered popular culture. Maggi Noodles' 'two minutes only' and Bajaj's 'Hamara Bajaj' are some of the great ads that are remembered to this day and created widespread brand awareness and loyalty. It is debatable whether online methods only can create such widespread consumer awareness backed by strong sales. Online movie promotions, for instance, generate awareness among people but will depend on reviews to pay and watch them (see Marketing Insight 1.3).

TABLE 1.2   *Difference between Traditional and Digital Marketing*

Traditional Marketing	Digital Marketing
Dependence on mass media, public relations (PR), flyers and so on to build brands and drive sales	Dependence on creating online word-of-mouth (WOM) and consumer engagement
One-to-many and one-way passive communications from company to consumer	One-to-one and two-way interactive communications; interaction between company and consumer
Based on product, price, place and promotion (4Ps)	Based on solution, access, value and education (SAVE)
Professional content made by advertising agencies	Consumer-generated content
Measured in terms of reach, frequency and sales revenues	Measured in terms of clicks, visits, likes, shares and consumer engagement
Employs models and celebrities	Employs online experts, users and influencers
Provides structured company information	Provides unstructured consumer information; informal language
Uses the sales funnel approach (awareness, interest, desire and action [AIDA])	Uses a circular approach based on consumer decision journey (CDJ)

This book does not distinguish between digital and traditional marketing but explains how digital enhances a company's marketing initiatives. It describes how traditional methods are evolving to remain relevant in the digital era.

It is clear that companies must use the web's unique capabilities in its marketing approach. Traditional methods interact with online methods to create customer experiences (CXs). The next section describes how these can be integrated.

ONLINE REVOLUTION

The basis of traditional marketing—mass media—has been losing ground over the years. Even if the TV habit had not declined, the invention of the remote control had given consumers the power to zap advertisements that came up embedded in their favourite entertainment shows. Newspapers also faced a digital onslaught as modern readers turned online for their dose of news and current affairs. The information technology (IT) industry reduced bulky computers into easy-to-carry, slick laptops and then into screens small enough to fit people's pockets. Thanks to laptops and mobiles, people can now choose what they want to watch at times convenient to them. The mobile device has become an extension of one's personality, as it contains access to almost everything that

FIGURE 1.4 *Integrating the Traditional and Digital Approach*

Source: https://www.thesocialtie.in/single-post/2017/08/07/Traditional-Marketing-vs-Digital-Marketing (accessed on 21 January 2021).

one may want to accomplish. Companies need to integrate both traditional and digital capabilities in today's world (Figure 1.4).

At the heart of this revolution is the smartphone. It has changed the way people go about their lives. They can now access information about anything at all times. Apart from posting pictures and videos about themselves, the smartphone enables them to make connections across the globe. Apps allow them to do many things on their devices, including buying things and engaging with companies. Now companies have two-way communication with customers as opposed to earlier one-way communication of mass media.

In terms of marketing, today, people have the means to communicate with and about brands. They can now post comments and product reviews, engage with brands or complain about negative experiences and thereby influence others. Kumar (2015) writes that one-way communication is a thing of the past; companies have to learn to live with two-way communications in which the power of brands has shifted to the consumer.

The new marketing rests on the mobile interface, peer influence, community-oriented marketing and customer relationships. To some extent, these were used in traditional marketing as well, but now the power of these methods has multiplied. Pearson (2011) writes, 'The fundamentals have changed, as have the means and methods to define targets, to create more productive encounters that provide more opportunities to sell, to develop deeper and more significant insights, and to exploit singular points of difference.' Companies have incorporated marketing strategies by recognizing the web's unique capabilities and improving customer engagement and experience in the process.

CXS ON THE WEB: THE WEB'S 'UNIQUE CAPABILITIES'

'The Internet offers a startling set of advantages as a marketing medium,' writes Ingari (1999). It is up to companies how they capitalize on these advantages. They have to actively explore how they can apply the Internet's power to their marketing programmes. Indeed, the Internet has led to a complete transformation of business models, as illustrated by the case studies of various companies that are presented in this book. Companies have to integrate their traditional marketing campaigns with the Internet's unique capabilities and also its limitations, summarized in Table 1.3.

The web's capabilities transform the function of marketing to a great extent. One of the most common concepts taught in marketing is that of product, place, promotion and price (4Ps). In the next section, we will discuss how this has changed for the new era.

TABLE 1.3 *The Web's Unique Capabilities and Limitations*

Capabilities	Limitations
Reach: The Internet helps companies extend their reach to previously unapproachable markets.	**Vanity features:** Web metrics consist of number of followers or those who like and engage with brands but do little to encourage sales.
Ability to target precisely: Companies can now select the precise customers or groups to target.	**Conversion cost:** Generating traffic is a difficult task. Ads may appear cheap, but the cost of acquiring customers gets multiplied many times.
Interactivity: Customers can now talk back to companies. The Internet is the most interactive of marketing media.	**User attentiveness:** Users flit from site to site, exploring whatever suits their fancy. Holding their interest is a big task for companies.
AIDA completeness: Traditional marketing can influence only one or two steps in the AIDA model. The Internet offers AIDA completeness; the company can influence each step of the purchase process and even post-purchase behaviour.	**Click through fraud:** Pay-per-click models were invented to measure the number of interested users in a brand. This has been used to generate artificial traffic and likes for brands.
Closed loop learning: The Internet allows 'closed-loop' learning, in which the company learns from each customer reaction.	**Ineffective banner ads:** Conventional ads remain weak substitutes for TV or print advertising, since few attract users' attention.

Capabilities	Limitations
Immediacy and relevancy: Since tracking can be done in real time, marketing actions are immediate and relevant.	**Control:** Control has shifted to customers. They choose the time and level of interaction. Negative comments are magnified.
Customer involvement: Since customers can block advertising messages, they are involved by obtaining permission from them.	**Spam:** Customers are quick to block brand content if they think that it is a spam.
Versatile: The Internet allows a variety of marketing interventions such as awareness messages, using multimedia, platforms for reviews, seminars and PR.	**Exclusive:** The online medium excludes millions of people who have no access to the Internet or are unable to use it. The problem is huge in poor countries.

INTERNET MARKETING MIX: 4Ps TO SAVE

The marketing mix is a framework provided by Jerome McCarthy which explains that managers can devise their marketing strategy by integrating four controllable variables called the 4Ps. This concept has endured since it was proposed in 1960. Later, three more variables were added to cater to marketing of services: people, processes and physical evidence. Companies have tried to modify these elements in the online context by adding a website or an online communication channel to the variables.

Such an approach ignores the unique capabilities of the Internet. A radically new approach is needed, which takes into account the capability and spread of the Internet. What businesses must do is to find out effective ways of using new technologies, just as they have used the telephone, newspapers and TV in the past. They have to approach marketing in new ways and discover new methods of reaching out to customers. This calls for a revisit of the 4Ps approach.

Today, marketing is better served by the SAVE framework, which focuses on solution, access, value and education described by Ettenson, Conrado and Knowles (2012). Pioneered by Motorola Solutions, SAVE can be used as a guide to restructure the marketing organization and consists of a radical change in approach. The transformation from 4Ps to SAVE is summarized in Table 1.4.

The changes in marketing mix are described as follows:

1. **Solution instead of product:** Today, consumers look for solutions. Product features do not mean much to customers if a product fails to solve their problem. The digital economy is replete with new businesses that are based on providing solutions (see Marketing Insight 1.3). The product approach makes companies focus on features, functions and technological superiority, whereas the solution approach focuses on building products and services based on customer needs and solving problems.
2. **Access instead of place:** Since people can access any product at any time by using their smartphones, access becomes more important. Online technology creates

TABLE 1.4   *How the Marketing Mix Has Changed*

Traditional Marketing (4Ps)	Digital Marketing (SAVE)
Product: Companies stress on product attributes	**Solution:** Consumers look for solutions for day-to-day problems
Place: Reaching products where they are consumed	**Access:** Multi-channel access, integration of channels and the importance of fulfilment
Price: Absolute price charged to customers	**Value:** Consumers look for value; hence, price is secondary
Promotion: Products are promoted and advertised over mass media	**Education:** Interactive communication between company and consumers

access through a multichannel presence that influences all stages in the customer's decision journey. Since customers want instant access and answers to their queries, companies have to, therefore, break silos and integrate all departments to provide access to customers. Place in the online context means company website, physical stores, third-party seller sites, e-commerce sites and even purchaser sites and auctions. An important aspect of place/access is the integration of all distribution and communication channels. This means that they use a combination of physical and online services to reach consumers.

3. **Value instead of price:** The Internet makes pricing transparent. Customers can search other sites instantly for discounts and deals. Many services are also offered free. So the price becomes subordinate to value. Pricing power is obtained when companies are able to communicate the value that the customer can derive. The focus on price places emphasis on tangible prices that customers pay and ignores the value that they derive from it. The Internet can influence the price/value combination by providing improved price transparency. Dynamic pricing can implement different pricing for different segments and customers.

4. **Education instead of promotion:** Promoting products through mass media involves interrupting people in whatever they were doing to send them advertising messages. Today, education replaces the old paradigm of promotion as companies provide customers with information that they value. The promotion thus becomes a marketing communication strategy instead of just pushing products. The Internet provides a new, direct and interactive communication channel through which a company can connect with consumers and build relationships with them.

When we start thinking in terms of the SAVE framework, we can discover business opportunities—many new businesses have emerged over the years (see Marketing Insight 1.4), which do not rely on the 4Ps but on providing solutions, access, value and education to customers. The SAVE framework takes into account the web's capabilities and leads to building CXs on the Internet.

MARKETING INSIGHT 1.4   *Solving Consumer Problems for Online Success*

Merely going online is not enough. Companies succeed digitally if they solve some outstanding problem for the customer. Some of these businesses that have used the web's capabilities to solve customer problems are described below:

- **Travel:** People seek information when they are planning a trip to an unknown place. Earlier, they depended on travel agents or brochures for this information. Deep information and traveller reviews were missing. Tripadvisor brings together information about places to visit and stay and thus solves a problem for users. Travel portals like MakeMyTrip help in planning trips by making flight information transparent. Yatra helps plan holidays both online and offline. Owners of houses had no way to let out spare rooms to travellers who did not want to stay in hotels; Airbnb solved this and became an instant hit.
- **Real estate:** The problem of finding homes and offices was solved by portals such as Magicbricks and 99acres. Prices were displayed, and transactions became more transparent.
- **Healthcare:** Information and advice regarding health and medicines were made available through Healthkart, 1mg and Lenskart.
- **Education:** Web capabilities provide education and certified courses to people who could not go to regular colleges. edX, Coursera, Meritnation and so on provide online services and hence solve the problem of distance. On the other hand, existing colleges and universities offer access to their facilities online for their students and staff.

Why is it necessary to think in terms of the SAVE framework in the digital era?

While adapting to the shift to digital, it is important to remember the traditional objectives, that is, keeping the customer needs as the centre of all marketing efforts. Channels have to be integrated to cater to the modern, always-on consumer (AOC).

■ INTEGRATION OF CHANNELS

From the point of view of consumers, the Internet is just another channel to accomplish whatever they are doing—buying things, paying bills, ordering a taxi and so on—if digital helps them in their tasks, they will seek it. They do not differentiate between channels but seek a combination of interactions across channels to complete their objectives. Thus, the answer is to integrate all channels rather than see digital marketing as something distinct and separate. 'Ultimately, strategies that integrate the Internet and traditional competitive advantages, and ways of competing should win in many industries,' writes Porter (2001). Even pure online players, such as Google, Amazon, Flipkart, Pepperfry and many other companies, rely on TV and newspaper advertising to generate online traffic (Figure 1.5) showing the need of integration of channels.

FIGURE 1.5 *Internet Giants Too Advertise in Traditional Media*

The future lies in combining the objectives of marketing with Internet and communication technologies. Digital marketing is not distinct from the company's marketing. Many companies continue to make this mistake. Integration of channels leads to achieving marketing objectives through an 'omnichannel' approach. This approach leads to meeting customer requirements and creating value. Digital marketing can be instrumental in value creation in a variety of ways, as discussed in the next section.

ADDING VALUE THROUGH DIGITAL MARKETING

A clear strategy is needed in order to create value through digital methods. This is covered in Chapter 2. Edelman (2010b) writes about four core sources of value through digital activities: integrate, empower, publish information and use data intelligence. They are briefly described as follows:

- **Integrate:** All activities must be coordinated to engage the consumer throughout a digital purchase journey. Department silos must be broken. Although customers interact with brands in various ways, completely different departments in an organization manage these interactions. Digital channels can unify the CX. All departments, consisting of marketing, sales and service, are facilitated by online channels. For example, traditional advertising must provide keywords for consumers to search online, and online interventions must guide customers to physical stores. Links should help consumers learn about and buy products, connecting them with reviewer and retailer sites.

- **Empower customers:** Consumers are empowered by becoming part of communities and platforms in which they can express themselves freely. They participate in discussions online, and companies respond to both positive and negative comments. Also, companies must empower consumers to build their own marketing identities and, in the process, to serve as brand ambassadors.

- **Become publishers:** Since consumers look for information, companies in effect become publishers of content, which goes well beyond advertisements. They must publish everything from static content to dynamic updates. Content and applications must flow across different sites and mobile platforms. They must act as multimedia publishers as they manage content across products, segments, channels and promotions.

- **Data intelligence:** The fourth way to build value is to make sense of the enormous data available. Companies can track customers both online and as they go about their daily lives. This data must be managed in real time. Algorithms identify search terms of consumers, and constant tracking of online comments is required. Control rooms have to be established to spot and react to online complaints or rumours. For this, companies must invest in data tools, skilled analysts and flexible processes that can facilitate rapid action. They must plan strategically to use the plethora of digital data now available and respond to the rapidly changing marketing environment.

CHANGES IN THE MARKETING ENVIRONMENT

Marketing methods have continued to evolve. Every new technology, from telephone to TV, has helped marketing to evolve. Now, the Internet has changed the marketing environment in a very big way. Today, companies have to cater to the 'always-on' customer in ways that had not been thought of before. Marketing has to respond to critical changes in the environment, which is discussed in detail in Chapter 5. This section describes how changes in the marketing environment impact changes in marketing.

Consumer Engagement

The Internet offers a way of engaging customers not only in sales and feedback but also in co-creation and co-innovation. Consumer engagement refers to all interactions that a prospect or consumer makes with a brand or company. In the online context, it refers to technologies and applications that are designed to increase these interactions, such as content generation, customer feedback, product blogs, acting as influencers and participating in brand communities. Engagements now take many forms: getting customers to like brands, share brand posts, write about their brand experiences, giving suggestions, co-developing and co-creating and recommending brands to others (Figure 1.6). Companies can promote relevant and consistent communication, and if people start posting comments positively, they build loyalty and fan following over a period of time. At the same time, contacts in the physical world must be managed well, such as experience in retail shops, after-sales service, salesmen and other channels.

Increased Consumer Power

The power of brands has shifted from companies to consumers. Earlier, brand communications originated from the company, but now, companies have to get used to the consumer generating content about the brand. Blogs and social media are used to share brand experiences, product recommendations and complaints. This conversation has assumed much larger importance than company communications since people rely on peer and community communications. For instance, a company may release advertisements extolling the advantages of its products, but if a negative comment or video becomes viral, all advertisements become useless. In a survey of consumers in the UK by Deloitte (2014), it was found that only 12 per cent of respondents trusted the manufacturer or service provider. This shows how power has shifted to consumers. Companies have to adjust to the fact that they do not control brand communication any longer.

Omnichannel Marketing

Omnichannel marketing refers to the integration of multiple channels in delivering CX. Consumers look for a seamless experience regardless of channel or device they are choosing. They may well start their purchase journey by an online search or interaction, but they will also be exposed to and interact with the brand or company on a website, mobile app, hoardings and print ads, TV and YouTube videos, social media and in physical stores. They will go back and forth till they make up their minds. Bonchek and France (2014) write, 'The buying process is no longer linear.' While digital marketing implies online interactions, omnichannel suggests that users may well look for products online but buy from a physical store and vice versa. As a consequence, 'clicks-only' businesses are setting up physical stores. In India, pure online players such as Yatra, Lenskart and Ferns N Petals have invested in physical stores (Figure 1.7). On the other hand, physical stores

FIGURE 1.6 *The Consumer Engagement Process*

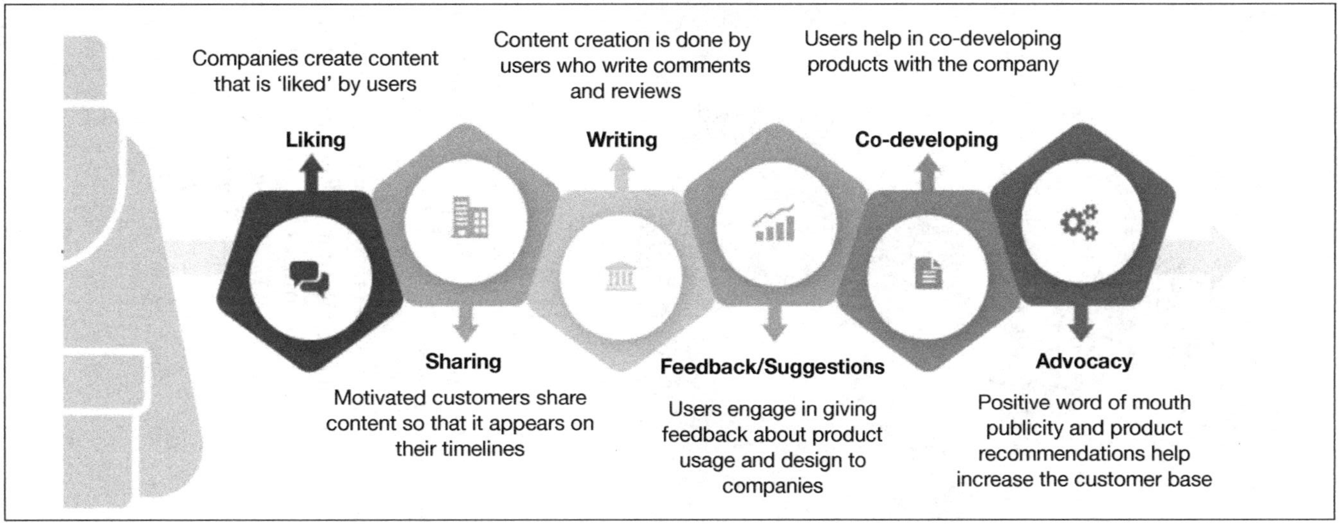

Liking

Companies create content that is 'liked' by users

Sharing

Motivated customers share content so that it appears on their timelines

Writing

Content creation is done by users who write comments and reviews

Feedback/Suggestions

Users engage in giving feedback about product usage and design to companies

Co-developing

Users help in co-developing products with the company

Advocacy

Positive word of mouth publicity and product recommendations help increase the customer base

FIGURE 1.7   *Yatra, an Online Portal, Has Physical Stores across India*

or bricks-and-mortar stores are investing in online channels, and we are, therefore, now witnessing what is called the 'clicks-and-bricks' stores, which is a term for a business model in which a company integrates both offline and online presences. Physical stores such as Westside, Shoppers Stop and Croma, for example, are found in both online and physical worlds.

The importance of omnichannel marketing is that a company must deliver a consistent and uninterrupted brand experience across many channels that the customer gets exposed to. It means converging of physical and online channels as well and a merger of traditional and online methods of marketing. But it does raise problems of measuring efficiency or return on investment (ROI). Customers may buy from physical stores, but there is no saying how they were influenced online, or they may buy from online stores, but we cannot measure how they were influenced in the physical world.

Smartphone Addiction

Companies have to find ways to get into the world of the consumer, which is, today, dominated by the smartphone. Efforts to advertise through mobile phones are rejected since users do not want any undesired intrusions in their personal space. This makes the task of companies quite difficult. The new marketing has to take into account the changes in consumer behaviour resulting from widespread smartphone use. Many people see it as an extension of their personality and find it difficult to do without it even for a few moments (see Chapter 4). This trend forces companies to rethink how they engage and connect with their customers. They have to look for ways to provide interesting apps or content that *makes the customer want to engage with the brand*. The challenge is to get a foothold in consumers' minds as they browse and interact with others online. This is easier said than done, of course, since people dislike spam and are quick to block unwanted messages and calls. There are two implications of this. First, if consumers share a picture of their brand experience on social media, it becomes unpaid advertisements for the brand. Companies have used this strategy quite effectively. Second, the concept of media gets redefined. Media is no longer a vehicle to send ads but is classified as paid, earned, shared and owned (PESO).

PESO Media

Along with traditional media, companies have to understand the nuances of PESO in the online context (Table 1.5).

TABLE 1.5   *PESO Examples and Benefits*

Media	Definition	Characteristics	Examples
Paid	Paid advertisements or content to influence audience	Targeted ads Pay-per-click	Banner ads Paid content Influencer marketing
Earned	Brand communications that are spread by consumers voluntarily	Voluntary posts by users High credibility Not paid for	Reviews and posts Articles and blog posts Recommendations WOM
Shared	Content that is shared by users on their channels	Helps in virality Authentic	Likes and shares Retweets
Owned	Channels and content that are controlled by the company	Control	Company website, YouTube channel Blogs and other owned channels

Paid Media

Paid media consists of content that is paid for by companies. Companies spend money to place banner ads on popular sites, use Google Adwords, banner ads, advertise on social media and hire influencers to spread their message. This type of intervention is akin to traditional marketing methods.

Earned Media

Earned media are the brand communications that are spread by consumers, and the company does not pay for them. It is 'earned' in the sense that the consumer shares the communication voluntarily without any effort of the company. Earned media is when people talk positively about the brand and influence others through WOM and 'viral' communications. The challenge for companies is to get people to comment and share. One way is to delight customers so that they genuinely feel like serving as mouthpieces for the company. Such comments will be authentic and spark others' interest.

Shared Media

Shared media is content that is shared by users on their pages. Companies posting their content online hope that consumers will start sharing their content, which can then be spread widely. When people share brand content with their acquaintances, it shows up in their feeds, and companies get extra advertising mileage. Any social media strategy must include methods to get brand content shared.

Owned Media

Owned media consists of channels and content that are controlled by the company. Websites, blogs, email lists and social media channels of companies are examples of owned media. Owned channels are used to execute campaigns, promote content, encourage WOM and engagement and thus fuel earned content.

In order to be effective, all these methods must work together. Companies have to leverage the level of influence each has across the decision journey of a customer. Paid media has to be used wisely because people tend to block such content. Even if they do not, getting people to act on it is difficult.

Social communications are used as supplements to existing media programmes. However, getting high reach on social media using organic methods has become increasingly difficult due to algorithmic changes to social newsfeeds that favour paid over organic brand communications. That is why using digital channels effectively remains a challenge.

USING DIGITAL MARKETING EFFECTIVELY

One troubling question that has plagued digital marketing is how to use it effectively. A number of digital marketing gurus offer books and courses, but most are limited to measuring the effectiveness of digital campaigns in terms of the number of visitors, shares or likes. This online WOM communication may work for movies, celebrities, artists, social movements and some other causes, but companies are more interested in measuring their paying customers. A key question remains: How does one convert this WOM or the Internet chatter into customers? Further, can a company encourage 'went-there/purchased' activity as compared to 'loved the brand'? It has been an uphill task: Even F-commerce or buying products on the Facebook platform has not quite succeeded (see the Closing Case).

In their research, Pauwels et al. (2013) found that Facebook likes and comments did not significantly affect store traffic. Tweets may be better than paid marketing, but it is difficult to track and understand exactly what consumers are saying about their product/brand. Content-specific WOM performed better than other methods. Among the conversation topics, 'love for the brand' had larger long-term traffic effects, but neutral conversations on 'went there/purchased' drove traffic in the short run.

These findings suggest that social media impact is not just about volume and valence: Knowing 'what' consumers say matters. Companies must invest in understanding how conversations affect their business, and how their marketing strategies influence online conversations. They also have to figure out how paid marketing may spark WOM in a way that can positively influence their brands.

Pikas and Sorrentino (2014) write that though businesses pay to advertise on popular social networking sites, the effectiveness of these advertising methods remains debatable. It is assumed that if the online advertising strategy of a company is formulated correctly, it can effectively target this large segment of the population that is active on social media. Their study found that the majority of respondents were not receptive to advertising on such sites. In fact, most were annoyed by online advertisements. The majority of respondents stated they would not like to be voluntarily exposed to information shared by businesses.

Blake, Nosko and Tadelis (2014) report the results of large-scale field experiments to measure the causal effectiveness of paid search ads. They found that conventional methods used to measure the impact of search engine maximization vastly overstate its effect, and that the effectiveness of search engine maximization is small for a well-known company like eBay and that it has been ineffective on average. However, they found a detectable positive impact of search engine maximization on new user acquisition and in influencing purchases by infrequent users, thereby showing that targeting uninformed users is a critical factor for successful advertising.

In search engine maximizing approach, the advertiser pays per click; that is, the expenditure rises with the number of clicks obtained. This means that the company ends up paying either for consumers who already know about the company advertised or to people who have no intention to buy (see Marketing Insight 1.2 on Shah Rukh Khan's movie). Advertising may appear to attract these consumers, when in reality, they would have found the company's website anyway. That is to say that there is no measurable short-term value in brand keyword advertising. Maiti (2017) writes in *Mint*, 'The story of six blind people describing an elephant has an interesting parallel in the world of digital advertising.'

◼ CONCLUSION

Aubrey and Judge (2012) write that the lesson from digital marketing is that technology should be used as a tool to deliver a seamless experience across channels, enabling trial, search, compare, review, order online or buy in-store. As such, in-store technology needs to be integrated and relevant to consumer needs and offer solutions such as increased convenience, product interactivity or better communication.

An omnichannel approach is becoming essential. Today's connected consumers seek out reviews of products and services before they make decisions. Companies need to support this desire throughout the customer's journey, especially the use of smartphones in the store to make shopping easier. Stores can encourage the use of photography in-store and QR codes to make product research and purchase quicker and easier. Brands also need to use the power of social media by integrating it into the retail and giving customers enough reasons to share brand-related posts on their pages. Such integrated stores can drive efficiencies in marketing. Brands that include e-commerce solutions into the physical store can reduce costs. Physical store networks serve as customer fulfilment centres. Kimmel (2010) writes that Web 2.0 is less a technology or a set of applications than a philosophy that 'is firmly rooted in the recognition of consumers' increasing connectedness, participation, and control over marketing functions'.

In sum, it can be said that far from its death, traditional marketing still has a role to play. It has got a new tool which may well transform it. The Internet is a powerful tool that will transform business just as the telephone has done since it was invented in 1876. In this book, we explore the exciting ways that technology is being used and how traditional marketing is getting impacted by it. This chapter shows that an integration of knowledge is needed across platforms.

◼ SUMMARY

This chapter explores the role of traditional and digital marketing. Digital methods can indeed help marketing in achieving its objectives, provided that companies understand the nature of digital methods and devise ways to use them innovatively. They have to avoid the hype created by Internet giants who flood us with information about the efficacy of digital methods in order to avoid creating a bubble of imaginary expectations. To succeed, businesses have to find a balance between traditional and digital methods.

The basis of traditional marketing—mass media—has been losing ground over the years but still remains important. People can now choose their own channels not only for news and entertainment but also to connect with friends and people of similar interests. The revolution has impacted marketing. Now, people have the means to communicate with and about brands. They can now post comments and product reviews, engage with brands or complain about negative experiences and influence others. The new marketing, therefore, rests on an integration of the mobile interface, peer influence, community-oriented marketing and customer relationships.

Digital marketing has evolved since its earliest days. Initially, companies used the Internet as a media channel. Subsequently, the Internet has been thought of as an information provider, a communication channel, social media, an engagement platform, a selling medium and, finally, a technology. Due to this, traditional marketing also has to change: The framework of 4Ps has evolved in SAVE. It has to cater to huge changes taking place in the fields of consumer engagement in an era of increased consumer power. Companies have to find ways of adding value through digital marketing and respond to changes in the marketing environment.

Media has also changed: To use online technologies effectively, companies have to understand and use PESO media. The chapter stresses the importance of adapting the huge changes taking place and to use digital technologies effectively by keeping marketing objectives firmly in focus.

■ KEY TERMS

Bricks and mortar: Physical presence of an organization or business in the marketplace.

Clicks and bricks: A term for a business model by which a company integrates both offline and online presence.

Consumer engagement: Consumer engagement refers to all interactions that a consumer or potential consumer makes with a brand or company.

Digital marketing: Digital marketing is defined as the use of digital technologies by companies to meet business objectives of revenue growth and profits. It includes marketing on the Internet through mobile phones, display advertising and any other digital medium.

Earned media: Earned media consists of channels not controlled by the company, including online review sites, social media, blogs and sites which give voice to the customer.

Electronic WOM communication: Electronic WOM consists of positive or negative statements made about a product or company on the Internet by users.

Omnichannel marketing: The integration of multiple channels in delivering CX is called omnichannel marketing.

Owned media: Owned media is one that is in control of the consumer, such as advertisements, promotions and websites.

Purchase funnel: The purchase funnel exhibits the purchase behaviour of consumers as they make purchase decisions, showing AIDA.

SAVE: The transformation of the 4Ps framework, which focuses on the solution, access, value and education.

CONCEPT REVIEW QUESTIONS

1. Compare traditional marketing with digital marketing. What are the points of difference between the two?
2. What is digital marketing? What are the tools of digital marketing?
3. How has digital marketing evolved since its start in the 1990s?
4. How has traditional marketing changed as a result of the popularity of online methods?
5. What is consumer engagement? How is it achieved?
6. What is omnichannel marketing?
7. What does online advertising consist of? Comment on the effectiveness of online advertising.
8. Describe the shift from 4Ps to the SAVE framework and its importance.
9. Describe the ways in which value is added through digital marketing.
10. How has media changed over the years? Describe the difference in paid, earned, shared and owned media.

CRITICAL THINKING QUESTIONS

1. Do you think that traditional marketing methods are dead, and online marketing is the future? Why?
2. Success in the online world is measured in terms of likes, the number of views of a video, the number of app downloads and building engaging communities. How can these be converted into paying customers? Support your answer with examples of companies that have succeeded in their efforts.
3. If digital marketing is as effective as it is made out to be, why are Internet giants using traditional media such as newspapers and TV to increase their sales? Why do they not depend totally on online marketing?
4. Discuss the statement in the context of digital marketing: 'Ignore basic economic principles at your own risk. Technology changes. Economic laws do not.'

PROJECTS AND ASSIGNMENTS

1. Several people have mentioned that digital marketing is being pushed by Internet giants, but it has failed in many cases. Read such papers and books and summarize their main points. What is your opinion?
2. Conduct a survey of your friends to find out how many of them have actually purchased things on products displayed on social media sites. Would you say that selling on such sites is common?
3. Scan newspapers and TV to see how many online brands/stores advertise on traditional media. Why do they do this when they can easily resort to digital marketing?

4. Find out about the best and most successful online campaigns. Suggest reasons why you think they were successful.

▌ REFERENCES

Aubrey, C., and D. Judge. 2012. 'Re-imagine Retail: Why Store Innovation Is Key to a Brand's Growth in the "New Normal", Digitally-connected and Transparent World.' *Journal of Brand Strategy* 1, no. 1 (April–June): 31–39.

Blake, T., C. Nosko, and S. Tadelis. 2014. 'Consumer Heterogeneity and Paid Search Effectiveness: A Large Scale Field Experiment.' National Bureau of Economic Research Working Paper 20171. Available at: http://www.nber.org/papers/w20171 (accessed on 21 January 2021).

Bonchek, M., and C. France. 2014. 'Marketing Can No Longer Rely on the Funnel.' *Harvard Business Review*. Available at: https://hbr.org/2014/05/marketing-can-no-longer-rely-on-the-funnel (accessed on 21 January 2021).

Buehler, D. R. 2014. *The Digital Delusion: How to Overcome the Misguidance and Misinformation Online to Become the Leader in Your Industry.*

Deloitte. 2014. *The Growing Power of Consumers.* Deloitte LLP. Available at: https://www2.deloitte.com/content/dam/Deloitte/uk/Documents/consumer-business/consumer-review-8-the-growing-power-ofconsumers.pdf (accessed on 28 January 2021).

Edelman, D. C. 2010a. 'Branding in the Digital Age.' *Harvard Business Review*. Available at: https://hbr.org/2010/12/branding-in-the-digital-age-youre-spending-your-money-in-all-the-wrong-places (accessed on 21 January 2021).

Edelman, D. C. 2010b. 'Four Ways to Get More Value from Digital Marketing.' *McKinsey Quarterly*. Available at: https://www.mckinsey.com/business-functions/marketing-and-sales/our-insights/four-ways-to-get-more-value-from-digital-marketing (accessed on 21 January 2021).

Ettenson, R., C. Eduardo, and J. Knowles. 2013. 'Rethinking the 4Ps.' *Harvard Business Review*. Available at: https://hbr.org/2013/01/rethinking-the-4-ps (accessed on 21 January 2021).

GroupM. 2019. 'GroupM's India 2019 Ad Forecast: Strong 14% Growth, over ₹10,000 Crores in New Investment.' Available at: https://www.groupm.com/groupm-indias-2019-ad-forecast/ (accessed on 21 January 2021).

Holt, D. 2016. 'Branding in the Age of Social Media.' *Harvard Business Review*. Available at: https://hbr.org/2016/03/branding-in-the-age-of-social-media (accessed on 21 January 2021).

Kimmel, A. J. 2010. *Connecting with Consumers: Marketing for New Marketplace Realities.* Oxford: Oxford University Press.

Kumar, D. 2015. *The Connected Consumer.* New York, NY: Business Expert Press.

Lee, B. 2012. 'Marketing Is Dead.' HBR Blog Network. Available at: http://blogs.hbr.org/2012/08/marketing-is-dead/ (accessed on 21 January 2021).

Maiti, S. 2017. 'Digital Advertising in 2017: Elephant in the Room?' *Mint*. Available at: https://www.livemint.com/Industry/QX0lOVJTUR2Mgn8Cm9fjTP/Digital-advertising-in-2017-Elephant-in-the-room.html (accessed on 21 January 2021).

Pauwels, K., E. C. Stacey, and A. Lackman. 'Beyond Likes and Tweets: Marketing, Social Media Content and Store Performance.' Marketing Science Institute Working Paper Series 2013. Available at: https://www.msi.org/wp-content/uploads/2020/06/MSI_Report_13-1251.pdf (accessed on 26 February 2021).

Pikas, B., and G. Sorrentino. 2014. 'The Effectiveness of Online Advertising: Consumer's Perceptions of Ads on Facebook, Twitter and YouTube.' *Journal of Applied Business and Economics* 16, no. 4 (August): 70–81.

Piskorski, M. J. 2011. 'Social Strategies That Work.' *Harvard Business Review*. Available at: https://hbr.org/2011/11/social-strategies-that-work (accessed on 21 January 2021).

Porter, M. 2001. 'Strategy and the Internet.' *Harvard Business Review* (March): 63–78. Available at: https://hbr.org/2001/03/strategy-and-the-internet (accessed on 21 January 2021).

Royle, J., and A. Laing. 'The Digital Marketing Skills Gap: Developing a Digital Marketer Model for the Communication Industries.' *International Journal of Information Management* 34, no. 2 (April): 65–73. Available at: https://doi.org/10.1016/j.ijinfomgt.2013.11.008 (accessed on 21 January 2021).

Shapiro, C., and H. R. Varian. 1999. *Information Rules: A Strategic Guide to the Network Economy.* Boston, MA: Harvard Business School Press.

The Conversation. 2014. 'Q&A: Philip Kotler on Whether Traditional Marketing Is Dead.' Available at: http://theconversation.com/qanda-philip-kotler-on-whether-traditional-marketing-is-dead-34121 (accessed on 21 January 2021).

Wymbs, C. 2001. 'Digital Marketing: The Time for a New "Academic Major" Has Arrived.' *Journal of Marketing Education* 33, no. 1: 93–106.

CLOSING CASE

F-COMMERCE: SOCIAL, NOT COMMERCIAL

A common myth that is floated around these days is that with over 2.6 billion users as in the first quarter of 2020, Facebook would be a country bigger than China. 'With over 600 million users connecting an average of one hour a day and providing a wealth of information on their tastes, Facebook has a huge potential for sale,' reads an advertisement. Theoretically, a platform with a potential to reach to a global user base of 2.6 billion people is a formidable asset for marketing people reach its users and sell products to them. The only thing is that it is not a country; it is a collection of users who like to post their pictures on it. Could it also help brands sell on its platform?

Facebook tried selling things on its platform, calling it F-commerce. Online sales on Facebook could be done without the user leaving the platform—in other words, people can buy stuff while they are communicating with their friends. Theoretically, if a friend recommends or shares a product on Facebook, the user can buy it then and there.

There was a lot of anticipation that Facebook would turn into a new destination or a place where people would shop, but it was like trying to sell stuff to people while they were hanging out with their friends. Some companies did set up their F-commerce pages on the site, hoping that sales would follow. It did not materialize. Facebook has never been able to become the online shopping emporium that was once predicted.

A flower-delivery service, 1-800-Flowers, struggled to make the leap into doing business on Facebook. It opened its Facebook store in 2009, and though it was one of the first to actually have an F-store, the company found that it was not very successful. People preferred to buy on its website rather than on the Facebook platform. Other ventures include Facebook Gifts, an online gift shop which had to be closed down in 2014. Facebook also tested with 'buy' buttons in newsfeed ads, but even those have not caught on.

Facebook chatbots were used, allowing Messenger bots to accept payments without leaving the app. People could use their credit card information stored with Facebook or Messenger to make instant purchases with the bots. Messenger also supported third-party payment options such as PayPal and Stripe as alternatives. However, Facebook has conceded that Messenger has not produced good e-commerce results.

The F-commerce experience of many companies has not been very successful. GameStop Corporation, a video game retailer, opened a store on Facebook as it had 3.5 million 'fans'. The store lasted only six months. The company did not get ROI that was needed from the Facebook market, so it was shut down quickly. It found that Facebook was a way to communicate with customers on deals, not a place to sell. Customers preferred to buy on its website rather than on Facebook platform, so its marketing ROI was not sustainable.

Other companies also found that having a large number of 'fans' did not translate into sales. Gap had 5.6 million Facebook fans but shut down its Facebook store. JCPenney, Banana Republic, Old Navy and Nordstrom have all opened and closed storefronts on Facebook. The stores' quick failure shows that the social network does not drive commerce.

F-commerce has not turned out to be a serious threat to Amazon or PayPal. Even though Facebook is the most-visited website in the world, it has not succeeded in e-commerce. Expectations that it could be a marketplace have failed. But despite efforts, e-commerce on its platform has not yielded results, except perhaps for small businesses.

Questions for Discussion

1. With a very large user base, why has F-commerce failed to take off?
2. What do you think is the scope of e-commerce on social media, considering that a large player like Facebook has not succeeded?
3. What can companies do to convert 'fans' into paying customers on social media?
4. What role can Facebook play in the marketing plans of companies? Can digital-only succeed?

Sources

Lutz, A. 2012. 'Gamestop to J. C. Penney Shut Facebook Stores.' Bloomberg. Available at: https://www.bloomberg.com/news/articles/2012-02-17/f-commerce-trips-as-gap -to-penney-shut-facebook-stores-retail (accessed on 21 January 2021).

Walsh, M. 2016. 'A Tough Sell: Why Facebook's E-commerce Dream Failed to Take Flight.' *The Guardian*, 1 October. Available at: https://www.theguardian.com/technology/2016/ oct/01/facebook-businesses-online-shopping-chatbots (accessed on 21 January 2021).

CHAPTER 2

Creating Digital Value

 OPENING CASE

COKE AND MERCEDES: CREATING DIGITAL VALUE

Companies can, today, create value by employing a number of digital technologies in all fields, from manufacturing to marketing. These new technologies include network 3D printing, robotics, smart products, advertising using virtual screens and 3D interactive models and employing data tools and analytics, covering all functions of a business. Using such technologies creatively, companies can change their product offerings and also change how things are designed, made, sold and serviced.

Combining these technologies can create value across business operations and also by efficiently making and delivering products matching customer needs.

This case study discusses two companies that have used technology to deliver customer value in completely different ways. They integrate business operations in ways that seemed unimaginable just a few years back. This is done through collaboration between channel partners, customers, and in many cases, competitors as well. Digitizing the value chain can result in innovation across levels and users as our two examples show. A well-connected inventory system, for example, can result in huge savings by optimizing manufacturing operations, reduce time to market and match supply needed by customers, reducing stock holding across operations.

In particular, product development and design are revolutionized as customers opt in for co-creation and co-design. Beyond the design and manufacturing phase, the digital value is created by connecting partners, as the following companies show.

#ShareaCoke

Coca-Cola introduced its 'Share a Coke' campaign in 2014 in collaboration with channel partners. Instead of its trade name, the company introduced bottles with 250 popular American names on them. This kind of thing would have been unthinkable just a few years back when products could not be customized. By doing so, the company added to the delight of consumers when they saw a bottle with their own name on it (Figure 2.1).

Consumers could search for bottles that had names of their friends or family members on them and share it with them. 'Share a Coke is a fun way to connect with friends and loved ones,' says its website. The fun moments could be captured in pictures, and people could share them and tweet about their experiences using the hashtag #ShareaCoke. The campaign was a huge success. Slowly, the company increased the number of names to 1,000. Customers could customize the names on bottles on Coca-Cola's online store. The results have been phenomenal.

The campaign encouraged consumers to share pictures of their enjoying the drink with their friends and family and post them on social media. This generated a lot of positive content, and customers loved the job of creating pictures and text with bottles featuring the

FIGURE 2.1 *Coke Was Able to Customize Bottles with Popular Names, Adding to Brand Excitement*

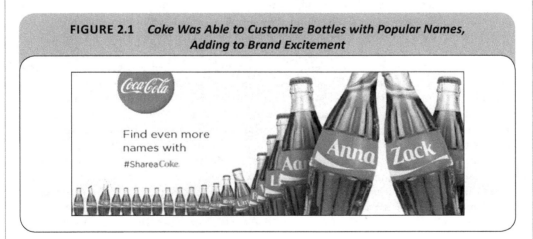

Source: https://cocacolaunited.com/blog/2015/05/18/share-coke-bigger-better-ever/ (accessed on 22 January 2021).

(Continued)

(Continued)

names of their loved ones. Consumers posted more than 500,000 photos with the #ShareaCoke hashtag, and the company gained some 25 million new Facebook followers.

The campaign was not about followers alone but encouraged people to buy and share the product. Customers loved to share their personal stories and connect with their friends and family members, and the names on bottles made it a personal sharing space. Combining it with offline, the company created a cross-country 'Share a Coke' tour in which customers could customize their Coke cans. Pre-printed cans carrying the labels 'Bestie', or 'BFF' also became popular. Later in 2017, consumers could hear a short jingle with their name in it, and the name labels were made removable in 2018 and could be stuck to clothing or personal items of consumers.

In Israel, large interactive signs greeted consumers by name, and in China, nicknames were printed on the bottles. A new variation included lyrics of a popular song that were printed on the labels.

The campaign was powerful as it combined technology for customizing the bottles, and this helped consumer engagement and sales growth.

Mercedes me

Mercedes has gone about digitizing the value chain in a different manner. It has focused on CX by providing 'Mercedes me Adapter' and 'Mercedes me connect' apps.

'Mercedes me' app is an e-sim based cloud connectivity solution. It offers over 25 unique features such as remote lock/unlock, parked vehicle locator, send destination to car, remote retrieval of vehicle status, valet protect, speed alert and continuously monitors the health of the vehicle. It helps in maintenance management by collecting remote vehicle diagnostics data on various parameters of vehicle running and sent to the service partner. This ensures that maintenance is done before a breakdown occurs. The company uses tele-diagnostics to track the wear of automotive parts so that they can be replaced before they breakdown.

Along with these, the system also provides breakdown management services, including accident recovery. If an accident occurs, a message is send automatically to the Mercedes-Benz emergency response centre with the vehicle's position and the number of occupants. The emergency call data is connected to a Europe-wide emergency response centre, ensuring quick relief.

Another feature is the Mercedes-Benz User Experience, a smart virtual assistant, 'Hey Mercedes'. It is an infotainment system launched in the 2019 A-class and subsequent models. As many people tend to anthropomorphize their cars, the assistant allows people to have conversations with their cars, and this tends to build a relationship with them. The live traffic information alerts users about the live traffic information and the estimated driving time. It supports the digital vehicle key which can be used to lock and unlock the Mercedes-Benz from one's smartphone and to start the engine. The user's smartphone becomes the car key. Some Mercedes-Benz vehicles can use Car-to-X communication to share information with one another and to warn users quickly about traffic jams and driving conditions.

While reading this chapter, try to answer the following questions:

1. How can value be added digitally to products?

2. What are the principles of digital value creation?
3. Relate the methods used by these two companies with the tools described in this chapter.
4. How can companies respond to the digital value challenge?

Sources

Coca-Cola website: https://www.coca-colacompany.com/au/faqs/what-was-the-share-a-coke-campaign (accessed on 22 January 2021).

Mercedes me website: https://www.mercedes-benz.com/en/mercedes-me/ (accessed on 22 January 2021).

Nanry, J., S. Narayanan, and L. Rassey. 2015. 'Digitizing the Value Chain.' *McKinsey Quarterly* (March). Available at: https://www.mckinsey.com/business-functions/operations/our-insights/digitizing-the-value-chain (accessed on 22 January 2021).

■ INTRODUCTION

The concept of value is central to marketing. It refers to the satisfaction that people get when they buy and consume products. If they are highly satisfied, they are willing to pay more for products and services. Companies marketing products must, therefore, ensure that the derived satisfaction from the benefits of a product or service must be greater than the costs incurred in obtaining it.

This is the premise on which modern marketing rests. Traditionally, the value was created by making better products either in terms of functionality, design or by adding psychological benefits. Michael Porter (1985) had introduced the concept of the value chain, which described the sequence of activities from design to production to selling and delivering products, adding value at each stage. With the advent of the connected, 'always-on' customer, companies have to find ways to add value in the digital value chain. However, Favaro (2016) makes an interesting point that companies should not plunge into the digital world without specifying how they intend to add value. He suggests that companies have to first affect the value proposition to the target customer through digital technology.

Digital value requires information systems that are open, connected and easy to learn and use. Systems have already been built that integrate computer-aided design, ERP and manufacturing systems so that they communicate with each other and with all partners. Porter explained that companies could build competitive advantage by adding value at each stage of their operations: the way they sourced raw material, in manufacturing and design and marketing and sales. It is an important concept, which shows how companies can build sustainable business models which competitors find difficult to copy.

The value chain can, thus, be seen as consisting of systems and activities and shows how each operation has an effect on costs and profit. Traditional businesses have followed this model and focused on primary activities: inbound logistics, production, outbound logistics, marketing, sales and service. These are supported by firm infrastructure, human resources (HR), technology development and procurement functions in creating value for both customers as well as the firm. The next section explains how value is added to products.

HOW VALUE IS ADDED TO PRODUCTS

To understand the concept of value, we have to understand how basic products become augmented products. A core product is one that fulfils a fundamental need of the customer. For instance, a camera is purchased for the pictures it takes. When features and services are added to the core product to make it more useful, it becomes an augmented product. So a camera can be provided with a carrying case, a battery, a memory card and a guarantee, which would make it much more useful for customers. Most products are marketed using the augmented product concept since core products are generic products and do not offer any advantage for the seller or value for the consumer. Products can be augmented as shown in Figure 2.2. How companies are able to customize products and thereby augment them is illustrated in our Opening Case on Coke and Mercedes.

FIGURE 2.2 *How Core Products Are Augmented*

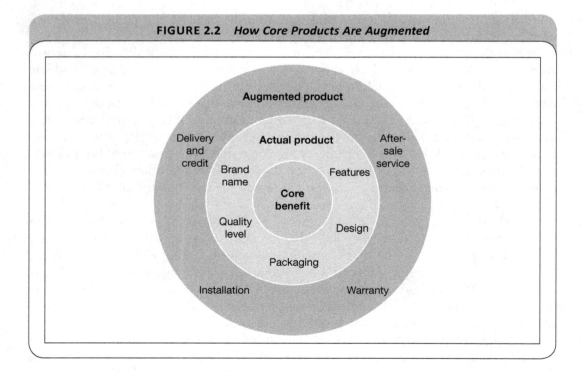

Today, digital capabilities must be added to each of the areas described above. Every point of creating and delivering value can be enhanced by digital technologies. While traditional companies must think of ways to increase value both for themselves and their customers by using digital tools, online-only businesses must add value in the way they solve problems for their customers. This is not an easy task, since the digital value is quite abstract and fluid. Customers may find a service or app useful at one time but will leave in droves if a better app comes along. Companies, thus, try to increase the number of users by providing incentives, but the question remains whether this is a sustainable way of doing business (see Closing Case).

Online tools help add considerable value to products by augmenting them, such as:

- Product presentation using virtual reality tools
- Comparison of attributes and prices
- Online payments or cash on delivery (COD)
- Quick deliveries
- Try and buy at customer's site
- Customizing the offering and adding features required by customers
- Suggestions for complementary products or services
- Co-creation and co-design of products
- Virtual touring

 Value

All these activities are of use to customers and give them a reason to buy. The digital value is added in this way by enhancing products, services and the entire industry.

In this chapter, we describe the concept of digital value and how companies are creating it digitally. The strategies for value creation are as follows:

1. Transforming the value chain from manufacturing to marketing
2. Enhancement of the physical value chain with a virtual value chain
3. Co-creation with stakeholders
4. Creating marketspaces
5. Network and sharing economies
6. Dynamic pricing

■ TRANSFORMING THE VALUE CHAIN

Products are enhanced by various digital technologies. Entire industries and value chains must undergo a transformation. This transformation is called *Industry 4.0* and shows that production, supply chains and CX can all be transformed by the digitization process. Digitization has resulted in great benefits in the industrial sector and new capabilities which promise to multiply them.

Industry 4.0 is the term used to describe the transformation in the industry as it increasingly employs automation and data exchange in manufacturing technologies.

Technologies such as robotics, the Internet of things (IoT), cloud computing and artificial intelligence (AI) and intelligent systems promise to revolutionize the entire industry value chain.

The industry is going through a transformation as digital technologies continue to expand and offer new ways of doing and controlling operations. Figure 2.3 shows the

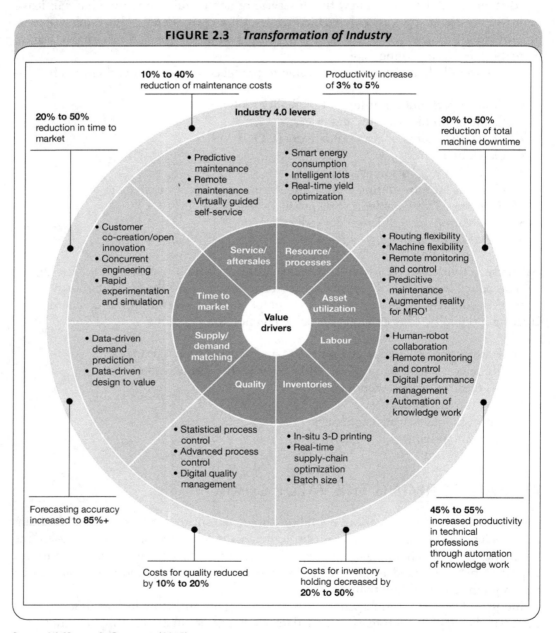

FIGURE 2.3 *Transformation of Industry*

Source: McKinsey & Company (2015).

drivers of value for Industry 4.0, given by McKinsey (Caylar, Noterdaeme and Naik 2016). Note that value is added at each stage of operations, from manufacturing to marketing.

1. **Manufacturing:** Data helps in increasing the optimum use of resources and energy, which can result in up to 5 per cent reduction in resources used.
2. **Maintenance and downtime:** Technology helps in reducing downtime, predictive maintenance, manufacturing and routing. Both downtime and maintenance costs are reduced dramatically.
3. **Automation of knowledge work:** Automation of knowledge work can bring about many opportunities, such as using robots effectively, automation and remote monitoring.
4. **Stock control:** Efficient supply chains can affect just-in-time deliveries, resulting in huge savings. Deploying 3D printing can further reduce inventories and delivery time.
5. **Quality control:** Quality control is made efficient by the use of statistical process control, digital quality management and will result in a huge reduction in quality costs and efficient manufacturing.
6. **Demand forecasting:** Data analytics, including data-driven demand prediction, paves the way for accurate demand forecasting, leading to savings across the supply chain.
7. **Time to market:** Co-creation and open innovation can help build the most relevant products for consumers. Time to market is considerably reduced by employing techniques such as concurrent engineering and quick experimentation and simulation.
8. **Productivity increase:** Productivity gains are experienced across the board as companies employ digital technologies in their manufacturing and marketing process.

Digital Value Creation

Digital value refers to the benefit that consumers get in using digital services and platforms. However, this calls for a radical change in company functioning; rather than protecting its knowledge, it has to open up and share information with stakeholders. The case study of P&G (Marketing Insight 2.1) shows a transparent approach that has helped its product development research. Transparency is the reason that consumers use a service or platform, and it consists of transformation at every stage of operation of a business that occurs due to digital technologies. It is built by (a) using technologies to capture new frontiers of the business world, (b) creating new avenues in imparting CXs and (c) building foundational capabilities that support the entire structure (Dörner and Edelman 2015).

Digital value has to be seen from two sides:

1. From the point of users, who must see a benefit in using online services
2. From the point of view of companies, who must generate revenue from their activities

For existing companies, the digital value is created by adding digital components to its model of business as described above. This can consist of ease of buying and making payments or providing services to customers by using online tools. Digital value can be created both in existing traditional companies as well as in online companies.

The digital value is the reason that a customer seeks the services of a company repeatedly. It is created not by influencing a one-time sale only. A McKinsey (2015) report mentions four core capabilities for digital value creation, which are as follows:

1. **Proactive approach:** Since customers are constantly shifting channels, companies have to be proactive in real time. Customers want immediate resolution of problems, and this requires quick responsiveness. It also involves delivering relevant communications and personalizing all moments of truth (MOT) in the customer decision journey. While the back office crunches data about customer needs and behaviour in real time, the company must proactively respond to this data.
2. **Dynamic interactivity:** Data from touch points shows how the consumer is interacting with the brand across channels. This builds a path for modifying interactions. Tracking customer interactions gives a stream of data that allows brands to deliver a better CX. The use of wearable technology and the IoT gives so much data that companies can adopt dynamic interactivity.
3. **Automation:** Modern technologies can help automate routine functions and interactions with customers. Given the number of consumers that are tracked with each at multiple touch points, tracking them requires automation. Automation helps solve problems and queries quickly, personalize communications and influence customer decision journeys across channels and devices. Customers get responses at any time and across any channel.
4. **Journey-focused innovation:** As companies track and influence CDJs, it allows them to be creative in their interactions. Existing customer journeys can give indications to sell complementary products, and thus, companies discover new areas in which to extend the relationship with their customers. A positive spiral is created, and companies can think of creating new avenues and platforms.

MARKETING INSIGHT 2.1 *P&G: Adding Value through Open Innovation and Co-creation*

Companies are redefining how they create value by seeking consumer participation in new product development. This case study describes P&G's initiative of Connect + Develop (C+D) open innovation programme so as to incorporate external expertise into their new products (Figure 2.4). The company describes the initiative on its website as, 'P&G is collaborating with individuals and companies around the world to develop innovative ideas and products.'

P&G's senior management team consisting of Larry Huston and Nabil Sakkab (2006) describe how the system came about. The company developed products based on its own

FIGURE 2.4   *The Website of P&G's C+D Model of Open Innovation*

Source: http://jugaadtoinnovation.blogspot.com/2012/09/open-innovation-panacea.html (accessed on 22 January 2021).

R&D departments, but by 2000, it was clear that the model was outdated. The innovation success rate was just about 35 per cent, and the company's stock had more than halved to $52 a share. A new strategy of innovation was required.

The result was a co-creation platform, the C+D model that could identify ideas from across the world in combination with the company's own R&D expertise, 'to create better and cheaper products, faster'. Sakkab (2002) writes that the system uses corporate intranet and reporting systems for knowledge sharing, community participation, technology entrepreneurs and open innovation with government and university sharing. This strategy is very helpful in the present times when product life cycles are short, and companies must have a pipeline of new products that they can launch. Brown and Anthony (2011) describe it as a process to 'marry the creativity of Edison's lab with the speed and reliability of Ford's factory'.

The company created six C+D hubs so that ideas would flow from different countries. This has helped the company to develop new products by making them 'simpler, more convenient, easier to access or more affordable.' P&G developed a washing powder for developing countries that could provide greater benefit at a lower cost, called Tide Naturals. It could reduce cost by developing a locally produced perfume for the powder. It introduced Swash in the USA, which was a quick and easy way to clean the clothes required for a developed country. A new business model called Tide Dry Cleaners was also developed.

The company could do this by creating a platform for technology entrepreneurs who could mine scientific literature, generate ideas and look for a local alternative of raw material. A secure platform was created to share technology with suppliers, giving a push to the process of co-creation. Several open networks were created to connect researchers globally.

(Continued)

(Continued)

Among them was NineSigma that shares technology briefs with partners and collaborators. If the idea works, the system connects with the company, and the product is developed for commercial launch. Its InnoCentive system puts up problems and scientists from across the world suggest solutions, which are tried and tested. The YourEncore platform brings together retired scientists and engineers from across companies, leveraging on their experience and wide exposure to different companies and systems. Another platform, yet2.com, is an online marketplace for intellectual property exchange for companies, universities and government labs. The Live Well programme was founded to design products and services for the elderly. It formed a collaboration with Citigroup, the design school of the University of Cincinnati and the Singapore government.

The C+D co-creation platform has been highly effective. The company's R&D productivity increased by 60 per cent, and the innovation success rate has doubled.

Why is it necessary for companies to have an open innovation strategy?

Sources

Brown, B., and S. D. Anthony. 2011. 'How P&G Tripled Its Innovation Success Rate.' *Harvard Business Review* (June). Available at: https://hbr.org/2011/06/how-pg-tripled-its-innovation-success-rate (accessed on 22 January 2021).

Huston, L., and N. Sakkab. 2006. 'Connect and Develop: Inside Procter & Gamble's New Model for Innovation.' *Harvard Business Review* (March). Available at: https://hbr.org/2006/03/connect-and-develop-inside-procter-gambles-new-model-for-innovation (accessed on 22 January 2021).

P&G website: https://us.pg.com/ (accessed on 22 January 2021).

Sakkab, N. 2002. 'Connect & Develop Complements Research & Develop at P&G.' *Research-Technology Management* 45, no. 2 (January): 38–45. Available at: https://doi.org/10.1080/08956308.2002.11671490 (accessed on 22 January 2021).

VIRTUAL VALUE CHAIN

The concept of value chain shows that value is added at every stage of operation by a company; it is created at every stage of physical and digital operations. Since physical processes can be made more efficient by digital technologies, a company's success lies in adding digital value at every stage of operations. This implies transforming the entire way of doing business using data, metrics and technology. By using new technologies, companies can develop new capabilities to improve customer service by understanding customer purchasing journeys and analysing touch points. In the process, companies build foundational capabilities that support the entire business structure.

The concept of creating value is described by Michael Porter in the value chain concept, which shows how companies add value at different stages such as inbound logistics, production, outbound logistics and sales and marketing. It consists of a series of primary and secondary activities through which companies can differentiate their operations and products and thus gain a competitive advantage. The value chain has been very successful in analysing individual value-added activities that can get customers hooked to products and brands. The model has been extremely helpful for companies to guide their investments and create processes that are valued by customers.

The virtual value chain is defined as an enhancement of the physical value chain by information-based value activities. The enhancement takes place as companies use IT to engage in a virtual world. The activities in the traditional value chain are extended and developed by the use of technology. Rayport and Sviokla (1994) write that every company today competes in two different worlds: a *physical* world consisting of resources that can be seen and touched and the *virtual* in which information is the resource.

Information is the raw material that must be used to provide service for users. For instance, BookMyShow (see Marketing Insight 2.1) connects seating plans and ticket availability information from theatres for consumers to easily book their tickets. It collects raw information and organizes it in a way that suppliers and consumers find useful, thereby creating value for both. Finally, it connects to physical resources (theatres) that people like to go.

The virtual value chain (Figure 2.5) can be understood as consisting of content, context, infrastructure and finally leading to CX, as explained below:

- **Content:** The product or service that is offered. This may be linked to the physical world.
- **Context:** The offering in the context of consumer needs, or how it solves a consumer problem.

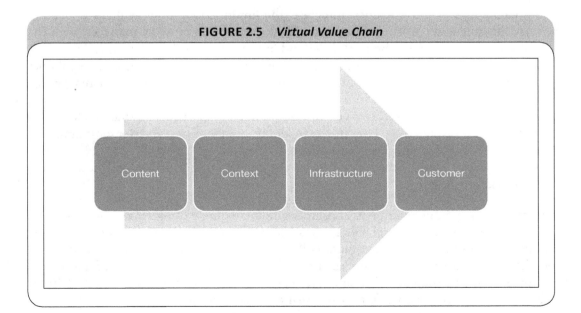

FIGURE 2.5   *Virtual Value Chain*

Content → Context → Infrastructure → Customer

- **Infrastructure:** The system that enables the transaction and includes facilities for physical display and distribution.
- **Consumer:** MOT by which a consumer interacts with physical and virtual channels of a company.

Every stage of the virtual value chain adds value and creates new value opportunities. The important thing to note here is that the physical and the virtual chain are not treated as distinct. Both the physical and virtual activities support each other to provide a complete CX. Liu and Wu (2010) write that today managers must have the capability to understand the interrelations between the two chains as this will help them see more opportunities for value creation as compared to operating within one chain only.

With IT becoming ubiquitous, value chains have changed profoundly. The first impact has been on using and integrating information in value chains. Through ERP systems, all the company's operations are integrated, which enables it to visualize all the activities and the value that each one is adding to the entire operation. A McKinsey report (Nanry, Narayanan, and Rassey 2015) notes, 'The aggregation and analysis of data across a product's life cycle can increase the uptime of production machinery, reduce time to market, and make it possible to understand the product's consumers.'

The virtual value chain is a model that shows how companies add value across all activities and consumer interactions (Figure 2.6). It gives a tool for companies to design their business processes for a sustainable advantage over the competition. Information is, generally, seen as a means of monitoring and control, but in the digital era, it becomes a source of generating value.

The value chain can be transformed by IT in the following four stages:

- **Collect:** When companies integrate the information, they build a system of collecting and collating information. This information provides managers with the ability to coordinate their activities and improve systems in an organization.
- **Integrate:** Second, companies integrate online capabilities into their physical ones to make them more efficient or customer-friendly, like online payments, online tracking or online co-creation.
- **Create:** Third, they create a virtual value chain that connects all stakeholders. This information creates a basis for developing communities and for engaging and co-creation with customers and others.
- **Automate:** Fourth, they integrate offsite manufacturing and AI in products and services.

The last step is gaining traction as consumers are increasingly using AI-enabled assistants such as Amazon's Alexa and Google Assistant. These have evolved into becoming marketing platforms. These assistants collect customer data every time an enquiry or purchase is made. Using this information, they are able to build detailed profiles of customers showing their brand preferences, a price–quality combination of a user, delivery schedules and so on. Such systems can learn to place orders on their own based on past usage and preferences, thus becoming an aid to the marketing of routine purchases. Dawar

FIGURE 2.6   *Value Is Added at Every Stage of Customer Interaction*

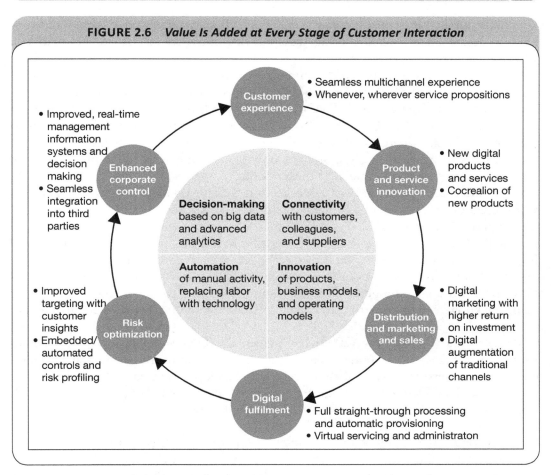

Source: http://www.theagileelephant.com/mckinsey-technology-impact-on-business-social-businesss-role/ (accessed on 15 April 2021).

(2018) explains that the assistant will evolve as a portal for shopping and advertising, all while collecting and analysing information. The virtual assistant can also suggest alternative products and play the role of a shopkeeper. Companies will then have to link and market to virtual assistants rather than consumers.

CO-CREATION

Earlier, companies designed products in-house by their R&D departments. Today, informed and networked customers are more than willing to give their inputs to companies. Customers feel empowered when companies involve them, so it is a win-win situation for both. Co-creation changes the way value is created, since now there is a combination of both internal and outside HR. Zimmermann et al. (2014) write that this 'synergistic public-private value creation requires a different starting point', and companies have to create mechanisms to bring together different stakeholders on one platform, which is the basis of co-creation.

Prahalad and Ramaswamy (2004) define co-creation as 'the joint creation of value by the company and the customer; allowing the customer to co-construct the service experience to suit their context'. That is, a company enlists customers to design products and services. This is done by means of an intranet or a collaboration platform similar to that of Facebook, where companies and customers interact. Companies may limit co-creation with some strategic customers only or have a common platform. We have described several cases of co-creation in this book.

Co-creation adds value and is a response to the changing nature of competition and value creation process due to digital technologies, leading to customized products and experiences. Prahalad and Krishanan (2008) write, 'Value is based on unique, personalized experiences of consumers. Firms have to learn to focus on one consumer and his/her experience at a time, even if they serve 100 million consumers.'

For example, Starbucks asks customers to design their own drink by clicking on add-ons (Chapter 6). If a large number of customers are choosing a particular combination, the company knows which drink to commercialize. Such interaction between companies and consumers is becoming common.

Prahalad and Ramaswamy (2004) have given the DART model for co-creation of value, which takes into account recent advances in communications technology, which enables customers to engage with brands and develop long-term relationships with companies. The DART model consists of four components: dialogue, access, risk assessment and transparency (DART), as explained below:

1. **Dialogue:** Communication technologies encourage interaction and engagement between companies and customers, as opposed to one-way communication, which was the norm earlier. Dialogue implies listening and sharing and the creation of a loyal community.
2. **Access:** This step means providing information and tools to customers and suppliers so that they have access to the company's resources. Customers can contribute to the co-creation process better if they have access to the design and processes of the company.
3. **Risk assessment:** If customers participate in the co-creation of value, they must be aware of risks to them and society. Companies should inform customers fully about the risks associated with products and services.
4. **Transparency:** Modern IT does not support secrecy and opaqueness. Transparency means firms should share all information related to costs, prices and profits. Companies and customers need to practice openness of information in all areas and build trust.

By combining elements of DART in any way, companies can create digital capabilities in many ways. For example, by combining access and transparency, investments in shares and securities have become very easy as opposed to the traditional method when orders had to be placed through brokers.

MARKETPLACE VERSUS MARKETSPACE

Many companies make the mistake of treating the physical and virtual chains as separate. It was thought that physical chains relate to manufacturing and delivery, while the real value came from online technology. Such thinking has caused problems for many online companies (see the closing case 'Brands without Profits'). That is why modern companies have to combine each activity of the physical chain to virtual value chains.

The physical world is the marketplace, and the virtual world is the marketspace.

Marketplace

A marketplace is a physical location which brings together sellers and buyers. Readers will be familiar with this term, as marketplaces are the traditional way of selling to consumers.

Marketspace

An e-marketplace or marketspace is an online platform on which sellers can give information about their products, and buyers can transact online to buy those products. Without intermediaries, the marketspace is a web-based platform which helps both suppliers and buyers.

An e-marketplace can host a large number of sellers who are not limited by location and can be based anywhere in the world. It becomes a showcase of products and helps consumers to find those products. Transactions are facilitated by online trading and payments. Examples of marketspaces are Amazon, Flipkart, eBay and other similar sites. These marketspaces allow connections between suppliers and buyers wherever they might be.

A marketspace becomes a platform for two-way conversations between companies and customers, and also among customers themselves. It is an online space through which sellers can list and sell their products and match them with the requirements of customers, who can describe their needs on it. Marketspaces help expand markets and can, theoretically, at least, sell any product from anywhere in the world.

Marketspace versus Marketplace

How is value created in marketplaces and marketspaces? It is not as simple as aggregating products to sell on a platform. A marketspace has to offer some value to consumers so that they are tempted to use it. Kim and Mauborgne (1999) describe a 'New Value Curve'

FIGURE 2.7 *New Value Curve*

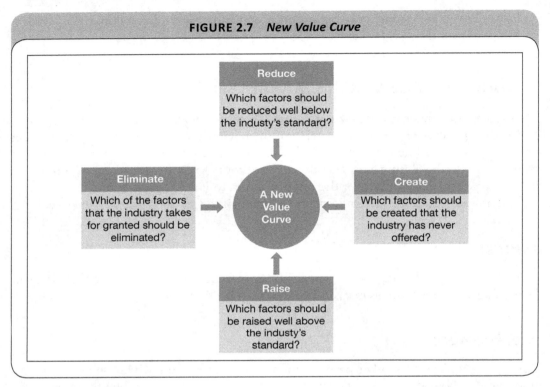

Source: Kim and Mauborgne (1999).

which shows how companies can create new marketspace. It requires new thinking and systematically going across boundaries. Hence, instead of looking at new technologies to help the business incrementally, they look for ways in which technologies will add value for customers. It helps understand the factors that must be reduced below the industry standard, raised above the industry standard, factors that should be eliminated or factors that should be created that the industry has never offered before (Figure 2.7).

A value curve is a simple tool that helps companies to work out a strategy that is different from competitors. Companies can *eliminate* costly features, redundant processes and barriers among departments to reduce their cost. They *raise* features such as product offerings, staff knowledge, timings and ease of use. They make attempts to *reduce* price, packaging cost and complexities of business. Finally, they *create* breakthrough value by innovating and solving problems for customers by using digital technologies. The case of Airbnb (Marketing Insight 2.2) shows how it was able to create a completely new marketspace.

The value curve model helps in creating marketspaces which were not discovered before. It is a simple means of deploying technology by companies, identifies gaps in the market and is an effective tool to find out about integrating digital technologies. Other ways of adding value are described in the next section.

MARKETING INSIGHT 2.2 *Creating Digital Value: Airbnb*

Digital technologies have given rise to new opportunities in businesses based on sharing resources. Since digital technologies connect both suppliers and consumers, sharing of resources becomes easy. Both intangible and tangible resources are shared in a win-win situation for both parties: the users get services cheaply, and the suppliers are able to use their idle resources to earn money. This new economy is called the *networked economy*. Using peer-to-peer networks, a number of companies, today, offer convenience and, in the process, drive down costs.

This case study describes Airbnb, which is a typical example of a marketspace in which people offer their rooms to travellers across the world. It is an online platform that lets people rent out their spare accommodation. Today, it partners with car rental services, restaurants, entertainment and tour sites to offer experiences to its users, becoming an online 'travel community' for global travellers.

The sharing arrangement allows people who have spare rooms to share them for a price, while the travellers get a chance to savour the local flavour of cities that hotels cannot provide. People have put up rooms not only in their apartments but also in villas and castles on Airbnb, offering unique travel experiences. The company was started in 2008 and now offers more than 6 million listings in 100,000 cities.

Airbnb lists properties with descriptions and photographs, which makes it appealing for users and are easy to choose. The site offers homes and travel experiences and has recently added online experiences as well. Online experiences consist of learning skills like baking or cartooning, attending a concert or a wine class, meeting 'dogs of Chernobyl' or experience 'meditation with sleepy sheep'. Hosts can avail services of professional photos on the site, improving the visuals and the spaces become more attractive for users (Figure 2.8). This also gives Airbnb a good click-through rate. The company uses Google display advertising that shows images from actual listings on the site, increasing international traffic considerably.

Airbnb started in 2007 when Brian Chesky and Joe Gebbia noticed that all hotel rooms in San Francisco were booked due to conferences and decided to share their apartment in an effort to help pay the rent. They bought some inflatable mattresses and offered visitors a 'homestay experience'. Airbnb was thus formed. They saw an opportunity in providing this service in other cities also and expanded the listings. It was not an easy journey, and it was only after experimenting with different models that they found success. To fulfil the bed-and-breakfast part, they designed cereal boxes, Obama O's and Cap'n McCains and used them to get their first funding. The company is estimated to be worth $38 billion in 2019 (Warren 2019).

Airbnb is a community of travellers who do not want to see places as tourists but as local residents, avoiding the formality of hotels. The users get a home away from home in a community based on trust and sharing. The revenue model of Airbnb rests on charging a service fee from both the hosts of properties and the guest.

The company has seen controversies as well. Some people have protested against the commercialization of their neighbourhoods. It has also resulted in increased rents in some areas. The system works on ratings given by both the travellers and the owners, and some have been blocked from the platform, causing further criticism.

(Continued)

(*Continued*)

FIGURE 2.8 *Airbnb Offers Services of Professional Photographs That Add Aesthetic Value to Properties*

Source: https://www.esquireme.com/content/40620-airbnb-will-now-have-a-party-house-rapid-response-team (accessed on 22 January 2021).

Airbnb has started offering host guarantee and host protection to meet the criticism it has faced. It now requires a government ID before booking, provides reviews and enforces house rules for guests. It also offers protection for property damage and liability insurance along with global customer support.

In 2016, an alternative, Fairbnb, tried to get over the criticisms faced by Airbnb. Its website describes its approach as: 'Fairbnb.coop is the cooperative accommodation booking platform that promotes and funds local initiatives and projects,' donating 50 per cent of its fee to communities visited by users.

Airbnb combines the advantages of a network economy: sharing, global awareness and decentralization. It has disrupted the hotel industry with its operations. In terms of listings, it has more rooms than the world's hotel chains, but its market share in many cities remains small. Its success has been part of the 'sharing economy' that is becoming highly popular now. Other companies such as Uber and Ola are part of this new sharing economy, which is based on the principle of a larger user base both on the demand and supply side. The success of Airbnb has been based on the following:

- Offering a personal home environment for users
- Reducing costs
- Appealing to young travellers who do not like to stay at hotels
- Offering the possibility of socializing for travellers
- Removing the middleman and commissions—in this case, the travel agent
- Genuine reviews based on an actual stay

However, despite being valued highly at more than $30 billion, Airbnb suffers the curse of many Internet businesses: CNBC (2019) reported that its quarterly losses doubled over the last year in the first quarter to $306 million and has postponed its initial public offering. Airbnb is in the company of big names such as Lyft, Uber and WeWork, which struggle to make profits.

How were the elements of the value curve exploited by Airbnb?

Sources

Airbnb website: https://www.airbnb.co.in/ (accessed on 22 January 2021).

CNBC. 2019. 'Airbnb's Quarterly Loss Reportedly Doubled in Q1, a Bad Sign as Investors Grow Wary of Money-losers.' Available at: https://www.cnbc.com/2019/10/17/airbnbs-quarterly-loss-reportedly-doubled-in-q1.html (accessed on 22 January 2021).

Fairbnb website: https://fairbnb.coop/ (accessed on 22 January 2021).

Warren, K. 2019. 'Brian Chesky Cofounded Airbnb in 2008.' Business Insider (28 August). Available at: https://www.businessinsider.in/brian-chesky-cofounded-airbnb-in-2008-to-help-pay-rent-on-his-san-francisco-apartment-and-now-hes-worth-4-2-billion-heres-what-the-ceos-life-is-like-from-partying-at-burning-man-to-taking-airbnb-stay-cations-/articleshow/70878010.cms (accessed on 22 January 2021).

■ MARKETSPACES AND THEIR ECONOMIC IMPACT

E-marketplaces facilitate buying and selling of products. Consumers can look at a very broad range of options and make comparisons based on various attributes. Since earlier sellers were limited by their geographical location and could serve only a limited area, with an e-marketplace, they can theoretically serve the entire global market, finding new buyers and increase their sales. Economic value is thus created for all parties—buyers, sellers, market intermediaries and society.

E-commerce has had a wide-ranging economic impact both in business-to-business (B2B) and business-to-consumer (B2C) markets.

While product availability has improved considerably, e-commerce has also impacted pricing and consumer behaviour. Customers have better choice and access to products that are produced anywhere in the world.

An OECD paper (1999) notes that because of the value that e-commerce provides, barriers have continued to fall for both buyers and sellers. While earlier e-commerce could be carried out by large players, today, anyone can register as a seller on an e-marketplace. Another important feature is that while earlier most B2B transactions occurred between known parties, today, e-commerce happens between a huge number of firms who may never know each other. The report says, 'The Internet has done for electronic commerce what Henry Ford did for the automobile—converted a luxury for the few into a relatively simple and inexpensive device for the many.'

The backbone of the e-marketplace is technology, so investments in e-commerce technology are increasing. Intermediaries like banks gain by providing platforms for e-payments and providing insurance for buyers and sellers. Transportation systems get connected and e-commerce has facilitated efficient supply chains in a very big way. It has fostered delivery services in towns and cities that reach millions of packets to customers each day, thus connecting small towns and communities which earlier did not have access to markets.

We further examine digital value from the point of view of an industry. In the next section, we examine the integrated way that value is added by the modern industry by using digital technologies.

■ VISIBILITY, MIRRORING CAPABILITY AND NEW CUSTOMER RELATIONSHIPS

The virtual value chain describes how companies integrate into the information world to perform value-adding steps, just as they would for physical value chains. Rayport and Sviokla (1995) explain that companies adopt value-adding information processes in three stages: visibility, mirroring and capability for establishing new customer relationships. They describe a radical shift in thinking from physical markets to virtual ones based on information. They define marketspace as 'a virtual realm where products and services exist as digital information and can be delivered through information-based channels'. The three stages are briefly described as follows:

1. **Visibility:** Visibility means using the information to keep track of business operations. Companies collect and use the information to control and monitor operations at different stages in the value chain. This gives the ability to visualize the company as an integrated operation, keeping control across the supply chain by integration information through ERP systems. The IT systems help to coordinate activities across business operations. The physical value chains are the precursors for making virtual value chains in organizations.

2. **Mirroring:** The second phase is the mirroring capability, in which companies substitute virtual activities for physical ones, that is, value-adding activities are shifted from the physical marketplace to the virtual marketspace. For example, the web page is a mirror of an activity that has existed in the physical world. Companies look for operations that can be done better and faster through online tools.

3. **New customer relationships:** Finally, companies are able to use the information to establish new customer relationships, resulting in acquiring new customers and getting additional business from existing ones. It involves providing a platform for customers and engaging them through it. The flow of information in the virtual value chain is used to deliver value to customers in new ways.

At the heart of the digital value chain is the networked economy, which allows diverse people to come together for common activities.

NETWORK ECONOMY

Another aspect of adding value to digital value chains is the network economy, which means that value is added to products and services through participation of people in social networks. An economic network consists of individuals, groups or other entities that interact for the common benefit of the community. The larger the network of interested members, the more is the contribution to innovation and co-creation. This represents a revolutionary change, as earlier companies did not have the means of getting partners and customers involved. Businesses can, therefore, capture value created by social networks in a variety of ways.

The importance of networks is highlighted by Satell (2014), who writes, 'Competitive advantage is no longer the sum of all efficiencies but the sum of all connections. To win in today's connected economy, you need to deepen and widen networks.' In the network economy, a company does not remain an isolated one but represents an ecosystem of useful networks. Competitive advantage is gained from these networks, and it is up to the company to find ways of adding value through their connections to widen their networks and get everyone involved.

A report by Deloitte (2017) says that businesses are developing their own networks that can be leveraged into serious profits. The networked economy results from an interconnected business ecosystem. 'This interconnectedness fundamentally flips the script,' it says, because the power gets shifted from producers to networked communities. Further, earlier, networks were of people and processes within a company, but now, they include people who are outside the company's direct control. It also means that companies would have to be completely transparent if they have to develop a trust of their partners and customers. Without this crucial element, companies cannot leverage their networks fully.

It is easy to see that the value of a network increases with the number of users. This is known as Metcalfe's Law, which says that the value of a network is proportional to the square of the number of connected devices. Hence, as a network grows, its value grows exponentially. There are, therefore, two tasks for a company: first, increase the people connected to its network and second, engage them meaningfully so that they contribute value to it. This law explains why the value of social media networks continues to expand with their number of users. It also points to the importance for companies to expand their networks.

A natural outcome of the networked economy is the ability to share skills, knowledge and resources among online communities. This has given rise to another aspect of value addition: the sharing economy. Airbnb is an example of this type of economic value addition. However, the sharing economy has spread far and wide, as described in the next section.

◼ SHARING ECONOMY

The network economy has given rise to a new form of business, called sharing economy.

Sharing economy is a system in which assets or services are shared between individuals through the Internet. People have been able to rent out their idle resources, such as bikes, homes and cars because of the rise of the sharing economy. The model is a peer-to-peer activity of sharing goods and services on an online platform.

Examples of sharing sites are Uber and Airbnb, which are explained in this chapter. They are platforms on which people can find rides and rooms. But the sharing economy is much more than that. Some examples of sharing are as follows:

- **Freelancing:** The sharing economy has encouraged freelancing. Some sites connect people and share the tasks they want to be done and for others to perform those tasks. Upwork lists work relating to writing, designing and coding and freelancers can bid on them. TaskRabbit lists tasks relating to repairs, dog walkers and similar things. Care.com connects care providers for children and elderly people.
- **Coworking:** Sites like WeWork offer office facilities for freelancers, entrepreneurs and telecommuters who do not wish to rent expensive space.
- **Lending:** Some sites offer people to give loans to those who need it. The lenders earn interest on the money loaned, while borrowers can get small loans without depending on banks. Some sites like Rang De focus on social loans which are facilitated on its platform.
- **Clothes:** Some sites allow people to rent, buy and sell used clothing. Sites like Lehengaonrent, Rent My Wardrobe, the Stylease and many others allow people to get a dress on rent which saves them the cost of buying it.
- **Kitchen appliances:** People can take a kitchen appliance for a short time instead of buying it on sites such as RentoMojo, GrabOnRent and Cityfurnish. This helps use spare appliances for people who do not wish to buy them.

These services are possible only with tools like algorithms and data analysis, writes Marr (2016). Both the users and the providers must be linked on a trusted platform that allows search, renting and payment. These platforms do not offer the goods or services themselves but act as facilitators. This is the basis of the sharing economy.

MARKETING INSIGHT 2.3   *Marketspaces: BookMyShow*

BookMyShow is an online ticketing platform owned by Bigtree Entertainment, Mumbai. It was founded in 1999 by Ashish Hemrajani, Parikshit Dar and Rajesh Balpande. The main business of BookMyShow is movie ticketing, but it also offers tickets for events, concerts, comedy shows, theatre, sports and so on.

The valuation of the company is ₹3,960 million (Ahuja 2018). It is the ticketing source for major events in four countries, including India, and is the market leader for online entertainment ticketing with over 3 billion page views a month. With competitors like Paytm pushing ticket sales aggressively, BookMyShow realized that it had to add value both to their venue clients and ticket buyers. It could do so by moving from a purely transactional model of selling tickets to providing information about customers to venues and about events to customers. It uses data analytics to provide venue clients with information about ticket pricing strategies.

BookMyShow had added content that people want. It is now a portal that provides information on movie releases, genres, theatre locations and layout and so on. Customers buy tickets online and pay a convenience fee to the portal. Launched in its present form in 2007, BookMyShow has become popular for online ticket booking. In 2010, it became the ticketing partner for some teams in IPL, and in 2011, it sold tickets for first-ever Formula One race, becoming its exclusive partner. The major source of earning, however, remains to be movie tickets, which contribute 60 per cent of its revenues.

It has an app which has been very popular with users and is very active on social media, with over 8 million likes on Facebook. The company engages with users on social media, sharing information and content about upcoming events.

The company has got funding from various sources over the years, raising funding of over $224.5 million in 6 rounds. The remarkable thing about BookMyShow is that it has survived the dotcom bubble of 2002 and the 2007 financial crisis and has got over the initial problems of the low Internet usage, unwillingness to use credit cards and poor broadband connectivity. The company has been instrumental in getting many theatres on board, linking them with e-ticketing software. Initially, the tickets were delivered to the users; later, they could print them and now simply show the code they get on their mobile screens.

Today, BookMyShow is the market leader in online ticketing. Its revenues have been increasing, going up to ₹6,190 million in 2019. But the expenses have also been rising and were ₹7,335.5 million, reporting a net loss of ₹1,151.9 million (ET Bureau 2019).

Today, BookMyShow faces challenges of rising competition and thinning ticket sales, and fewer people want to go to theatres to see movies.

How can the company survive the onslaughts of similar sites and reduction in the movie-going habit?

Sources

Ahuja, A. 2018. 'BookMyShow Posts 20% Jump in Revenues at ₹400.7 Crore for FY18.' *Mint*, 29 October. Available at: https://www.livemint.com/Companies/kvxojL3TJyE-hXIg37m6u8O/BookMyShow-posts-20-jump-in-revenues-at-4007-crore-for-FY.html (accessed on 20 January 2021).

ET Bureau. 2019. 'BookMyShow Parent's Loss Narrows, Topline Rises.' *The Economic Times*, 11 December. Available at: https://economictimes.indiatimes.com/small-biz/startups/newsbuzz/bookmyshow-parents-loss-narrows-topline-rises/articleshow/72432355.cms?from=mdr (accessed on 20 January 2021).

To succeed, businesses must have an OVP, which is the primary reason that users should visit a site. All companies should develop such a reason because it explains the motivations of a buyer to engage with a company.

ONLINE VALUE PROPOSITION

To convey the value to customers, a company must develop a crisp yet strong value proposition. OVP is a statement describing the online benefits provided by a company and how it delivers those benefits uniquely in a clear, easy-to-understand manner differentiating itself from competitor offerings. OVP describes the target segment and the pain points solved by the company.

Like a positioning statement used in traditional marketing, OVP is a persuasive value proposition that customers understand. It shows customers and prospects why the business offers a better way of doing things.

Examples of some easily understood value propositions are:

- **Bitly:** Shorten, share, measure
- **Macbook:** Light years ahead
- **Vimeo:** Make life worth watching
- **Weebly:** The easiest way to make a website

OVP statement communicates the core values of the business. It answers the question clearly: 'Why should a customer use the online offering?' There has to be a compelling answer to this question so as to appeal to users. Companies have to think through their OVPs and express it succinctly and help solve a customer problem.

While concentrating on digital value creation, many businesses forget the actual cost of serving customers. The cost of creating digital value should be less than what the platform earns by way of user fees and other revenue streams. Both online and offline costs must be recovered. In the next section, we will discuss the second aspect of value creation: that to the company.

PRICE AND CUSTOMER VALUE

Online businesses earn money from the following two sources:

- **User fees:** Commissions charged by portals for their services, like booking a room, buying movie tickets or making e-payments.
- **Advertising fee:** When other companies want to advertise on the platforms because of the large number of users they have, the platforms earn advertising fee.

Some platforms, such as Facebook and Twitter, do not charge any user fee and try to build revenue from advertisers. Other sites, such as BookMyShow, Airbnb and others charge users a fee for using their services. For them, advertising revenues are incidental.

Online companies, thus, have to decide about their revenue models, the prices to be charged and if so, how much. It is a tricky decision because history is dotted with a large number of companies that managed to gather a very large number of users but could not make money, while others have started charging user fee and seen the number of users decline. Others such as BookMyShow and Airbnb (see Marketing Insights 2.2 and 2.3) charge commissions but find that marketing costs are so high that they cannot make profits.

Pricing, therefore, becomes an important variable in the online environment as it determines the business model a company should have. Traditionally, pricing has been based on several strategies, which are summarized as follows:

- **Cost-plus pricing:** In this method, a company estimates all its costs in manufacturing and delivering the product and adds a percentage to it to set its price. Cost-plus pricing ensures that the company or retailer is able to earn the required profit margin. This method, though simple, ignores what competitors may be charging for the product. Online prices have to be more sensitive to competition as a consumer can easily search for similar products and substitutes. Cost-plus pricing is, however, an easy method and gives a thumb rule for pricing decisions.
- **Target return pricing:** When a company sets a target of its ROI and determines price so that the target return can be achieved, it is called target return pricing. This pricing, too, suffers from the shortcoming that it ignores competitor pricing and that sometimes, the target return may not be achievable. Online businesses target the number of users they should have on their platforms, but as sales forecasts, this number tends to go haywire.
- **Value-based pricing:** This pricing strategy is different from the first two as it does not focus on returns but on the value that its customers perceive in them. This strategy is successful for big brands and products that have an emotional pull to them. It is successful online as well, and many entrepreneurs sell customs-made products to customers who see much value in them.
- **Competitive pricing:** As the name implies, this method is based on the price that competitors charge for similar or substitute products. This strategy has to be followed in online markets because the information is available easily. Weak brands or generic products must follow this pricing method. Traditional retailers have to adapt to this pricing method because customers easily check online prices on their smartphones even as they are inspecting goods in physical stores.
- **Lead generation model:** In this method, the company provides information online and interested users contact the company for further information or intervention of a salesperson. Users are engaged online, and leads are generated, and these are followed up by the company sales staff. This method is commonly used in B2B sales.

ONLINE PRICING STRATEGIES

Online pricing can make use of any of the above methods but must take into account the advantages that the online environment offers. One of the major advantages online is that prices can be changed several times a day. Thus, companies can extract more value. For instance, companies can offer time-based, urgency of purchase and dynamic pricing while selling online. These type of pricing methods are called time-based online pricing or dynamic pricing.

Dynamic Pricing

Dynamic pricing is a pricing strategy in which the prices of products are changed in response to the real-time demand and supply. First introduced by American Airlines in the 1980s, it allowed the carrier to change flight rates based on various factors. This helped the company to improve its profit margin considerably.

Today, dynamic pricing is practised by a host of companies and industries. According to Mehta, Detroja and Agashe (2019), Amazon changes product prices about every 10 minutes, resulting in an increase in revenues of 25 per cent. Walmart, too, follows dynamic pricing.

These companies track and analyse large volumes of data, including a customer's shopping pattern, demographics, competitor prices, inventories and many other factors. Amazon has one billion gigabytes of data on their items and users. Its software analyses a large number of factors every 10 minutes and changes prices, accordingly, ensuring that they are always at an optimal level and contribute to better profits.

A strategy followed by Amazon is to raise prices on uncommon products, but prices of common products are kept lower, making people believe that they are getting the best prices for all products. Since most searches are for the most common products, users get the impression that Amazon has the best prices for all products. Amazon can make data-driven suggestions and also follows an anticipatory shipping model.

- **Data-driven suggestions:** Another way of serving consumers is to make recommendations for products based on their search history. Amazon makes suggestions with its feature, 'Customers Who Bought This Item Also Bought,' suggesting complementing products. It also uses data from Kindle—based on the words that people highlight on it, the company can predict customer needs.
- **Anticipatory shipping:** Need-prediction based on data has also led to Amazon's patented technique, the 'Anticipatory Shipping Model'. When the company predicts future purchases of a customer, it stocks those items in a warehouse from where it can be despatched quickly whenever the order comes. It becomes clear that big data analysis can lead to adding tremendous economic value both for customers and the supplying companies.

Big data also gives companies knowledge of market trends and real-time supply–demand, helping them to adjust prices for maximum profit. When demand is low, the seller can drop prices, and when demand is high, the prices can be increased.

Dynamic pricing is useful to make price adjustments due to changes in environmental conditions. By reducing the prices of slow-moving stock, it can clear stuck inventories or respond to competitor prices faster. Today, online retailers use technology and data to understand each customer, pattern of purchase and demographic characteristics to make their pricing decisions.

Some online pricing strategies are described as follows:

- **Competitor-based pricing:** At least for common goods, companies continuously monitor prices set by competitors and change accordingly so that customers are able to see low prices when they search for or visit the site.
- **Time-based pricing:** Another way is to adjust prices with time. For instance, if companies know purchase patterns for different times of the day, prices can be changed for those timings. Time-based pricing also refers to altering the prices of products depending on how long they have been in the market.
- **Peak pricing:** Users of cab-hailing apps are aware of peak pricing, which means varying prices according to demand fluctuations. Simply put, it means increasing prices when demand is high and lowering when demand is lagging. Demand for cabs, for instance, will increase on weekends or when it is raining. Companies increase their prices during such events.
- **Segmented pricing:** Since companies can track the geographic location of the users and their profiles, prices of the same product will differ according to the area.
- **Penetration pricing:** While introducing a new product in a locality, companies might like to keep the price low so that they get a large number of customers. Later, prices can be adjusted according to demand.
- **Need-based pricing:** Prices can be increased if the company can figure out how urgent the customer need is. Amazon and other sellers, for instance, charge a higher delivery cost for 'same-day delivery'. During festivals, the delivery cost can be increased because people want their products quickly.
- **Psychological pricing:** This pricing method considers the psychology of the consumer while setting the price. By tracking social media posts through big data analytics, companies are able to know the emotional state of customers. This can then be used to adjust prices for those customers.
- **Neuroscience-based pricing:** Neuroscience can tell us which combination of prices a customer is most likely to choose. Companies can, thus, offer multiple combos of a product, and the customer can then be 'nudged' to the most profitable one. Customers may feel they have the freedom to choose their combos, though they are being manipulated by programming based on neuroscience.

Companies can choose any of the methods described above or combine them to work out their strategies. But they are not without danger. Peak pricing, for instance, has been soundly criticized, and customers have turned away from apps that fleeced them. Such negative publicity tends to become viral and, in the process, destroys brands.

Companies can follow multiple pricing strategies according to their market position and company objectives.

■ CONCLUSION

Shifting to virtual value chains requires a radical change in thinking by companies and their managers. Traditionally, companies have thought of the Internet as another media to advertise or communicate with customers, but the enhancement of value chains implies that every business activity can be used for digital value addition. The collaboration with stakeholders is, therefore, one of the most important elements that can add value for companies, which will result in improvement in product and service innovation, the R&D process and business operations. Customer loyalty increases as a consequence, which translates into revenue streams.

The chapter also calls for a re-examination of pricing and business models. Many portals and platforms have followed the model of acquiring customers by offering free services, hoping to build a network which can later be monetized. Fuelled by venture capital, such businesses are loved by customers but are unable to make money. It is a matter of conjecture when the patience of investors runs out or whether online models can convert their followers into revenue streams before that. But more importantly, a relook and radical transformation of business models is certainly the need of the hour.

■ SUMMARY

This chapter explains the concept of digital value. Digital value has to be seen from the point of users, who must see the benefit in using online platforms, and from that of companies who must generate profits from their activities. It can be visualized by means of the virtual value chain, which is an extension of the value chain concept given by Michael Porter. The virtual value chain shows that value is added at every stage of customer interaction and data analysis helps add value across the product's life cycle. The virtual value chain consists of content, context, infrastructure and finally, leading to CX.

Value can be added digitally by enhancing products, sharing products and services, building platforms and marketspaces, encouraging stakeholders in the process of co-creation and other methods.

Companies can add value-adding information processes in three stages: visibility, mirroring and capability for establishing new customer relationships. Online technologies encourage people to connect through virtual communities and form their networks, which are used to engage customers. It has also led to the rise of the sharing economy in which people share their resources with people who need to borrow them.

Creating digital value requires a complete transformation of business. Dubbed as Industry 4.0, it refers to a transformation in the industry as it employs automation and data exchange in manufacturing technologies. In modern industry, value is created at each stage from manufacturing, automation, inventory and quality control, to marketing and customer engagement. This chapter also describes how OVP is made.

However, digital value has to be seen in relation to costs incurred online. Many companies operate with venture capital funds but continue making operational losses. Pricing techniques have been discussed. Many companies have taken the route of providing services for free with the hope that once they have a large number of users, they can sell advertisements on the platform. Despite the large rounds of funding received by such platforms, they have been unable to monetize their models. This chapter argues that business models must be carefully designed; otherwise, they will end up making losses.

■ KEY TERMS

Co-creation: The joint creation of value by the company and the customer, allowing the customer to co-construct the product or service to suit their context.

Digital value: Digital value refers to the benefit that consumers get in using digital services and platforms.

Dynamic pricing: A pricing strategy in which the prices of products are changed in response to the real-time demand and supply.

Industry 4.0: The term used to describe the transformation in the industry as it employs automation and data exchange in manufacturing technologies.

Marketplace: A marketplace is a physical location which brings together sellers and buyers.

Marketspace: An online space through which sellers can list and sell their products and match them with the requirements of customers.

Mirroring: The act of substituting virtual activities for physical ones. That is, value-adding activities are shifted from the physical marketplace to the virtual marketspace.

Network economy: A system in which value is added to products and services through the participation of people in social networks.

OVP: A statement describing the online benefits provided by a company and how it delivers those benefits uniquely in a clear, easy-to-understand manner differentiating itself from competitor offerings.

Value chain: An analysis of a firm's systems and activities to show how each operation has an effect on costs and profit, and how companies can build competitive advantage and sustainable business models.

Virtual value chain: A model that shows how companies add value across all activities and consumer interactions and is aided by aggregation and analysis of data. It is an enhancement of the physical value chain by information-based value activities.

Visibility: Visibility means using the information to keep track of business operations. This information is used to control and monitor operations at different stages in the value chain.

■ CONCEPT REVIEW QUESTIONS

1. What is a digital value? How is it added to products?
2. Describe a virtual value chain. Explain how value is added at every stage of customer interaction.
3. Distinguish between marketplace and marketspace. How can companies create a marketspace?
4. How does a virtual value chain get integrated into the physical value chains?
5. What is the network economy? How is a value added to a company by the network economy?
6. Describe the sharing economy. Give examples of different types of sharing economy.
7. What is OVP? What basic question should it answer?
8. Describe the methods of price determination and their relevance in the online environment.
9. What is dynamic pricing? Describe the types of dynamic pricing strategies.
10. Describe the process of co-creation. How is it done? Illustrate your answer with examples.

■ CRITICAL THINKING QUESTIONS

1. Why is it important to study pricing strategies while analysing online value? How are they linked to business models? If you have to design a platform, would you offer services for free or have a user fee-based system? What are the advantages and disadvantages of the two systems?
2. The examples given in this chapter show that many companies are able to gather a large number of users and still make losses. Is this a sustainable model of business? What is the solution to the problem of online brands without profits?
3. Critically examine the statement of Michael Porter (2001): 'Many companies have subsidized purchase of their products and services in hopes of staking out a position on the Internet and attracting a base of customers.' Comment on how this builds sustainable businesses.
4. The chapter explains that value is added in all activities of Industry 4.0. Apply this concept to a company of your choice and see whether the savings mentioned can actually be achieved. What is your assessment?

■ PROJECTS AND ASSIGNMENTS

1. Study the portals of airline ticketing over a fortnight. Check the prices of flights on a route and see how they fluctuate over the days. Can you understand why and how

does the portal change prices? Is it advisable to buy tickets close to the date of the flight or should one buy in advance?

2. Study the business models of some famous platforms such as Uber, Paytm, BookMyShow and others. Study their financial reports. Suggest how they can make profits.
3. Select a company of your choice. Draw its virtual value chain, showing how value is added at each stage of its physical and online operations.
4. Search for products and services that have resulted out of the process of co-creation. Describe the steps taken by the companies and the inputs from customers. Do you think co-creation is practical?

■ REFERENCES

Caylar, P., O. Noterdaeme, and K. Naik. 2016. 'Digital in Industry: From Buzzword to Value Creation.' McKinsey Digital. Available at: https://www.mckinsey.com/business-functions/mckinsey-digital/our-insights/digital-in-industry-from-buzzword-to-value-creation (accessed on 22 January 2021).

Dawar, N. 2018. 'Marketing in the Age of Alexa.' *Harvard Business Review* (May–June). Available at: https://hbr.org/2018/05/marketing-in-the-age-of-alexa (accessed on 22 January 2021).

Deloitte. 2017. 'Elevate Your Business with the Connections of a Networked Economy.' Available at: https://www2.deloitte.com/us/en/pages/risk/articles/networked-economy-connections-benefits.html (accessed on 22 January 2021).

Dörner, K., and D. Edelman. 2015. 'What "Digital" Really Means.' McKinsey Digital. Available at: https://www.mckinsey.com/industries/technology-media-and-telecommunications/our-insights/what-digital-really-means (accessed on 22 January 2021).

Favaro, K. 2016. 'Don't Draft a Digital Strategy Just because Everyone Else Is.' *Harvard Business Review* (16 March). Available at: https://hbr.org/2016/03/dont-draft-a-digital-strategy-just-because-everyone-else-is (accessed on 22 January 2021).

Kim, W. C., and R. Mauborgne. 1999. 'Creating New Market Space.' *Harvard Business Review* (January–February). Available at: https://hbr.org/1999/01/creating-new-market-space (accessed on 22 January 2021).

Liu, L., and J. Wu. 2010. 'Virtual Value Chain and Competitive Advantages in the Context of E-commerce.' 2010 IEEE 17Th International Conference on Industrial Engineering and Engineering Management. Available at: 10.1109/ICIEEM.2010.5646044 (accessed on 22 January 2021).

Marr, B. 2016. 'The Sharing Economy: What It Is, Examples, and How Big Data, Platforms and Algorithms Fuel It.' *Forbes*. Available at: https://www.forbes.com/sites/bernardmarr/2016/10/21/the-sharing-economy-what-it-is-examples-and-how-big-data-platforms-and-algorithms-fuel/#2d5073cc7c5a (accessed on 22 January 2021).

McKinsey & Company. 2015. 'Industry 4.0: How to Navigate Digitization of the Manufacturing Sector.' McKinsey Digital. Available at: https://www.mckinsey.com/~/media/McKinsey/Business%20Functions/Operations/Our%20Insights/Industry%2040%20How%20to%20navigate%20digitization%20of%20the%20manufacturing%20sector/Industry-40-How-to-navigate-digitization-of-the-manufacturing-sector.ashx (accessed on 22 January 2021).

Mehta, N., P. Detroja, and A. Agashe. 2019. *Swipe to Unlock: The Primer on Technology and Business Strategy.* Scotts Valley, CL: CreateSpace Independent Publishing Platform.

Nanry, J., S. Narayanan, and L. Rassey. 2015. 'Digitizing the Value Chain.' McKinsey Quarterly (March). Available at: https://www.mckinsey.com/business-functions/operations/our-insights/digitizing-the-value-chain (accessed on 22 January 2021).

OECD. 1999. 'Economic and Social Impact of Ecommerce: Preliminary Findings and Research Agenda.' OECD Digital Economy Paper No. 40. Available at: http://dx.doi.org/10.1787/236588526334 (accessed on 22 January 2021).

Porter, M. E. 1985. *Competitive Advantage: Creating and Sustaining Superior Performance.* Hauppauge, NY: Nova Science Publishers.

Prahalad, C. K., and M. S. Krishanan. 2008. *The New Age of Innovation: Driving Co-created Value through Global Networks.* New York, NY: McGraw Hill.

Prahalad, C. K., and V. Ramaswamy. 2004. 'Co-creating Unique Value with Customers.' *Strategy and Leadership* 32, no. 3: 4–9.

Rayport, J. F., and J. J. Sviokla. 1994. 'Managing in the Marketspace.' *Harvard Business Review* (November–December). Available at: https://hbr.org/1994/11/managing-in-the-marketspace (accessed on 22 January 2021).

Rayport, J. F., and J. J. Sviokla. 1995. 'Exploiting the Virtual Value Chain.' *Harvard Business Review* (November–December). Available at: https://hbr.org/1995/11/exploiting-the-virtual-value-chain (accessed on 22 January 2021).

Satell, G. 2014. '3 Things You Should Know about the Network Economy.' *Forbes* (7 July). Available at: https://www.forbes.com/sites/gregsatell/2014/07/07/3-things-you-should-know-the-network-economy/#1e3246175ff5 (accessed on 22 January 2021).

Zimmermann, A., P. Gomez, G. Probst, and S. Raisch. 2014. 'Creating Societal Benefits and Corporate Profits.' *MIT Sloan Management Review* (March). Available at: https://sloanreview.mit.edu/article/creating-societal-benefits-and-corporate-profits/ (accessed on 22 January 2021).

 CLOSING CASE

BRANDS WITHOUT PROFITS

Generating digital value is quite a different ball game as compared to building value in the traditional way of doing business. Earlier, businesses would buy raw materials, process them, add value and sell to customers, and thereby make a profit. Economies of scale were achieved, and mass production helped drive down cost.

The digital model does not rely on manufacturing. It has to create value in the virtual world, using data and information to meet customer needs. One online business model is to gather a large number of users and then try to monetize the numbers, which is referred to as the network economy. This has worked well for many online companies and is also the dream of start-ups, but for many companies, profits remain elusive despite earning a huge following. The question then is: what is digital value, and how can companies create it?

To build their networks, many online businesses have taken the route of offering discounts and cashback to attract users. Describing the tendency to gather users by providing unrealistic incentives, Porter (2001) wrote that, 'Many companies have subsidized purchase of their products and services in hopes of staking out a position on the Internet and attracting a base of customers.' But without a revenue model, such methods only lead to ruin. The tendency of many companies is to offer deep discounts or offer services for free in the hopes of acquiring huge number of customers and then make a profit somehow. Venture capital has been used to finance such offerings.

The taxi-hailing service, Uber, has been a huge success in changing people's approach to urban transportation. Its valuation at one time was thought to be $100 billion. Indeed, the success of taxi-hailing services has changed the way people commute: many people across the world do not prefer to drive their own car to avoid traffic and parking problems in congested areas. Uber is an example of a highly successful digital marketing strategy and operates in many countries. Still, it has lost money: it has burned cash of $7.9 billion since 2009, writes *The Economist* (2019). Will it ever make profits?

Similarly, Paytm has been hugely successful in changing payment habits in India. The app that offers digital payments and an online store is used by millions of people. The results of One97 Communications Ltd, which owns Paytm, show a revenue ₹33,148 million in 2018. But it too is losing money: it reported losses of ₹16,060.5 million in the same period (Chanchani 2018).

Both Uber and Paytm are big brands in the sense that both are well known. They are leaders in their own fields. But customer loyalty is questionable since Uber customers and taxi drivers would easily switch if better discounts or more business is offered by other apps. Similarly, customers of Paytm would easily switch if they get better cashback elsewhere. Uber Eats, which offers delivery of food from restaurants to consumers, also may see little profits, since both restaurants and drivers must be paid.

Online businesses and brands thus face a challenge of making profits before better apps are developed and building customer loyalty. Such businesses face the danger of becoming commodities rather than brands. That is because customers want apps that solve their problems, and if a better app comes along that does the same or similar things in a better way, they will switch.

Questions for Discussion

1. Is the strategy of acquiring customers a sustainable one? How can the customer base of these companies be converted into revenue?
2. Are digital companies falling into the trap of becoming brands without profits? How can online businesses add value?
3. Are online ventures hiding the real costs of doing business?
4. What is the roadmap for the future for such ventures?

Sources

Chanchani, M. 2018. 'Paytm's Losses Go up 270% to ₹3,393 Crore Driven by E-tail Business.' *The Economic Times*, 29 October.

Porter, M. 2001. 'Strategy and the Internet.' *Harvard Business Review* (March). Available at: https://hbr.org/2001/03/strategy-and-the-internet (accessed on 22 January 2021).

The Economist. 2019. 'Can Uber Ever Make Money?' *The Economist*, 27 April. Available at: https://www.economist.com/business/2019/04/27/can-uber-ever-make-money (accessed on 22 January 2021).

CHAPTER 3

Customer Relationship Management and Digital Tools

Digital technologies generate data, and companies analyse it to develop methods to retain customers and build loyalty. This chapter describes how companies can build CRM strategies through digital methods.

After reading this chapter, you will be able to learn about the following:

☐ CRM and its importance in modern marketing

☐ Need to develop a communication strategy

☐ CRM systems and predictive analytics

☐ Cross-selling, upselling and moving customers up the loyalty ladder

☐ Social customer relationship management (SCRM) and its applications

OPENING CASE

USING CRM TO PREDICT CONSUMERS' NEEDS

In the movie *Minority Report* (2002), a character, John Anderson, played by Tom Cruise, walks into a Gap store. He is recognized immediately by an automated eye scan and is greeted by name. His preferences and purchase history are displayed on a screen (Figure 3.1), and specific ads are targeted to him. The movie is in the realm of science fiction and describes a system that can precisely predict crimes *before* they are committed. Although the movie is a science fiction, companies today track information about customers from multiple sources and have systems that are able to recognize, track and predict what customers would need even before those needs are expressed.

CRM systems are now being used extensively to know customers and predict what they need. By crunching data at increasingly faster speeds, they are able to give accurate customer profiles and even make predictions about them. Duhigg (2012) described an interesting anecdote, in which the US retailer Target sent mailers for baby-related products to a young

FIGURE 3.1 *CRM Systems Recognize Customers and Make Recommendations Based on Your Purchase History and Preferences*

Source: https://productplacementblog.com/movies/gap-store-in-minority-report-2002/ (accessed on 25 January 2021).

girl who was still in school. Her father was furious and wanted to know why the company was sending such mailers to his daughter. 'Are you trying to encourage her to get pregnant?' he asked. The company apologized, but he found out that his daughter was, indeed, pregnant. How did Target know about the pregnancy?

The answer lies in CRM systems that track data about customers at all times. Some data is available with retail companies—they know about customer preferences by analysing shopping baskets revealing details about the most intimate consumption patterns; they have credit histories and demographic details, and they know which promotions are the most effective for particular customers. Moreover, they track consumer sentiments in real time. Based on these, companies can predict what you are likely to buy most from them.

Today, data mining goes beyond this. Companies mine data from multiple streams—the customer's Internet search history, social media posts, demographic information, friend lists and much more. The combined data gives insights into customer behaviour which can lead to accurate predictions. In this case, Target analysed purchase patterns of women who had signed in the baby registry. The data revealed that such women tend to buy large quantities of unscented lotion at the beginning of their second trimester. They also tend to buy vitamin supplements in the first 20 weeks. Data analysis also revealed that women tend to buy scent-free soap, cotton balls and hand sanitisers when they are close to their delivery date. Using this information, Target could predict consumer needs and sent mailers to women regarding baby products knowing that the delivery date was getting near.

Large companies routinely analyse customer data. Customers do not mind sharing their phone numbers and email IDs at the billing counter, and this gives companies the means to track them. Using both publicly available data and data provided by the customer, the phone

(Continued)

(Continued)

number or guest ID is linked to demographic information including the customer's age, marital status, number of children, physical address and details of salary and credit history. Web history shows up the most intimate interests of the customer. Add to this data that can be bought, such as education records, job history, subscriptions and medical history, the company has comprehensive information about its customers. GPS-enabled mobile phones provide information on customer location and habits. Integration of face recognition technologies will further provide details of where customers go and with whom. Finding out what they would be buying next becomes easy, given the enormous data that companies have access to. And by analysing purchase patterns of similar people in the same demographics, many inferences can be made.

As technology advances, companies can make more and more accurate predictions. Several firms are taking the lead in developing such technologies. A US-based firm, Euclid, offers a free analytics solution that helps 'understand your customers beyond transactions'. Other companies, including ShopperTrak, RetailNext, Prism Skylabs and others are working to offer retail analytics solutions. This means that retailers can easily implement analytics to track various aspects of customer behaviour.

The only issue here is: What do consumers think of this continuous surveillance? There are two possibilities. One is that customers do not mind sharing their data and like the convenience of getting things that they like, at a time when they need them most. The second possibility is that customers feel uncomfortable that companies know so much and that privacy concerns become important so that governments enact privacy protection laws, limiting the use of personal data, as has been done in many European countries.

While reading this chapter, try to answer the following questions:

1. How do companies build their CRM systems, and what are they capable of?
2. What are the tools and technologies that companies use to track their customers and their habits?
3. How do companies predict what customers may require in the future?
4. Is it ethical to use customer data? Is it ethical, for instance, to predict the pregnancy of a girl and try to sell things to her?

Sources

Datoo, S. 2014. 'How Tracking Customers In-store Will Soon Be the Norm.' *The Guardian*, 10 January. Available at: https://www.theguardian.com/technology/datablog/2014/jan/10/how-tracking-customers-in-store-will-soon-be-the-norm (accessed on 25 January 2021).

Duhigg, C. 2012. 'How Companies Learn Your Secrets.' *The New York Times*, 16 February. Available at: https://www.nytimes.com/2012/02/19/magazine/shopping-habits.html (accessed on 25 January 2021).

Hill, K. 2012. 'How Target Figured Out a Teen Girl Was Pregnant before Her Father Did.' *Forbes*, 16 February . Available at: https://www.forbes.com/sites/kashmirhill/2012/02/16/how-target-figured-out-a-teen-girl-was-pregnant-before-her-father-did/#3fc53b996668 (accessed on 25 January 2021).

INTRODUCTION

Marketing has always depended on building relationships with customers. This is done by traditional retailers by remembering their customers and their preferences, greeting them personally and making gentle recommendations based on their past purchase behaviour. As retailers grew big, relationships became difficult to manage because of sheer volumes and disinterested sales clerks. Data came to the rescue and provided a method to know about customers and track them.

Whenever people buy something from large stores, the cashier asks their details which were stored in a database. Such systems are being used even today, which generate birthday and anniversary greetings for customers with the assumption that it develops customer loyalty. While there may be some customers who may get influenced by such greetings, many others do not appreciate an impersonal message from a faceless company. Others may simply use the discount offered on their birthday but do not become loyal customers. Such CRM systems are, thus, a drag on profitability. Moreover, since companies had no means to update information, they ended up sending birthday greetings to dead people or anniversary greetings to people who had divorced.

In the era of digital marketing and e-commerce, although customers may seldom meet salespeople, companies get a wealth of online data. Through this, they can analyse customer habits and preferences, leading to focused interactions and building relationships with them. This is the foundation of electronic customer relationship management (e-CRM), which integrates data from all sources to provide the company with a holistic view of customers in real time. E-CRM uses digital technologies to collect data from web sites, email, data mining and analytics in order to improve interactions with customers that are not seen as intrusive. Without realizing, customers build trust with those websites, which is the basis of relationships (see the Opening Case). Rigby, Reichheld and Schefter (2002) write that CRM also reduces the costs of acquiring and serving customers as it builds loyalty and reduces customer attrition, which contribute to profitability.

Modern CRM is not a database but is a system that uses data analytics to understand customer activity, predict the needs of consumers and make targeted and customized offers for them. It develops precise communications that customers value and sharpens the advertising of companies.

WHAT IS CRM?

CRM is defined as a company-wide strategy of managing interactions with potential and existing customers to improve profitability. Its objective is to build customer retention, loyalty and advocacy and, thus, drive profitability by decreasing costs of customer acquisition and retention. The CRM strategy puts customers at the centre of all business operations and provides customer focus to organizations. All customer touch points are integrated and managed to deliver consistent customer experience across platforms.

Data from touch points are analysed to build the CRM system. The e-CRM system is defined as the process of gathering data and using data analytics to build customer profiles and devising strategies and methods to move customers up the loyalty ladder. Greenberg (2010) describes it as, 'a philosophy and a business strategy, supported by a technology platform, business rules, workflow, processes and social characteristics, designed to engage the customer in a collaborative conversation in order to provide mutually beneficial value in a trusted and transparent business environment'. However, CRM should not be pursued because everybody else is doing so. It should have clear objectives. Rigby and Ledingham (2004) write that CRM systems should (a) be strategic, (b) solve some problems, (c) justify their cost and (d) have a future plan.

Modern CRM systems are an outcome of three tools: relationship marketing, direct marketing and database marketing. Because of the sheer volumes, large businesses rely on marketing automation to track and know their customers. Today, technology allows companies to send tailor-made messages for individual customers. Since these individual customers spend most of their lives on social media platforms, companies make their social pages hoping to attract users.

■ CRM FUNCTIONS

Data analysis can help support a host of CRM functions—marketing, sales, delivery and service support (Figure 3.2).

- **Marketing:** Marketing campaigns such as emails and other messages are created automatically depending on consumer behaviour.

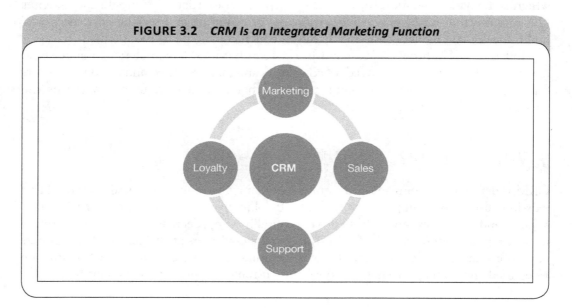

FIGURE 3.2   *CRM Is an Integrated Marketing Function*

- **Support:** Customer support is to be automated using past data. For instance, customers are identified based on their telephone numbers, and when they call, their purchase history and needs are displayed for the service representative so that appropriate customer support is provided without delay.
- **Sales:** Reports are generated on all activities performed by the company, including leads, conversions, sales and service. Leads are managed for optimum sales performance leading to increment in efficiencies.
- **Loyalty:** CRM helps customers climb up the loyalty ladder by managing CDJ, contract management, lead scoring, forecasting and so on.

CRM becomes the basis of many applications, as shown in Table 3.1.

TABLE 3.1   *Key CRM Applications*

Function	Application
Contact management	Information on leads, when to contact and what the message should be
	Personalize contacts with customers, making them feel important
Customer opportunity management	Identify customer opportunities
	Lead scoring ranks prospects on the basis of the perceived value of each lead
	Focusing on users that are most likely to convert, making sales operations more efficient
	Decide the level of engagement
Lead management	Identify high-quality leads based on the readiness to buy
	Identify the best customers by using demographic and psychographic data
Reports and dashboards	Real-time reporting with marketing dashboards
	Managers can view the activity of customers in real time
	Measure traffic and conversion ratio
	Quick and better business decisions
Sales analytics	Sales reporting shows sales data in real time
	Calculate the efficacy of campaigns and learn what works and what does not
	Create better sales campaigns which interest consumers
	Social media data, polls and website traffic can be managed
Sentiment analysis	Tracking and analysing customer feelings about the brand
	Monitor and analyse online chatter of consumers as they interact with each other through automated systems
	Track and understand conversations to measure the effectiveness of campaigns and products

E-CRM

When CRM is digitized, it is referred to as e-CRM. It uses Internet-based technologies such as emails, websites, chat rooms, social media, discussion forums and other channels to achieve the objectives of keeping in touch with customers. A well-structured and coordinated process of CRM results in automation in the processes of marketing, sales and customer service. An effective e-CRM increases the efficiency of the communication by improving the interactions with customers, leading to customized products and services that meet the customers' individual needs.

E-CRM is the term used to describe application of Internet-based technologies to achieve CRM objectives.

E-CRM improves interactions with customers and helps in developing customized products and services to their customers. Stringfellow, Nie and Bowen (2014) writes that CRM systems have three building blocks, which are as follows:

- Insight about consumers
- Information about customers' decision-making
- Information processing capability

E-CRM systems track customers over their decision journeys in real time. It results in the creation of an analytical database that helps in optimizing communications to the customer. CRM is, sometimes, mistaken to be database management or a substitute for sales, but it is actually a system of optimizing customer interactions.

Benefits of E-CRM

A good CRM has many benefits. Some of these are as follows:

- It improves customer relations, service and support, customer satisfaction (CSAT) and loyalty.
- It improves customer orientation in the entire organization.
- It improves precise and individually tailored offerings that match customers' needs.
- It improves efficiency and cost reduction, leading to profitability.
- It improves lead generation, sales support and builds a friendly company image.
- It improves identification of best customers and helps a company focus on them.
- It drives customer-centric innovation.

The purpose of e-CRM is to use technology to deliver high-quality customer experience across all channels and touch points. Each touch point must be managed well because every interaction can enhance or break the relationship.

NEED OF CRM

It is often said that it is cheaper to retain an existing customer than to recruit a new one. To get new customers, a company must spend money on advertising and sales effort whereas existing customers need no such expenses or effort. That is why it is essential to retain customers and build systems giving them reasons to stay with a particular company or brand. A good CRM contributes to increased profitability and growth. There are several reasons why companies need CRM, which are as follows.

- **Knowing customers and their needs:** The primary objective of CRM systems is to know customers and their precise needs. This helps in sending relevant communications to them and devising offers that they will respond to. Customers like to buy from companies that they trust.
- **Communication with customers:** Through CRM systems, companies can develop systems to establish two-way communications with their customers. Customers find themselves valued if they know companies are listening to them. They are likely to buy from companies that customize products for them.
- **Focus on profitability:** CRM helps identify customers that are more profitable than others and focus on them. Also, it makes customers buy more from the company. Retaining customers means stopping customers from leaving and bringing back those who have switched their customs. An example of this is banks which offer preferential services and special lounges for customers having high net worth. Extra facilities are offered so that loyalty is built in such customers.
- **Customization of offerings:** When companies know their customers, they can customize their products and services.
- **Reducing customer attrition:** CRM imparts a company-wide customer orientation. Customers are the responsibility of not only the sales department but also the entire organization. All policies are made, keeping the customer firmly in focus. CRM helps break down departmental silos and helps all employees to become customer oriented. As a consequence, everyone in the company cares for customers which result in the reduction of customer attrition rate.
- **Building long-term relationships:** A good CRM helps in building long-term relationships with customers. Suggestions of customers are sought to design new products, leading to co-creation. If customers feel involved with the firm, they are less likely to leave for a competitor. They also tend to buy more and stay longer with a company.
- **Increase in customer lifetime value (CLV):** When customers are loyal and spend more with a company, it increases customer equity and CLV, which is the sum of customers' expense with a company over their lifetimes.

- **Building competitive advantage:** CRM provides a safety net for companies during slowdowns and recessions. As they have a large base of committed customers who do not get lured away by competitors, their survival is assured.
- **Better corporate image:** When consumers become advocates, they contribute to corporate image. Loyal customers defend the company in case of adverse comments on social media, post favourable reviews and influence others. In this way, they provide free publicity and advertising for the company.
- **Trust:** An underlying assumption of any relationship is trust. Relationship marketing is based on continuous interaction and mutual trust between company and customer, which results in a long-term, mutually beneficial relationship.

■ CONVERTING DATA INTO INFORMATION

The basis of e-CRM is the collection and analysis of data from all consumer activity to offer products to customers at the precise moment they need them. It integrates information from all touch points—advertising, sales and customer service—using web-based technologies to interact with and understand customers.

A good CRM system discovers insights about consumers, analyses data and optimizes operations for better profitability, as explained below:

- **Discover:** Companies try to find useful insights about consumers through their online interactions. They follow consumer trends and also track individual interactions so that they can predict their needs and address their issues. For example, consumer complaints or online rumours may become viral if they are not contained. By tracking issues and responding to them well in time, such wildfires can be controlled.
- **Analyse data:** A CRM system requires strong data analytics that tracks data across channels. As people browse the web or interact with company blogs or website or post on social media, data analytics integrates and makes sense of all these data streams.
- **Optimize:** The CRM optimizes operations and improves efficiency. For instance, instead of advertising indiscriminately and sending messages to all and sundry, targeted advertising can be designed, which reaches only the right consumers at the moment they are ready to purchase.

The objective of CRM is to build retention and loyalty. This is built in a step-by-step manner, just as climbing a ladder. The stages of loyalty can be visualized as a ladder and companies use CRM systems to gradually move customers to higher steps.

■ LOYALTY LADDER

The loyalty ladder shows how a prospect progresses from having a little interest in a company's products to becoming a customer and gradually moving up through different stages of loyalty to finally becoming die-hard loyal customers (Figure 3.3). These stages are described as follows:

1. **Suspect:** Initially, people may show a little or no interest in a brand or company and may not be aware of it. At this stage, they are suspects in the sense that they could become interested if the company made some efforts.
2. **Prospect:** When people show some interest, such as searching online, asking for friends' opinion, visiting a store or making an enquiry, they become prospects. They are still not customers as no purchase has happened so far.
3. **Customer:** Those prospects who make a purchase become one-time customers but do not show loyalty.
4. **Client:** When customers show a tendency for repeat purchases, they are referred to as clients.
5. **Advocate:** Some customers like to recommend the brand to their friends and relatives. When this happens, they become advocates.
6. **Fans:** When customers show deep loyalty and start thinking of brands as an extension of their personality, they become fans. Fans show what is called 'brand love' by Roberts (2007) and like to flaunt the brand, join brand communities and show off their brands and products, influencing others. He writes that great brands

FIGURE 3.3   *Loyalty Ladder Shows Different Stages of Customer Loyalty*

Source: http://marketingtips4authors.blogspot.com/2013/04/where-are-your-customers-on-loyalty.html (accessed on 15 April 2021).

needed to create 'loyalty beyond reason' and that this was the only way to differentiate themselves in the future. The task of most of the companies is to build this kind of brand love.

A good CRM strategy consists of motivating people to go from one stage to the next and finally reach the highest stage of loyalty.

■ E-LOYALTY

Earning loyalty on the Internet seems to be quite difficult since customers can shift from one site to another with a mere click of a mouse. But this is not so. Reichheld and Schefter (2000) write, 'The Web is actually a very sticky place in both the B2C and B2B spheres.' Indeed, customers like to consolidate their purchases with one primary supplier, so that the supplier's site becomes part of their daily routine. This can happen when the site offers unique services, ease of operation and integration with the physical world. That is to say that e-loyalty is generated by earning the trust of customers and offering a consistently superior experience to customers.

Kumar (2015) writes that cultivating loyalty is an economic necessity because acquiring customers on the Internet is very expensive. Online businesses can be profitable only when they cultivate loyal customers who spend on the site regularly. Loyalty on the web is a function of the following:

- **Trust:** Easy payments and refunds, resolution of problems, consistency and confidence in dealing with the online company generate trust in consumers.
- **Transparency:** Customers appreciate correct and instant information, with honest reviews and opinions, with assistance when required.
- **Enduring relationships:** CRM helps build enduring relationships, which results in loyalty.

Many companies have indeed achieved this. Customers rate sellers on these sites, and the ratings are available for all to see. eBay holds the payments made by customers in an escrow account until the customer is satisfied with the purchase. This transparent system has helped build trust among millions of customers.

Google remains a big threat in the online environment because users may give loyalty a pass and click on an alternate search result or an online promotion. Hence, companies have to create stickiness on their websites so that the customer does not go to a search engine like Google. If online players are able to build trust—based on quick deliveries, quality products, smooth returns and refunds and so on—they get their customers to move up the loyalty ladder. Hence, loyalty accumulates into greater profits over the long run. Shankar, Smith and Rangaswamy (2003) show that loyalty towards an e-retailer maybe stronger than towards a traditional retailer. That is what makes e-CRM important to build.

ECONOMICS OF E-LOYALTY

The next step is to understand the economics of e-loyalty. The basic purpose of CRM is to build customer retention and loyalty, which in turn contribute to profitability. Reichheld and Schefter (2000) recognize that 'long-term e-commerce profit hinges on customer loyalty.' Their study showed that businesses incur a very high cost to acquire customers. This cost consists of advertising, identifying prospects, pitching them and so on. Hence, customer relationships remain unprofitable initially. It is only when customers buy repeatedly that the relationships become profitable. They report a startling, interesting finding, 'increasing customer retention rates by 5% increases profits by 25% to 95%.' That is why CRM is so important for companies.

The benefits of customer loyalty are as follows:

- Retaining customers is cheaper
- Loyal customers are less deal prone
- WOM publicity and referrals
- Selling additional products with less marketing effort
- Earns goodwill

Another reason for strong CRM is that the cost of acquiring customers on the Internet is far greater than in traditional marketing (see Marketing Insight 3.1). With an acquisition cost of $700 per customer and an assumed return of 10 per cent, companies need to sell greater than 10 times as much just to break even.

MARKETING INSIGHT 3.1 *Cost of Acquiring Customers*

While discussing online businesses and the economics of e-loyalty, many business operations report revenues but disregard the cost of acquiring new customers. In traditional models, customers are attracted by advertising, and the cost is deferred over a large number of conversions. On the Internet, advertising cost is paid on individual clicks or SEO leads. Thus, the cost of acquiring customers on the Internet is huge—a fact that is often overlooked by online operations. Hoffman and Novak (2000) have analysed this cost and write that, on average, online operations spend more than $100 to acquire a new customer, and some spend upwards of $500.

The case of CDNow, a popular music company at one time, is an eye opener. In 1999, it was the fourth most visited shopping site. It had garnered a sizeable following—700,000 visitors and 5 million page hits every day. It had reached a valuation of $1 billion and was very popular with music buffs. Yet, it went bust and showed the weakness of the dotcom business model. In 2000, it was reported that the company had run out of cash, and by June of that year, Bertelsmann Music Group acquired the company for $117 million, which was 90 per cent less than its valuation just two years earlier. The company was, finally, acquired by Amazon.

(Continued)

(Continued)

CDNow had underestimated the cost of acquiring and retaining customers. The online ad rates may appear low when measured over 1,000 clicks, but such ads have very low conversion rates. With a 1 per cent click-through rate and a 1 per cent conversion rate, the cost of acquiring customers becomes 10,000 times of the quoted rate.

A rough calculation shows how these rates do not make business sense. If an online ad is bought at a rate of $70 per thousand visitors, it means that the company pays seven cents for each person exposed to its banner. This seems cheap enough, but when we factor in the figure that 1 per cent of the people who saw the banner ad actually clicked through to the CDNow site, the cost becomes $7 per visitor. But this is not all. Since everybody who clicks does not buy, and the conversion rates are very small, again about 1 per cent, the cost of acquiring a new customer becomes a whopping $700.

Assuming that margins on products sold by the company are 10 per cent after deducting operating and delivery cost, the company needs to sell $7,000 worth of goods to each customer just to break even. Only if customers are retained over a few years will the company hope to sell $7,000 of goods to each. This shows that CRM is even more important in the online world than in the offline world.

This case study shows why the CRM programme must retain customers over the long term. Instead of relying wholly on paid media or click-through ads, companies must take steps to earn recommendations and WOM publicity.

How can companies reduce the cost of customer acquisition on the Internet?

Source

Hoffman, D. L., and T. P. Novak. 2000. 'How to Acquire Customers on the Web.' *Harvard Business Review* 78, no. 3 (May–June): 179–185.

These reasons are compelling enough to have efficient CRM systems that build customer relationships. Many online ventures make losses in the beginning and become profitable only when customers buy again. This is because the costs of acquiring customers in online environments are much higher in e-commerce than in traditional business, ranging from 20 to 40 per cent more. Many businesses are not able to sustain such losses and fold up. Others, such as Amazon, Google and Facebook suffered losses for many years before turning profitable. But once a critical mass of loyal customers is created, all companies have to do is to make them buy repeatedly or use their networks to generate profits.

■ CRM IN THE AGE OF DATA

It becomes clear from the previous section that loyalty—which was once the realm of the shopkeeper who remembered his/her customers and could make suggestions to them—is done by technology today. Companies have systems to gather and analyse information generated by customers across different channels as they go about their purchase cycles.

Data from the company's website—telephone, chat, retail shops, credit card usage, social media and other sources is collected and analysed in real time. Companies are, thus, able to track customers' personal information, buying history, spending habits, emotional states and practically, everything about a person through online tracking and data analytics. Any CRM system, thus, will try to get customers to:

- Come to the site whenever they look for products rather than use a search engine
- Continue to spend money on the site
- Try and buy new products when they are offered
- Recommend the site to other customers, which adds to revenues

CRM needs bigdata for personalization and customization of products and services and to deliver customer experiences. As data analytics develop, both advertising and customer experience can be made more targeted and specific. Already a number of tools are available that companies are using. The technologies can encourage a number of micro-relationships as well, such as encouraging customers to co-create advertising or encourage dialogues among customers themselves. There are a number of applications in CRM that are fine-tuned by data analysis. Some of these are as follows:

1. **Customer service:** Data enables integration of marketing, sales and customer service. This is a very big step in building relationships because customers do not see these three as separate departments but part of one company. A bad experience with one results in a bad image of the company or brand. Data integrates all touch points so that the customer is not dialling different numbers for sales support or getting service. In the past, customers having complaints were treated like ping-pong balls among different departments of the same company. When a customer is looking for a quick resolution, this becomes frustrating and generates negative publicity. The integration of data builds trust in customers. Further, AI systems learn as they go along, making the service delivered better with time.

   For example, a new development of technology in the field of customer service is the introduction of chatbots. These are automated response systems which analyse past customer patterns and behaviour and suggest solutions based on them. AI-based chatbots follow customer decision journeys and solve customer queries. Chatbots learn to adapt to individuals and thus meet their specific needs just like human representatives.

2. **Personalized advertising:** As data helps to learn about customers, it paves the way for creating personalized advertising messages. Ads are created that target individual consumers and specific goals. New technologies such as Alexa and Google Assistant deliver interactive marketing content and can make recommendations tailored for individual customers.

3. **Dialogue-centred marketing:** Another way that data is used is through targeting of specific communities through platforms such as YouTube, Facebook and others. This is not targeted individually but to communities which can lead the way for

generating dialogues. This, in turn, will lead to better customer engagement and help in establishing the brand.

4. **Predicting sales:** CRM systems backed by data analytics have the ability to predict consumer behaviour. Kumar, Venkatesan and Reinartz (2006) describe a new way of predicting a specific purchase by a specific customer with an accuracy of about 85 per cent. Using this approach, companies offer exact products to specific consumers so that only specific messages are sent. This can increase revenues and avoid the harm done by mindless advertising and over-communication.

5. **Building relationships:** An important aspect that is missed is that relationships are not built by data or computers alone. Companies want to have relationships with customers, but mostly, it is a one-sided relationship because people do not want to be treated as sales targets. Effective CRM ensures that customers feel they get value for money by having a relationship with a brand. This is the foundation of the relationship, which will lead to better retention rates and loyalty.

Building relationships means that customers are not sent advertising messages without their permission. Three concepts, permission marketing, cross-selling and upselling, are described in this section.

i. **Permission marketing:** Permission marketing is a marketing technique in which consent is taken from consumers to send them advertisements of goods and services. That is, consumers agree to receive a company's marketing messages activities, sometimes for an incentive. Permission marketing is the opposite of interruption marketing, in which marketing communications are sent to consumers without their consent and disrupt their activities.

ii. **Cross-selling and upselling:** Cross-selling and upselling are used to sell additional or more expensive products to customers. They are used to increase sales from customers. Since companies track their customers through effective CRM programmes, they get to know their needs and are able to suggest additional or complementary products (cross-selling) or suggest better and more expensive options (upselling). For example, a lady looking for a dress will find many options when she searches a fashion site. When she clicks on a dress, she may be shown similar but more expensive dresses or matching accessories to go along with it. These are examples of both cross-selling and upselling, and many e-commerce sites follow the practice. These are described as follows:

Cross-selling means selling additional products to an existing customer. Related or complementary products are often suggested to customers, and they are tempted to buy them. Camera dealers, for instance, may suggest that customers buy memory cards or batteries/chargers along with their cameras. In this way, they increase their revenue. Online companies like Amazon have a suggestion like 'Customers Who Bought This Also Bought…' as a method of cross-selling.

Upselling is the practice of encouraging customers to buy a more expensive option. The salesman or the website highlights the advantages of the higher model, tempting customers to upgrade and pay more. Online tools like comparison of models are aimed at making people buy the more expensive option.

Both upselling and cross-selling are tools for increasing revenue but must be used carefully. One reason is that customers who do spend more money often have regrets later on and may decide to avoid the store or the salesperson who made them do so. Instead of pushing customers in this way—which may actually spoil relationships—it is better for a company to build relationship capital that goes a long way than a one-time transaction.

6. **Relationship capital:** Relationship capital is defined as the sum of all of the relationships of all of the people connected with a firm. Relationships with all stakeholders are considered. We have already talked about CRM, but relational capital includes stakeholders beyond customers. These include partners, suppliers, community, government, media, institutions and practically anyone who knows about the company. A company must manage interactions with all these by sharing knowledge, collaborating, seeking advice and the creation of connections (Figure 3.4).

Relationship capital or social capital consists of intangible assets such as shared values and accumulated knowledge that form the reputation and trust that a company has developed over time. It cannot be calculated with any accuracy but rests on the assumption that long-term revenues depend on solid relationships. For example, good relations with suppliers will ensure that they help in new projects and do not mind making investments for long-term collaboration. Companies must make efforts to build positive relational capital by means of stories and experiences and build online communities (see Marketing Insight 3.2).

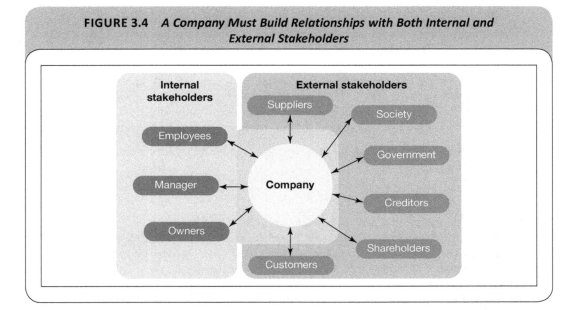

FIGURE 3.4 *A Company Must Build Relationships with Both Internal and External Stakeholders*

MARKETING INSIGHT 3.2   *Online Communities*

An online community is a virtual community of people with common interests whose members interact, work together, pursue their interests and solve each other's problems over the web. It is like having a 'family of invisible friends' who share common interests. While online communities are formed on their own, companies try to form brand communities so that customers can interact around the common theme of the brand. Such communities attract people who feel very strongly for the brand and what it stands for.

Goodson (2012) writes that traditional marketing has given way to 'movement marketing', a marketing model that starts with an idea in culture and then ties that back to the brand. He writes that brands can 'identify, crystallize, curate and sponsor movements, accelerating their rise'. Seth Godin (2008) calls it 'tribe-building', and the tribe becomes a community of people who identifies with the brand. That is why it has become important these days for brands to identify with social causes. Communities have become a means of building fierce customer loyalty.

Communities show that marketing in the digital era has changed in two profound ways: (a) marketing is about participating in a dialogue with consumers and (b) it is no longer about transactions but about building relationships.

While there are many active online communities on a variety of subjects, some examples of brand communities are as follows:

- **Sephora:** Sephora has a very successful online community called BeautyTalk in which one can learn about make-up, share ideas, ask questions and get answers from other users. People can upload their pictures wearing Sephora make-up products, and the photos provide links to the products used.
- **Lego Ideas:** Fans of Lego upload their designs, browse and vote on other designs. In an example of co-creation, the ideas with the most votes are marketed by the company. The person who gave the idea gets a share of the sales.
- **Starbucks:** Lovers of coffee can share and discuss their ideas through 'My Starbucks Idea.' When a company involves customers for ideas, they feel valued and connected. Starbucks is also involved with a number of social initiatives, like the volunteer matching service through which partners and community members engage to help those outside the community. It also has an annual #redcupcontest holiday cup decorating contest and allows users to post pictures around products like #psl (pumpkin spice latte) photos.
- **Walt Disney:** Disney has a global community tied together by people's love for their characters, movies and theme parks. It hosts an annual gathering, the Official Disney Fan Club so that members of the Disney community join in for a celebration.

What are the characteristics of brand communities? Are they effective? What are the pitfalls in creating brand communities?

Sources

Godin, S. 2008. *Tribes*. New York, NY: Portfolio Books.
Goodson, S. 2012. 'Marketing Is Dead. Now What?' *Forbes*. Available at: http://www.forbes.com/sites/marketshare/2012/08/13/marketing-is-dead-now-what/ (accessed on 25 January 2021).
Lego website: https://ideas.lego.com/ (accessed on 25 January 2021).
Sephora website: https://www.sephora.com/community (accessed on 25 January 2021).
Starbucks website: https://ideas.starbucks.com/ (accessed on 25 January 2021).

CRM AND THE CUSTOMER LIFE CYCLE

The customer life cycle is a term used to describe the progression of steps that a customer goes through from deciding to buy products to the stage of building loyalty.

The customer life cycle consists of five stages: reach, acquisition, conversion, retention and loyalty (Figure 3.5). This involves reaching out to get people's attention, understanding their needs to make an offer, turn them into paying customers and then making them stick to become loyal and returning customers. Customer retention becomes a circle to get the customer to move through the cycle again and again. The five stages are briefly described as follows:

1. **Reach:** At the initial stage, people have to be made aware of the company and its products. Advertisements, online interactions, recommendations and WOM publicity of past customers are important elements here. The objective is to let people know about the brand so that it is in the consideration set of existing and potential consumers.
2. **Acquisition:** Once the consumers are aware of a company or brand, the next step is to make them buy. The company must progress from consumer awareness to the buying stage and acquire paying customers. The company may push by encouraging conversations and interactions through sales representatives or by offering sampling or testing of products.
3. **Conversion:** This is the stage when people overcome the deciding stage and actually buy the product. At this stage, the customer moves from 'think' to 'buy'.

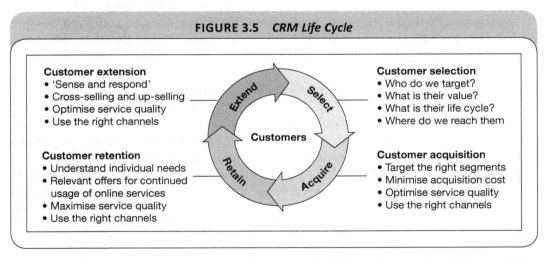

FIGURE 3.5 *CRM Life Cycle*

Source: https://kompy.info/chapter-1-introducing-internet-marketing.html?page=3 (accessed on 25 January 2020).

4. **Retention:** After users are converted into customers, the challenge is to retain them. Thus, companies must focus on CSAT. This step is also important because companies want customers to speak well of their products, thus generating WOM publicity. Any issue of the customer must be solved quickly. Companies must try to retain their customers as it costs less to retain existing customers than to acquire new ones.

5. **Loyalty:** Customers exhibit loyalty if they buy repeatedly from the company. The benefit of this is that loyal customers will buy additional products as they begin to trust the company's brand name. More importantly, they will help multiply the business by recommending the products to others.

The CRM life cycle is managed by understanding the types of CRM and the role played by each in contributing to relationships.

■ RELATIONSHIP MARKETING

Collaborative CRM is also called 'relationship marketing' which means retaining customers and maximizing CLV. This becomes very important in online marketing since customers can switch loyalties simply by clicking a search result. Online relationship marketing works in several ways, as described below:

- **Social networking:** Since a very large number of people use social network sites, companies build their presence on such sites hoping that they can extend their presence. Consumers can join the company's pages or profiles, engage with content, post comments and pictures and interact with one another. Compelling content that attracts users is the secret of social networking. Companies also entice consumers by organizing competitions or offering discount coupons, but these are short-term strategies. Long-term retention occurs only if people are motivated to interact with a company's social media pages.

- **Customization:** Online technologies allow customization. Users can simply click on their choice of colour, design, size and so on, and the product is delivered to their doorstep. Companies dealing in fashion, automobiles, luxury goods and many others allow customization of their products. Delivering an experience or product tailor-made for customers leads to better customer retention.

- **Surveys and suggestions:** Companies design online questionnaires and surveys to get customer feedback about their products and services. Suggestions are also sought regarding their operations. Some companies go one step ahead and involve their customers in co-creation or designing their products and offerings.

- **E-vouchers:** A tested way of encouraging online engagement is to offer discount vouchers or to organize competitions to increase sharing of content or interaction with a company's products. Companies can track their customers who are dormant and send a voucher that makes them buy from the company again. However, distributing discounts on social media can be a short-sighted strategy since customers may use the vouchers and fail to establish a long-term relationship.

- **Chat:** Increasingly, users are noticing a chat window on company websites that enables them to send messages to a representative and get their queries answered. This can be text messages or video interactions. Such interactions can encourage sales since customers feel that the company is responsive.
- **Service:** Online technologies help deliver customer service. Companies allow customer logins so that they can review their product histories, make complaints and track them.

COLLABORATIVE WEB AND THE E-ENTERPRISE

Collaborative web refers to the tools and technologies that provide organizations with the ability to collaborate with employees, customers or other stakeholders using the Internet. Several web-based tools are available which are used to connect and collaborate with various parties in real time. Companies use them for communication, sales and CRM, customer service, satisfaction and a host of other collaborations. Companies can share resources both internally and externally and collaborate using voice and text chat. Multi-user conferences can be organized.

Enterprise collaboration refers to the similar tools and technologies that are used to collaborate with employees. Several collaboration platforms and enterprise social networking tools are available that can be used through a company-wide intranet or even the Internet. The system enables employees to share resources with one another and work together on developmental projects. This collaboration is not limited by geographic boundaries—multinational corporations can collaborate with their employees across continents. Today, companies are using groupware, video conferencing and collaborative working technologies. Internal social media and networking are also used.

SOCIAL CRM

When companies integrate social media channels into their CRM platforms, it is known as SCRM.

Companies combine their CRM systems with elements of social media and use social networks, communication and build communities for stronger customer value and relationships (see P&G's connect and develop case study [Marketing Insight 2.1] in Chapter 2). Companies use SCRM to engage with customers, track information shared by them and encourage them to post content related to brands. This develops customer relationships and customer value.

Traditional CRM gathers *transactional* information such as purchase history and basic demographic information. With social media, a company can gather additional information on *habits* and *sentiment,* including their attitudes, likes and dislikes and views on various topics and issues that impact the organization. Furthermore, an organization can have a two-way online conversation with their customers or prospects.

Treacy and Wiersema (1995) describe three value disciplines: product leadership, operational excellence and customer intimacy. While all three are aided by good CRM, the building of customer intimacy is perhaps the most crucial. Customer intimacy combines the value of best service with a flexible operating model that enables doing what it takes for each selected customer.

SCRM aids traditional CRM as it improves interactions and service through social media platforms. It leads to a more personalized marketing strategy than traditional CRM. It goes beyond dealing with data and information and instead improves relationships through conversations and engagements. The conversations and relationships are not just company-to-consumer but include consumer-to-consumer (C2C) conversations. Companies can communicate directly with their followers on social media and also listen to them and track their comments about the company or brand. SCRM is more of a strategy for customer engagement and tracks interactions with review platforms. SCRM helps in providing fast customer service and enables customers to share their experiences with millions online (Table 3.2).

The activities involved in SCRM are as follows:

- Monitoring customer conversations on social platforms
- Sifting through the conversations to identify users who are most likely to buy
- Solving customer problems and finding service and support from other customers
- Involving customers in new product development or give suggestions for improving offerings
- Encouraging C2C conversations to form an e-business collaboration with stakeholders
- Enhancing customer experience and add value to the brand
- Encouraging consumer advocacy so that users recommend the company's products and services to others

TABLE 3.2   *From CRM to Social CRM*

	CRM	Social CRM
Basis	Customer-provided data	Data mining across the web
Responsibility	Marketing and sales	Everyone in the company
Control	Company	Customer
Time	Office timings	Customer interaction at all hours
Channels	Company-defined channels	Omnichannel
Communication	Company directed	Targeted, personalized and two-way

SCRM—the world in which customers operate—has given rise to digital ecosystems. Companies go beyond products and try to create ecosystems of services. The objective is that customers get all services from one company without having to leave their virtual worlds.

SCRM AND NEW PRODUCT DEVELOPMENT

In the past, manufacturers made products based on designs they made themselves and developed by their R&D departments. Very often, these did not fully meet needs and expectations. As a consequence, failure rates of new products were extremely high, sometimes as high as 80 per cent. Very often, these failures could be attributed to lack of user information and based on incorrect assumptions about needs and usage patterns. Poetz and Schreier (2012) write that ideas created by professionals show significantly lower customer benefit than user ideas. The new product development process is shown in Figure 3.6. Consumers are involved in the first three stages of the process.

In some cases, products were designed based on market research done through surveys or interviews. But surveys could go notoriously wrong if not done properly. And once the

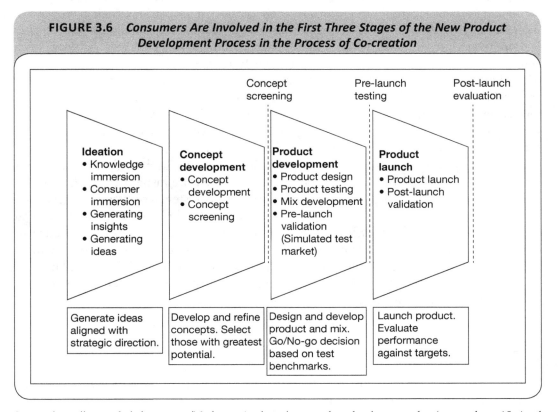

FIGURE 3.6 *Consumers Are Involved in the First Three Stages of the New Product Development Process in the Process of Co-creation*

Source: https://www.ashokcharan.com/MarketingAnalytics/new-product-development.php (accessed on 15 April 2021).

product was developed companies did not seek suggestions on prototypes from the initial survey participants.

Co-creation or involving consumers in product development helps in overcoming many of the shortcomings of new products from the perspective of the consumer or the user. Today, technology allows companies to collaborate with consumers and establish a viable partnership for new product development. Consumers provide ideas about functions and features and make products acceptable to them, resulting in better functional design and higher chances of success in terms of sales. Lilien et al. (2002) found that new products developed 3M in collaboration with lead users had higher innovativeness and resulted in better sales than those developed by 3M internally.

■ DIGITAL ECOSYSTEMS

SCRM lays the foundation of digital ecosystems. Greenberg (2010) writes that customers live in their ecosystems surrounded by the channels chosen by them. The customer is at the hub, accessing his/her preferred channels. One such ecosystem is an online community. Companies have to find ways to get into this ecosystem. Customers are no longer 'targets' for making a sale but firmly in control of their ecosystem and choose their own ways of interaction. How companies make them interested in brands is the challenge so that users feel motivated to interact with brands. The advantage is that every activity, from generating likes to visits, can be measured through metrics.

A digital ecosystem can be described as a group of interconnected digital resources that are available on one platform. It consists of suppliers, partners, enterprises, customers, service providers and apps that provide services to subscribers. While customers get services within their ecosystem, service providers get revenues. Web customers, usually, get accustomed to one primary supplier and buy from it regularly. They develop trust and familiarity in dealing with one or a few suppliers. The challenge in the online environment is that the first search for a product should be on a trusted site rather than on Google.

For example, HDFC bank has created a digital ecosystem consisting of securities trading, a payment app called PayZapp, tax filing and utility bill payments. It also has an e-commerce site called SmartBuy. Such an online ecosystem provides convenience to customers as they get many services all linked to their accounts. The revenues generated add to profits. Many companies have created digital ecosystems around their core business.

All social media activity must be measured for its contribution to revenues and profits. SCRM metrics help companies by tracking real-time data.

■ SCRM METRICS

SCRM is used to get people talking about brands. The metrics used to measure the level of successful customer engagement are as follows:

- **Traffic:** Companies can measure the traffic generated from social media platforms. This shows that users are drawn from social media platforms to seek information on the company's pages. People who show interests are the leads that salespeople can follow for conversions.
- **Conversions:** The second metric is to calculate how many leads actually buy the product. With this metric, companies can measure whether their social media interventions are converting into sales and are generating value or not.
- **Engagement:** User engagement with the sites, including time spent by users and the kind of comments generated, show how users engage with the company's social media pages.
- **Active followers:** Active followers are those who post comments and pictures. SCRM shows what percentage of users are active followers and engaging with the company's content.
- **Brand mentions:** The number of times that a brand is mentioned in the comments shows how many users are talking about the company or its brands, and the number of shares earned.

Through SCRM metrics, companies are able to classify customers based on their profitability. This becomes important because companies are able to focus on the most profitable ones. A method to do this is described in the next section.

FOCUSING ON RIGHT CUSTOMERS

CRM systems highlight the need to focus on the right customers. Companies can identify the types of customers using data analytics. Reinartz and Kumar (2002) write that companies need to differentiate between profitable loyal customers and less profitable ones. They describe four types of loyal customers, as shown in Table 3.3.

TABLE 3.3   *Four Types of Customers*

True friends: True friends are those customers who speak highly of a company and its products and recommend them to others. These are die-hard customers who go to any extent to praise and recommend brands.	**Butterflies:** Butterflies are customers who have bought a company's products but keep shifting their customs to competitors. They do not show consistent loyalty.
Barnacles: Barnacles are loyal customers, but they look for discounts and offers, and they are not profitable for a company. An example of this is a customer who buys one cup of coffee and keeps occupying space and use free Wi-Fi at a cafe.	**Strangers:** Strangers are neither loyal nor profitable. For example, customers who walk into shops, browse for long and then make a small or no purchase.

Once companies can classify customers in such categories, they can develop strategies to deal with them. True friends are loyal because they are comfortable in dealing with a company. Companies can institute a plan to turn them into 'true believers' by rewarding them for their loyalty. There are several ways of doing this: special previews for selected customers, price promotions, exclusive events and so on. At the same time, companies should not overdo this. Increasing communications and mailings with customers put them off and consider them as interruptions rather than of any practical help.

For 'butterflies', the strategy should be to make them buy more for the time they spend with a company. They are pushed to buy more because they may not return for a while. In the case of 'barnacles'—customers who block a company's bandwidth but buy little, the strategy should be to find out if they can spend more. Otherwise, it is best that the company gets rid of the barnacles. Tjan (2011) writes in his article 'It's Time to Fire Some of Your Customers' that to increase revenue quality of a business, some 15 per cent of a customer base can be trimmed every year. 'A higher quality of revenue means a better long-term business,' he writes. Indeed, freeing up bandwidth taken up by hyper-complaining or low-revenue customers means that the company can spend more resources on its profitable customers.

Finally, for 'strangers'—who are neither profitable nor do they show loyalty—companies should identify them and decide not to spend resources on them. At the same time, 'firing customers' does not mean throwing them out but to impose conditions so that profitable customers select priority channels while others do not.

Data analytics give such insights as consumer purchases, frequency, value and profits. In the next section, we will discuss Internet strategies which facilitate CRM.

■ OPERATIONAL, COLLABORATIVE, ANALYTICAL CRM

There are mainly three types of CRM applications—operational, analytical and collaborative.

Operational CRM

Operational CRM combines data from all business processes that contribute to the direct functioning of a company. It maintains a record of interactions that directly impact the functioning of the organization. It includes manufacturing, marketing and sales, customer service and supporting functions. The purpose of operational CRM is to integrate all data relating to operations and to make it available to different departments. It enables transparency and quick decision-making. Most ERP systems offer this type of integration and enable their automation.

- **Sales automation:** Automating the sales process involves setting processes for acquiring new customers and engaging with existing ones. It integrates several CRM sales modules such as lead management, contact management, quotations and sales forecasting. Sales CRM helps in establishing a contact system with prospects and customers to increase the efficiency of sales personnel.

- **Marketing automation:** Marketing automation integrates products and offers and is able to approach potential customers. Campaigns can be managed and measured, and companies can decide the most effective channels to communicate with prospects.
- **Service automation:** Service automation helps improve service as and when customers need it, resulting in building relationships with them. It helps in resolving issues and problems, automates customer call management and monitors service quality.

Analytical CRM

Analytical CRM consists of data mining from every level of the organization; it analyses the data and provides processed data for insights and intelligence. Users in different departments or areas can generate reports pertaining to their area. The main function of this type of CRM is data analysis and reports. These reports help the management in decision-making, and users can optimise their areas.

Collaborative CRM

Collaborative or strategic CRM is a system which enables collaboration among all stakeholders for value creation. All information from customer touch points is shared by all departments so that they are able to present one integrated image in front of the customer even if they are not responsible for customer dealings. Since everyone collaborates with each other, customers are not bounced between departments. This can become an invaluable resource for knowledge for an organization. For example, a customer complaint is not limited to the service domain but may provide invaluable suggestions to manufacturing for improvement in the products. Earlier, each department worked independently, and as a result, knowledge from one department seldom flowed to the other, causing customer dissatisfaction and also revenue loss. Collaborative CRM also results in co-creation and collaborative solution to many problems. It is best placed in building long-term relationships with customers.

■ PREDICTIVE ANALYTICS

CRM and retention strategies depend on predictive models, which are data-based models that can anticipate customer behaviour and needs. A simple example of a predictive model consists of anticipating a consumer to buy a tube of toothpaste every month based on his/her past purchase data. Two predictive analytics models that help in customer retention are propensity models and collaborative filtering.

1. **Propensity models:** Propensity models are used to predict customer behaviour based on information collected. It can be used for customer engagement, conversion and retention. For instance, if a company can predict which customers are likely to leave, it can take steps to prevent defection—in the case of telecom companies, if it can be predicted which customers are likely to port out, they can be held back by making a special long-term offer for them. Another application is to spot the 'next best action' in advertising, that is, to plan the next conversation with the consumer.

2. **Collaborative filtering:** Collaborative filtering means to make recommendations to encourage customers to buy additional products. In this method, recommendations are made by using filtered data from many users or a collaboration of users. Data of hundreds of people are used to segment customers and then to make specific recommendations. Many sites are using this method; recommendations can be found on many diverse sites from movies to consumer products.

Personalization: Personalization means offering tailored marketing on an individual basis. It leads to making engagement with customers more relevant. Data-driven marketing allows tailor-made messages and products for every single customer based on his/her preferences and background. Personalization does not mean that customers should be merely addressed by their first names, but it should lead to making relevant offers, increase conversion rates and order values and also increase marketing ROI and CLV.

Data mining: Data mining—finding meaning from large and varied data sets—can lead to making predictions about customers (see the Opening Case). The power of predictive analytics is described in Marketing Insight 3.3.

These and other methods lay the ground for next-generation CRM, which is likely to be even more accurate and more sophisticated.

MARKETING INSIGHT 3.3   *The Power of Predictive Analytics*

Predictive analytics is based on data analytics to predict market trends and customer needs before they are expressed, thereby helping companies to manufacture and stock goods. The use of predictive analytics is limited only by the imagination. Here are some applications of this technology (Morgan 2018):

-   **Reducing churn rate:** Tracking customer data helps in predicting which customers are most likely to switch brands. Using AI-powered algorithms, Sprint can identify such customers and makes efforts to make retention offers tailor made for each customer. Further, AI predicts what customers want by using data from their search histories and generates an offer matching with what they want. This has resulted in reducing the churn rate at Sprint and created fans out of customers.
-   **Transforming prospects to customers:** Harley Davidson uses an AI application called 'Albert' to identify and target customers directly. Albert is able to identify high-value

customers who are potential customers. Identifying the moment when they are ready to buy, the company makes direct contact through a sales representative. The probability of making a sale is very high, as prospects are approached when they are in the process of making up their minds. The system works for the benefit of both parties— the company gets a sale, while customers get personalized service.

- **Detecting faulty parts:** Volvo tracks operational data on cars sold to predict car servicing needs and also identifies the parts that must be replaced. The company has an early warning system that analyses data and is able to predict which part is likely to breakdown. Based on this, Volvo makes recommendations to customers to have their cars serviced or repaired before they break down.

- **Personalized recommendations:** Netflix is another company that uses data extensively. It uses data from a large number of sources such as demographics, viewing history, reviews, ratings and preferences to create shows and promoting them. Data from each user is collected and analysed by an algorithm powered with AI, which is able to predict what shows the customers are most likely to watch next. In this way, it customizes its recommendations for each user. It is a very accurate and effective system, given that about 80 per cent of what is viewed is a result of its recommendations. This system creates fans of customers, reflecting in its continuous growth, resulting in customer loyalty and retention.

- **Helps in finding right products:** Sephora, the French multinational chain selling personal care and beauty products, uses technology to help customers find products suited to their lifestyle and skin tones. It creates profiles for each customer and updates them based on purchase history, search and preferences and predicts what customers are most likely to need. This is shown in 'Recommended for You' section. Its loyalty programme is also based on data, and the company is able to send rewards and messages designed for each individual customer.

- **Handles complaints, queries and fraud prevention:** Data analytics is used by banking companies to track and resolve complaints. Automated systems help in solving queries and complaints by bankers all over the world. Customer data is displayed on a dashboard which helps to understand customer activity and predict their needs. Interestingly, the system can predict fraud and prevent it. American Express uses the system to identify and warn customers that are most likely to be defrauded. This personalized approach is appreciated by customers, while American Express is able to achieve very low fraud loss rates.

- **Dynamic pricing and upgrades:** AI-powered analytics help identify the best offers for customers. Airlines and hotels use AI to adjust dynamic pricing. Customer data helps predict the types of upgrades that individual guests would appreciate. The hospitality industry collects data from customers to improve service and customer experience.

Can you think of other applications of predictive analytics?

Source

Morgan, B. 2018. '10 Examples of Predictive Customer Experience Outcomes Powered by AI.' *Forbes*, 20 October. Available at: https://www.forbes.com/sites/blakemorgan/2018/12/20/10-examples-of-predictive-customer-experience-outcomes-powered-by-ai/#65ce38e15d0b (accessed on 25 January 2021).

NEXT-GENERATION CRM

Traditionally, CRM systems have been based on databases. Companies asked customers to provide their addresses, birthday and anniversary dates. The idea was to push sales by offering them discounts on their special dates. However, a major problem was related to updating the database. Customers moved out, changed their marital status or just died. Companies ended up often sending happy birthday greetings to dead people or sending anniversary greetings to people who had subsequently divorced. The CRM was transaction oriented and seldom resulted in building long-term relationships.

With people now sharing their data and status online voluntarily, this has changed. Today, companies have the means to know about customers in real time. Businesses just have to tap online information to know not only the demographic data of customers but also their emotional state. They have a goldmine of information, and it is up to companies how they use it.

The objective of CRM has, thus, changed from being transactional in nature to relational (Table 3.4). Companies use data not to push one-time sales but seek a long-term relationship by which they can maximize customer lifetime value. Innovative methods are used to generate and deliver value to customers.

Traditional CRM systems provided data to the company's sales representatives which they used to turn prospects into customers. A lot of cold calling was involved. Today, CRM allows companies to deliver specific customer experiences without cold calling because they already know what the customer wants. It keeps the customer's current and future needs always in focus. Since technology allows communication with individual customers, personalized communications and experiences are developed which people find helpful rather than intrusive.

Today, companies are not concentrating on one-time sales. The new business model consists of offering a user experience. The customer is firmly in focus and is at the centre

TABLE 3.4　*Traditional and Next-generation CRM*

	Traditional CRM	Next-generation CRM
Customer relationship	Transactional	Relational
Time frame	One-time sales	Long-term relationship building
Focus and objective	Sales, profitability	Customer lifetime value
Advertising and communications	One-way	Targeted, individual specific, two-way
Customer engagement	Limited	Co-creation
Basis	Data mining and analytics	AI

of every interaction—digital, sales personnel, advertising, product interaction or service. All the touch points are integrated, and all transactions are recorded, which becomes the basis of data analysis. Next-generation CRM relies on AI.

AI in CRM

AI makes it easier to predict user behaviour. It can provide real-time tracking of CDJs and provide a 360-degree view of customer engagement. It can result in a number of outcomes, as shown in Figure 3.7.

Next-generation CRM will also see a number of new applications. Some of these are already being used. *Intelligent automation* allows companies to automate many marketing functions, from promotion to sales. It provides assistance in sales, classifying leads and assisting in understanding customer segmentation and behaviour. *Natural language processing* allows companies to interact with customers, just like humans. It generates precise responses to customer queries by analysing textual content. *Semantic analysis* reveals brand sentiment by tracking comments on social media sites. Other technologies will result in still more accurate tracking of customers.

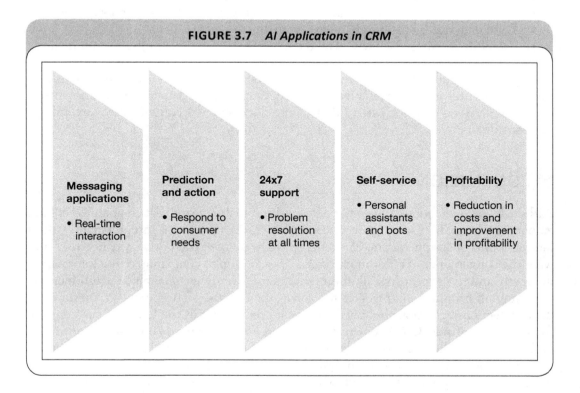

FIGURE 3.7   AI Applications in CRM

Messaging applications	**Prediction and action**	**24x7 support**	**Self-service**	**Profitability**
• Real-time interaction	• Respond to consumer needs	• Problem resolution at all times	• Personal assistants and bots	• Reduction in costs and improvement in profitability

DATA WAREHOUSING AND REAL-TIME PROFILING

Data profiling occurs when a company reviews its existing database to check inconsistencies, integrate various datasets and see how they can be used in different applications. The purpose of data profiling is to (a) discover, (b) understand and (c) organize the data in an organization. Through this, a company checks the types and content of data that a company has and how these are interrelated. This is done in real time because the amount of data and their sources are increasing all the time. Without data profiling, the company may end up with disjointed data from different sources and not be able to use them effectively.

Companies already deal with huge data sets sources such as email, blogs, social media, big data technologies and physical records generated by a host of sources. The IoT adds a very large number of devices generating data all the time. All this data has to be correctly formatted and standardized so that it can be integrated with the needs of the organization.

Data profiling is diagnostic in nature so that data problems can be fixed so that the databases are used effectively for a company. The purpose of data profiling is to:

- Use data for multiple purposes and users, making it more searchable
- Improve data quality and integrate it with new applications
- Clean the existing data to make it accurate and maintain it in standard formats
- Fulfil data needs for future projects or queries
- Establish an enterprise view of all data, with rules for data governance for quality

Data profiling results in creating an active data warehouse in a company. It establishes a source of business intelligence and results in optimum use of data across departments. It can be understood in three parts: (a) structure discovery, (b) content discovery and (c) relationship discovery.

CONCLUSION

Although CRM encourages customer relationships, it also means that companies get large amounts of data. There have been concerns about lack of privacy as Internet giants collect large amounts of customer data. Customers have to get over their privacy concerns if they want the convenience of tailor-made offers. Thus, it is up to companies to use information discreetly and not appear to stalk their customers. Already in some places, customers are switching off from networking sites to protect their privacy. The European Union has a data protection regulation that puts control of private data in the hands of customers. If such trends continue, CRM systems that depend on data analytics may need a rethink.

The trade-off, then, is between giving up large chunks of personal data in exchange for customer convenience. Usually, people do not pay much attention to privacy clauses when they sign up on sites. But with technologies such as facial recognition and continuous GPS tracking, nothing will remain hidden from modern CRM systems. Social unrest in many parts of the world has led to governments using such technologies to track dissenters and punish them. If, as a result of such tracking, people start switching off their devices, the basis of digital CRM collapses.

It is difficult to predict the future, but it is certain that companies will have ever more data about their customers. How this data is used, and how customers respond to systems that stalk them in real time, remains to be seen.

SUMMARY

CRM is an outcome of relationship marketing. It is a system that uses data analytics to understand customer activity, predict the needs of consumers and make targeted and customized offers for them. Its objective is to build customer retention, loyalty and advocacy and thus drive profitability in an organization. E-CRM used Internet-based technologies to achieve CRM objectives.

When social media channels are integrated into CRM platforms, it is known as SCRM. SCRM is used to engage with customers, track information shared by them and encourage them to post content related to brands. But the challenge for companies is to analyse the vast amounts of data and use it to push customers gently up the loyalty ladder to become die-hard fans. Achieving e-loyalty is difficult but can be achieved by trust and transparency, resulting in enduring relationships.

However, an important aspect is achieving profitability. The cost of acquiring customers is far higher on the Internet than in the physical world, and this has caused grief to many online companies. That is why focusing on the most profitable customers is important.

Predictive models, which are data-based models that can anticipate customer behaviour and needs, help identify customer needs before they are expressed. This helps in creating targeted advertising and offers. This is the basis of next-generation CRM, which helps to deliver specific CXs without cold calling because companies already know what the customer wants.

In the long run, companies need to build their relationship capital, which is the sum of all of the relationships of all of the people connected with a firm. The collaborative web offers companies the tools and technologies that provide organizations with the ability to collaborate with all stakeholders. It also helps in the co-creation of products by involving customers in the product development process.

KEY TERMS

Analytical CRM: It is a system that consists of data mining from every level of the organization; it analyses the data and provides processed data for insights and intelligence.

Barnacles: These are a type of customers who look for discounts and offers, and they are not profitable for a company.

Butterflies: It refers to customers who sometimes buy a company's products but keep shifting their custom to competitors.

Collaborative filtering: It helps in making recommendations to encourage customers to buy additional products using filtered data from many users or a collaboration of users.

Collaborative or strategic CRM: It is a system in which all information from customer touch points is shared by all departments.

Collaborative web: It refers to the tools and technologies that provide organizations the ability to collaborate with employees, customers or other stakeholders using the Internet.

Cross-selling: It means selling additional or complementary products to an existing customer.

Customer life cycle: It is a term used to describe the progression of a customer while considering, purchasing, using and maintaining loyalty to a product or service. The customer life cycle consists of five stages: reach, acquisition, conversion, retention and loyalty.

CRM: A company-wide strategy of managing interactions with potential and existing customers, with the objective of building customer retention, loyalty and advocacy, and driving profitability.

E-CRM: It is a system that uses digital technologies to collect data from all sources to provide the company with a holistic view of customers in real time.

Loyalty ladder: The loyalty ladder is a concept that shows how a customer progresses from being merely interested in a company's products to becoming a customer and gradually moving up to different stages of loyalty to finally becoming die-hard loyal customers.

Operational CRM: It is a system that combines data from all business processes that contribute to the direct functioning of a company.

Predictive analytics: These are data-based models that can anticipate customer behaviour and needs.

Relationship capital: It is the sum of all of the relationships of all of the stakeholders of a firm.

Sentiment analysis: Sentiment analysis is the process of tracking and analysing customer feelings about a company or brand by monitoring online chatter of consumers through blogs, social media, chats and comments.

Strangers: Strangers are neither loyal nor are they profitable, like customers who browse for long and then make a small or no purchase.

True friends: This is a type of customer who speaks highly of a company and its products and recommends them to others.

Upselling: It is the practice of encouraging customers to buy a more expensive option than what they had planned.

CONCEPT REVIEW QUESTIONS

1. Define CRM. How has CRM changed in the digital environment?
2. What are the functions of CRM? How are these tied to business objectives?
3. What is e-CRM? What does it consist of?
4. Justify the statement: 'CRM systems also highlight the need to focus on the right customers.'
5. What are the key applications of digital CRM?

6. Describe the loyalty ladder and the different stages of customer loyalty. Illustrate your answer with an example.
7. What is cross-selling and upselling? Give examples. What is the downside of cross-selling and upselling?
8. Define predictive analytics. What does it consist of, and what is its use?
9. Describe CRM and the customer life cycle. What are the different stages of the customer life cycle?
10. What does next-generation CRM consist of? What is the difference between traditional CRM applications?

CRITICAL THINKING QUESTIONS

1. With companies tracking every bit of data of customers, would privacy concerns force companies to back down? Or does the future mean that people lose all their rights of privacy? What are the harms of that?
2. E-commerce companies realize that customers become profitable only in the long term. Thus, they acquire customers giving cashback and discounts, hoping that they would become profitable later on. How far is this strategy practical? Can you describe in which cases they have succeeded and in which cases they have failed?
3. It is commonly believed that 'customer is king.' But it has been suggested that companies classify customers and fire the barnacles and strangers. How do you reconcile these two opposing schools of thought?
4. What is the difference between operational, analytical and collaborative CRM? How do they interact to deliver an integrated consumer interface?

PROJECTS AND ASSIGNMENTS

1. Study the CRM systems of some selected companies. Are these systems based on database management, or are they proactive systems based on AI?
2. Visit a popular cafe like Café Coffee Day or Starbucks and observe the customers. Can you identify the true friends, butterflies, barnacles and strangers? What is the approximate percentage of each category? How much time on average does each spend in the cafe?
3. Modern CRM became very popular in the 1990s, and companies made huge investments in buying software. But investments started falling by 1999. It was a few years later that CRM had a comeback. Trace the reasons why interest in CRM fell, and why it has become a hot technology these days. Compare the earlier capabilities with present CRM capabilities.
4. Look at some CRM software such as Salesforce, SaaS, NetSuite and others and list their applications. Compare the offerings of each.

REFERENCES

Greenberg, P. 2010. *CRM at the Speed of Light: Social CRM Strategies, Tools, and Techniques for Engaging Your Customers*. New York, NY: McGraw Hill.

Kumar, D. 2015. *Consumer Behaviour*. New Delhi: Oxford University Press.

Kumar, V., R. Venkatesan, and W. Reinartz. 2006. 'Knowing What to Sell, When, and to Whom.' *Harvard Business Review* (March): 131–150. Available at: https://hbr.org/2006/03/knowing-what-to-sell-when-and-to-whom (accessed on 25 January 2021).

Lilien, G. L., P. D. Morrison, K. Searles, M. Sonnack, and E. Von Hippel. 2002. 'Performance Assessment of the Lead User Idea-generation Process for New Product Development.' *Management Science* 48, no. 8 (August): 1042–1059.

Poetz, M. K., and M. Schreier. 2012. 'The Value of Crowdsourcing: Can Users Really Compete with Professionals in Generating New Product Ideas?' *Journal of Product Innovation Management* 29, no. 2 (March): 245–256.

Reichheld, F. F., and P. Schefter. 2000. 'E-Loyalty Your Secret Weapon on the Web.' *Harvard Business Review* (July–August). Available at: https://hbr.org/2000/07/e-loyalty-your-secret-weapon-on-the-web (accessed on 25 January 2021).

Reinartz, W., and V. Kumar. 2002. 'The Mismanagement of Customer Loyalty.' *Harvard Business Review* (July). Available at: https://hbr.org/2002/07/the-mismanagement-of-customer-loyalty (accessed on 25 January 2021).

Rigby, D. K., and D. Ledingham. 2004. 'CRM Done Right.' *Harvard Business Review* 82, no. 11 (November): 118–122.

Rigby, D., F. Reichheld, and P. Schefter. 2002. 'Avoid the Four Perils of CRM.' *Harvard Business Review* (February). Available at: https://hbr.org/2002/02/avoid-the-four-perils-of-crm (accessed on 25 January 2021).

Roberts, K. 2007. *Lovemarks: The Future beyond Brands*. Brooklyn, NY: powerHouse Books.

Shankar, V., A. K. Smith, and A. Rangaswamy. 2003. 'Customer Satisfaction and Loyalty in Online and Offline Environments.' *International Journal of Research in Marketing* 20, no. 2 (June): 153–175.

Stringfellow, A., W. Nie, and D. E. Bowen. 2004. 'CRM: Profiting from Understanding Customer Needs.' *Business Horizons* 47, no. 5 (September–October): 45–52. Available at: https://doi.org/10.1016/j.bushor.2004.07.008 (accessed on 25 January 2021).

Tjan, A. K. 2011. 'It's Time to Fire Some of Your Customers.' *Harvard Business Review* (23 August). Available at: https://hbr.org/2011/08/its-time-to-fire-some-of-your.html (accessed on 25 January 2021).

Treacy, M., and F. Wiersema. 1995. *The Discipline of Market Leaders*. New York, NY: Perseus Books.

 CLOSING CASE

CRM IS THE SECRET BEHIND AMAZON'S SUCCESS

Many companies offer loyalty cards whenever you make a purchase. These are usually free. Amazon is one company that actually charges customers to make a relationship with the company. The Amazon Prime membership is a relationship programme that charges customers ₹999 a year.

Amazon correlates customer data from various sources and uses it to establish a CRM system successfully. Over the years, it has developed customer loyalty and has dominated online shopping wherever it operates. Today, apart from providing home deliveries of all products from 'A to Z', Amazon provides streaming video—its products such as Kindle and Alexa have become quite popular—and is the world's largest provider of cloud infrastructure.

For many customers, Amazon has become the first choice to look when they want to look for products online. How has the company achieved this? The answer is its huge variety, competitive process, ease of use, quick transactions and quick deliveries. Products are of good quality, and money is refunded quickly if transactions fail. That is the reason that people have come to trust Amazon for their purchases. Above all, it has a CRM system that remembers customers' purchases and habits, provides quick payments and refunds and makes recommendations that people find useful.

Amazon offers a streamlined buying process which people rely upon. It has a huge product range, which has helped it to capture more than half of all spending in the USA. Founded in 1994, Amazon started by selling books and has added products ever since. Amazon is now counted among the 'Big Five' of Internet companies that include Apple, Google, Facebook and Microsoft. It has become the largest Internet retailer in the world.

Amazon's CRM System

Customers think of Amazon as 'user friendly, great selection and convenience'. This is the basis of its approach and its CRM system. With huge storage of data and its analysis, it would not be wrong to say that it is actually a tech company that also sells products. Over the years, Amazon has built its system around customer convenience. It uses customer data and provides customers a streamlined shopping journey with easy order tracking. Its CRM system is characterized by:

- **User interface:** It has a clean user interface that is easy to use and navigate, with well-organized product categories. It can be used by just about anyone, with a quick search that ensures best results for customers, with images to match. There is no mis-selling.
- **Customer focus:** Amazon keeps its firm focus on CX, called bordering on 'customer obsession'.
- **Data analysis:** Amazon's CRM constantly analyses customer information from browsing habits and product search, order history and products placed in the 'wish list'. Even if customers do not place orders, they provide information to the company. This information is used to deliver CX.
- **Recommendations:** Amazon makes product suggestions based on users' search history, orders and wish lists. Its system is able to suggest 'Customers Who Bought This Item Also Bought', making it easier for people to buy complementary products. This feature increases sales and is based on data analytics.
- **Customer needs:** Amazon's system is so tuned to customer needs that one does not need to call customer services. Tracking orders, managing payment methods, order

(Continued)

cancellation—everything can be done by the customer using a streamlined system. This makes the buying process easy and stress-free for customers.

- **Reviews:** Another way of helping customers is by providing reviews. Customers can read reviews of verified past buyers and learn about products, thereby making informed decisions for themselves. These reviews are trusted as they are from genuine users. Needless to say, this adds to the trust that the retailer has earned.

Questions for Discussion

1. How can companies use relationship management techniques to build long-term customer loyalty?
2. How CRM uses data analytics to track customer needs?
3. How can CRM build loyalty among customers?
4. What will CRM look like in the future?

Source

https://www.softwareadvisoryservice.com/case-studies/case-study-how-crm-is-the-secret-behind-amazons-success/ (accessed on 27 January 2021).

CHAPTER 4

Online Consumer Behaviour

Understanding consumers and their behaviour forms the basis of marketing. This chapter describes the changes in human behaviour because of hyperconnectivity that have led to changes in consumer behaviour.

After reading this chapter, you will be able to learn about the following:

❏ Changes in human behaviour and consumer behaviour of the 'always-on' customer
❏ Online factors that impact online purchase and intentions, and what people buy online
❏ Drivers of online purchase behaviour, including personal, product, medium, merchants and environmental characteristics
❏ Reasons for buying online
❏ Online customer service experience

OPENING CASE

DOVE'S REAL BEAUTY: GETTING PEOPLE TALKING

More than ever before, brands have to ensure that people are engaged with them and talking about them. To achieve this, it is important to understand consumers and their behaviour. Companies have to understand what gets people talking, sharing and liking brands. That is why campaigns that are successful tend to have personal messages propagated over multiple channels. This case study describes an extraordinary digital campaign of Dove Real Beauty, which has succeeded in engaging customers across the world. It uses the power of digital billboards, sharing videos to tell stories and utilizing social media effectively.

First, it was important to know about consumers. So it commissioned a survey which found that only 2 per cent of the women interviewed considered themselves beautiful. If

(Continued)

(Continued)

women started talking about beauty and accepted their bodies as they were, could Dove become more relevant to them?

The idea came from the 2004 exhibition that Dove and Ogilvy & Mather had organized showing pictures taken by female photographers called 'Beyond Compare: Women Photographers on Real Beauty', to explore female beauty and women's perception towards it. It led to the development of the Dove Real Beauty campaign, which became highly successful, and people started talking about society's concept of beauty. The campaign tries to get over perceptions of beauty created in advertisements that use photoshopped images of beautiful models, resulting in women comparing their own bodies with those images and concluding that they are not beautiful. The campaign tries to get over this and asks women to 'imagine a world where beauty is a source of confidence, not anxiety'.

The campaign for Real Beauty is one of the most talked-about modern marketing success stories, says Bahadur (2014). The campaign has exploited diverse communication channels; it used digital billboards, social media and online videos. Shorter videos were shown on TV. In 2006, its video, 'Evolution', went viral even before 'viral' meant what it means today. Its 2013 ad, 'Real Beauty Sketches', which shows women describing their appearances to a sketch artist, became the most-watched video ads of all time.

The campaign used digital billboards to start its 'Tick Box' campaign featuring images of women with two tick-box options next to them asking questions like 'fat or fit?' and 'withered or wonderful?' Passers-by could text their vote to a listed number, and the results appeared next to the image on the billboard. The campaign touched a chord: it led 1.5 million visitors to the campaign for Real Beauty website. The images and the concept hit home. Since the campaign contains something that people can connect with, it led to huge customer engagement, brand love and subsequently, brand loyalty.

Dove is the only mainstream brand that talks about society's definition of female beauty. It features women who were not models but ordinary citizens (see Figure 4.1). It partnered with organizations such as the Girl Scouts and Boys & Girls Clubs of America to organize activities, including discussions about online bullying and photography projects capturing the beauty girls see in the world around them.

Next, the brand used YouTube to tell stories. 'Daughters' is a series of interviews with mothers and their daughters; 'Onslaught' takes a look at how the beauty industry targets young girls, and 'Evolution' showed how make-up and digital alterations can transform an average woman to look like a supermodel. These were highly successful on YouTube. The Dove Real Beauty Sketches had 67 million views, and the Evolution video had 19 million views at the time of writing this case study. For many young women, Dove Evolution struck a chord within them and made them aware of the way that images were manipulated in the media.

Another social media campaign, #DovePositiveChange, has a unique execution. Its short film, 'Selfie', explores how a group of girls takes selfies matching with online beauty standards. At first, it shows girls taking selfies from various angles to get their best slim profile. Then they are joined by their mothers, and the film becomes sweet and uplifting.

The case shows how an established brand could move into people's hearts by understanding consumers and talking about issues affecting them, deploying the power of digital methods.

FIGURE 4.1 *Dove Campaign Involved Readers through Both Online and Offline Methods*

Source: https://getevangelized.com/povs/guest-posts/legendary-advertising-paradigms-deepalinaair/attachment/dove-grey-gorgeous (accessed on 27 January 2021).

While reading this chapter, try to answer the following questions:

1. Why is it important to study consumer behaviour while devising digital campaigns?
2. What is the combination of elements of behaviour and digital methods that were used by Dove in their campaign?
3. How did the brand encourage consumer involvement in the brand?
4. Why is it necessary to use both online and offline media to influence the modern consumer?

Sources

Bahadur, N. 2014. 'Dove Real Beauty Campaign Turns 10.' *The Huffington Post*, 21 January. Available at: https://www.huffpost.com/entry/dove-real-beauty-campaign-turns-10_n_4575940 (accessed on 27 January 2021).

Matthews, N. 2014. 'The Campaign That Will Change Your Mind about #Selfies... and Maybe Make You Cry.' *Elle* (21 January). Available at: elle.com/fashion/news/a18879/dove-selfie-real-beauty-campaign-video/ (accessed on 16 February 2021).

■ INTRODUCTION

Consumer behaviour is defined as consumers' response to marketing stimuli. It explains how people make their purchase decisions, what influences them and what makes them buy. This involves studying human psychology—a difficult task, given that it is almost impossible to figure out what goes on inside the human brain.

The success of marketing has depended on understanding consumer behaviour. Companies undertake studies to understand why and how people buy products. Advertising campaigns are created after studying theories of learning, motivation, personality, lifestyle and perception. Humanistic models take into account emotions and moods as well.

These theories and constructs are quite relevant even today and give us insights about consumer behaviour. However, human behaviour has undergone huge changes with the spread of the Internet and smartphones. Now, people are busy in their virtual worlds, checking them compulsively every few minutes and showing anxiety if the phone is misplaced even for a short time. Instead of going to retail stores for products and brands, the first interaction between a consumer and brand is likely to be on a smartphone. Media consumption patterns have also changed over the years. This chapter looks at the changes occurring in human behaviour and how companies must change strategies to get into the world of the modern 'always-on' consumer.

■ HOW HUMAN BEHAVIOUR HAS CHANGED

One major change in human behaviour has been in the way that people interact with each other, and also the way they interact with companies and brands. Yan (2012) writes of the 'unprecedentedly pervasive and profound influence of the Internet on human beings'. The Lookout (2012) found some of the following interesting changes in people:

- A majority of respondents said that they cannot complete an hour without checking their phones. Younger people were found to be the most addicted.
- More than half of the respondents said they check their phones in bed, before going to sleep, after they wake up, even in the middle of the night. About 20 per cent of the people check their phones immediately after sex and about 40 per cent while on the toilet.
- People even check their phones while having meals and during religious services.

Aiken (2016) explains how human behaviour has changed online as people prefer online dating and interaction, pointing to a complete change in social interaction methods. Online gaming is fast becoming more popular than physical games. The mobile is the new drug: average users check their phones more than 1,500 times a week.

This exposure has led to consumer culture spreading its tentacles further into society. One consequence is that children are becoming aware as consumers much earlier than in the past because of their exposure to the Internet. A new market selling products to children and their parents has opened up: *The Economic Times* (Mukherjee and Jacob 2012) reports that a number of companies, including Panasonic, Sony, Bajaj, Disney, Piramal Healthcare and Chicco are custom-making TVs, ceiling fans, light fittings, washing machines, cologne and even sunscreen lotion for children. Teenagers, too, show a marked change in behaviour. A culture of looking good on social media has taken root.

Levin and Kilbourne (2009) write that teens are being sold cosmetics, padded bras, risqué costumes and t-shirts with sexy messages. They write, 'Corporations capitalize on this disturbing trend, and without the emotional sophistication to understand what they are doing and seeing, kids are getting into increasing trouble emotionally and socially.'

Society, as a whole, has been impacted due to the abundance of mobile phones. While they help in many tasks such as paying bills, ordering things or making reservations, it has also caused people to live more in virtual rather than physical worlds. These changes in human behaviour show that people have changed as consumers. This has had a profound change in how marketing must operate.

■ CONSUMERS IN AN ONLINE ENVIRONMENT

Online buying behaviour is the behaviour exhibited by consumers while browsing websites with the intention of buying products and services. Some new shopping behaviours are also emerging (see Marketing Insight 4.1). Lee (2012) writes that 'traditional marketing is dead' because traditional marketing methods no longer work. Today, people do not pay attention to marketing messages in the mass media, which has fragmented, and confidence is decreasing by the day that marketing spends will bring in results.

Connected consumers, through their mobile phones, move back and forth between stages of the purchase process. A study of consumer behaviour in the online context, therefore, must include the following:

1. The personal characteristics of buyers and their habits
2. Environmental factors that impact consumer decision-making
3. Analysis of consumer data left as they browse the Internet
4. Online and offline experiences that influence consumers

Correia (2017) calls today's consumer as 'the fluid consumer', who has little brand loyalty but high expectations. The problem is that companies are not built for fluid consumers. New levels of consumer engagement and empowerment have to be devised using smarter technologies to cater to consumers, who move easily between different types of transactions and channels (see Figure 4.2). They are indifferent to channels and flit between them; so companies have to present a unified picture of online and offline integration.

Consumers today are more informed and like to review, compare, consult and contrast purchase activity anywhere, including online interactions and physical stores. This means that digital and social influence is more important than ever before. Labrecque et al. (2013) write that this amplifies consumer power: social media and ubiquitous connectivity has not only enhanced access to information but also allowed consumers to create content and amplify their voices.

FIGURE 4.2 *Fluid Consumers Move Easily between Different Types of Actions and Channels*

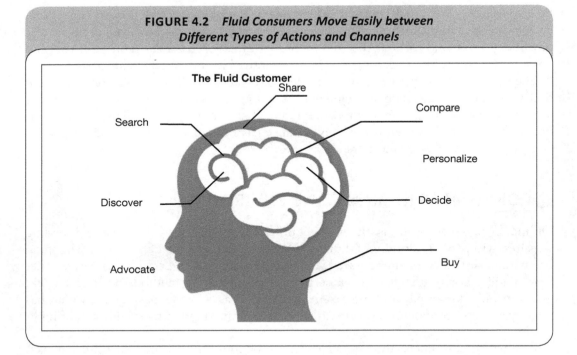

The changes are coming in quick and fast. Edelman (2010) writes that the phenomenal reach, speed and interactivity of digital touch points make brand experience essential to marketing. In the past, companies built brand awareness which would pull consumers to stores, but the changing environment means that companies have to influence touch points. The traditional construct of the purchase funnel becomes redundant as consumer move in circular paths to accomplish their purchases.

MARKETING INSIGHT 4.1 *New Trends in Consumer Behaviour*

One consequence of changing human behaviour can be seen in shopping behaviour such as *showrooming*, *webrooming* and *smartphonatics*.

- **Showrooming:** Physical retailers are worried about a phenomenon in which people visit their stores, check out products and prices on display, try them but buy them online. In this way, consumers experience the product physically and use their phones to get the best deals online. But it works to the disadvantage of the store: it invests in infrastructure and ambience, only to find customers walking out without a sale. Consumers take pictures of designs and check online prices even while they are in the store itself.
- **Smartphonatics:** Smartphonatics are people who change their financial, payment and shopping behaviour as a result of owning a smartphone. They differ from other

consumers as they quickly adopt mobile payments and financial services and are driving the adoption of mobile banking and payments systems. Financial and retail institutions have to adapt or risk being left behind. Showrooming poses a real threat to physical stores. They provide services but lose sales. As a result, several bricks-and-mortar retailers are losing sales and profitability, and some have had to shut shop. However, since people shift between online and physical channels seamlessly, it is difficult to assess how much influence each of them exercises on the purchase decision. How can retailers respond? One way is to provide complete transparency and equip salesmen with tablets to assist customers to search for online prices, but at the same time, they can explain the benefits of buying in-store. This will keep customers interested and make purchases on site.

Retailers are also setting up their own online stores and vice versa. The store directs customers to its own website and encourages them to order there; so the physical store becomes a supplement to the online world. Stores can improve their customer service, expand their product lines, and offer after-sales service. This can counter the trend of showrooming to some extent.

- **Webrooming:** A process called 'reverse showrooming' or 'webrooming' is also happening. This describes the phenomenon when consumers search online, but then buy products from physical stores. This requires employing knowledgeable sales staff, integration of online and offline orders, in-store Wi-Fi, smartphone discounts and making shopping a social experience, hence the need for integration of channels.

How can retailers get over the problem of showrooming?

PURCHASE FUNNEL TO DECISION JOURNEYS

Traditionally, consumer behaviour has been understood through the concept of 'marketing funnel' (Figure 4.3). This explains how consumers move in their purchase journeys. They are exposed to a large number of brands in the beginning, and then they narrow their choices as they proceed to buy. The funnel also exhibits the purchase behaviour of consumers—a large number of people become aware through advertising, but this number reduces as they move to successive stages of showing interest, generating desire and finally, taking action, which is called the AIDA model. The funnel becomes progressively narrow as a person moves from the awareness stage to actually buying.

Does the funnel capture the touch points and key buying factors in the digital era? Court et al. (2009) write that consumers, today, start their purchase process

FIGURE 4.3   *The Purchase Funnel Represented by AIDA*

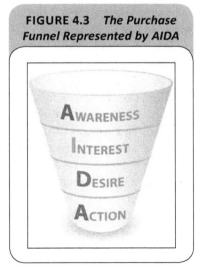

by searching on the Internet or getting influenced by someone, say, by seeing a picture of a friend using the product on social media. This leads to an online search and discussing the product on a chat group. Information and reviews are sought for. The consumer moves back and forth in these Internet interactions.

Today, consumers move towards their goals by following circular loops rather than a linear journey described in the AIDA model. The new marketing, thus, has to consist of engaging customers around consumer experience planning. By enhancing the customer's experience and enjoyment, the stage of advocacy is achieved. A brand promise has to be delivered by omnichannel, closely integrated with each other so that they coherently and consistently deliver that experience to consumers.

■ A NEW CONSUMER MODEL: CONSUMER DECISION JOURNEY

CDJ is a circular path, write Court et al. (2009). According to them, the CDJ combines 'all elements of marketing—strategy, spending, channel management, and message—with the journey that consumers undertake when they make purchasing decisions but also of integrating those elements across the organization.'

CDJ is an important development to understand hyperconnected consumers who look for information from multiple sources and interact across channels in their decision journeys. They interact with various parties at every stage of the purchase process. The decision-making process is, thus, more complex because it can change at every stage. Companies have to shape these journeys and influence each stage, write Edelman and Singer (2015).

'A special kind of consumer has taken a major role in the marketplace—the new info shopper. These people just can't buy anything unless they first look it up online and get the lowdown,' writes Penn (2009). His survey of shoppers revealed that 70 per cent of consumers search online for virtually everything, looking at product reviews and other information before making a purchase. Window shoppers have become 'windows shoppers', he writes, showing the all-pervasive influence of the Internet in our lives. Further, the research found that 70 per cent of users consulted product reviews or consumer ratings before they make their buying decisions.

The CDJ captures the many influences on the consumer in the decision process. Going from one step to the next is not a step-by-step process. They have two-way conversations with peers and reviewers, and companies have to change their approaches. The authors describe the consumer decision-making process as a circular journey with four primary phases: consider, evaluate, buy and experience. This becomes a loop so that one customer's experience sharing becomes another's consideration stage (Figure 4.4).

Edelman (2010) elaborates that CDJ can be described as consider, evaluate, buy, experience and enjoy, share and advocate, as explained below.

FIGURE 4.4 *The Consumer Decision Journey*

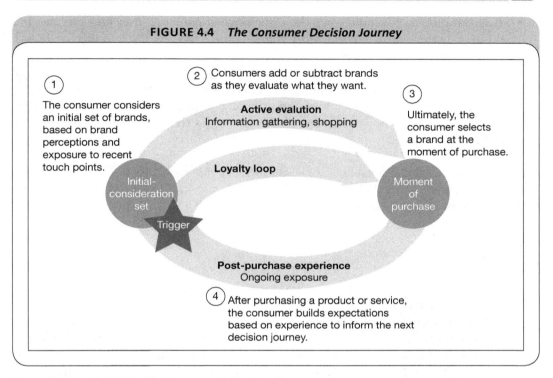

- **Consider:** Marketing activities help to get a brand into the consideration set of the consumer. This involves ads, store displays, trials and demos, recommendations of friends, interacting with salespersons, social media and sampling.
- **Evaluate:** The next stage is when the customers evaluate their choices, seek advice and read reviews from various sources. The role of opinion leaders, retailers, friends and so on becomes important at this stage. The consumer continuously adds new brands to the consideration set while leaving out others.
- **Buy:** After evaluation, they make their choice and decide to buy. The final purchase is made after deliberation either online or offline. The role of omnichannel marketing, therefore, becomes important.
- **Enjoy:** After buying, the consumer enjoys the experience of using the product and showing it off. The company will be interested in how the product is consumed or displayed and should ensure that it happens publicly. Kumar (2015a) writes that this is a crucial step in the consumption cycle, which is ignored by the purchase funnel analogy. Companies, now, have the means to influence consumers as they experience the product and share their feelings. Getting customers to pose with their purchases and post pictures online, thus, becomes a crucial element of marketing strategy.

- **Advocate:** If the consumers like the experience of purchase, they post pictures and positive reviews, share them with friends and advocate the product or brand, contributing to WOM publicity.
- **Bond:** Bonding or attachment with a product refers to consumers' emotional connect or a positive feeling experienced by them through consumption. Personalization helps in building emotional connect—our case study on Coke (Chapter 2) shows how customers loved the bottles that had their names or those of their loved ones.

Each step in the CDJ is a contact with a customer, referred to as MOT. That is where the efforts of a company meet the user, and it is a point which can make or break the buying decision. The next section discusses managing these MOT.

■ MOMENTS OF TRUTH

The CDJ identifies contact points between customers and companies, called MOT. MOT occurs every time a customer comes into contact with a brand. Carlzon (1987) wrote that each MOT is an opportunity to form an impression and can lead to a favourable outcome.

If a person wanted to buy a product in the pre-digital era, advertisements or displays at stores were their first MOT. Today, however, consumers start their consumer journeys by an online search for information of a product. Thus, Google (2012) added another MOT, which it calls 'the zero moment of truth (ZMOT)', when a customer searches for a product online. The MOT can be summed up as follows:

- **Zero moment of truth (ZMOT):** ZMOT is the moment when the consumer searches for a product or service online or comes across it on social media.
- **First moment of truth (FMOT):** FMOT is when the consumer buys the product.
- **Second moment of truth (SMOT):** SMOT occurs when the customer uses the product and experiences it.
- **Third moment of truth (TMOT):** TMOT occurs when consumers share their experiences of buying and using the brand.

Once a company identifies MOTs, it can find ways to influence them. For example, if a company can find the exact words that are used by consumers to search for its product or brand, it can optimize those words in search engines.

Moran, Muzellec and Nolan (2014) write that digital technologies are enabling the creation of a credible consumer-led information cycle. When consumers share their experiences on social networking sites, they help in starting others' purchasing journeys. In this way, online personal networks are used for brand guidance and purchase, resulting in consumer-generated publicity for the company. Lipsman et al. (2012) explain that managing MOTs can increase the depth of engagement and loyalty among fans, generate incremental purchase behaviour and leverage the ability to influence friends of fans. One's

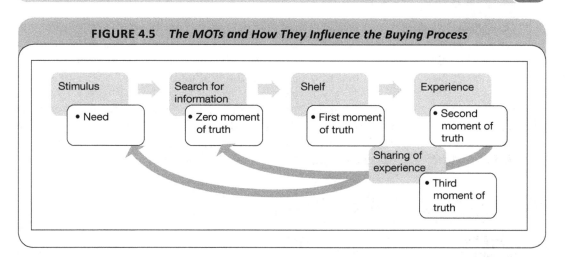

FIGURE 4.5 *The MOTs and How They Influence the Buying Process*

TMOT may well trigger the ZMOT of another as a friend gets exposed to the post, triggering a cycle of electronic WOM influence (Figure 4.5).

This represents a fundamental shift in how consumers interact with brands. Companies have to adjust to this new buying behaviour and change their communication strategies accordingly. The implications of understanding MOTs are as follows:

- **Influencing the MOT cycle:** Companies' marketing activities must include managing the MOT journeys and CX in the digital era. Since a TMOT of one customer can be a ZMOT for another, companies need to make every MOT meaningful. They have to encourage online conversations, which require a strategy to engage customers to make them share brand experiences. However, this strategy should not be intrusive; otherwise, customers will simply turn away.

- **Encourage electronic WOM:** Electronic WOM consists of positive or negative statements made about a product or company online by users. They may be posted by customers, but even non-customers tend to post comments based on their impressions. Electronic WOM consists of interactions through blogs, online reviews, social media posts and messages posted on online groups. Since electronic WOM has the power to reach a large number of people, it is imperative for companies to track and influence what is written and spoken on the Internet. Negative experiences have the tendency to get shared widely which cause harm to the company.

- **Converging of channels:** ZMOT may occur online, but the MOT cycle shows that all interactions with the brand are important. This implies the converging of channels. While it is important to engage customers online, experiences across channels—whether online or offline—must be pleasant. A Millward Brown report (2016) shows that Facebook + TV advertising can be used to extend reach beyond traditional TV; hence, offline MOTs should not be ignored.

- **Emphasis on data:** Tracking MOTs imply that companies have information about the nature of each interaction. Earlier, this data was hard to find. Now, data analytics allow companies not only to track all MOTs but also to have accurate profiles of customers, leading to a virtual customer data mine.

Analysis of MOTs helps in understanding online consumer behaviour. Our next step is to find out what makes people look for and buy products. This is discussed in the next section. However, while we discuss mostly consumer behaviour in this chapter, we must also be aware of B2B buying behaviour, which is explained in Marketing Insight 4.2.

MARKETING INSIGHT 4.2   *Online B2B Buying Behaviour*

B2B refers to commercial transactions between businesses as opposed to B2C, which is companies dealing with consumers. B2B is defined as the selling of products, services or information between two companies rather than companies selling to consumers. B2B transactions imply that the goods and services are not meant to be consumed by the buyer, but they are used by the buyer to further produce goods and services that are sold to consumers. Thus, if you buy some flour to bake a cake for your family, it is a B2C transaction, but if a baking firm buys flour to make cakes and sell them to others, it becomes a B2B transaction. B2B transactions consist of raw materials, machinery and accessories, consumables and services, which the buying company uses to process and add value and resell them in the form of finished products to consumers.

B2B purchases are more complex than B2C transactions. Buyers of automated machinery do not walk home as buyers from a flea market: They expect installation, application, parts, repair and maintenance and help in remaining competitive. It is, therefore, a long relationship not limited to a few transactions. The purchase decision is, thus, not to buy something, but a decision to enter into a bonded relationship.

B2B behaviour in the digital era has also changed. Digital technologies have impacted B2B in a big way, which is explained as follows.

- **Information:** B2B buying happens on the basis of product specifications and performance standards. Thus, B2B buyers look for information that helps them take a decision. Sellers must post all relevant information, including payment terms and safeguards on their sites which will help buyers.
- **Networking:** The buying decision in B2B environments is not taken by an individual but by a group of employees of the organization or a formal committee responsible for making purchases, called the 'buying centre'. B2B suppliers have to communicate with committee members and meet their objectives. For example, the production manager will look for a machine that is easy to operate, but the finance manager will look for savings. Online networking technologies assist in transparent communication with all committee members. The seller can be interactive and respond to queries from various parts of the organization, including technical, finance, purchasing and senior management.

- **Ratings and reviews:** B2B buyers have to be sure about their supplies. They look for ratings and reviews of not only products but also the dependability of suppliers. This is aided by online B2B platforms. Suppliers have to ensure that they get good reviews from buyers or will find their orders dwindle.
- **Compliance requirements:** Supplier companies must meet compliance requirements such as sustainability, diversity, working conditions and safety. All such requirements are posted on their sites and can build a source of competitive differentiation. Adherence to fair trade practices is also required.
- **Fast service:** The Internet allows supplier companies to respond faster should they face any issues at the manufacturing stage. Supplier companies can track live updates from installed machinery and provide quick action.
- **Transparency:** An advantage of the online world is that price, delivery and omnichannel transparency are maintained. Buyer companies can track their orders in supply chains. E-procurement is the order of the day now.
- **ERP and AI:** ERP systems have helped connect stakeholders in manufacturing. Now, AI-enabled platforms manage the entire buying process. Stock levels are automatically tracked, and orders are raised seamlessly. Invoicing, payments and accounts are linked in the entire B2B process.
- **IoT and preventive maintenance:** Another characteristic of B2B behaviour is that the customer expects service over the lifetime of the product. For instance, an airline buying a plane from Boeing or Airbus will look for error-free operations much after it is bought. The airline looks for preventive maintenance so that the planes do not crash. IoT and a maintenance dashboard assume much greater importance in B2B business than in B2C business. Manufacturers install sensors in machinery that are monitored digitally. Any change in performance immediately alerts manufacturers and their customers that corrective action is needed.

How is B2B buying behaviour different from B2C buying behaviour?

ONLINE CONSUMER BEHAVIOUR

In this section, we will consider the behaviour and motivations of people as they go online and search for products. Korgaonkar and Wolin (1999) describe the motivations for using the Internet. They found that people used the Internet because of social escapism, security and privacy, information, interactive control, socialization and economic motivation. This implies that sites that provide privacy, activities to connect with people and post comments and easy transactions with quick delivery are likely to be favoured by customers than those who merely list their products like mail-order catalogues.

Studies have found a number of other motivations for online search and buying products. Joines, Scherer and Scheufele (2003) found that informational motivations are positively related to shopping, followed by interaction and control, showing that consumers wanted to get all the information and be in control of the purchase decision,

FIGURE 4.6 *Factors Affecting Consumer Decision Journeys*

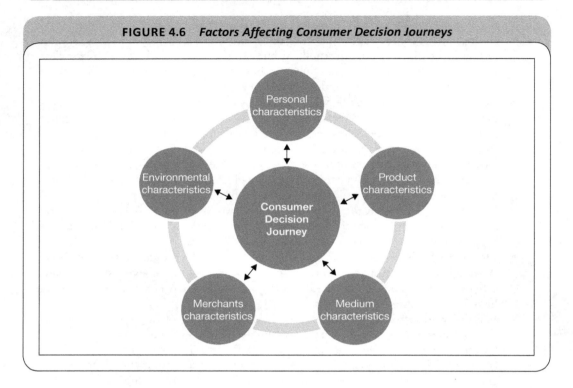

without interference from ads or salespeople. Many people prefer the Internet to avoid push marketing by salespeople.

Kumar (2015) writes that understanding online consumer behaviour involves understanding:

- What is the consumer browsing?
- What type of channel does the consumer prefer?
- What type of products appeal to consumers?
- What drives consumers online and what are their habits?
- What are the factors affecting online purchases?

This leads us towards developing a framework for online consumer behaviour. This shows how an individual interacts with and uses the Internet. In this framework, we see that CDJ is affected by five variables. Each stage of the CDJ is influenced by any of the surrounding variables (Figure 4.6).

All the variables interact with consumers at every stage of their CDJs: consideration, evaluation, purchase and advocate. The consumer moves back and forth between touch points and also between the brand and channels. All interactions, including offline ones, have to be handled well at every stage in order to influence consumers.

This leads us to develop an online consumer decision model that takes into account the constant interaction of several factors on the buying decision.

ONLINE CONSUMER BEHAVIOUR MODEL

An online consumer behaviour model integrates CDJ with personal characteristics and with the offline world (Figure 4.7). The model explains that CDJ is influenced by (a) personal characteristics, (b) physical marketing stimuli and (c) web experience consisting of the online marketing mix.

The model shows that consumers interact on various levels during their decision journeys. Personal factors play their role—some people are more prone to experimenting with new channels than others. While physical channels maintain their importance, the web experience leads customers to:

- View products with zoom and 3D views
- Examine the contents of the packaging and installation guidance
- Full product description and ingredients
- Reviews and testimonials from customers
- Endorsements from brand ambassadors and influencers

FIGURE 4.7   *An Online Consumer Behaviour Model*

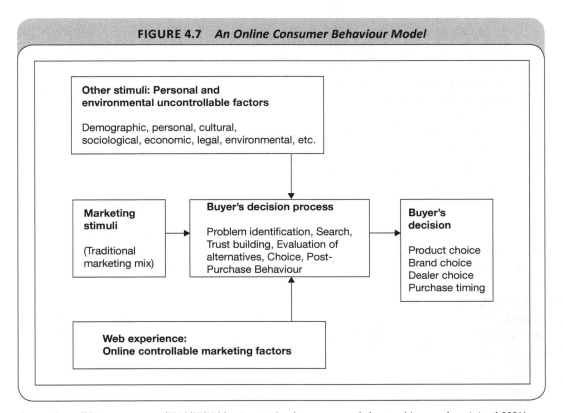

Source: https://theintactone.com/2018/07/07/cb-u4-topic-6-online-consumer-behaviour/ (accessed on 4 April 2021).

- Social media links and feeds
- Third-party endorsements, awards and testimonials

All the physical and online factors play a part in the purchase decision. We examine the following five types of influences in the context of consumers:

- Personal
- Environmental
- Medium
- Merchant
- Product

Personal Characteristics

Studying personal characteristics helps answers the question, 'Why do people buy online?'

In marketing, consumers are usually classified on the basis of their income, lifestyle and other consumer characteristics that affect their purchase. Gehrt et al. (2012) have investigated why people buy online and the dominant behaviours of Indian consumers. These are as follows.

- **Value singularity:** People are positively motivated by value: They look for cheaper prices on the Internet. Such consumers tend to value security and use the web to pay utility bills, buy air or rail tickets and books.
- **Quality orientation:** People look for known brands or products that have high quality. Young professionals who have sizeable incomes but are hard pressed for time are likely to look for quality. Price is relatively unimportant for them. They like to purchase holidays, utilities, experiences and consumer electronics online.
- **Recreational orientation:** People with recreational orientation enjoy shopping and like looking for new products. They like to browse online stores and explore websites and products and, sometimes, end up making a purchase.

The online purchase process is influenced by additional factors such as personality traits, knowledge of the Internet and trust. It also includes a person's need for time saving, demographic factors such as age, gender, education and income, the acceptance of new technologies as well as the individual's attitude towards the adoption of IT. Values, lifestyle, attitude, psychological factors, motivation and behavioural characteristics are part of personal characteristics. Some people are not trustful while buying online, and factors such as quality of products or payment security inhibit them, but perceived convenience may help to overcome their fears. Other consumers are attracted to a variety of products, price savings, deals and discounts and the speed of purchases. These are summarized in Table 4.1.

TABLE 4.1 *Personal Characteristics and Their Online Impact*

Personal Factors	Impact
Age	Older online shoppers search for a few products, but they actually purchase as much as the younger consumers do.
Gender	Male and female consumer behaviour differ online.
	The type of products bought also varies between men and women.
Income	Higher incomes lead to a higher probability of online purchase. Volume sales are also higher.
Education	Literacy is required for online transactions.
Culture	An individualistic culture is conducive to online commerce in comparison to a collectivistic culture.
Motivation	Convenience is a driving force of e-commerce; recreational and economic shoppers are also very active. Experiential shoppers and innovators look for information online.

- **Age:** It is generally believed that younger consumers would be more open to online transactions than older consumers. However, Sorce, Perotti and Widrick (2005) found that while older online shoppers search for significantly fewer products than their younger counterparts, they actually purchase as much as the younger consumers do. So although older consumers were less likely to search for a product online, once they had done so, they were open to buy it online. They can be classified as goal-oriented shoppers, who look for four objectives for online shopping: *convenience, information access, selection* and the *ability to control* the shopping experience. Companies offering all the four would, thus, be able to attract large numbers of online shoppers. Younger shoppers can be seen as hedonic shoppers, who are motivated by fun, brands and service.
- **Gender:** Traditionally, women are thought to be more involved in household shopping and shop from traditional stores. However, in the online space, men tend to make more purchases and spend more money online than women. Men were more convenience-oriented and less motivated by social interaction, while women were just the opposite. Women did not find online shopping 'as practical and convenient as their male counterparts'. Women were reported to have a higher level of web apprehensiveness.
- **Income:** Online shoppers tend to have higher incomes than traditional store shoppers, which can be seen from the fact that the most popular items purchased online, such as books, appliances, holiday and leisure travel, PC hardware, mobiles and software. This could be because affluent people have had Internet access in India so far. As the Internet habit spreads, this is changing towards grocery and household goods.

- **Culture:** Culture represents a shared set of values that influence societal perceptions, attitudes, preferences and responses. According to Hofstede's culture model, two dimensions, individualism–collectivism and masculinity–femininity have been used to predict online consumer behaviour. Online shopping is more evident in an individualistic than in a collective culture. Educated and empowered societies will have more female online shoppers than traditional male-oriented societies.
- **Online segmentation:** Aljukhadar and Senecal (2011) have provided a basis for segmentation of online customers. Their study reveals that online consumers form three global segments:
  o **Basic communicators:** Consumers who mainly use email to communicate, consist of mostly educated people and older people.
  o **Lurking shoppers:** Consumers who use the Internet to navigate and to heavily shop, consisting of educated males or females who belong mainly to the higher income and age groups.
  o **Social thrivers:** Consumers who use the Internet to interact socially by means of chatting, blogging, video streaming and downloading. The social thrivers belong to the youngest age group (< 35 years old) and fall in the lowest income bracket.

Companies can use this basis of segmentation to allocate their marketing expenditure effectively. Marketing and advertising strategies can be developed according to the customer's online segment.

In general, it may be said that consumers who are most likely to use e-commerce are those who are motivated by the following: (a) product specifications, (b) opinions of friends and peers, (c) discounts, cashback and promotions and (d) inability to access physical stores.

That is why consumers' demographic and socio-economic characteristics may be less important than behavioural characteristics in the online context since these are likely to play a more relevant role in online usage.

The individual's motivations have to be matched with commercial activities. For example, campaigns to get people to consume products and then post their pictures while they are in the act, use the need of people to show off and feel cool about it. In other words, companies have to remain relevant to consumers and get them engaged with their brands. The challenge can, well, be understood when we realize that how a consumer prefers to interact with a brand depends on the individual, not the company. As Kotler (2002) had explained, 'Internet users in general place greater value on information and tend to respond negatively to messages aimed only at selling… In online marketing, it is the consumer, not the marketer, who gives permission and controls the interaction.'

Product/Service Characteristics

Certain products are more conducive for online sales than others, which helps us to answer the question: 'What do people buy online?'

TABLE 4.2 *What People Buy Online*

Category	Approx. Percentage
Train and air tickets, hotel reservations	60
Mobile phones and accessories	25
Apparels, accessories, personal and healthcare	10
Others, including laptops, jewelry and books	5

Source: Author estimates based on new reports.

Typically, products that require information search are more popular on the net. This category includes travel bookings, books, consumer electronics, mobile phones, financial services and others. Firms that merely leveraged information have, thus, gone out of business with the advent of the Internet. For example, travel agents have had to shut down their offices as people can now easily customize their travel plans online, search for information and choose modes of travel or hotels based on their personal needs.

A study of online purchases helps us determine the product characteristics that are important for consumers. People buy online if it helps solve some problem in their life. This could be related to non-availability, quality, difficulty in procurement, price, ease and convenience.

One of the most popular searches relate to online travel information. Having confirmed tickets and reservations saves the problem of standing in queues and uncertainty. A large part of e-commerce is accounted for rail and air tickets, in addition to hotel reservations. The balance online retail consists of apparel, accessories, electronics, books and so on (Table 4.2). The mobile phone is a favourite online purchase since people can search for a large number of models and get discounts and deals. Also, popular online are personal accessories, consumer durables and computing devices.

Among the categories that are not shown in the table but represent high growth in the future are groceries, financial services and entertainment. Online groceries are a growing category and are the focus of giants such as Reliance, Amazon and others. The category percentages could well change in the future as habits and services offered increase.

Merchant Characteristics

Analysing merchant qualities helps us answer the question, 'Why are some websites more popular with customers than others?'

Trustworthy merchants and brands encourage people to buy online. Strauss and Frost (2012) write that there are three cornerstones for attracting customers online. These are as follows:

- **Reputation:** Reputations are built by being transparent and honest. Companies must make authentic claims and deliver on brand promises. How companies join online conversations is the key to online marketing, and reputations are built if these interactions are honestly managed.

- **Relevance:** The second challenge is to remain relevant in the consumer's world. Irrelevant communication is, at once, blocked, but relevant information gets a chance to be seen. For example, if a site makes recommendations based on the customer's past purchases, they are likely to be seen as relevant.
- **Engagement:** Communication between three groups—company, consumers and their social circle—must be kept alive. Social media sites are a boon for this kind of conversation but using social media for commercial purposes is not very easy. Further, engagement in itself is not enough, and conversions drive the market.

The most important role is played by trust. Hahn and Kim (2009) write that consumer trust in an offline store translates into online stores as well. Brands that have established trust, thus, tend to do better on the Internet. Initially, people have reservations about sharing confidential information like credit card details, but trust overcame such fears. Consumers feel confident with online shopping if the company has developed trust with them.

Other online merchant characteristics are summed up in Table 4.3.

Online merchants give consumers the freedom to combine attributes and services that they seek. Fashion sites, for example, offer combinations of clothes and accessories

TABLE 4.3   *Merchant Characteristics*

Characteristics	Variables
Delivery	Timely and accurate deliveries, quick order confirmation, shipping notification and tracking orders, complaint tracking and logistics
Quality	Design, material, colour, fit and durability
Time savings	Easy search, easy ordering and payments, quick orders and check-outs, fixed time delivery and automated problem resolution
Comparison shopping	Ability to compare, information availability, listed prices and bargains, and discounts
After-sales service, customer support	Integration with offline service centres, easy registration of complaints and timely service across cities, returns, breakages and delivery tracking
Product descriptions	Accurate product descriptions
Payment options	Easy payments, secure payment gateways, cards, e-wallets, EMIs, COD, stored payment and billing information, coupon codes and gift cards
Wish lists	Shopping lists and deferred purchases
Real-time inventory	Updated inventory and balance in stock
Engagement and experience	Technological features and ease of use, and navigation

that consumers can mix, match and order. Information and reviews can tend to augment products. To provide a real-life experience, companies are using technologies such as virtual displays. Technology is also used to customize products by 3D printing as per individual needs. Offline initiatives like COD help customers try out products at home.

Companies get over consumer resistance by making recommendations or informing them about what their friends have bought. Making wish lists is another way in making customers positively inclined towards online purchases.

Medium Characteristics

Medium characteristics help us answer, 'How is the Internet conducive for delivering consumer experience?' It consists of web design, ease of navigation, ease of placing orders and reliability.

Online interaction and experience influences buying decisions. Zhu and Zhang (2010) found that online reviews are more influential when consumers have relatively greater Internet experience, showing that people love the Internet experience. Joines, Scherer and Scheufele (2003) studied the time spent by users on the Internet. They found that Internet activities consist of accessing entertainment, getting information about hobbies and jobs, news and other information, travel bookings and information, health or family care, and connecting with local communities.

Medium characteristics consist of elements shaping the customer's virtual experience. Constantinides (2004) writes that customers are influenced by functionality, including information availability, emotions, cues, stimuli, and products and services combinations. This integrated experience can be delivered through usability, interactivity, trust, aesthetics and the traditional marketing mix elements (see Table 4.4).

Identifying the online experience components and understanding their role affecting the customer decision-making process are important steps in developing and delivering an online experience that is attractive to users. Morgan-Thomas and Veloutsou (2013) write that online environments are, by their nature, information-based service environments that are linked with technology and technological innovation. Companies thus have to understand the medium characteristics and invest in delivering customer experience.

TABLE 4.4 *Determinants of Web Experience*

Stimuli	Responsiveness	Psychological Factors	Appearance	Functionality
Marketing mix	Interactivity	Trust	Aesthetics	Usability, search
Promotion	Service and sales	Security	Design	Site navigation
Fulfilment	Customization	Safety	Presentation	Payments
Social media	Network and community	Returns and refunds	Design, ambience	Speed, accessibility

Online customer service experience (OCSE) is defined as the customers' overall mental perception of their interaction with the service provider. Klaus (2013) writes that two sets of factors play an important role—functionality and psychological factors (Figure 4.8).

Psychological factors consist of trust, value for money and context familiarity, which are described as follows.

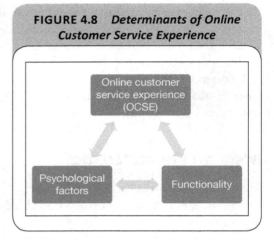

FIGURE 4.8 *Determinants of Online Customer Service Experience*

- **Trust:** Online channels have to get over a lack of trust that arises because of physical distance, payment concerns, lack of personal contact and after-sales service. Trust is developed if uncertainties attached to these are removed. Explicit guarantees, safety certificates and clear terms of delivery and service are likely to reassure consumers and help to reduce the uncertainty associated with purchasing in online environments.
- **Value for money:** Customers prefer any channel if it offers better value in comparison with other channels. Buying desired products at discounted prices was seen as emotionally significant and contributed towards a positive experience.
- **Context familiarity:** Context familiarity means how a website can create a service experience similar to that of buying in a physical store. This includes a number of attributes, such as online visual representation, consistency in style and quick answering of queries.

Functionality factors consist of usability, product presence, communication, social presence and interactivity, which are described as follows.

- **Usability:** Usability relates to ease of use of the website. Attributes affecting usability are site speed, ease of use and hyperlink design. The website should enable easy and quick navigation and browsing. The greater the perceived usability of the website, the greater is the likelihood of visitors and purchase. Image interactivity and the 'look inside' feature helps customers examine the products.
- **Communication:** Communication regarding payment and deliveries is important as it reduces the uncertainty associated with online purchasing. A confirmation email gives customers a sense of dealing with a person, not the computer.
- **Social presence:** A customer's virtual interaction with other shoppers through comments, product reviews and social media linkages is called social presence. It helps in the purchase decision process, in particular in the information search and alternatives evaluation stages.

- **Interactivity:** Interactivity refers to the responsiveness of the website for users. Personal information is used to tailor communications and recommendations. Psychological factors play an important role in overcoming customers' reluctance to use online channels.

Environmental Characteristics

The question to be answered in environmental characteristics is 'What makes people transact online?'

The answer lies in discovering the influence of economic variables, peer groups, education, payments systems, security and financial issues. Environmental factors such as economic, culture, social influence and media play an important role in affecting consumer purchasing decisions. These factors are relevant in the context of online consumer behaviour. Some of these are briefly described as follows.

- **Economic variables:** Individual purchasing power and economic indicators impact online behaviour. In villages, wages and purchasing power are limited, and many farmers are under debt. Reliable courier services are also missing. In such a scenario, almost two-third of the population that lives in rural areas lack resources or ability for online purchases.
- **Social variables:** Social variables, such as education, knowledge and attitude about online buying and peer group, influence and affect the choice of channel. WOM is an important factor to encourage online sales; hence, social factors tend to be extremely useful.
- **Cultural variables:** Online purchases tend to be popular in individualistic cultures. In collective cultures, as in rural India, it impacts inclination for online commerce. People prefer to buy whatever is available locally.
- **Government restrictions:** The Indian government imposes restrictions on e-commerce companies, and issues of taxation spoil the discounting model. Restricting certain goods online implies that supply chains cannot be built.
- **Technological:** Non-availability of broadband and electronic payments impacts online purchases. In rural areas, for instance, Internet services are slow and, in some areas, not available at all. Villagers also do not have credit, debit cards or e-wallets, and trust in these still has to be established.
- **Other variables:** Other environmental variables consist of availability of information, government regulation towards e-commerce, legal constraints and situational factors.

In addition, there are sudden changes in the environment that affect propensity to use online services. For instance, the impact of coronavirus encouraged people to stay at home and use contactless retail (see Marketing Insight 4.3). This caused a huge shift in consumer behaviour globally. On the other hand, data leakages may well prevent people from sharing their data online.

The above discussion explains the influences on online consumer behaviour. All the factors have to be approached simultaneously. Many companies are able to achieve this, which is reflected in the success of e-commerce in India. The next section describes the growth of online transactions and explains why they are becoming popular.

The above factors that affect CDJs help us understand the rise of e-commerce, which has picked up in recent years.

MARKETING INSIGHT 4.3 *Coronavirus and Digital Marketing*

The spread of the coronavirus has caused huge changes in consumer behaviour. This change will continue, well, in the future. In the short term, consumers have seen falling incomes which has shifted their consumption patterns towards grocery and household supplies. There has also been a drastic cut in spending on apparel, footwear and travel.

In the long term, many other changes are occurring which will change shopping forever. Digital buying and contactless delivery are becoming popular. It is only a matter of time before consumers take to online ordering with curbside or store pickup, drive-through services and increase deliveries of household items. Further, as work from home increases and social gatherings are shunned, there will be less demand for apparel, cosmetics, shoes and the like. These trends will stay for a long time.

A Mckinsey & Company report (2020) shows that 91 per cent of Indian consumers have changed their shopping behaviour. It says that the Coronavirus has resulted in changes in consumer behaviour in five distinct ways: (a) preference for value buying and essential goods, (b) shift to digital and omnichannel, (c) decline in brand and store loyalty, (d) rise of health and caring economy and (e) a 'homebody economy', as people avoid travel and crowded places.

Sheth (2020) writes that new habits will emerge. Consumers will exhibit modified shopping habits as they follow safety and social distancing guidelines. At the same time, new habits will also emerge. Shopping will entail screening and temperature checks, trying of apparel and unnecessary touching of objects will be discouraged.

In this scenario, consumers will opt for safe shopping options and are switching to digital options in a big way. E-commerce is poised to grow in leaps and will offer innovative choices. A survey by PwC (2020) shows that half of the consumers avoid leaving home and work from home almost entirely. People are also avoiding public transport and meeting friends, which means that restaurants and pubs will lose their popularity.

Although the shift to online was happening rapidly even without the coronavirus, the changed behaviour now promises to boost this even further. Companies will have to offer innovative methods of contactless shopping and delivery, like drone deliveries, in the future.

How will contactless shopping impact consumers and businesses?

Sources

Gupta, S. 2020. 'Explained: How the Covid-19 Pandemic Has Changed Consumer Behaviour.' *Indian Express*, 19 July. Available at: https://indianexpress.com/article/explained/explained-how-the-covid-19-pandemic-has-changed-consumer-behaviour-6510354/ (accessed on 28 January 2021).

PwC. 2020. 'Evolving Priorities: COVID-19 Rapidly Reshapes Consumer Behavior.' Available at: https://www.pwc.com/us/en/industries/consumer-markets/library/covid-19-consumer-behavior-survey.html (accessed on 28 January 2021).

Sheth, J. 2020. 'Impact of Covid-19 on Consumer Behavior: Will the Old Habits Return or Die?' *Journal of Business Research* 117 (September): 280–283. Available at: https://doi.org/10.1016/j.jbusres.2020.05.059 (accessed on 28 January 2021).

■ E-COMMERCE

E-commerce or electronic commerce is the buying and selling of goods and services as well as the transmitting of funds or data over an electronic network. These business transactions occur either as B2B, B2C, C2C or consumer to business.

Despite the initial hiccups, Indian consumers have taken to e-commerce in a big way. A number of factors, such as demonetization, government regulations, which prohibited deep discounting and restricting the contribution of a single seller on online marketplaces to 25 per cent, and consumer sentiment, played a role. However, its steady growth shows that e-commerce has become quite popular not only in metros but also in small towns.

A number of factors have contributed to the success of e-commerce in India, which are as follows:

- An almost infinite variety of choices
- Serves most geographic areas
- Freedom from pesky salesmen
- 'Try and buy' and cash on delivery facilities
- Very quick deliveries
- Offers complete information about products
- Increasing Internet penetration and 4G services
- Lowering the cost of smartphones

A PwC-ASSOCHAM report (2014) says that the online world represents an 'ever-evolving, information symmetric and globalised world of e-commerce'. The realm of competition has shifted to better customer service by shortening delivery times. Low delivery prices, doorstep delivery, traceability and reverse logistics have become the most important elements of differentiation for e-commerce players.

The top sites that find favour customers are: Amazon, Flipkart, Myntra, Snapdeal, Paytm and others. E-commerce sites that meet expectations of online shoppers succeed better than others. These expectations are discussed in the next section.

■ EXPECTATIONS OF ONLINE SHOPPERS

The use and spread of e-commerce depend on understanding consumer expectations from it. The rise in online buyers shows that their confidence in online buying is increasing.

A report by Forrester Research (Wigder and Bahl 2011) points out that consumers exhibit a typical behaviour while shopping online and have various expectations, which are as follows:

- **High expectations:** Indian consumers have high expectations from online commerce as e-commerce sites try to gather a large number of users. Customers expect freebies and discounts, deals from banks and free deliveries as they shop online. For instance, many banks offer additional discounts if their cards are used to shop on certain sites.
- **Product returns:** Consumers expect easy product returns. Some online retailers offer such facilities despite high costs in order to build consumer confidence.
- **Free delivery:** Consumers expect free shipping and quick delivery of online orders. Even though this adds to cost, websites have to offer this facility in order to compete.
- **Low prices:** Easy availability of information makes consumers search for low prices. Websites offer comparison facilities and low prices along with deals and offers that make consumers expect discounted prices. Whether this is sustainable in the long run is doubtful: Many entrants have already shut shop as they found low prices and high costs of free delivery unsustainable.

As their expectations are mostly being met, people are shedding their inhibitions and are finding reasons to shop online. We can sum up the reasons for buying and not buying online in Table 4.5.

The industry is solving some of the problems that arise in an online environment. Payment methods have been made easier and secure, as described in the next section.

■ E-PAYMENT METHODS

Indian online consumers prefer COD as the payment method. Some sites, therefore, give a little discount for people who pay by debit or credit cards. The major chunk of online payments is made through Internet banking, debit card or credit cards (Figure 4.9).

Projections show that the share of mobile wallets in digital payments is increasing. The COD method is declining but is still preferred by a majority of Indian consumers. The use of debit and credit cards and online banking methods show slight increases.

The chart shows that Indian consumers are finding confidence in using e-payment methods. This is aiding e-commerce to spread in the country. It is also adding to an online service experience.

TABLE 4.5   *Reasons for Buying and Not Buying Online*

Reasons for Buying Online	Why People Do Not Buy Online
Ease and convenience, saving time	Lack of trust and security issues
Better prices, deals and discounts	Late or wrong deliveries, product not as per expectations
Comparison and availability of a large variety	Quality of products not as shown on the site
Easy search, quick deliveries	Bad shopping experience, lost lists, site freezing
Better information and specifications	Payments deducted but not received, online frauds
Reviews and opinions of others	Touch, try, feel and smell factor
Avoiding pushy salespersons	Non-availability of broadband, not being technology savvy
Secure payment methods, EMI and COD options	Lack of after-sales service, difficulty in returning faulty products

FIGURE 4.9   *Payment Preferences of Indian Customers for Online Transactions*

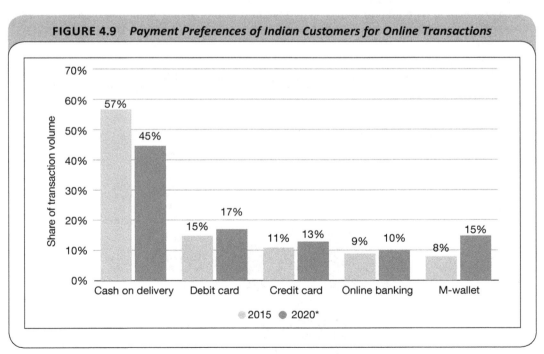

Source: https://www.statista.com/statistics/257478/preferred-payment-methods-of-online-shoppers-in-india/ (accessed on 28 January 2021).

Note: *refers to estimated figures for 2020.

Sometimes, online firms build offline stores to help consumers have the touch and feel experience (see Marketing Insight 4.4), deliver after-sales service and to facilitate convenient returns and deliveries. Companies are, therefore, facilitating online product reviews, videos and more advanced sizing and fitting tools.

MARKETING INSIGHT 4.4   *Adding Tangibility to Online Trades*

Consumers do not differentiate between online and offline channels. Online players find that they must integrate their online offerings with real-world commerce. Many such sites are now not only simulating offline buying experiences to provide touch-and-feel comfort to consumers, but they are also opening physical outlets to woo potential buyers and tackle negative perceptions about online shopping.

CNBC (2014) reports that despite the shift towards online shopping, a number of online brands are moving into the physical space. Online retailers are finding that growth comes from multiple channels. Many brands have realized that to build volume and scale, they need to have an offline presence as well. Physical stores bring them the opportunity to expose their brands.

Ferns N Petals an online player, has a physical presence in various cities (Figure 4.10). It has tied up local florists to display its signage in an effort to connect with customers in the real world.

Zivame.com, an online retailer of bras, panties and thongs, is conducting lingerie-fitting workshops for female customers. The company realized that women are used to buying offline,

FIGURE 4.10   *A Ferns N Petals Store in Mohali*

so it needs to talk to them in the language and environment they are comfortable with. This activity spreads awareness about the brand and also gives the brand a face and credibility.

Yatra.com has opened physical stores also to aid online buying to reach out to people looking for additional information or offering tailor-made travel plans. Yatra holiday lounges can now be seen in many cities and towns of India.

Zovi, an apparel retailer, rolled out a virtual trial room to enable its buyers to check out how selected merchandise looked on them via an interactive webcam. In addition, there was a brand awareness campaign, including a TV commercial. Its merchandise was displayed at kiosks at malls and high-footfall sites. The company realized that having an offline presence gave them credibility and also took them closer to their customers who could touch and feel the product offerings.

Myntra (taken over by Flipkart) has been advertising on TV and has a 'style studio', which is a virtual dressing room aimed at making online shopping more interactive. The style studio enables users to click their pictures using a web camera, select a product they want to try and see how it looks on them. It also enables users to share their look with friends on Facebook and Twitter. It also offers a 'try and buy' service in which consumers shop for a product online, get it delivered at their home, try it out and then decide about buying it. This enables customers to get over their reservations about the looks and style of the apparels they are buying.

Why are online companies adding physical stores to their portfolio?

Sources

CNBC. 2014. '10 Online Retailers Going from Clicks to Bricks.' Available at: http://www.cnbc.com/id/101573601 (accessed on 28 January 2021).

Singh, Rajiv. 2012. 'Online Retailers Like Zovi, Myntra Offer Simulating "Touch & Feel" Comfort to Consumers.' *The Economic Times*, 14 November. Available at: https://economictimes.indiatimes.com/online-retailers-like-zovi-myntra-offer-simulating-touch-feel-comfort-to-consumers/articleshow/17430319.cms?from=mdr (accessed on 15 April 2021).

INTEGRATING CHANNELS

One important aspect of the change in consumer behaviour is that businesses, today, cannot be Internet only or physical only. This is because people use all channels: They may not buy online but will certainly look for information and reviews before buying from a store. Thus, the figures for online retail hide the consumers who do their research online at home but buy offline. For example, apparel is one category in which people look for styles online, but the purchase decision is taken after trying the dresses out. So while the purchase may contribute to physical stores, the buying process started on online channels.

Gulati and Garino (2000) write that the distinction between dotcom and physical stores is rapidly fading. Customers are concerned with the products and services they get, so they do not distinguish between offline brands and online purchases. 'Success in the new economy will go to those who can execute clicks-and-mortar strategies that bridge the physical and the virtual worlds,' they write.

Companies, therefore, try to combine offline experiences with their online trade to enhance the shopping experience. Koufaris (2002) writes that consumers have dual roles: as a traditional shopper and as a computer user. Both enjoyment of the physical shopping experience and usefulness of the website are important. Thus, offline brand presence works in tandem with online efforts. Any online consumer behaviour model must reflect this.

CONCLUSION

In the changing environment, when customers have limited attention spans, and human behaviour is centred on their smartphones, companies face a tough challenge to get in the world of customers. But smartphones also provide an opportunity for innovative companies to involve and engage them.

Kimmel (2010) writes that channels are personally chosen by consumers. An understanding of consumers interact with brands and companies is, therefore, of extreme importance. Consumers increasingly are in control of when and how they receive marketing messages and tend to block formal marketing efforts. Companies have to overcome this challenge by investing in improving the online customer service experience. In the final analysis, companies that understand their consumers and use the medium effectively will continue to engage and serve their customers in the future.

SUMMARY

The Internet has caused a huge change in human behaviour. Now, people check out their phones every few moments, showing compulsive behaviour and anxiety if the phone is misplaced even for a short time. Today, people are connected with a vast network of information, while multitasking creates 'an artificial sense of crisis'. Today's generation exhibits the 'always-on,' anywhere, anytime, anyplace consumer behaviour. The hyperconnected generation is immersed in what is happening on their pocket screens, immersed in themselves (Vollmer 2008).

In this scenario, consumers do not pay attention to marketing messages, leading to the claim that traditional marketing is dead. Consumers, today, are more informed and like to review, compare, consult and contrast purchase activity anywhere, including physical stores. Online consumer behaviour is influenced by five variables: personal, product, medium, merchant and environmental characteristics. A study of these reveals what and why people take to online purchases.

Personal characteristics refer to the personal characteristics of the consumer. These include income and purchasing power as well as personality, values, lifestyle, attitude, psychological factors, motivation and behavioural characteristics. Medium characteristics refer to the human–computer interaction, and how user interface design affects consumers, and these include reputation, relevance and engagement. Usability, communication, social presence, product presence and interactivity also determine whether a website will become popular with customers. Product characteristics refer to the type of products that require information search are more popular on the net. Merchant attributes include trust, security, service and deliveries that differentiate one online player from another.

The study of online consumer behaviour shows what people buy online, the products that are more conducive for online trade and why they buy them.

▓ KEY TERMS

AIDA: The purchase funnel is the traditional consumer behaviour model represented by four stages of the consumer buying process, consisting of awareness, interest, desire and action.

B2B: This refers to the selling of products, services or information between two companies rather than companies selling to consumers.

Consumer behaviour: Consumer behaviour is defined as consumers' response to marketing stimuli.

CDJ: Online consumer behaviour is represented by a circular model called CDJ which consists of consider, evaluate, buy, enjoy, advocate and bond.

E-commerce: E-commerce is the buying and selling of goods and services as well as the transmitting of funds or data over an electronic network.

Environmental characteristics: These are the factors outside the control of the online business that affects online transactions, such as laws, economic factors, education, social and cultural variables.

Medium characteristics: These are the qualities of the Internet as a medium for online transactions. It consists of web design, ease of navigation, ease of placing order and reliability.

Merchant characteristics: These are the attributes of online businesses that make them attractive to buyers.

MOT: It is the points of contact between customers and companies.

OCSE: It is the customers' overall mental perception of their interaction with the online service provider.

Personal characteristics: These are consumer characteristics that affect online purchase or intentions, consisting of personality traits, income and purchasing power, values, lifestyle, attitude, psychological factors, motivation, behavioural characteristics, knowledge of the Internet and trust in the online purchase process.

Product/service characteristics: These are the product attributes that makes it more conducive to buying and selling online.

Showrooming: This is the phenomenon in which people visit their stores, check out products and prices on display, try them but buy them online.

Smartphonatics: These are the people who change their financial, payment and shopping behaviour as a result of owning a smartphone.

Webrooming: This is the phenomenon when consumers search online, but then buy products from physical stores.

CONCEPT REVIEW QUESTIONS

1. Why is it necessary to study consumer behaviour for online marketing? What does the study of online consumer behaviour consist of?
2. What are the changes taking place in human behaviour that are impacting marketing?
3. What products do people buy online in the Indian e-commerce market? Why?
4. How do personal characteristics impact online consumer behaviour?
5. What type of consumer is likely to transact online? Make a consumer profile of a typical online consumer.
6. Explain the drivers of online buying. What are the factors that prevent people from buying online?
7. What are the factors to be considered while analysing the online customer service experience? Explain with examples.
8. What are the merchant attributes that influence online purchases?
9. Why is the integration taking place between online and offline stores? What aspects of consumer behaviour are forcing this change?
10. Explain the elements that affect the web experience. How do they enhance CX?

CRITICAL THINKING QUESTIONS

1. Websites can, because of their nature, deliver limited CX. Most show the products and buy buttons. In such a scenario, how can they differentiate the buying experience? What are the elements that go into building positive customer online experience?
2. Given the fact that people do not like marketing messages when they are interacting with friends on their smartphones, how can companies actually send them marketing messages? Do you agree with the statement that traditional advertising is dead?
3. Critically examine the statement, 'Brand communication is no longer controlled by companies but by customers.' What are your views? If this is so, what can companies really do to influence customers?
4. How is online consumer behaviour different from traditional consumer behaviour? Comment on online segmentation and behaviours that have changed because of online interactions.

PROJECTS AND ASSIGNMENTS

1. Conduct a survey of your classmates about online buying behaviour. Identify those people who have made online purchases. Find out from them what they bought,

why they bought it, the factors that went into their decision and post-purchase behaviour. What do you learn from the survey?

2. Study the websites of some online merchants. How are the sites similar, and how are they different? Prepare a report showing their differences in the choice of products, target markets, customer service and other factors.

3. Study some online campaigns. Assess whether they are merely giving information or are engaging their customers in some way. List down the approaches of the advertisements that you think were successful in involving their customers.

4. Visit some physical retail stores. How many of them have facilities to engage their customers online? Do offline and online initiatives dovetail to influence consumer behaviour?

■ REFERENCES

Aiken, M. 2016. *The Cyber Effect: A Pioneering Cyberpsychologist Explains How Human Behaviour Changes Online*. London: John Murray.

Aljukhadar, M., and S. Senecal. 2011. 'Segmenting the Online Consumer Market.' *Marketing Intelligence & Planning* 29 (June): 421–435.

Carlzon, J. 1987. *Moments of Truth*. Cambridge MA: Ballinger.

Constantinides, E. 2004. 'Influencing the Online Consumer's Behavior: The Web Experience.' *Internet Research* 14, no. 2 (April): 111–126.

Correia, T. 2017. *The Fluid Consumer: Next Generation Growth and Branding in the Digital Age*. London: Kogan Page.

Court, D., D. Elzinga, S. Mulder, and O. J. Vetvik. 2009. 'The Consumer Decision Journey.' *McKinsey Quarterly* (June). Available at: https://www.mckinsey.com/business-functions/marketing-and-sales/our-insights/the-consumer-decision-journey (accessed on 27 January 2021).

Edelman, D. C. 2010. 'Branding in the Digital Age.' *Harvard Business Review* (December). Available at: https://hbr.org/2010/12/branding-in-the-digital-age-youre-spending-your-money-in-all-the-wrong-places (accessed on 27 January 2021).

Edelman, D., and Singer, M. 2015. 'Competing on Customer Journeys.' *Harvard Business Review* (November). Available at: https://hbr.org/2015/11/competing-on-customer-journeys (accessed on 27 January 2021).

Gehrt, K. C., M. N. Rajan, G. Shainesh, D. Czerwinski, and M. O'Brien. 2012. 'Emergence of Online Shopping in India: Shopping Orientation Segments.' *International Journal of Retail & Distribution Management* 40, no. 10 (August): 742–758.

Google. 2012. *ZMOT Handbook: Ways to Win Shoppers at the Zero Moment of Truth*. Available at: https://www.thinkwithgoogle.com/marketing-strategies/video/2012-zmot-handbook/ (accessed on 27 January 2021).

Gulati, R., and J. Garino. 2000. 'Get the Right Mix of Bricks & Clicks.' *Harvard Business Review* (May). Available at: https://hbr.org/2000/05/get-the-right-mix-of-bricks-and-clicks (accessed on 28 January 2021).

Hahn, K. H., and J. Kim. 2009. 'The Effect of Offline Brand Trust and Perceived Internet Confidence on Online Shopping Intention in the Integrated Multi-channel Context.' *International Journal of Retail & Distribution Management* 37, no. 2 (February): 126–141.

Joines, J. L., C. W. Scherer, and D. A. Scheufele. 2003. 'Exploring Motivations for Consumer Web Use and Their Implications for E-commerce.' *Journal of Consumer Marketing* 20, no. 2: 90–108.

Kimmel, A. J. 2010. *Connecting with Consumers: Marketing for New Marketplace Realities*. Oxford: Oxford University Press.

Klaus, P. 2013. 'The Case of Amazon.com: Towards a Conceptual Framework of Online Customer Service Experience (OCSE) Using the Emerging Consensus Technique (ECT).' *Journal of Services Marketing* 27, no. 6: 443–457.

Korgaonkar, P. K., and L. D. Wolin. 1999. 'A Multivariate Analysis of Web Usage.' *Journal of Advertising Research* 39, no. 2: 53–68.

Kotler, P. 2002. *Marketing Management* (13th edition). Upper Saddle River, NJ: Prentice Hall, p. 325.

Koufaris, M. 2002. 'Applying the Technology Acceptance Model and Flow Theory to Online Consumer Behavior.' *Information Systems Research* 13, no. 2 (June): 205–223.

Kumar, D. 2015a. *Consumer Behaviour*. New Delhi: Oxford University Press.

Kumar, D. 2015b. *The Connected Consumer*. New York, NY: Business Expert Press.

Labrecque, L. I., J. vor dem Esche, C. Mathwick, T. P. Novak, and C. F. Hofacker. 2013. 'Consumer Power: Evolution in the Digital Age.' *Journal of Interactive Marketing* 27, no. 4 (November): 257–269.

Lee, B. 2012. 'Marketing Is Dead.' HBR Blog Network, August. Available at: http://blogs.hbr.org/2012/08/marketing-is-dead/ (accessed on 27 January 2021).

Levin, D. E., and J. Kilbourne. 2009. *So Sexy So Soon: The New Sexualized Childhood and What Parents Can Do to Protect Their Kids*. New York, NY: Random House Publishing Group.

Lipsman, A., G. Mudd, M. Rich, and S. Bruich. 2012. 'The Power of "Like": How Brands Reach (and Influence) Fans through Social-media Marketing.' *Journal of Advertising Research* 52 (March): 40–52.

Lookout. 2012. Lookout Mobile Mindset Study. Available at: https://www.tecnostress.it/wp-content/uploads/2012/12/lookout-mobile-mindset-2012.pdf (accessed on 27 January 2021).

Millward Brown. 2016. *Making the Most of Facebook Video Content*. Available at: campaignbrief.com/millward-brown-research-shows/ (accessed on 20 April 2021).

Moran, G., L. Muzellec, and E. Nolan. 2014. 'Consumer Moments of Truth in the Digital Context: How "Search" and "E-Word of Mouth" Can Fuel Consumer Decision-making.' *Journal of Advertising Research* 54, no. 2: 200–204.

Morgan-Thomas, A., and C. Veloutsou. 2013. 'Beyond Technology Acceptance: Brand Relationships and Online Brand Experience.' *Journal of Business Research* 66, no. 1 (January): 21–27.

Mukherjee, W., and S. Jacob. 2012. 'Companies Like Panasonic, Sony, Bajaj, Disney Custom-making TVs, Fans, Lights, Cologne for Children.' *The Economic Times*, 27 April. Available at: https://economictimes.indiatimes.com/industry/cons-products/electronics/companies-like-panasonic-sony-bajaj-disney-custom-making-tvs-fans-lights-cologne-for-children/articleshow/12888393.cms?from=mdr (accessed on 27 January 2021).

Penn, M. 2009. 'New Info Shoppers.' *The Wall Street Journal* (8 January). Available at: https://www.wsj.com/news/articles/SB123144483005365353?mod=googlewsj (accessed on 27 January 2021).

PwC-ASSOCHAM. 2014. 'Evolution of e-commerce in India.' Available at: http://www.pwc.in/assets/pdfs/publications/2014/evolution-of-e-commerce-in-india.pdf (accessed on 28 January 2021).

Sorce, P., V. Perotti, and S. Widrick. 2005. 'Attitude and Age Differences in Online Buying.' *International Journal of Retail & Distribution Management* 33, no. 2 (February): 122–132.

Strauss, J., and R. Frost. 2012. *E-Marketing*, 153–155. 6th edition. New Delhi: PHI Learning.

Vollmer, C. 2008. *Always On: Advertising, Marketing, and Media in an Era of Consumer Control*. New Delhi: Tata-McGraw Hill.

Wigder, Z. D., and M. Bahl. 2011. 'Trends in India's eCommerce Market: How Online Retail in India Is Evolving Differently from Other Major Markets.' Forrester Research, Cambridge, USA. Available at: https://www.forrester.com/report/Trends+In+Indias+eCommerce+Market/-/E-RES78361 (accessed on 20 April 2021).

Yan, Z. 2012. *Encyclopedia of Cyber Behaviour*. Hershey, PA: IGI Global.

Zhu, F., and X. Zhang. 2010. 'Impact of Online Consumer Reviews on Sales: The Moderating Role of Product and Consumer Characteristics.' *Journal of Marketing* 74, no. 2 (March): 133–148.

CLOSING CASE

HEINEKEN'S 'OPEN YOUR WORLD' CAMPAIGN

A major challenge in online marketing is to engage people. Innovative methods are required. Some companies have succeeded in achieving this better than others. This case study describes the case of Heineken, which involved people in a powerful campaign.

To get people talking, Heineken used a commercial to answer the question, 'Can the social problems of the world be resolved over a drink?' It suggests that a good drink might help bridge divides between people with opposite views on some of the most controversial issues. For example, two participants—a feminist and one who calls today's feminism 'man hating'—were paired together. The six participants—a right-winger paired with a left-winger, a climate change denier with an environmentalist and a transgender woman with a man who opposes transgender rights—all start by working together to build chairs, a table and a bar.

The ad asks, 'Can two strangers with opposing views prove that there's more that unites than divides us?' It then leads to the tagline that there is 'more that unites us than divides us' (Figure 4.11).

In the ad, titled 'Worlds Apart', Heineken stages a social experiment by pairing three sets of strangers who have conflicting views on feminism, climate change and transgender rights.

FIGURE 4.11　*Heineken Encourages People to Open Up and Accept Differences*

Source: http://www.theheinekencompany.com (accessed on 28 January 2021).

(Continued)

(Continued)

They do not know about those differences when they are given a task of converting a warehouse and assemble a bar and a set of stools. In this 'social experiment', each pair is given some furniture to assemble and a questionnaire to complete together. Then, seated at the bar they have just built, they watch a short film in which their partner's opposing point of view—that climate change is 'total piffle'; that women 'need to remember we need you to have our children'—is revealed for the first time.

The participants are then given a choice: 'You may go, or you can stay and discuss your differences over a beer.' All six choose to hash it out respectfully; one pair is even shown to swap numbers. The underlying theme is that there is no gap that cannot be bridged over a Heineken.

The film, which is about four and a half minutes long, is 'a real-life social experiment that features real people', says the company. The objective was to know if people could get along together even if they had entirely opposite views and whether they could bond if they were unaware of those self-imposed labels. The campaign only ran online.

The people in the Worlds Apart film are natural, and Heineken merely plays the friendly facilitator of difficult conversations. It is a film that viewers found relatable. It helped Heineken to associate with a cause. It helps the brand to establish a deeper meaning and connect with consumers.

Heineken went a step further. It included a Facebook chatbot connecting people from diverse backgrounds, in partnership with The Human Library, 'a positive framework for conversations that can challenge stereotypes and prejudices through dialogue', says its website.

The film shows that people accept each other's differences. They learn that life is not black and white and accommodate different points of view.

The ad shows that companies can and should use online media creatively and effectively. Online campaigns can host long films and get over the time limitation that TV places. But the campaign has to be powerful enough to involve audiences. Positive WOM publicity can be gained by such campaigns with a positive image of the brand.

Not all efforts to cause marketing succeed. In Australia, for instance, Coopers Brewery invited beer drinkers of opposing views to 'disagree most agreeably', with a video of politicians debating the issue of same-sex marriage. The 'Keeping It Light' campaign gained wide condemnation as the company was seen as pushing religious messages. The ad was well-intentioned but was widely criticized on social media.

Questions for Discussion

1. What consumer behaviour elements were used by Heineken in creating this campaign?
2. Considering that there are many ads which people watch and forget, what did the Heineken ad do correctly?
3. What do you learn about involving people from the campaign?
4. Why is it necessary to involve people in online campaigns?

Sources

Hunt, E. 2017. 'That Heineken Ad: Brewer Tackles How to Talk to Your Political Opposite.' *The Guardian*, 28 April. Available at: https://www.theguardian.com/media/2017/apr/28/that-heineken-ad-does-it-land-with-the-audiences-other-beers-cannot-reach (accessed on 28 January 2021).

Kim, E. K. 2017. 'Powerful Heineken Ad Proves People "Worlds Apart" Can Still Come Together.' *Today*, 27 April. Available at: https://www.today.com/news/heineken-beer-ad-shows-people-bridging-political-divides-t110872 (accessed on 28 January 2021).

Ruiz-Grossman, S. 2017. 'New Heineken Ad Shows Power of Connecting across Political Divides.' *Huffington Post*, 27 April. Available at: http://www.huffingtonpost.in/entry/heineken-ad-worlds-apart-bridge-divides_us_5900eac2e4b0026db1dda41e (accessed on 28 January 2021).

CHAPTER 5

Digital Marketing Environment

Digital technologies have resulted in profound changes in the business environment. This chapter discusses how businesses are impacted due to this.

After reading this chapter, you will be able to learn about the following:

☐ Changes in business environment due to changes in technology, people and media
☐ Dotcom evolution over the years and the dotcom bubble
☐ How marketing mix, market research and business models have undergone major changes
☐ Concepts of digital Darwinism and digital divide
☐ Digital property and its protection

 OPENING CASE

NIKE'S DIGITAL INITIATIVES

Nike is among the world's largest manufacturer of athletic footwear and apparel. It is among the best-known brands in the world, with an iconic logo and one of the most memorable taglines in history, 'Just Do It'. Both the Nike Swoosh logo and tagline endear it to its customers and convey a sporty image, achieving differentiation in a crowded market. This case study explains how Nike has maintained its position in a digital environment, in which both customers and the methods of marketing and advertising have changed. How did Nike adapt to the changing environment?

Nike realized early that brands could no longer sustain on the basis of great media campaigns. As consumers shifted to digital, the company knew the future lay in consumer engagement through online channels. Indeed, Nike has increased the share of digital in its advertising budget. It has placed brilliant ads online, which connect with the audience emotionally and are built around the theme of individual aspiration. People love to share and talk about these ads, which rarely feature products and the messaging is simple, but they

FIGURE 5.1 *Nike's Phenomenal Shot Can Be Viewed in Different Ways*

Source: https://www.thinkwithgoogle.com/marketing-strategies/app-and-mobile/nike-phenomenal-shot/ (accessed on 15 April 2021).

appeal to viewers on a psychological level. More importantly, it did not simply use the Internet as an information disseminating medium or a platform for its emotional ads, but the company transformed its approach to advertising, imbibing technology in the process. The case study shows that companies do not have to *adapt* to the changed environment but *transform* themselves and seek technological collaboration so as to thrive in a dramatically changed business environment.

An example of this is Nike's partnership with Google in the 2014 FIFA World Cup to involve users to create a 'Nike Phenomenal Shot'. Using a real-time delivery tool in the Google Display Network, users got a 3D display ad on their screens within seconds of a Nike athlete scoring a goal (Figure 5.1). The users could rotate the players in 3D imaging, personalizing the images with special filters, captions and stickers. These images could then be shared on social media. The campaign was a huge success, and it showed how digital technologies could be used to engage fans resulting in building relationships with them.

At the same time, Nike has also invested in online assets. It has created an exclusive online community called Joga. Its website, jogaworld.com explains what it is about: 'Joga is a movement system made up of the benefits of yoga combined with the biomechanics of sport.… It is the only type of "yoga" an athlete should be doing and a dominating force in the fitness industry.' The virtual community allows the users to share photos and videos, and create personal websites. Joga is the result of its soccer campaign Joga Bonito (play beautiful) and reflects the passion of its members. The content is provided by Nike, and the technical aspects are managed by Google. Joga shows the love and passion for soccer and is not just an

(Continued)

(Continued)

online advertisement platform. It is an example of connecting with consumers, a philosophy that has helped Nike in using the digital space effectively.

Another initiative was Nike+, allowing users to monitor their bodies through a sensor as they exercised. It was created in partnership with Apple and has now morphed into a membership programme by which users can get exclusive products, guidance and advice and can 'access 100 on-the-go workouts' according to its website. Nike+ had a mass appeal since it was relevant to the target market and allowed interactivity and community.

In its approach, Nike shows an understanding of online capabilities. It does not use online merely like traditional media, but to connect directly with consumers, learn about them, engage them and, in the process, create fans and brand advocates. It is an effective way to move from ad-based marketing to creating consumer experiences.

In his book, *Always On*, Vollmer (2008) writes, 'Nike's message is not just the advertising tacked on to consumer content. The advertising is the content.' The strategy helped Nike stay in step with its customers who wanted online experiences and deeper connections. Nike's example shows that digital must be integrated into the brand's strategy and be a building block of experiences and not an appendage to its existing advertising campaign. Since digital technologies allow direct connect with customers, Nike uses the platform optimally by engaging with its customers.

Nike has shown a strategic shift in response to the changed business environment. As Vollmer explains, 'We are now at the beginning of a consumer-centric digital age in which the traditional approaches to marketing products and services are no longer viable.'

The new business environment is the one in which consumers control the interaction with the brand and can do so through a number of devices at a time of their choosing. Each intervention can be measured in terms of marketing ROI, which creates opportunities for effective marketing and advertising. Online technologies enable better targeting, segmentation and measurability. This means that marketing needs new ways of operating; the traditional method of playing with the 4Ps no longer works.

Nike has been successful in shifting to online technologies and developed its own ways to reach and engage customers. It is a complete paradigm shift. It does not rely on incremental ways in which online technologies aid traditional business. Earlier, companies were content in knowing how many people saw and recalled an advertisement; now, they can measure the ways that people are engaging with their brands. As Vollmer explains, 'Marketing is being reborn as a consumer-centred craft.'

Nike shows that companies must adapt to the changed marketing environment effectively. Some of the things that the company did was:

- Create meaningful stories: Nike sells more than a product; it sells aspiration.
- Earn WOM by creating compelling 'watercooler moments'.
- Make some really fun ads that people love sharing and talking about.
- Become socially conscious and highlight social causes.
- Invest in constant innovation and use technologies creatively.
- Use social media for conversations and engagement.
- Partner with technology companies to create platforms.

While reading this chapter, try to answer the following questions:

1. How has the marketing environment changed and how can companies adapt to it?
2. How have changes in consumers, technology and media impacted marketing?
3. What is the online marketing mix and business models that have become more relevant today?
4. How do consumers want to interact with brands, and what can brands do to encourage this engagement?

Sources

https://www.jogaworld.com/ (accessed on 28 January 2021).
https://www.nike.com/in/membership (accessed on 28 January 2021).
https://www.thinkwithgoogle.com/marketing-resources/experience-design/nike-phenomenal-shot/ (accessed on 28 January 2021).
Vollmer, C. 2008. *Always On*. New York, NY: McGraw Hill.

◼ INTRODUCTION

One of the greatest questions that managers face in the area of marketing is: How to adjust to the rapidly changing business environment? There was a time when the environment was more or less stable, and consumers were more or less predictable. People worked in offices and returned in the evening to relax in front of the TV or read a newspaper or magazine, and marketing messages were sent to them through mass media. It was pretty effective: a company like P&G pioneered daytime serial dramas on radio and TV and since they were sponsored by P&G's soap brands, such dramas are known as 'soap operas' even today. P&G built some of the most powerful brands placing its advertising during the highly popular long-running dramas.

Marketing companies knew which channels people were watching and could base their advertising decisions based on what they knew about the media and their consumers. Today, however, both are fragmented. For many young consumers, the media means mobile phones. Instant messaging and social media have drastically changed media consumption, leaving companies in confusion as to how and where to advertise. Many companies fell into the trap of going online with information or content, gathering many 'likes' in the process but a little contribution to brand building or top-line growth.

They also had to contend with shifting sands as technology and consumers changed rapidly. Popular sites such as Yahoo and Myspace fizzled out while new apps and platforms grew out of nowhere to capture consumers' imagination. Consumers became immersed in their online world and shunned interruptions in the form of advertisements. Hyperconnected, they came to be known as 'always-on' people. In the changed environment, consumers could engage with companies if and when they felt like and were quick to voice their experiences online. As technology gained the capability to track every move made by consumers, privacy concerns began to take hold. Companies had to manage all of these and still find ways of reaching out to their potential and existing customers.

This chapter describes the environment in which present-day marketing must operate. Vast changes have occurred in the business environment, including changes in technology, consumer behaviour, business economics and media. Understanding the changes taking place in the environment helps figure out how best to operate under these rapidly changing and interesting times.

◾ DOTCOM EVOLUTION

The business environment has been changing over the years, ever since the Internet was developed and launched. Although it was invented to send data packets of information between computers, it was only a matter of time that it would be used for commercial purposes. Soon, companies started marking their online presence through dotcom domain names: A dotcom is a company whose business model is based on the Internet. It is called a dotcom because commercial domain names end with '.com'. This section describes how the environment has evolved over the years due to the emergence of digital technologies.

Electronic data transactions started in the 1960s. Information was exchanged through computer networks and the earliest application was email. Electronic data interchange enabled sharing of documents between computers. The ARPANET was developed by the US military with the objective of sharing information should there be a nuclear attack. The ARPANET started using Transmission Control Protocol and Internet Protocol in 1982, and this has remained the technology that is used even today.

By the 1980s, computers were seen in universities across the world and were used for email and processing data. In 1979, the US company CompuServe became the first one to offer email capabilities and was offering wide-area networking capabilities by 1982. It later developed message boards and chat rooms for PC users. The Electronic Mall was introduced in 1984, which was not very successful, but it was the precursor of online retail as we know it. Commercial Internet use was allowed in 1991 by the National Science Foundation, which led to the development of e-commerce and other commercial capabilities. The first online retail transaction is thought to have happened in 1994.

The earliest browser was Netscape. It has a protocol called Secure Socket Layer which kept online transactions secure and allowed the capability of encryption of personal information online. Credit card processing capabilities came shortly thereafter and paved the way for secure retail transactions on the web. This was an important milestone which opened up opportunities for e-commerce. Amazon was founded in 1994 and eBay in 1995.

Both of these companies pioneered and revolutionized e-commerce. Amazon sold the first book in July 1995 and started creating the first full-scale online retail business model. It started selling books across 45 countries, and people liked the collection, ease of ordering and quick deliveries. Amazon kept adding features to its site, and users could search the site and go through reviews. The company went public in 1997, and it kept increasing the products on its site. Today, Amazon is a one-stop destination for practically anything that a person might need and even provides streaming video content.

eBay took a different route and started a site that allowed people to list their products and buyers could bid for them. AuctionWeb, as it was known, became very popular, and eBay had 220 million users by 2007. By 1997, Dell had faced success in selling computers that people could customize on its site, and it became the first company to achieve sales of $1 million online in a single day. The dotcom revolution had begun.

The success of these companies laid the foundation of e-commerce. People followed in droves to start dotcoms, but they were met with varying degrees of success; many companies folded up but a few survived; understanding the new technology and making e-commerce profitable was not everyone's cup of tea. Although entrepreneurs loved the idea of starting a business by simply launching a website, getting paying customers to the site remained a daunting task.

The introduction of broadband services gave more people access to the Internet. This gave a boost to computer usage and dotcom growth. Companies did not want to miss out on this new way of doing business, in which they could be in touch with customers directly. E-commerce entrepreneurs, spurred by the success of a few companies, too wanted to be a part of this revolution.

The Internet also opened the way for collaborations. Amazon was the first to use affiliate marketing, meaning allowing other sites to refer Amazon products and earn commissions on sales. Today, affiliate marketing is a big contributor to business; for Amazon, it contributes about 40 per cent of the total sales revenue.

For consumers, the Internet made the task of getting information easily available. People could search for products and compare competing offers. This shifted the power into consumers' hands. Businesses that leveraged on information such as travel agents and brokers soon found themselves out of business. There was much euphoria about the new model of business, and entrepreneurs rushed in, creating a bubble.

◼ DOTCOM BUBBLE

Our discussion of dotcom evolution would be incomplete without a description of the dotcom bubble. A number of companies and entrepreneurs had entered the online space, hoping to get a share of the pie. The success of early movers such as Amazon and eBay generated euphoria about the online business. People came up with ideas and found easy funding from investors, who assumed that profits could flow in easily. This, however, was unrealistic; many entrepreneurs and investors did not understand the Internet at all. Speculation was built up from 1997 to 2001 and was encouraged by reports of huge money made by both entrepreneurs and engineers online. The bubble burst in 2002. A large number of these new companies without sustainable business models folded up. Stocks of Internet companies collapsed and left investors with a hole of some $5 trillion.

The bursting of the dotcom bubble showed that the expectations that had built up were imaginary, to begin with. Many of these dotcoms had no business model or any stable revenue streams. Further, as shown by Hoffman and Novak (2000), the costs of promoting a business online were far greater than had been imagined. It was thought that starting an online business would automatically attract users and make money for investors. The reality hit in 2001 and broke many dreams as thousands of dotcom companies failed.

During this time, online activities moved from personal computers to laptops to tablets. With the advent of mobile phones and their widespread usage, the business had to evolve into the world of mobiles and social media. This was the emergence of a new business landscape, powered by mobile.

■ MOBILE

By the 2010s, dotcoms had moved to a new platform: mobile. As smartphone users multiplied, e-commerce started catering to 'anytime, anywhere commerce'. This was a boon to the 'always-on' population since people could conduct transactions even when they were on the move. Smartphones were the new frontier for dotcoms, and companies had to evolve. In 2015, Google released a search algorithm update that encouraged mobile-friendly pages, boosting the ranking of such pages so that users could browse on their mobiles and get the readable text without tapping or zooming or horizontal scrolling. This update was referred to as 'Mobilegeddon'.

Mobile changed consumer behaviour, as Chapter 4 shows. It is now estimated that the majority of shoppers use mobile phones to conduct their transactions. Google has become the first point of contact as users search for products on it, called 'ZMOT'. It has become the initial starting point of the CDJ when consumers search Google before buying and look for reviews, user recommendations or offers and deals.

■ SOCIAL MEDIA

Another development took place that revolutionized the way business was conducted. This was the popularity of social media. People took to social media platforms, spending more time on them, and companies wanted a share of that too. We have covered social media in Chapter 6. Along with Google, consumers are today more likely to interact with brands on social media before their purchase decision. They seek friends' advice and recommendations by sharing pictures and content. Social media has become another important factor in e-commerce.

An important lesson from the study of dotcom evolution is that entrepreneurs need to have a practical business model in place before they take the online plunge. It is easy to get influenced by the number of users of the Internet and hope that any business would do well, but this is not true. Further, some businesses get overwhelmed by popularity measures such as the number of likes they get on social media or the number of downloads of their apps. However, likes do not translate into revenues, nor does the number of downloads ensure usage. People often give unthinking likes on online content, without any intention to buy. A humorous video, for instance, will be shared widely, but it may or may not translate into sales. Apps can be uninstalled as easily as they are downloaded. Hence, online businesses without business models struggled to generate revenues. On the other hand, companies that used IT for competitive advantage stood to reap tremendous benefits from the online revolution.

INFORMATION FOR COMPETITIVE ADVANTAGE

It is increasingly being understood that companies can use data profitably. Consumers leave online traces of data in almost every activity they do, thanks to the connected world. Smartphones and IoT ensure that companies have a lot of information about people and the products they use. Online activity, connected watches, household appliances and cars add to the data generated every second. By analysing this data, companies can meet consumer needs better, sell more and make more profits.

The Economist (2017) calls data as the new oil. 'Internet companies' control of data gives them enormous power. Old ways of thinking about competition, devised in the era of oil, look outdated in what has come to be called the "data economy" have made data abundant, ubiquitous and far more valuable,' it writes.

Data analytics and AI help companies to gain insights and extract value from data. Today, data can predict the precise moment when a customer is ready to make a purchase decision or when a car or jet engine needs servicing. This can add to a competitive advantage. How companies use data will determine their sustainable competitive advantage. The idea is to have better data analytics methods than those of competitors. To do this, we have to understand how the marketing environment has changed and what are the drivers forcing this change.

DRIVERS OF NEW MARKETING ENVIRONMENT

Marketing environment has changed dramatically in recent years. Many of the established principles of business have changed. Companies have to understand what drives the new marketing environment. The marketing environment is discussed with respect to changes taking place in three broad areas: technology, people and media. Another aspect, macro changes in the online environment, will be discussed in the next section, which are affecting business globally. These are summed up in Table 5.1 and explained below.

Online marketing operates in an environment that is impacted profoundly by changes in these four factors (Figure 5.2).

TABLE 5.1 *Drivers of New Marketing Environment*

Technology	People	Media	Macro Trends
New communication channels	Always on	Apps and platforms	Digital Darwinism
Consumer control	Multitasked	Media consumption patterns	Digital divide
New business models	Mobile addicts	Top down to co-creation	Digital property
Omnichannel approach	–	Communication mix	–
E-payment systems	–	–	–
Technological advances in retail	–	–	–

FIGURE 5.2 *Online Marketing Environment and the Factors Affecting It*

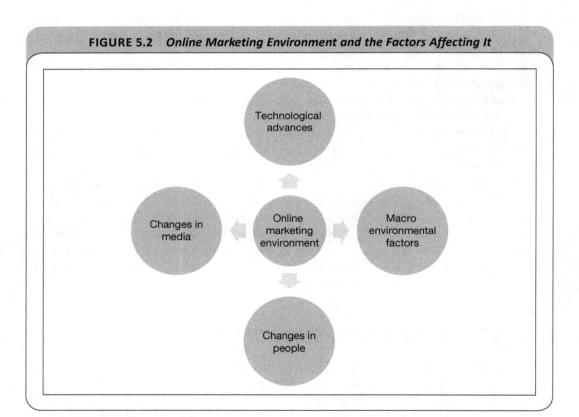

■ TECHNOLOGICAL ADVANCES

Today, digital technology is providing new ways of doing business, and companies must adjust to this changing environment. The change in technological environment over the years is summarized in Table 5.2.

TABLE 5.2 *Evolution of the Technological Environment*

Web 1.0	Web 2.0	Web 3.0
Up to 2001	2004	2006
Static web	Interactive web	Intelligent or semantic web
Creation of first websites, the first web browsers, protocols, standard markup languages	Changes ways of utilization of the Web, second generation of web-based services: online collaboration, sharing, social networking	Portable, personal web, focused on the individual, apps, widgets, activity streams, 3D applications
Read-only web, posting printed media online, creation of home pages	Read–write web, interactive platforms, blogs	Read–write–execute web, collaboration and co-creation
Owning content, portals and directories	Sharing content, RSS feeds	Personalized web
Shopping carts, commercialization of the Web and Web business models, huge investments in dotcoms, dotcom bubble, lasted till 2001	Media sharing, communities, wikis, online conversations, WOM, interaction with companies and brands	Data mining and analytics, AI-based technologies, natural language processing, machine learning, rules-based inferences, personal agents

The table shows developments up to Web 3.0. But the change goes on. Web 4.0 promises to further disrupt business. Foundations have already been laid to use data more extensively. Face recognition technologies will track customers in the physical world, and IoT promises to track their homes, their appliances, body parameters and their environment. Robotics will become popular, and people will start using robots for a variety of applications. Technologies like self-driving cars will fructify. The advent of intelligent machines means that in the future, people will interact more and more with new interfaces.

Technology is advancing in previously unimaginable ways. If the connected world had opened up new markets, AI promises to do much more. New apps and platforms continue to be invented. Technological advances have already eliminated entry barriers for many businesses and achieved lower operating and distribution costs. New ways of doing business have led to the sprouting of new businesses that disrupt the business models of established companies. These digital disruptions are happening so fast that it is sometimes difficult to keep track. For instance, it would have seemed unimaginable that small, ride sharing apps would emerge as competitors to car manufacturers, as many people make do without owning cars today. Similarly, start-ups offer value to today's 'always-on' customers in many different and new ways, threatening traditional companies.

This section discusses drivers of the business environment due to huge technological changes. Today, companies must grapple with changes in the digital environment, including the following:

- **New communication channels:** Technology has transformed communication channels. These channels have the capability to provide personalized messages and are today interactive and two-way. This means that companies can listen to and keep track of online conversations. They must respond to queries and issues quickly because pending matters are quickly highlighted by consumers and may damage companies by becoming viral.

- **Consumer control:** Earlier, companies had full control over their brands and marketing communications. Customers had little say or control over a company's marketing programmes. They received marketing communications passively, which changed their opinions about products and resulted in sales. Today, top-down control does not work, and customers are the new power centres, creating communications and spreading messages on their own. Companies try to influence the online chatter, but they have no means to get into the lives of their customers unless they get specific consent. Companies have to get used to this new power structure.

- **New business models:** The digital revolution has resulted in new business models that can be understood on three drivers: (a) the value proposition consists of offering products and services on demand, (b) customers can be targeted as very small segments or micro-segments and even on the individual level thanks to technology and data from multiple sources and (c) networked customer relationships since companies can deliver relevant and individualized offers.

- **Omnichannel approach:** Omnichannel is a business approach that integrates all channels with the objective of providing a seamless shopping experience on all channels, including physical stores, websites, apps, mass media and virtual media. This implies that all customer information is integrated and available across channels.

- **Advancements in e-payment technologies:** A major technological change that has helped online business has been the development of e-payments. Digital payment systems consist of cards, e-wallets, online banking, UPI payments which have grown over the years. Some countries are becoming cashless economies. Secure digital payments encourage e-commerce and have been a major driver for change.

Online payments began in the 1990s. The earliest e-payment system was PayPal, which facilitated secure payments online. People could make and accept payments by creating an account on its site. It became popular as eBay started using it. PayPal was an easy, quick and secure e-payments system. It kept innovating, adding new currencies, mobile payment apps, payment buttons, and systems to reduce fraud. eBay acquired PayPal in 2002. Later, it was made a separate company.

Digital payments grew quickly, and a large number of companies entered the field. Credit and debit cards are also used, and banks have invested in sophisticated and secure systems. However, there is a danger that the financial information provided by a bank account or credit card when used online can lead to its misuse. Many sites store payment details of customers to make it easy for them to make transactions. If these are hacked, data of millions of people is exposed. Such cases have happened with alarming frequency.

Online payment systems have also grown in India. Many companies like Paytm, PhonePe, Freecharge and so on provide e-wallet and payment services. Banks have started their own payment apps such as HDFC banks' PayZapp. Google and Ola, too, offer quick online transactions.

Payment systems have evolved in several ways to aid e-commerce.

o **COD:** For customers who did not use e-payment systems, the e-commerce industry started a COD service in which a customer buys online but pays in cash when the good is delivered.

o **E-wallets:** E-wallets allow people to store cash electronically. These apps can store cash virtually, and payments can be sent to other devices. Transactions can be done through mobile phones, and hence, they can replace physical wallets. Such systems are secure and are now being used widely. Such systems are used for micropayments—small payments for which credit cards are not feasible or economical. They are a boon for people who lack banking access as such people can operate e-wallets by using their thumbprints to make transactions.

o **Virtual cards:** Banks issue credit cards virtually that are stored on phones. Such cards can be used for transactions by authorizing payment by using their mobile screens.

o **Virtual banking:** A virtual bank is an entity that offers traditional banking services online and may not have a physical branch. While traditional banks offer virtual banking services, many companies do not have physical branches at all and run through apps. Virtual banking is a boon for small businesses and people in remote areas who do not have access to banking services. Such banks are simple to operate and offer the security required. Electronic micropayments or small payments, required for small daily tasks, have been a boon to millions of poor people as they can keep their money securely in their e-wallets (see Marketing Insight 5.1). Services such as Paytm and M-Pesa have been very important for digital inclusion.

o **Cryptocurrency:** Another development in the payments system is the development of cryptocurrency or a digital decentralized currency that is not controlled by banks. Using blockchain and cryptography, automated and untraceable digital payments can be made. A blockchain is secure as data cannot be modified on it. Bitcoin became the first digital currency and is operated without the interference of any government or a central bank. The Bitcoin has been in circulation since 2009, and many companies are planning to launch their own cryptocurrencies. Facebook, for instance, has launched its digital currency called Libra. Cryptocurrency is thought to be the future in digital payments. How it shapes up and whether it gains mass circulation remains to be seen.

• **Retail technological advances:** Technological developments are fast changing the shape of retail. Digital signage, robotics, buy-online-pick-up stores, drone deliveries, interactive mirror displays and augmented reality are part of the rapidly changing technologies that promise to revolutionize businesses. We will discuss these developments in Chapter 10.

MARKETING INSIGHT 5.1 *E-payments and Social Inclusion*

Micropayments are non-cash transactions involving payments of small amounts up to about ₹250. They facilitate small purchases and payments are made by a card or through an app. People can pay for their daily goods purchases through these apps. With Paytm, PhonePe, Google Pay, Amazon Pay and other systems becoming popular, micropayments get over the problem of dealing with currency notes and coins. It is not surprising to see small shops and service providers connected to electronic payments these days.

Micropayments have come as a big boon to people who do not have access to conventional banking. Poor people, rural folk and those living in remote areas constituting at least 70 per cent of the population, now have a way of keeping their money secure and making transactions as and when required. Now, these app-based micropayments companies also provide loans, saving accounts, insurance and remittances facilities. This has led to a major benefit for developing countries: social inclusion of hitherto disadvantaged populations. The linkage to Aadhaar has further helped the targeted transfer of government benefits for such segments (see the Closing Case).

The remote savings bank works with the help of banking correspondents, who carry mobile machines with fingerprint scanners (Figure 5.3). For depositing or withdrawal of money, the fingerprints of both the customer and correspondent are required. The account is updated immediately, and the payment is settled at the customers' doorstep by the correspondent.

However, since margins are low, companies operating in micropayments have to build a huge subscriber base in order to be profitable. This poses severe challenges for the sector. Profits are hard to come by, even for the most popular apps.

Among the problems faced by micropayment service providers are training correspondents and providing them with POS machines. Enrolment of a large number of shops is also important; otherwise, the e-payment accounts would have limited value. Educating people

FIGURE 5.3 *A Payments Bank with Micro ATM*

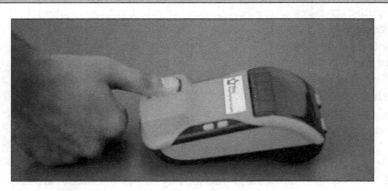

Source: https://www.indiamart.com/proddetail/fino-payments-bank-csp-with-micro-atm-and-fingerprint-device-and-printer-20224918648.html (accessed on 15 April 2021).

in rural areas to adopt the service is another challenge. Further, there is the problem of getting telecom signals. In many rural areas, signals are weak or non-existent.

It is expected that many problems will be overcome in times to come. The e-payments system has become popular in many areas as it gets over the problem of storing money. Regulatory pressures have also eased. For small businessmen and consumers, an e-savings bank is quite helpful in their day to day activities.

What are the advantages of micropayments systems? How can these services become profitable?

Sources

Businessworld. 2014. 'A Small Fortune.' 8 November. Available at: http://www.businessworld.in/article/A-Small-Fortune/08-11-2014-69540/ (accessed on 16 February 2021).

Iyer, R. 2020. 'Here's How to Help India's Rural Population Go Digital.' World Economic Forum, 7 January. Available at: https://www.weforum.org/agenda/2020/01/help-india-rural-population-go-digital/ (accessed on 8 February 2021).

◼ CHANGE IN CONSUMERS

We have discussed changes in human behaviour in Chapter 4. Here, we discuss changes in consumers as part of the business environment and how companies should respond to these changes. 'Never has a communications system played so many roles in our lives—or exerted such broad influence over our thoughts—as the Internet does today,' writes Nicholas Carr (2008). By looking around, we see these changes every day. Globally, people can be seen engrossed in their own little screens, shutting the outside by wearing headphones. Personal interaction now means forwarding messages on social apps, while checking phones has become a compulsive habit. People lack inner cultural inheritance, writes Foreman (2005), because we have all become 'pancake people'—spread wide and thin over a vast network of information. Companies have to adapt accordingly to the pancake people, who are self-engrossed, multitasking, 'always-on' consumers, with very short attention spans.

- **Always on:** Today's generation is digitally connected all the time, using multiple devices, which they check several times a day. How companies get into the lives of these AOCs requires a radical change in approach. Vollmer (2008) dubbed them as 'Always-On Consumers' and are defined by the following characteristics:
  o **Looks for instant gratification:** Information must be available at all times as consumers look for immediate solutions.
  o **Requires simple solutions:** Customers look for intuitive self-service options and transparent cross-channel connectivity; they do not want to deal with different departments.
  o **Concerned about privacy:** Customers today have privacy concerns. They are willing to share a lot of information about themselves with companies but want to be reassured that their privacy will not be compromised.

o **Integration between physical and virtual worlds:** The new generation of consumers want to interact seamlessly between physical and virtual worlds. They want solutions in both worlds.

o **Multiple screens:** Today, people are often engaged with multiple screens at the same time. TV, laptops and mobile devices are always in working mode. This means that marketing strategies must link all media. A TV ad may ask people, for instance, to send an SMS or check out a link online.

o **Interactive communication:** Customers expect interactive communications at all times. Queries must be responded to in real time, content must be interactive, and people want to engage with companies and products.

- **Multitasking:** Multitasking, or doing several things together, has become the buzzword today. Stone (2009) describes how multitasking changes human behaviour. She writes of 'an artificial sense of crisis' that today's generation exhibits because of continuous, immediate and non-stop interaction. People live in a state of high alert, doing multiple complex actions at the same time, motivated by a desire not to miss anything. Multitasking is a reality of modern life, whether it is talking on the phone and driving, writing an email and participating in a conference call or carrying on a conversation at dinner and texting under the table. Companies face huge challenges in communicating to the present day's highly-strung, multitasking generation. Many companies have tried to satisfy the constant sharing/texting urge by offering rewards to people who share their pictures with products or make profile pictures with products and brands, thereby manipulating this multitasking need to generate free advertising.

- **Mobile addicts:** A major change in consumer behaviour is that people are mobile addicts. Attention spans are short as people compulsively check their phones every few minutes. Horrigan (2009) found that 39 per cent of the people have a symbiotic relationship with their phones and wireless access devices.

    The challenge before companies is to get into the lives of this self-absorbed, hyperconnected generation, and nobody is paying attention to them. Brand messages are seen as intrusions. As we have explained in this book, companies have to get into the conversations that people are having with each other and abandon the concept of traditional advertising.

    To do this, we need to know the traits of online behaviour. Joachimsthaler (2014) studied AOCs and classified them into five categories. Their usage shows the ways in which consumers use digital means such as devices, social networks and apps and interact with brands (Table 5.3).

The study shows that half of the online users—deal hunters and mindful explorers—do not feel the need to connect with brands or engage with a company's branded content. They tend to ignore online advertising and branded content. Both marketing and traditional research methods thus become obsolete. Companies have to find innovative ways to get into the lives of online natives.

TABLE 5.3 *AOCs and Their Online Behaviour*

Customer Category	Online Behaviour
Social bumblebees	• Active buyers (three–four times a week) • Spontaneous users of the Internet and e-commerce • Shop from their iPads or mobile phones • Very social online, spend over seven hours a day online • Broadcast their opinions and to share their private data • Consist of 22% of AOC
Mindful explorers	• Intensive information seekers about new products • Keep a low profile online, safeguard their personal data • Use the Internet as a source of information and entertainment • Buy after careful deliberations • Use social networks sparingly • Consist of 27% of AOC
Deal hunters	• Driven by deals and discounts, look for the most value • Active on social media, have the most online friends • Spend time looking for best prices, deals and coupons • Do not overly engage with brands • Consist of 13% of AOC
Focused problem-solvers	• Not very active on social media, prefer email • Spend the least time online • Prefer offline shopping • Exhibit loyalty to brands • Consist of 18% of AOC
Ad blockers	• Have a small but active circle of online friends • Make a few purchases online • Dislike advertising and branded content • Rational shoppers • Consist of 20% of AOC

Source: Adapted from Joachimsthaler (2014).

Concepts of brand building have also changed; it can no longer rely on managing perceptions and attribute shaping. Today, value is created, now, through a new communication mix consisting of interactivity, experience, co-creation and customization. Advertising-led brand building and communications are rendered quite irrelevant. A study of the digital media industry thus becomes vital.

DIGITAL MEDIA INDUSTRY

Today, media includes text, pictures and multimedia and their transmission. New media applications offer instantaneous transmittal, and this has disrupted the way that the world does business.

Digital media is defined as content that is transferred through the Internet or computer networks. It consists of any media which depends on digitization. Such content is transmitted across electronic devices and includes websites, images, video and audio, video games and social media. Digital media can be created, distributed, viewed, and stored on electronic devices. Digital media includes practically everything on the Internet:

- Advertising
- Video and video games
- Over-the-top (OTT) TV
- Web pages, software and web development
- Graphic design
- Apps and app development
- Social media
- Interactive media
- E-learning
- Others

We have classified digital media characteristics in Table 5.4 and explained in this section.

- **Objectives:** The objectives of modern communication have changed. Earlier, media had the role of informing and educating people. Today, the new media engages people in interactive communication. This means that companies have to learn new ways of using media, and merely imparting information is not good enough. The changing media means that big shifts have occurred in two disruptive ways:
  - o **From corporations to consumers:** Companies have to get used to the idea that they are no longer in control of their communications or brands. The control of

TABLE 5.4 *Media and Change Drivers*

Media Characteristics	Change Drivers
Objectives	From communication and information to engaging people
Power and control	1. From corporations to consumers 2. From media houses to big five of information technology
Two-way, instant communication	Apps, communication platforms, telecom companies, social media
Media consumption	From print and television to social, online and OTT platforms
Operations and control	Top-down, mass communication to individual, customer-centric operations

communications is firmly in the hands of the customers. No matter what companies may claim, consumers are free to post anything about any company or brand. The power of these individual communications cannot be underestimated since these posts can become viral in no time and can influence more people than official communications of companies.

o **From media houses to big five of IT:** Earlier, media houses held sway over the population. They were instrumental in forming opinions and were vehicles for advertising. This power has now shifted to 'big five' of the modern economy: Apple, Alphabet, Microsoft, Facebook and Amazon. These companies, constituting more than 40 per cent of the NASDAQ, have gobbled up and are gobbling up the rest of the economy. These companies hold immense power, and other companies have to learn to live with them.

- **Two-way, instant communication:** Companies have a number of tools for two-way, instant communication. Apps allow customers to perform specific tasks and connect with companies. Communication platforms provide a host of services such as blogging, publishing, sharing, reviewing and providing opinions. Telecom companies have become the backbone of the digital revolution, providing data services that run all digital devices. Social media platforms have emerged as the preferred platforms for interactive communication.

- **Media consumption:** Media consumption has changed from print and TV to social, online and OTT platforms. Satellite TV is giving way to streaming video services, offered by Amazon, Netflix and others. Social media and online platforms command the lion's share of media consumption today. They provide personalized content, including videos, relegating print and TV to secondary positions. OTT services go 'over' the set-top box through which cable and TV providers operate. These subscription-based services provide on-demand videos and content. Consumers appreciate the personalized, ad-free content and are not dependent on what TV channels might want to show them. People still watch TV, but now they are able to pick and choose the content that they want to see. Traditional TV watching has declined in the developed world, and many households in India, too, have opted for OTT services. Moreover, much of video content is consumed on mobile screens. TV and the small screen are now connected, with people switching between screens as and when they please. Younger consumers are leading this trend.

- **Operations:** An important change in the media environment is that the top-down approach has changed. Companies could earlier dictate terms to consumers but now find that consumers have all the information and can make informed decisions on their own. They do not like to be talked down to, which has necessarily meant that operations become customer centric. Companies also learn to communicate with each individual with tailor-made campaigns. Many managers involve consumers in creating advertising campaigns (see Marketing Insight 5.2).

MARKETING INSIGHT 5.2   *AXE Canada: Customer-led Marketing Campaigns*

Marketing campaigns in which customers are involved in producing content are called customer-led campaigns. In such campaigns, customers participate in content creation or provide advice and viewpoints or participate by way of competitions. Such campaigns generate interest as customers engage with brands. They participate in the campaign voluntarily, and hence are trusted because they are genuine users. User-generated content creates trust and reliability and may well become viral.

Axe Canada got young men involved in the brand by asking them to record themselves praising their friends. The idea was that demonstrating praise and affection did not make them any less of a man. The #PraiseUp campaign was based on doing something young people seldom do—praise others (Figure 5.4). The campaign was based on an insight gained by Unilever that young men liked to connect with their friends and could participate in activities and say things that they may not have been comfortable in the past. It was an attempt to get over the outdated thinking that young men do not like to praise others.

Traditionally, males are brought up to believe that sharing emotions goes

FIGURE 5.4   *Axe Campaign*

Source: https://twitter.com/axecanada/status/864691953992056833 (accessed on 15 April 2021).

against their manhood. This was challenged by the Axe campaign. It found that a majority of young men are comfortable in complimenting their friends. Toronto athletes Marcus Stroman and Kyle Lowry became the first to participate in this campaign. They participated in a series of online videos encouraging others to praise their friends. The campaign was based on the findings that male support and friendship was common, and that boys usually had supportive male friends.

The participation was phenomenal. People recorded their video, giving praise to their best friends without telling them. The praises that were lavished consisted of honesty, unique skills and appearance. These were posted on Snapchat, Instagram, Facebook and Twitter, using the hashtag #YouGotSomething with the challenge to the friends to post a similar video.

The campaign resulted in positive vibes among friends and also got them to engage with the brand.

However, such campaigns should be used with care because customers may sometimes make content with negative connotations. User-generated content has the possibility of becoming viral—but also for the wrong reasons. If the dangers are avoided, companies can be innovative and use the Internet in a clever manner. Since the Internet gives consumers a voice, why not use this voice for marketing brands?

Are customer-led campaigns effective? What are their advantages and disadvantages?

These changes in the business environment mean that marketing must undergo a radical change. The next section describes the principles and drivers of the new marketing environment and shows how it has undergone massive changes over the years.

PRINCIPLES AND DRIVERS OF DIGITAL MARKETING ENVIRONMENT

Several writers have tried to identify the principles and drivers of the digital marketing environment. Table 5.5 summarizes two approaches.

Both the 4C and 4S do not really capture all the drivers of modern marketing. Kalyanam and McIntyre (2002) have proposed the 4Ps + P2C2S3 model, which is a slight improvement over these models. These include 4Ps and two more Ps, namely *personalization and privacy*, 2Cs consisting of *customer service* and *community* and 3Ss, that is, *site, security* and *sales promotion.*

However, the complexity of the online environment shows that there is much more that marketing has to deal with. Although these models are improvements over traditional approaches, they ignore the myriad tools and technologies that are at the disposal of companies for marketing in the digital era. A paradigm shift is therefore needed to take

TABLE 5.5 *Principles and Drivers for the Digital World*

4C Model (Lauterborn 1990)	4S Model (Constantinides 2002)
Consumers' wants and needs: Companies should be more focused on what consumers want and offer solutions.	**Scope:** Includes (a) strategic and operational objectives for online operations, (b) tracking market potential, (c) readiness for e-commerce and (d) strategic role of e-commerce for the company.
Cost to satisfy: Companies should try to decrease the cost to customers.	**Site:** Interface between company and customer, platform for communication.
Convenience to buy: Online technologies should increase convenience for customers.	**Synergy:** Integration of the website with internal processes and databases and business partners.
Communication: Digital technologies are used to communicate with customers.	**System:** Technology, technical requirements and website administration.

FIGURE 5.5   *Drivers of the New Marketing Environment*

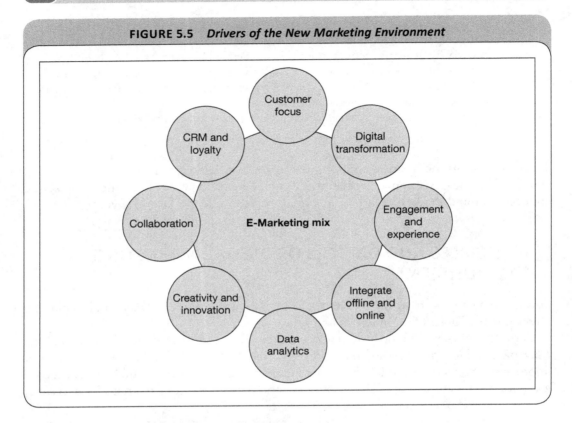

full benefit of online marketing tools because the controllable marketing elements are entirely different from the physical world. A radical new approach is suggested by Lewnes and Keller (2019). They describe 10 principles of modern marketing which gives an idea about the controllable factors that companies have at their disposal. We have developed a comprehensive model based on these principles (Figure 5.5). It represents the controllable factors that marketing must integrate to achieve competitive advantage and also represent the environment in which marketing must operate.

- **Customer focus:** Companies must make customers central to their functioning, listen to them and involve them in co-creating. They develop the ability to see things from the lens of a customer and build long-term relationships. Online technologies are used to create value but more than that to communicate that value and to deliver it. Companies can build competitive advantage by focusing on tools that improve communication and delivery.
- **Digital transformation:** Companies have to use technology to create customer experiences, communicate with stakeholders and use data to track customer behaviour. But more than that, technology creates the base for *a complete business transformation*, including people, processes and technology. Companies must use new technologies in business models, such as AI, chatbots and augmented reality.

These can build competitive advantage in modern times, but not through incremental steps but by involving all departments and stakeholders.

- **Engagement and experience:** Every customer's touch point, whether online or offline, must be integrated to provide a single, comprehensive customer experience. Every single web search, comment or tweet, online and offline exposure to the brand, the company's social purpose and its social media presence can be integrated to deliver immersive customer experience. In today's world, experience marketing provides a means to differentiate offerings from those of competitors.

- **Integrate online and offline worlds:** No company is purely online or offline. An important aspect of the marketing strategy is to integrate online and offline operations. Customers can browse online and buy from a physical store or vice-versa; the idea is that both worlds complement each other.

- **Data analytics:** Today's companies must use data to keep track of the business environment. Econometrics and attribution modelling is used in a wide range of applications to test products, predict trends, develop targeted communications to precise segments and engage with customers.

- **Creativity:** Creativity still rules in marketing. Companies try new ways to create connections with customers, and data shows them which methods are working and which are not. McKinsey & Company's (Gregg et al. 2018) survey of S&P 500 companies showed that companies that had combined data with creativity achieved a rate of revenue growth that was double of companies that had not. Consumers and communities are harnessed through co-creation platforms to contribute to the creative process.

- **Collaboration:** A radical change in approach is the realization that companies cannot do it alone in the new digital environment but create collaborations with others. It is not enough, for example, to sell on a company website or store but use an online aggregator such as Amazon and Flipkart as well. Companies thus form collaborations with companies, technology providers and others and try to achieve synergy. Acquisitions also help in enhancing technical and marketing capabilities.

- **CRM and loyalty:** CRM and e-loyalty have been discussed in Chapter 3.

Digital technology has also forced a change in the way that market research can be conducted. The several methods that use technological changes are discussed in the next section.

MARKETING RESEARCH ON THE NET

Traditional market research consists of making questionnaires and getting responses from customers by conducting surveys. Many companies have moved the same technique on the Internet. It becomes easy to post a few questions and ask people to give their responses. Online surveys are a convenient and low-cost way to get opinions of people. But they are not reliable if the respondents are not focused or motivated. For example, people tend to tick random answers on online surveys if they are not motivated enough, nor may they belong to the target market. It is a lazy person's survey technique and has little value if samples are not chosen carefully. If online surveys are paid for, a number of non-users will fill up online questions hoping to make some money.

Online surveys simply try to replicate physical surveys and are at best armchair surveys. But using traditional market research on the net is also to ignore the enormous capabilities of digital technologies. The huge data availability and analytics capabilities available today can provide so many consumer insights that surveys and questionnaires cannot accomplish. That is why a radical change in market research capabilities is called for.

There are two ways that market research can be conducted on the Internet: (a) researching information available on the web, and (b) using data mining and analysing data left by consumers willingly or unwillingly as they use the Internet.

Researching Information on the Internet

The easiest method to use the Internet is as a secondary data source. A company can get enormous information simply by searching the net, such as:

- Competitor information including financial statements
- Consumer demographic data, social profiles, needs and interests
- Tracking consumer reviews, blogs, shares and so on

The following methods are useful for gathering information easily available on the net:

- **Keyword search:** A simple use of search engines can show how people are finding particular products or services and utilize those words for better search engine visibility. A company can find out its own ranking and the mentions it has received over a period of time. It can discover product niches and usage that may not be easily visible. A keyword search can also help discover how many existing sites use those keywords. Further, it will help find cheaper suppliers for raw materials, and since it shows similar manufacturers all over the world, the company can learn of best practices and adopt those.
- **Competitor search:** Competitor search gives information about the strategies of competing companies, including pricing and advertising activity. Links to a competitor's website can also be identified. Even the financial reports of listed companies are available online.
- **Blog search:** A search of blogs yields information about what people are thinking about particular products and services. Some blog-specific search engines are available: Technorati and Nielsen BuzzMetrics tracks blogs and are helpful in knowing public opinion. Nielsen BlogPulse offers tools and analytics for blogs that companies can use.
- **Social media analysis:** Social media analysis refers to the process of collecting data from social media platforms and evaluating that data for gaining consumer insights. However, social media data comes with a lot of noise, such as spam and trolls.

Companies need to develop capabilities for accurate analysis and gaining consumer-based insights.

Using Data Mining and Analysing Data Left by Consumers

Companies also have access to data exhaust from user activities. Companies use data analytics to mine the consumer information in the following ways:

- **Data mining:** Data mining is the process of analysing varied streams of data and large data sets to yield useful information. A lot of data is left behind by users unknowingly on the Internet. Called data exhaust, it includes the traces left behind by their online activity, payment methods, photographs and so on. When this data is used for gaining insights, it is called data mining. Without conducting any surveys, companies can learn about a host of activities.
- **Audience research:** Companies can find out media consumption patterns by tracking set-top boxes, apps and Internet usage. Broadcast Audience Research Council puts out figures showing the popularity of channels and individual programmes running on them. Through data mining, companies can know who is visiting particular sites, and how much time they are spending on those channels.
- **Product research:** Feedback on products need not be taken through surveys: Companies can simply track what people are posting on their social media sites. Companies can seek feedback on consumer preferences and feedback on new products by launching websites that encourage users to choose among flavours or packages and click on their preference. Companies can also use profiling techniques to identify segments that use particular brands.
- **Psychological profiling:** Personal data available online can be used in psychological profiling of customers. Profiles of customers can be built on the basis of lifestyle, income and other attributes.
- **Scanner research:** Scanner research means using scans of transactions at shops to find purchase patterns of customers at those stores. This yields data on consumption habits and leads to better inventory control. Scanning data also reveals the effectiveness of sales promotion methods and develop a correlation like 'People Who Bought This Also Bought That' leading to better grouping and displays at shops.
- **Consumer satisfaction research:** Survey-based satisfaction research often yields wrong data since customers may give wrong answers. Data-based satisfaction research consists of tracking reviews, blogs, pictures of products posted on personal sites of consumers and reveals the true picture about what people are thinking of products and brands.

We have so far discussed changes in marketing due to changes in digital technologies. Another important aspect of this is the effect it will have on industries on a larger scale. We will discuss three concepts here: (a) digital Darwinism, (b) digital divide and (c) digital property.

DIGITAL DARWINISM

Global e-markets operate in a rapidly changing environment. Long established business tools such as the 4Ps and Porter's five forces model no longer capture the complexity of the business or the rapidly shifting sands of the business environment. Businesses must adapt to these evolving changes if they are to remain competitive in the online landscape.

The world of business is entering an era of 'digital Darwinism', a time in which technology and society are changing faster than businesses can adjust, threatening their survival. This is causing a large number of companies to become defunct. Darwin's theory of natural selection states that life forms must adapt to the environment otherwise they face extinction. In a similar way, companies today must 'adapt or die', that is, adapt to the digital environment or they would fade away. Indeed, many companies have lost their mojo in recent decades. 'Digital Darwinism does not discriminate. Every business is threatened,' writes Solis (2020).

DIGITAL DIVIDE

Digital divide refers to the gap between those who have access to digital technologies and those who have not. The World Economic Forum (White and Pinsky 2018) estimated that approximately half of the world's population does not have digital access. A report by McKinsey (2014) mentions several barriers to the Internet adoption contributing to the digital divide directly: incentives, low incomes and affordability, user capability and infrastructure. We have explained these barriers as follows.

1. **Geographical factors:** People are cut off from digital access because of their location. Globally, some areas do not have the digital infrastructure. Nationally, many remote villages are not able to get mobile signals because telecom companies find it uneconomical to install towers at every remote location.

2. **Economic factors:** Many people are unable to afford either digital devices like smartphones or find data costs too high. As a consequence, they remain cut-off from the digital revolution taking place around them. World Vision (2018) reports that globally, 10 per cent of the population is living on less than $2 a day, and 1.3 billion people in 104 developing countries live in multidimensional poverty.

3. **Social factors:** Many societies practice social exclusion and create disincentives for certain segments of the population regarding the use of technology. Abbas (2019) reports of a study conducted by the Centre for the Study of Developing Societies which found that upper castes in India are twice as likely to have exposure to social media as compared to Dalits and tribals. *The Independent* (Lewis 2016) writes that there have been reports from several states of India, including Rajasthan, UP and Gujarat, that girls have been banned from using mobile phones. Women in Suraj village in Gujarat face fines of ₹2,100 if they use the mobile phone. India TV News

(ANI 2019) reports that another village in Gujarat, Jalol, has banned the use of mobile phones by unmarried girls and that such use would constitute a crime. Such factors contribute to the digital divide.

4. **Political factors:** Several leaders and governments impose restrictions on the use of digital technologies as a means of keeping political control. India has become the world leader having the most Internet shutdowns, writes *The Guardian* (Safi 2019), but the trend is global. Many countries limit or shut down the Internet if it does not suit their purposes.

5. **Individual factors:** There are several individual factors that contribute to the digital divide. First is illiteracy. If people are illiterate, they will find it difficult to access the Internet. Second, many old people are unable or unwilling to use new technology.

6. **Privacy concerns:** Privacy concerns arise if people feel that companies and governments have too much of their data which can be used against them. For instance, a user's medical history may be accessed by financial companies, and higher rates for loans or insurance products will be charged as a result. Employers, too, can access their employees' social posts. As a result of such concerns, people are switching off their devices or deleting their accounts. This contributes to the digital divide.

The digital divide is contributing to inequality and social exclusion in societies. Since the Internet can impact the lives of the poor and the disadvantaged positively both within a country and between different nations, the digital divide creates deep inequalities. Today, there is a big difference between 'information haves' and 'information have-nots' in society. This is becoming serious because it excludes parts of society from both private and government schemes and services. Thus, the poor will continue to become poorer, and they will continue to be denied resources that would otherwise be available to them.

DIGITAL PROPERTY, EMERGING ISSUES

The digital property consists of data, Internet accounts, pictures, music, literary works, web pages, software, multimedia and other types of files that can be stored or transmitted digitally. This data is stored locally on a computer's hard drive, removable media or remotely and accessed on the Internet. The data or property is governed by contractual rights and intellectual property rights.

As with traditional forms of property, the digital property has value, and the ownership can be transferred upon a person's death. But if a person has not provided details of his/her accounts and their passwords, it becomes difficult to locate or access this property.

Internet accounts are created based on contracts between the individual and the service provider. Email accounts, financial accounts, websites, blogs, social networking accounts, registered domain names, video game and other virtual world accounts fall under this category.

In e-marketing, the digital property consists of digital assets used in marketing, such as campaigns and content. It includes:

- **Email templates:** The content and method of email advertising and templates.
- **Video:** Video content, advertisements or instructional videos, recordings are all part of the digital property.
- **Newsletters:** Printed or electronic newsletters that are sent to customers or associates, including electronic pamphlets.
- **Brochures:** Any text or pictorial matter used to market products and services.
- **Webpage:** Any web pages or websites created are also digital properties.

All this constitutes digital property and is protected by laws on intellectual property rights.

The digital property rights are still evolving but are protected as patents, copyrights and trademark brands. Disputes arise when other companies try to use the same methods or content in marketing.

- **Patent violations:** Software inventions can be patented. Amazon developed a system of 'one-click buying,' which enables customers to make purchases in a single click without entering credit card and billing information each time they bought something. The company patented this technology in 1999. However, other companies were quick to replicate this system by developing their own software. Barnes & Noble developed a similar system, but Amazon sued the company for patent infringement. The lawsuit was settled in 2002. The instance shows that companies must protect their marketing content and innovations by a patent and other rights; otherwise, they can easily be copied.
- **Licensing infringements:** Internet and web applications interconnect with digital devices. New web applications are also classified as digital property, and if patented, they can be licensed to other companies. Companies are under obligation to follow the licensing conditions.
- **Trademark infringement:** Trademark infringements occur when another company—usually a competitor—uses a company trademark to enhance its own image. This becomes important in the digital age when search words lead companies to their sites. If these words take the traffic to alternate sites, it becomes a problem for the company that owns the trademark or trade name.
- **Copyright infringements:** Copying of content, illegal posting of somebody else's content violate copyright laws. Virtual content is easily shared online. In recent years, online distribution of music, books and video has attracted lawsuits. In the digital world, duplication and distribution cost nothing and can occur in an instant.

As intellectual property law was written to protect and maintain fair marketplace practices, the Internet's continued growth rates warrant refining the laws that protect digital property rights. In effect, failure to properly define digital property rights can result in slowed economic progress as companies and individuals become less inclined to introduce new products in the marketplace. Consumers, too, run the risk of purchasing sub-par merchandise in cases where pirating and illegal distribution practices go unnoticed in the online world.

CONCLUSION

The growth of the Internet has led to new ways of doing business. Practically, every business stands to gain from using digital technologies, which are very much part of the business environment today. How these technologies are used depends on the companies, but the opportunities are huge.

What can be learnt from the experience of successful digital transformations is that the Internet is not used as an incremental business resource. It has to be treated as a central business strategy. Technology is advancing rapidly, and it is up to the innovation of managers to use the newly available resources fruitfully. Communication and market research techniques can be completely and radically changed. Only when businesses learn to do this, they will make full use of the online environment.

SUMMARY

This chapter describes the changing environment of business because of digital technology. Data has often been called the 'new oil', and it changes every aspect of doing business. The marketing environment is described in three major areas: (a) changes in technology, (b) changes in human behaviour and (c) changes in media platforms and usage. Technology has changed communication ways and channels, transferred control from companies to consumers, created new business models and increased importance of omnichannel approach. People are now hyperconnected and 'always-on', multitasked and mobile addicts. Media apps and platforms, consumption patterns and co-creation of content have changed the way people interact with the media.

This has impacted the online marketing mix, which must include eight controllable variables: customer focus, digital transformation, customer engagement and experience, integration of online and offline practices, data analytics, creativity, collaboration and CRM.

Market research has also undergone changes. Surveys and questionaries have been replaced by online information, data mining and social media analytics. Global marketplaces face digital Darwinism, in which technology and society are changing faster than businesses can adjust, threatening their survival. The question of the digital divide also becomes an important one, which refers to the gap between those who have access to digital technologies and those who have not. Factors contributing to the digital divide have been discussed.

Finally, digital property rights, as they relate to marketing, have been discussed. Companies have to safeguard their methods and content. The digital property must be patented and protected by intellectual property rights just as in the case of physical property.

KEY TERMS

Affiliate marketing: It is the process of promoting others' products or services and earning a commission on sales.

Cryptocurrency: It is a decentralized virtual currency that is not controlled by banks.

Customer-led campaigns: These are marketing campaigns in which customers are involved in producing content.

Data mining: Data mining is the process of analysing varied streams of data and large data to yield useful information.

Digital Darwinism: It is the time in which technology and society are changing faster than businesses can adjust, threatening their survival.

Digital divide: It is the gap between those who have access to digital technologies and those who have not.

Digital media: It is the content that is transferred through the Internet or computer networks.

Digital property: It refers to the data, Internet accounts, pictures, music, literary works, web pages, software, multimedia and other types of files that can be stored or transmitted digitally.

Dotcom bubble: It is the unrealistic growth of the stock market caused by huge investments in Internet-related companies which had no business models, and hence collapsed in 2002.

Dotcom: It is a company whose business model is based on the Internet and is so called because commercial domain names end with 'com.'.

E-payments: These are digital payment systems that consist of cards, e-wallets, online banking, UPI payments and so on which have grown over the years.

E-wallet: It is a digital app that can store cash virtually.

Omnichannel: It is a business approach that integrates all channels with the objective of providing a seamless shopping experience on all channels, including physical stores, websites, apps, mass media and virtual media.

Omnichannel: It is a business approach that integrates all channels with the objective of providing a seamless shopping experience on all channels.

OTT: OTT platforms provide content to consumers bypassing or going 'over' the set-top box through which cable and TV providers operate.

Virtual banking: It is a virtual bank, an entity that offers traditional banking services online and may not have a physical branch.

CONCEPT REVIEW QUESTIONS

1. How has the marketing environment changed due to digital technologies, and what are companies doing to adapt to them?

2. Describe the dotcom evolution and how the business environment has changed over the years due to the digital revolution.
3. What are the factors that drive the marketing environment of today?
4. Describe the various e-payment systems and their advantages.
5. How has human behaviour changed because of digital technologies?
6. Describe the digital media industry and its components.
7. What are the controllable factors that companies can manipulate for digital marketing?
8. How is market research conducted on the Internet? Which information is easily available, and how can modern technologies be used to provide consumer insights?
9. Explain the concepts of digital Darwinism and the digital divide. What are the factors that impact them?
10. What is a digital property? Why has it become important to protect digital property rights?

CRITICAL THINKING QUESTIONS

1. Do you agree with the statement that data is the new oil? What does it imply? Can data become central to the future economy just as oil has dominated the world economy?
2. Critically analyse the 4C, 4S and other models of marketing mix proposed by various authors. Which one do you think is most appropriate and why?
3. Data capabilities can provide deep consumer insights that traditional market research methods can never hope to accomplish. What are the disadvantages of traditional methods? Why are surveys and questionnaires still being used despite their severe limitations?
4. Examine the business models of some online companies. Identify their revenue streams and estimate their costs of marketing. Give your opinion about whether they are surviving on venture capital or whether they can sustain over the long term.

PROJECTS AND ASSIGNMENTS

1. Select a well-known online business like MakeMyTrip or BookMyShow. Analyse the marketing environment factors for it in detail, and explain how they impact its future business prospects.
2. Observe customers in a mobile or laptops shop. How many actually end up buying a product? Ask them the reasons for buying products physically and how many intend to buy online and why.

3. Ask your friends how they get their daily news and entertainment. What is the percentage of your friends who like traditional media such as newspapers and TV channels, and how many have never used traditional media?

4. Visit a grocery store and interview the owner. Find out how much percentage of sales is done physically by the store and how much is done online. Has online posed a threat to the physical store?

◼ REFERENCES

Abbas, G. 2019. 'Upper Castes Continue to Dominate Social Media Usage, Muslims More Exposed Than Dalits and Tribals: Study.' News 18 India, 21 June. Available at: https://www.news18.com/news/india/upper-castes-continue-to-dominate-social-media-usage-muslims-more-exposed-than-dalits-and-tribals-study-2191313.html (accessed on 8 February 2021).

ANI. 2019. 'Thakor Community in Banaskantha Bans Unmarried Girls from Using Cell Phones.' 16 July. Available at: https://www.india.com/news/india/thakor-community-in-gujarats-banaskantha-bans-unmarried-girls-from-using-cell-phones-3719104/ (accessed on 8 February 2021).

Carr, N. 2008. 'Is Google Making Us Stupid?' *The Atlantic* (July–August). Available at: https://www.theatlantic.com/magazine/archive/2008/07/is-google-making-us-stupid/306868/ (accessed on 8 February 2021).

Constantinides, E. 2002. 'The 4S Web-marketing Mix Model.' *Electronic Commerce Research and Applications* 1, no. 1 (March): 57–76.

Foreman, R. 2005. 'The Pancake People.' Edge the Third Culture, August. Available at: https://www.edge.org/3rd_culture/foreman05/foreman05_index.html (accessed on 8 February 2021).

Gregg, B., J. Heller, J. Perrey, and J. Tsai. 2018. 'The Perfect Union: Unlocking the Next Wave of Growth by Unifying Creativity and Analytics.' McKinsey & Company. Available at: https://www.mckinsey.com/business-functions/marketing-and-sales/our-insights/the-most-perfect-union (accessed on 8 February 2021).

Hoffman, D. L., and T. P. Novak. 2000. 'How to Acquire Customers on the Web.' *Harvard Business Review* (May–June). Available at: https://hbr.org/2000/05/how-to-acquire-customers-on-the-web (accessed on 8 February 2021).

Horrigan, J. B. 2009. 'The Mobile Difference.' Pew Research Center, 25 March. Available at: https://www.pewresearch.org/internet/2009/03/25/the-mobile-difference/ (accessed on 8 February 2021).

Joachimsthaler, E. 2014. 'Divining the Future: The Always-On Consumer.' *Forbes* (27 February). Available at: https://www.forbes.com/sites/onmarketing/2014/02/27/divining-the-future-the-always-on-consumer/?sh=7c4a85614814 (accessed on 8 February 2021).

Kalyanam, K., and S. H. Mcintyre. 'The E-Marketing Mix: A Contribution of the E-Tailing Wars.' *Journal of the Academy of Marketing Science* 30, no. 4 (October): 487–499. Available at: https://doi.org/10.1177/009207002236924 (accessed on 8 February 2021).

Lauterborn, B. 1990. 'New Marketing Litany: Four P's Passe: C-words Take over.' *Advertising Age* 61, no. 41: 26.

Lewis, K. 2016. 'Married Women in a Gujarat Village Now Face Fines of around £21.60 for Breaching the New Rule.' *The Independent*, 22 February. Available at: https://www.independent.co.uk/news/world/asia/girls-and-unmarried-women-in-india-forbidden-from-using-mobile-phones-to-prevent-disturbance-in-a6888911.html (accessed on 8 February 2021).

Lewnes, A., and K. L. Keller. 2019. '10 Principles of Modern Marketing.' *MIT Sloan Management Review* (April). Available at: https://sloanreview.mit.edu/article/10-principles-of-modern-marketing/ (accessed on 8 February 2021).

McKinsey. 2014. 'Offline and Falling behind: Barriers to Internet Adoption.' McKinsey & Company, August. Available at: https://www.mckinsey.com/industries/technology-media-and-telecommunications/our-insights/offline-and-falling-behind-barriers-to-internet-adoption (accessed on 8 February 2021).

Safi, M. 2019. 'India's Internet Curbs Are Part of Growing Global Trend.' *The Guardian*, 19 December. Available at: https://www.theguardian.com/technology/2019/dec/19/india-internet-curbs-are-part-of-growing-global-trend (accessed on 8 February 2021).

Solis, B. 2020. 'Tips to Help Brands Excel in 2020.' The Drum. Available at: https://www.thedrum.com/opinion/2020/02/28/tips-help-brands-excel-2020 (accessed on 8 February 2021).

Stone, L. 2009. 'Beyond Simple Multi-Tasking: Continuous Partial Attention.' November. Available at: https://lindastone.net/category/attention/continuous-continuous-partial-attention/ (accessed on 8 February 2021).

The Economist. 2017. 'The World's Most Valuable Resource Is No Longer Oil, but Data.' 6 May. Available at: https://www.economist.com/leaders/2017/05/06/the-worlds-most-valuable-resource-is-no-longer-oil-but-data (accessed on 8 February 2021).

Vollmer, C. 2008. *Always on: Advertising, Marketing, and Media in an Era of Consumer Control*. New Delhi: Tata-McGraw Hill.

White, E., and O. Pinsky. 2018. 'Half the World's Population Is Still Offline. Here's Why That Matters.' World Economic Forum. Available at: https://www.weforum.org/agenda/2018/05/half-the-world-s-population-is-still-offline-heres-why-that-matters (accessed on 8 February 2021).

World Vision. 2018. 'Global Poverty: Facts, FAQs, and How to Help.' 21 November. Available at: https://www.worldvision.org/sponsorship-news-stories/global-poverty-facts (accessed on 8 February 2021).

CLOSING CASE

AADHAR: THE WORLD'S BIGGEST ID DATABASE

For the poor, proving that they exist is a major issue. The World Bank estimates that about 15 per cent of people in the world cannot prove their identity. Without official identification, the poor face exclusion from many government schemes and private sector initiatives and are left behind in education, health and livelihood matters. Hence, poor people are stuck in temporary and demeaning professions, such as cleaning, rag picking and the like. They cannot sell goods on the roadside, nor can they collect disability benefits, and children are denied admission in schools. In India, most people have relied on 'ration cards' issued by the government for getting essential food items from the public distribution system.

Aadhaar is a unique identification number consisting of 12 digits issued by the Unique Identification Authority of India set up by the Indian government. It is issued free of cost for residents and is a digital database that includes name, photograph, date of birth, address and also biometric information consisting of 10 fingerprints and two iris scans. Some 1.25 billion identity cards have been issued as of December 2019. The system not only provides an identity to people but also enables 'target delivery' of government services. With an Aadhaar, a person can have access to education, pension, subsidies, school meals, bank accounts, healthcare and more.

(Continued)

(Continued)

Aadhaar has simplified identification as it can be accessed anywhere, and people can reprint it anytime they want. Earlier, a person had to rely on ration cards. If it got lost or damaged, people would be left without an identity.

Aadhaar has helped in targeted delivery. Government-run ration shops can now verify the user's identity by mean of a fingerprint scanner, and once logged in, the shopkeeper's computer displays the rations he/she is entitled to. Payment is made from an online savings bank account again authorized by a fingerprint scanner. Such technical advancement has been made possible by the introduction of Aadhaar. Consumers in villages now have bank accounts and use e-payment systems all connected to the national identification system. The system puts India much ahead of other countries. It has also eliminated leakages from the system since only the enrolled person can use the authentication by means of a fingerprint scan. Earlier, only about one-fourth of the money was properly distributed, thanks to rampant corruption. Fictitious children in schools and fictitious voters have been eliminated.

Aadhaar was meant to be voluntary, but the government now insists its use in a variety of applications. Now, the Aadhaar has been made mandatory for many other purposes such as booking train tickets and applying for a mobile connection. This leads to the question about the privacy of personal data and its misuse. The Aadhaar database has a strong infrastructure and serves authentication requests from all over India. But the system is not without its limitations.

Limitations

Although Aadhaar has been a huge success in terms of enrolments, it has left many people including children and old people, minorities, tribals, the visually and physically disabled and others who have lost their birth certificates or other identifying documents. For example, the fingerprints of many workers and old people are cracked, and they are unable to get enrolled or verified in Aadhar. Leprosy sufferers who have lost fingers or sight too are not enrolled in the system. Street children and homeless people, too, find it difficult to get Aadhaar because they simply do not have an address. Street children are destined to work in landfills because government schools have made Aadhaar mandatory for admission.

The system is also subjective. Documents uploaded can be accepted or rejected on the whims of the verifying officers.

This has spawned a number of court cases. The court ruled against compulsory Aadhaar in schools saying that welfare services should not be tied to it. However, the system continues. More services are being tied to the Aadhar, from opening bank accounts to government jobs. There have been reports of children being denied mid-day meals in schools as they did not have Aadhaar.

Another problem is that the system requires both electricity and a working Internet connection, both of which are not available in many remote villages. The system is also not foolproof since authentications fail for about one-third of the time.

Questions for Discussion

1. Has the Aadhar succeeded in its stated objectives? What can be done to make it more useful?

2. What other government and private services can be offered through Aadhar? How can it be a tool of social inclusion?
3. Newspapers have reported that some people are denied services and rations as their Aadhar did not work. How can such problems be avoided?
4. In light of increased government surveillance of citizens, how can they protect their right? Should an electronic database like Aadhar be made voluntary?

Sources

Ghosh, P. 2018. 'Aadhaar: In the World's Biggest Biometric ID Experiment, Many Have Fallen through the Gaps.' Scroll.in, 24 February. Available at: https://scroll.in/article/868836/aadhaar-in-the-worlds-biggest-biometric-id-experiment-many-have-fallen-through-the-gaps (accessed on 8 February 2021).

The Economist. 2017. 'India's ID System Is Reshaping Ties between State and Citizens.' *The Economist*, 12 April. Available at: https://www.economist.com/asia/2017/04/12/indias-id-system-is-reshaping-ties-between-state-and-citizens (accessed on 8 February 2021).

CHAPTER 6

Social Media and Marketing

Social media is the preferred destination for consumers. Companies realize that they have to incorporate it into their communications strategy, but attempts to advertise on it are usually rejected. This chapter describes how companies can use social media in their marketing efforts.

After reading this chapter, you will be able to learn about the following:

❑ Social media channels and tools and how they can be used in marketing

❑ How companies can move beyond likes and shares, and use social media more effectively by becoming a social brand

❑ Social media as a tool for prospecting, sales, as a supplement to media spend and as a soft metric for effectiveness

❑ Crowd cultures and community involvement

❑ Social media tools and metrics, dashboards and command centres

OPENING CASE

ENGAGING CUSTOMERS ON SOCIAL MEDIA

Social media attracts millions of people worldwide. Companies look for ways to engage customers through social media platforms. Kujur and Singh (2017) write that four factors play an important role in consumers' online participation and engagement: (a) vividness, (b) interactivity, (c) entertainment and (d) information. Brands try to build on these to increase awareness and engagement.

 four factor to engage customers

One of the most effective social media campaigns has been that of Starbucks. Its My Starbucks Idea, started in 2008, which helped to increase customer engagement and build relationships in a big way. It invited consumers to submit a new idea for a coffee flavour on its website, view ideas submitted by others and vote for them and see ideas that have been recommended. By doing this, the company could engage customers and make them feel involved with product development of the company.

Schultz and Gordon (2011) write that the company was stuck in a groove and lacklustre financial condition. It wanted to remain relevant and fight the increasing competition from McDonald's and Dunkin' Donuts. To meet these challenges, the company started an online crowdsourcing platform to involve customers and to get product ideas from them. Its website (ideas.starbucks.com) asks users to 'share your ideas, tell us what you think of other people's ideas, and join the discussion'. The company has received hundreds of thousands of ideas since the programme was started, according to a Credera report (2017). At the five-year anniversary of the site launch in 2013, My Starbucks Idea had generated more than 150,000 ideas and 277 of those ideas were implemented by the company.

According to a post on the HBS website (2016), the programme helps to *incentivize participation* to submit ideas and engage with the brand by actually implementing the ideas received; to *create value* by allowing customers to voice their ideas and to *capture value* through customer engagement and loyalty.

Another company that uses social media effectively is L'Oréal. It engages its consumers through video advertising, using global influencers and interacting through personalized communications. It has developed a social marketing model called 'Listen-to-Engage' with the idea that it must listen to consumers to understand what they expect. The company integrates the departments of product development, marketing and customer service and uses the CX management platform, Sprinklr. This tracks comments made on social media to monitor how the brand is performing and what consumers are feeling. Interesting conversations are detected and the company selects those in which it wants to participate. It uses social media to amplify the brand message, use influencers and provide customer service. L'Oréal has achieved what is sought after by many companies: a unified CX that also breaks down internal departmental divisions.

In India, L'Oréal encouraged user conversations asking questions such as 'Who is the person that keeps you rooted?' People could post their answers with the hashtag, #KeepsMeRooted. Another initiative asked people to post their pictures under the title 'What's Your Bollywood Look?' The company's Facebook page provides a style guide, links to celebrity pages, product information and links for buying products. It has 35 million followers.

On Twitter, L'Oréal provides beauty tips and tries to create a buzz with contests and promotions. Another innovative campaign was laying a virtual red carpet from India to the Cannes Festival. Fans across its social media channels had to cover the entire distance in 10 days with the reward of getting exclusive festival coverage.

An article in *Forbes* (Trefis Team and Great Speculations 2017) states that L'Oréal's social media initiatives 'are paying off and giving it a competitive edge' by involving customers. The engagement leads to a two-way communication resulting in ideas and suggestions for product improvements.

Every company must figure out how best it should use social media to meet its objectives. This case study shows how companies can engage customers on social media platforms not only to make brand names popular but also to engage them in product development.

(Continued)

(Continued)

While reading this chapter, try to answer the following questions:

1. How can companies use social media to involve others in co-creating products? How can it be recreated in other companies?
2. Can social media help in market research? How?
3. Does this strategy not endanger the company if rumours and misconceptions spread?
4. What are the advantages and disadvantages of involving consumers?

Sources

Credera. 2017. 'Winning with Digital in an Era of Customer-Led Disruption.' Available at: https://www.credera.com/wp-content/uploads/2016/12/Winning-with-Digital-in-an-Era-of-Customer-Led-Disruption.pdf (accessed on 20 January 2021).

HBS. 2016. 'My Starbucks Idea: Crowdsourcing for Customer Satisfaction and Innovation.' Available at: https://digit.hbs.org/submission/my-starbucks-idea-crowdsourcing-for-customer-satisfaction-and-innovation/ (accessed on 20 January 2021).

Kujur, F., and S. Singh. 2017. 'Engaging Customers through Online Participation in Social Networking Sites.' *Asia Pacific Management Review* 22, no. 1 (March): 16–24. Available at: https://doi.org/10.1016/j.apmrv.2016.10.006 (accessed on 20 January 2021).

Schultz, H., and J. Gordon. 2011. *Onward: How Starbucks Fought for Its Life without Losing Its Soul.* New York, NY: Rodale.

Trefis Team and Great Speculations. 2017. 'L'Oréal Is Benefitting from a Higher Digital Spending.' *Forbes* (8 February). Available at: https://www.forbes.com/sites/greatspeculations/2017/02/08/loreal-is-benefitting-from-a-higher-digital-spending/#58643c6743c1 (accessed on 20 January 2021).

■ INTRODUCTION

Social media is defined as the creation, sharing and exchange of information and ideas on online social networks. It consists of texts, visuals and audios created by companies and individuals to be shared on social networking sites. It allows two-way collaborations and connections between companies and consumers, and therefore has changed marketing in profound ways.

Social media is a powerful force of marketing in the digital era. Increasingly, people turn to social media for a variety of reasons. People now refer to social media when searching for products. But companies have found that it is not a vehicle for advertising messages, and consumers may instead use it to receive information and advice from their connections about products and brands. Social media includes a broad range of activities to connect customers and other stakeholders.

Three value disciplined

Treacy and Wiersema (1995) described three value disciplines: product leadership, operational excellence and customer intimacy as sources of unique value. Social media contributes to all three as shown in this chapter (see Opening Case). It is not just a broadcast channel or a sales and marketing tool. Many companies have treated it like other media, pushing advertising messages through it, but that has not really worked. Instead, they have to treat social media as a means of a two-way communication in which authenticity, honesty and open dialogue take the place of advertising.

SOCIAL MEDIA PLATFORMS

Social media not only allows companies to hear what people say but also enables them to respond. There is thus a paradigm shift in the marketing approach, and it involves figuring out how different channels and platforms of social sharing (Table 6.1) can be used for marketing purposes.

A study by PriceWaterhouseCoopers (2016) states that the shift is nothing short of a revolution: mobile phones are getting more popular as a purchasing tool. Social media helps in product selection. People who interact with it tend to have a positive impression of the product or brand: they are four times more likely to spend more money on purchases.

ROI – Return on Invest ment

UNDERSTANDING SOCIAL MEDIA

Despite the importance of social media in marketing, companies still struggle with it because they do not know how to use the new medium for marketing purposes. There are two distinct players.

1. On the one hand are social media marketing 'experts' who sing praises of the potential of social networking sites. They are able to generate likes and shares of online content.
2. On the other hand are marketing professionals who seek to build brands and increase marketing ROI, but are clueless about how to extend social media beyond likes and shares to sales performance.

Strategies are usually designed by one or the other without an integration of objectives. As a consequence, companies end up creating content that is well liked but does not translate into sales; or sending marketing messages that are ignored or end up in the 'spam' folder. Ad blockers and caller identification apps block efforts to advertise, and messages on social media space are usually deleted or reported as spam.

Piskorski (2011) writes that the efforts by companies to connect with consumers on social media are rejected because people want to connect with other people, not with companies. A survey conducted by Pikas and Sorrentino (2014) found that the majority

TABLE 6.1   *Popular Social Media Tools and Platforms*

Social Media Tool	What It Does	Application in Marketing
Blogs	A platform for dialogue and discussions on a specific topic. Expert opinions, experiences and reviews are shared through blogs.	Find relevant blogs, listen to conversations, influence Link RSS feeds
Facebook	The world's largest social network. Brands create pages on it and users can 'like' their pages and engage with brands.	Create brand profiles, invite users, engage communities
Twitter	A micro-blogging platform that allows exchange of information through short messages, images and video.	Follow, join social causes useful for sending updates or links
YouTube and Vimeo	Video hosting and watching websites.	Brands share videos for advertising, information and product demos
Flickr	An image- and video-hosting website and online community.	Share product pictures and usage
Instagram	A photo- and video-sharing app.	Product pictures, advertising, product usage and updates are shared
Snapchat/ WhatsApp	Mobile apps used to send messages, photos and videos to friends.	Short messages, updates, pictures and videos are shared
Pinterest	A pinboard-style platform, which is used for collecting images that can be categorized into separate boards.	Huge influencer in social shopping, featuring 'Buy' buttons on certain pins
LinkedIn groups	A place where groups of professionals share information and participate in conversations.	Useful for developing contacts, networks, user information
Discussion forums/reviews	Provide reviews on products and brands.	Listen to customers, post authentic reviews

of respondents were not receptive to advertising on social media sites. Their study suggests that companies like Google vastly exaggerate the effectiveness of search advertising. The majority of respondents were annoyed by online advertisements saying that they would not like to be voluntarily exposed to information shared by businesses. In other words, using social media for advertising and brand building is not very easy. Stauffer (2012) explains that social media methods are at odds with traditional campaign methods. As a result, many marketing communications on social media are 'social' in name only and are actually communication from brand to consumer, and hence fall flat.

The impact on consumer sales has also been called into question. Social media sites offer brands a source of customer intelligence and feedback; however, research finds no evidence that following a brand on social media changes people's purchasing behaviour. John et al. (2017) write, 'Social media doesn't work the way many marketers think it does. The mere act of endorsing a brand does not affect a customer's behaviour or lead to increased purchasing, nor does it spur purchasing by friends.'

Kumar (2016) writes that companies thus struggle to understand how to get people involved with their brands on a platform that is essentially social, not commercial. To use it effectively, they must try to answer the following questions:

- What do people do on social media?
- How to get people on social media engaged with brands?
- Why should people seek out a company or a brand on social media?
- What makes a customer willing or reluctant to interact with brands socially?
- Does social engagement really result in increase in sales or loyalty for a company?
- How can social media be used to assist marketing strategy of a company?

When these questions are addressed, we can see possibilities for linking social media activities with business applications (Table 6.2). Indeed, there are many ways that companies can use social media platforms to involve their customers, but interventions must not look like advertising (see Marketing Insight 6.1). Brands have to behave like people and make efforts to become 'social'. They have to mirror what people do on such sites, such as building friends and followers, supporting, engaging customers and seeking their help. To succeed, brands must start building trust and relationships and become *social brands*.

TABLE 6.2   *Social Applications Have Wide Applications That Connect a Wide Range of Business Applications*

Application	Activity	Business Application
Social networking	Connecting with friends, family and acquaintances	Build connections with customers and business associates
Ratings, reviews and discussion fora	User-generated opinions	Share reviews, rectify errors, connect with experts and users, solve problems
Blogs, wikis, videos	User-generated content	Involve experts and influencers, invest in keywords
Co-creation, crowdsourcing	Engaging users with companies	Generate business and product ideas, create user-generated advertising and influence
Communities	Connecting with like-minded people	Build communities and relationships around brands/causes

MARKETING INSIGHT 6.1   *Social Media Methods for Marketing*

Companies use social networking sites to become more likable to potential customers, both in B2C and B2B sales. Sales reps use social sites to present their qualifications and build trust. In B2B, salespeople use such sites to collaborate with each other and to know who they need to see within a company. Stokes (2013) writes that social media can be used to research, plan and strategize for brands and campaigns, use the web to drive traffic and leverage the available channels to build strong customer relationships, optimize data and analysis to improve marketing efforts. This can be done by the following methods.

1. **Targeted ads:** Social media allows the targeting of very specific audiences. With 'hypertargeting' or 'microtargeting', ads can be placed with precise segmentation parameters such as location, gender, age, education, relationship status, relationship interests and keywords.

2. **Appvertising:** Appvertising, or mobile application advertising, enables advertisers to place ads inside phone applications. This may also increase users' engagement.

3. **Social actions:** Placing ads on sites where people discuss related social activities. For instance, companies may advertise a hand sanitizer on a site discussing disease control.

4. **Engagement ads:** Ads that lead to customer engagement with visually rich, immersive experiences are called engagement ads.

5. **WOM:** An unpaid form of promotion in which customers tell other people how much they like a product or service. On social media, WOM implies people writing about products and sharing experiences, which becomes a form of promotion. Correctly handled, such advertising can quickly go 'viral'.

6. **Meme feeds:** An Internet meme is an idea, activity, catchphrase or piece of media that spreads from person to person via the Internet. Companies check to see what ideas people are discussing and can send meme feeds. For example, coronavirus spread has encouraged a number of memes and short messages to impart information to worried people.

7. **Crowdsourcing:** Another element of a social strategy is the crowdsourcing of ideas, which is the practice of obtaining information from a large number of followers or people. By listening to the crowd and asking for their suggestions, companies gain insight into customer needs and desires.

8. **Microtasking:** Companies can also resort to *microtasking*, which involves breaking a big task down into tiny components and asking many people to complete a few components, sometimes for payment. For example, a company may pay some users to evaluate the sentiment behind mentions in social media.

9. **Brand communities:** Some companies build brand communities by getting people together who have a keen interest in and affinity for a brand. Such people interact with brands and provide ways to improve the company's offerings. Sometimes, communities offer rewards to crowdsource ideas (see Chapter 3).

10. **Facebook page-like campaigns:** Page-like campaigns are popular within Facebook advertising. Brands and advertisers have invested large amounts of money collecting likes. Likes are still widely considered an indicator of brand loyalty and growth opportunity.

SOCIAL BRAND: BRANDS AS PERSONS

Customers spend much of their time on social sites, sharing comments and pictures, and connecting with friends and acquaintances. They have online conversations with each other. So the question is: *How do companies connect with them when they are so busy with each other?*

Van Bockel (2014) writes that brands today have to become social brands. A social brand is one that is seen as a person on social media, creating content, connecting with its customers and having two-way conversations. People will connect with brands only if the company/brand can engage with them on social media. Van Bockel introduces the concept of the *brand bank account* in which deposits are made by adding content that is valuable to its audience. Withdrawals are the negative comments posted.

The idea is that brands should make more deposits than withdrawals. Instead of merely posting advertising, a social brand has to interest people, fulfil promises and gain trust. If customers are happy with the product, they will post positive comments that add to the deposits of the brand. The approach has to be completely different from traditional marketing: instead of asking 'how can we make people buy from us?', companies should focus on 'how can we do something for people who buy our products or services?'

This is quite different from the way traditional marketing has operated. Managers have to learn how to think of brands as social brands. DeMers (2015) writes that social brands should have seven important qualities: trust, personal, unique, caring, responsive, authoritative and valuable. In short, they should have human social qualities. The concept of social brand takes into account the interests and needs of people, offering value and enriching others' lives, building relationships that people will seek and share with others. The key challenge changes from trying to get buyers to engaging people.

Shih (2009) writes that business is eminently social since sales depend on referrals and recommendations. Companies must use social networking sites to build *social capital* or the 'currency of business interactions and relationships'. Social capital is defined as consisting of links, shared values and understandings in society that enable individuals and groups to trust each other, and thus work together.

The reason that brands must transform themselves into social brands is that people spend huge amounts of time on social media. A study reported on *Social Media Today* (Asano 2017) shows that teens spend up to 9 hours a day on social platforms. It states that 30 per cent of all time spent online is now on social media interaction, facilitated by mobile devices. The average person spends nearly two hours (approximately 116 minutes) on social media every day, and this may well increase in the future. The total time spent by consumers on social media is more than the time they spent on eating and drinking, socializing and grooming. Among the social media platforms, time spent on YouTube was on average about 40 minutes, followed by Facebook with an average of 35 minutes a day. The time spent per day on Snapchat and Instagram was 25 minutes and 15 minutes, respectively, while users were estimated to spend 1 minute on Twitter (Figure 6.1). An average young person was found to check the smartphone more than 150 times a day.

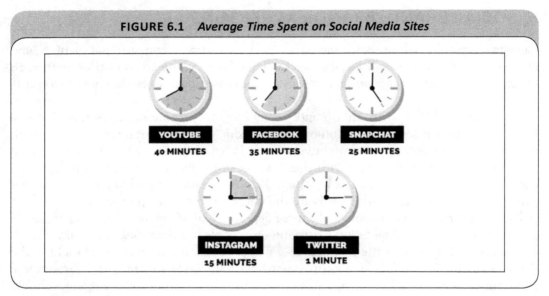

FIGURE 6.1 *Average Time Spent on Social Media Sites*

Source: Asano (2017).

Yet, using social media for marketing is not easy. While it is true that people are spending much of their time on social networking sites, companies have struggled to get advantages in marketing ROI. People like to look at content and also share it if they like it, but the impact on revenues has been limited. The next section describes the puzzle of social media.

SOCIAL MEDIA PUZZLE

Social media has found multiple uses: communication, collaboration, education, entertainment, sharing content, seeking advice and even searching for products and opinions. It is already redefining the way people live and do business. However, marketing on social media still remains a riddle.

Consumers have migrated to social media in a big way and so have businesses. It is estimated that social media ad spend by brands was over $36 billion in 2017. According to the CMO Survey (2017), companies are now spending 10.5 per cent of their budgets on social media, which is expected to increase in the future. It is a common belief that social media is the medium of the future; companies can ignore it at their own peril.

However, social media has failed to meet earlier projections according to the survey. It shows that companies do not know how to manage social media: many companies still manage social media as a separate activity. The average level of integration of a company's marketing strategy with social media was found to be only 3.9 on a scale of 7. Vizard (2017) writes that companies consistently overestimate how much of their budget they will spend on social media as they struggle to integrate it with the rest of their strategy.

Although social media is a unique source of customer intelligence and feedback, research does not find evidence that following a brand on social media changes people's purchasing behaviour. As a consequence, companies are cutting down on their social media spends. For example, in 2017 (Bruell and Terlep 2017), P&G cut $140 million in digital ad spend (see Marketing Insight 6.2). Other companies have also experienced similar concerns. Digital ad spends, though expected at one time to overtake print and TV advertising, are still just a fraction of traditional advertising. A social media strategy is needed to unravel this puzzle. The strategies that have been followed on social media are described further.

MARKETING INSIGHT 6.2   *P&G Cuts $140 Million in Digital Ad Spend*

Consumer goods giant P&G and the biggest advertiser in the USA has reported that it cut approximately $100 million to $140 million in digital advertising spend in the last quarter of 2017. Johnson (2017) writes that the reasons given were related to brand safety and ineffective ads. The company experienced fake traffic driven by bots and objectionable content, leading to the decision to pull back on its online advertising spending. The company says that its move to cut digital marketing spend had little impact on its growth rate, proving that those digital ads were largely ineffective.

Companies like P&G face challenges with regard to transparency with ads on social media. First, they wanted all platforms to provide independent measurement of the reach of the ads. Second, they found that ads were often placed next to objectionable material, giving the impression that the company endorsed that content.

P&G's CEO David Taylor stated that the ads suffered because they were not effective and were actually giving the company a bad name. The outcome: pull out of social media. Discarding the formula of advertising spend or share of the voice, the company now wants all its messages to add value to its stakeholders in some way.

However, some of P&G online campaigns have been quite effective. Its personal care brand Always used YouTube and other platforms for its 'Like a Girl' campaign (Figure 6.2). It helped the company to associate itself with a social cause and was highly successful (see Opening Case).

Why did P&G cut its digital ad spend? What could they have done?

Sources

Bruell, A., and S. Terlep. 2017. 'P&G Cuts More than $100 Million in "Largely Ineffective" Digital Ads.' *The Wall Street Journal* (27 July). Available at: https://www.wsj.com/articles/p-g-cuts-more-than—100-million-in-largely-ineffective-digital-ads—1501191104 (accessed on 20 January 2021).

Johnson, L. 2017. 'Procter & Gamble Cut Up to $140 Million in Digital Ad Spending Because of Brand Safety Concerns.' *Adweek* (28 July). Available at: http://www.adweek.com/digital/procter-gamble-cut—140-million-in-digital-ad-spending-because-of-brand-safety-concerns/ (accessed on 20 January 2021).

(Continued)

(Continued)

FIGURE 6.2 *The #likeagirl Campaign Connected with a Social Cause*

Source: https://www.youtube.com/watch?v=XjJQBjWYDTs (accessed on 21 January 2021).

SOCIAL MEDIA STRATEGIES

Social media strategies can take many forms. Fulgoni (2015) calls them the 'Five S's of Social Marketing':

- Social media as a supplement to media spend
- Social media as a substitute for media spend
- Social media as a saviour (for dying or niche brands, non-profits)
- Social media as a soft metric of effectiveness
- Social media as a sales driver

We discuss these strategies in this section.

Social Media as a Supplement to Media Spend

Companies use social media either to generate buzz about something they are doing or as a supplement to their offline advertising.

The first method is to use traditional media to encourage online interaction. Since TV still remains the medium for generating high reach in a very short period of time, such advertising helps the company to encourage online users as well. That is why many online brands have to use traditional channels. Social amplification complements traditional advertising reach.

The second approach consists of using social media to build awareness of the campaign to a level where TV coverage is earned. For example, when an idea or a campaign becomes viral, TV channels are forced to cover it. That is why brands use humour or celebrities hoping that they are entertaining enough for TV to cover. Paid social media is used to encourage earned and owned social communications with the logic 'start a fire and then rely on our social tribes to fan the flames'.

Social Media as a Substitute for Media Spend

Many companies, non-profits and small businesses use social media as a substitute for media spend to avoid the high cost of advertising. People selling hobby products such as home-made cakes and candles use social media as a substitute for traditional advertising. Innovative campaigns help such businesses reach their target audience cheaply. It is quite effective for NGOs and non-profits as it attracts people who identify with the cause. For example, the US Navy used social media to recruit 1,291 cryptologists. It designed an alternative reality game to connect with cryptology minds who could try and solve the puzzle. It used Facebook, Twitter, Instagram and Tumblr to send out a series of clues, tips and updates. These were shared widely, helping the earned media to amplify the campaign. Facebook Analytics, the campaign, reached 113,494 unique individuals without any use of any paid media. However, such a strategy works only for niche marketing.

Social Media as a Saviour

Social media is sometimes used as a means of reviving a dying brand. Such brands can target niche targets and ensure a steady business, where using traditional media can be very expensive. For example, the Immigrant Council of Ireland used the dating app Tinder to raise awareness of sex trafficking. The campaign created a number of fake profiles of women on Tinder. The first profile picture was that of a normal girl, which interested men to click on it, and the subsequent photos proceeded to tell a story of an abused woman.

Social Media as a Metric of Marketing Spends

Advertising effectiveness can be measured directly on social media. Companies keep track of likes, retweets, posts, shares and impressions to know how popular a post is. But these metrics are useful only if no other promotional elements are used. For measures of brand impact on sales performance, social media metrics are not of much help since they are used in combination with other media. At the same time, the simple measure of the number of followers or friends is not a reflection of the true popularity of a brand.

Paid social media advertising can be measured more accurately because a social media platform is able to identify the consumers who were exposed to a paid piece of communication. Cookies can track consumers who are exposed to a paid social message by identifying their in-store buying through retailer loyalty cards or other methods.

Social Media as a Sales Driver

Social media has the potential to help in sales. Since it is a means of two-way communication with customers, all aspects of personal selling and sales management can be used. Importantly, social media is not limited to technologies available for public consumption such as Facebook, LinkedIn, Twitter, Google+ , Pinterest and others but also includes internal social media and network tools being offered by Salesforce.com and other companies.

Andzulis, Panagopoulos and Rapp (2012) write that every stage in the sales cycle and every tactic can be affected by social media—understanding the customer, sales approach, needs discovery, presentation, closing and follow-up—can be influenced through social media. Figure 6.3 shows the evolution of social media as used in the sales process.

Social media channels are now used for various sales functions. Safko and Brake (2009) suggest some ways which social media helps in.

- Knowing customers and building strong relationship with them
- Tracking preferences and needs, and knowing their beliefs
- Creating a channel of communication and solving problems for customers
- Educating customers about the use or value of products and services
- Interaction with customers and seeking their recommendations
- Delivering sales promotion offers and implementing loyalty schemes
- Mitigating crisis situations by quelling rumours
- Salespeople can build rapport, answer queries, gain the prospect's attention and introduce themselves to customers

However, the real power of social media lies in sales prediction. If companies know when customers will require products, they can make targeted offers. Indeed, such models are being developed. Kumar et al. (2006) describe a mathematical model that predicts consumer behaviour, and 'the odds of successfully predicting a specific purchase by a specific customer at a specific time to about 80%'. Davenport, Mule and Lucker (2011) say that advances in IT and data analytics can help companies make 'highly customized offers that steer shoppers to the "right" merchandise at the right moment, at the right price, and in the right channel'. Such a system can help reduce the advertising spend and impact marketing ROI positively. At the same time, companies can reduce the number of times they contact a customer since over-communication is an irritant.

The contribution of social media in sales is described further.

1. **Lead generation and prospecting:** Using social media, salespersons can gather contact information of a customer that helps in lead generation and prospecting. Sales professionals can research accounts prior to meeting and gather recent news and happenings about prospects. They can listen to customers, monitor issues, answer questions and concerns, and establish rapport before making the sales pitch.

FIGURE 6.3 *Evolution on Social Media in Sales*

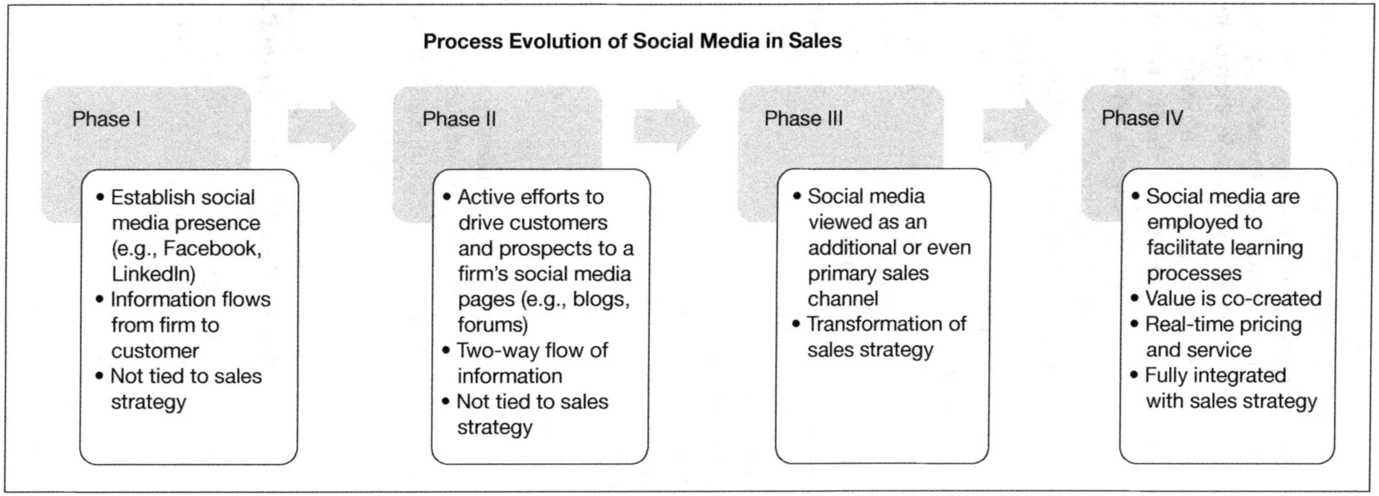

Process Evolution of Social Media in Sales

Phase I
- Establish social media presence (e.g., Facebook, LinkedIn)
- Information flows from firm to customer
- Not tied to sales strategy

Phase II
- Active efforts to drive customers and prospects to a firm's social media pages (e.g., blogs, forums)
- Two-way flow of information
- Not tied to sales strategy

Phase III
- Social media viewed as an additional or even primary sales channel
- Transformation of sales strategy

Phase IV
- Social media are employed to facilitate learning processes
- Value is co-created
- Real-time pricing and service
- Fully integrated with sales strategy

Source: Andzulis et al. (2012).

2. **Approach:** Salespeople can approach customers on social media in a variety of ways. They can build trust by meeting the small needs of a customer, sharing links, responding to requests or answering queries and thereby building a reputation for being responsive and caring. For example, Salesforce.com has an application called 'Faceconnector', which helps in finding shared interests with customers and building relationships. Networking events can be shared on networking sites. CRM data are dynamically updated from personal data posted on profiles.

3. **Building CRM:** Every interaction on social media is part of CRM. It is used to establish trust and build relationships by being open and transparent. The company must however break departmental barriers and reduce bureaucracy, learn to be responsive and present a unified picture across different departments. Further, the sales effort can be supplemented with real-time feedback from other customers, competitors and experts. A company must offer information, enable reviews from other customers and build trust.

4. **Presentations:** Presentations are enhanced as prospects' comments can be incorporated, leading to quick resolution and shortening of sales cycles. Social media can be used to supplement presentations. A firm and its client can work together to arrive at solutions, rather than delivering a one-sided proposal to a customer. The presentation process becomes much richer and its contents become the shared work of both sides.

5. **Closing and follow-up:** Sales close is facilitated as the salesperson can overcome objections and clarify the terms on social apps. Testimonials can be sent and customers can be contacted, and the close can be expedited by interacting at various points in the CDJ. Sales follow-up and customer service are helped by two-way communication on social media, referrals are made and opportunities for cross-selling and upselling are uncovered.

Companies use these and other methods to engage users on social media. All of these must fall into a comprehensive social media strategy. A number of companies offer tools that are helpful in business (Marketing Insight 6.3). All of these are not stand-alone but must fall within a social media strategy which is discussed next.

MARKETING INSIGHT 6.3 *Social Media Tools for Businesses*

Social media tools are required to create or post content. Forbes Agency Council (2017) lists the best social media management tools that can help a company make the most of its social presence.

1. **Buffer:** Buffer helps schedule and manage social media posts across platforms, and each post can be individually customized for different platforms. It also shares content at the best possible times throughout the day and tracks links to make visible the content that gets the most traction.

2. **Content calendar:** A content calendar can be created in Google Docs or Microsoft Word. It allows for scheduled releases and newsletter blasts.

3. **Google Analytics:** Google Analytics helps manage social media and provides data that are helpful in driving traffic to platforms. Google Analytics is used to calculate traffic and conversions, as well as ROI on marketing ad spends.

4. **Hootsuite:** Hootsuite allows users to schedule posts across all major platforms. It has a robust training platform that teaches how to think about social marketing as a whole.

5. **Hoover's Connect:** Hoover's Connect is a database of companies and contacts, and links it to a company's own extended network. Hoover's Connect traces the strength of relationships and the optimal path to reach a prospect.

6. **HubSpot:** HubSpot helps companies to publish and monitor reporting data that track the most productive channels and also track the posts drive actual sales leads.

7. **Iconosquare:** Iconosquare provides analytics to monitor the content of multiple accounts in one place, scheduling posts.

8. **IFTTT:** 'If This Then That' (IFTTT) helps manage social media platforms, apps and websites. It links services together to generate a trigger-based action. For example, if a company creates or publishes a blog, which becomes the trigger, then IFTTT will automatically create a tweet.

9. **KnowEm:** KnowEm allows companies to check the username or brand name over 500 social media websites.

10. **MeetEdgar:** MeetEdgar uses machine learning (ML) to read through brand content and generate social media updates, saving time.

11. **Raven:** Raven provides reports from PPC, SEO and social media channels. It also allows a company to access data and schedule posts on digital media channels.

12. **Social Report:** Social Report helps to track the performance of social media pages on a simple dashboard.

13. **SocialFlow:** SocialFlow analyses user behaviour and optimizes each post based on real-time data to predict the best time for publishing content. Posts are thus optimized for time, relevance and audience.

14. **Sprinklr:** Sprinklr is a management tool for all social channels, providing help for posting and metrics reporting.

15. **Sprout Social:** With Sprout Social, companies can monitor clients' social media mentions and engage with brand advocates. It also helps tool to streamline real-time communication.

16. **TweetDeck:** TweetDeck allows companies to follow several conversations on Twitter and schedule content.

17. **Klout:** Klout provides ratings on online social influence based on analytics. The 'Klout Score' measures the social media network and correlates the content created with the way users interact with it.

18. **ReadyPulse:** ReadyPulse enables companies to find the best influencers and user-generated content on social networks and helps to amplify these to promote products.

How many of these are useful? Can you think of a service for social media interaction?

(Continued)

(Continued)

Source

Forbes Agency Council. 2017. '15 Social Media Management Tools That Can Help Your Business Thrive.' Available at: https://www.forbes.com/sites/forbesagencycoun cil/2017/05/15/15-social-media-management-tools-that-can-help-your-business-thrive/#51747b952b13 (accessed on 20 January 2021).

■ SOCIAL MEDIA STRATEGY

Social media strategy is tricky as companies must find ways to intervene in the online conversations that customers have with each other. Very often, social media interventions are made without considering the impact on marketing, but an approach that focuses on marketing ROI is recommended. Moorman, Ross and Gorman (2014) explain the elements of strategy in using social media.

- **Influence CDJs:** Any social media strategy must take the customer on a decision-making journey. If it does not do this, it may be better to give it a miss.
- **Clear objectives:** Social media must be used with a specific objective. If building brand advocacy is the objective, for example, companies must have a strategy to use opinion leaders to amplify the company's message and increase customer loyalty.
- **Social media toolkits:** Just as companies have brand toolkits, they should create social media toolkits that include templates for Facebook and Twitter posts. These kits help to create a more cohesive brand image across platforms.
- **Integrate social media with brand teams:** The most successful social campaigns are executed by marketing people who understand brands (see Opening Case on Maersk). Otherwise, social media and marketing strategy often work in different directions.
- **Conversion to purchase:** Social media is a key touch point that can influence purchase. A metric about the contribution to sales revenue must be integrated with the company's marketing strategy.
- **Experiment:** It is much easier to experiment with social media since the execution costs are small. By doing this, companies can more accurately determine which social media posts and campaigns have the greatest impact on their marketing strategies. Using influencers (Marketing Insight 6.4) is a strategy by which impressions and sales are achieved.

A list of the market functions that are included in the social media strategy are shown in Table 6.3. They can be a source of competitive advantage if companies go beyond likes, mentions and shares. The use of generating crowd interest shows that it can be an effective tool to expand marketing reach.

TABLE 6.3 *Social Media Strategy and Marketing Functions*

Marketing Function	Traditional Approach	Social Media Approach
New product development	In-house by company's R&D	Customers contribute product ideas
Positioning	Created by company	Created and shared by customers
Market research	Surveys	Data mining
Targeting	Mass media campaigns	Customized communication
Content	Company created	Customer created

MARKETING INSIGHT 6.4   *Exploiting the Power of Influencer Marketing*

In the times of social media, companies look for people with huge followings on social sites such as Instagram or YouTube and try to get them to adopt the brand, write about it and post pictures and videos, hoping that the followers will also start buying the brand. Apart from celebrities, brands are now hiring popular bloggers and social media stars to sell their products.

Influencer marketing has emerged as an important marketing method on social media. It is defined as the use of people with a high following on social media to drive a brand's message, that is, some people are motivated to adopt a product or brand, and others are influenced to buy the brand by seeing them use it. Agrawal (2016) writes that celebrity influencers or the ones with many followers have more power because they get people's attention. Fashion brands and jewellers have for decades provided free dresses or jewellery items for film stars, knowing their pictures will influence their fans. Similarly, influencers are used to flaunt brands to get others to buy them.

Influencers do not market directly to consumers. Instead, they post content on their channels that will help the brand to spread its message to their followers. Influencer marketing consists of using two elements: social media marketing and content marketing.

Influencers spread the word through their own personal social channels and are therefore thought to be more effective than other forms of digital advertising. Key individuals are paid to leverage their influence among their followers. It is different from WOM marketing where consumers spread messages about a brand, and also from advocate marketing, which aims to encourage loyal customers to share their love of brand or product.

Influencers may be customers, but they are actually people who have achieved large following on social media. They are trusted by their followers who seek their advice and suggestions. Some influencers are known to charge large amounts of money from brands to promote their content. An influencer strategy consists of the following:

- Identifying important influencers in a particular field
- Engaging influencers to use the brand or paying them to promote the brand online
- Creating a secondary marketing campaign with influencers to drive greater awareness
- Tracking key metrics of sales influencer or brand awareness

(Continued)

(Continued)

Since the followers of influencers trust them, brands can gain, following through them, a targeted and interested audience. The strategy also bypasses ad-blocking software and is more effective than online ads.

Social media influencers exist on all social platforms. They also write on specialist sites and blogs on fashion, athletics, entertainment, fishing, yoga and spirituality. Brand Equity (2017b) reports that, thanks to the blossoming of Instagram, fashion is increasingly being marketed through influencers. Some fashion influencers have a few million followers each, with brands paying more than $200,000 per post. Collaborations between big brands and influencers are expected to increase in the future.

Instagram has created a new class of marketing that sees brands investing heavily in collaborations with big names in the online space. Companies report an extreme pull effect for products through digital influencers, making the brand accessible to a larger audience. It is better than the promoted content, which may be ignored by the audience. For their part, influencers have to be selective because the audience can easily reject them if they promote bad products or if they are seen to be too commercial. They have to make sure that the products are good and that they align with the style and thought process of the channel.

Influencer marketing tends to blur the lines between ads and posts that have caught the attention of government regulatory agencies. Roberts (2017) reports that such endorsements are seen as 'sneaky' and the Federal Trade Commission of the USA is cracking down on such campaigns. It wants the 'influencers' to clearly disclose when they are pushing a product and has asked prominent Instagram users to 'clearly and conspicuously disclose their relationships to brands'. Mega influencer Kim Kardashian, who regularly endorses products on Instagram, was the subject of a complaint in 2015 over an endorsement for a morning sickness drug for not disclosing her post as a sponsored ad. Other countries may well follow suit.

Should influencers be treated as other forms of advertising and be subject to disclosures?

Sources

Agrawal, A. J. 2016. 'Why Influencer Marketing Will Explode in 2017.' *Forbes* (27 December). Available at: https://www.forbes.com/sites/ajagrawal/2016/12/27/why-influencer-marketing-will-explode-in–2017/#2e4b458520a9 (accessed on 20 January 2021).

Brand Equity. 2017a. 'How "Influencer Marketing" Is Swiftly Taking Over the World.' *The Economic Times*, 27 May. Available at: https://brandequity.economictimes.indiatimes.com/news/marketing/how-influencer-marketing-is-swiftly-taking-over-the-world/58863920 (accessed on 20 January 2021).

———. 2017b. 'Trend Spot: Fashion re#tagged.' *The Economic Times*, 27 November. Available at: https://brandequity.economictimes.indiatimes.com/news/business-of-brands/trend-spot-fashion-retagged/61843121 (accessed on 20 January 2021).

Roberts, J. J. 2017. 'The FTC Says Celebrity Social Media Ads Are Still Too Sneaky.' *Fortune* (20 April). Available at: http://fortune.com/2017/04/20/ftc-instagram/ (accessed on 20 January 2021).

CROWD CULTURES AND MARKETING

In the world of social media, the content created by the company is unwelcome. But if people can somehow be motivated to associate themselves with a brand and post content, it would be more acceptable to users and their communities. Branding efforts on social media have very little pay-offs, writes Holt (2016). He writes that the answer is 'cultural branding' or *crowd culture*, which involves authentic content created by people rather than by brands. Crowd culture develops when people in online communities share their personal experiences with brands. Slowly, other people are attracted to the stories and communities are built around brands. It becomes a kind of shared culture based on the shared beliefs of people with respect to a brand or a company.

Brands succeed when they become part of crowd culture when people share stories and experiences with their online groups. Getting associated with a social cause helps: it attracts people and creates a kind of a brand subculture. But the task is not easy since very few of the social media posts relate to brands. This can be seen by the fact that people follow celebrities in hordes, but few brands have that kind of following.

The challenge before brands is to associate with a trend and build a community around it, involving people. Micro-cultures such as sports, movies, music and social causes can be used to build such communities and hope that they become big enough to be of use to mass market brands. Great care has to be exercised because the overt use of celebrities or trends can also backfire.

To get people to talk about a brand on social media, the brand idea must appeal emotionally to people and be meaningful to them. Campaigns that are remembered and shared are made around a social cause and have an emotional creative execution. Such ads touch people's hearts, and that becomes a reason for sharing with their friends.

The method is effective both in B2C and B2B realms as crowd culture makes people feel connected to companies. That is why companies need to look at ways to implement crowd cultures effectively. Done properly, kit becomes a powerful PR tool.

BUILDING STRONG COMMUNITIES AND CUSTOMER BASE

Building communities is important because more and more people are being influenced by their friends and peers. Consumers today tend to ignore traditional sales and marketing communications but turn to online communities. The importance of communities is reflected in the fact that many members become advocate for brands. They 'create peer influence in their markets, and make important contributions in areas like product development', explains Lee (2013). He describes four levels of customer relations (see Figure 6.4). Communities help customers at level 4, that is, of building their social capital by engaging them in support groups and making them feel part of a meaningful community.

Communities are able to build fierce brand loyalty. They also contribute to collective innovation that helps companies build new product and service experiences. Instead of

FIGURE 6.4 *Four Levels of Customer Engagement*

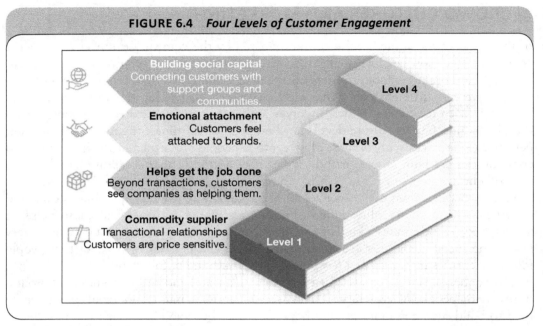

Source: Adapted from Lee (2013).

being passive consumers, they contribute value to companies. Blasingame (2017) writes that users have no incentive to visit a company's website repeatedly, but if they join its community, they give permission to connect with other users and with the company. It also implies that they are open to messages through direct messages and social media. This permission is used to send updated content and links that may trigger return to the website again.

Kozinets, Hemetsberger and Schau (2008) describe four types of online consumer communities: crowds, hives, mobs and swarms. The online communities are described below.

- **Crowds:** Crowds are large groups of people who are attracted to a certain cause or activity. They collaborate on projects, but there is less of collective innovation. When properly motivated, they can be used to generate content or ideas for ads, or they can contribute towards social causes.
- **Hives:** Hives refer to online communities formed for a specific goal. These groups are small in size but high in skill and can produce innovations or get involved with other creative projects. The development of open-source software is an example of hives. Hives can also produce content such as videos or podcasts that are shared widely to gain mass audiences. For example, Nike has a community 'Niketalk', which is 'The Ultimate Sneaker Enthusiast Community' with forums, a lounge and profile posts. Users post their shoe designs, discuss them, participate in design contests and thus help in co-creation.

- **Mobs:** Mobs have a focus on a product. They can create content for it. Coffee lovers, for instance, have their own community online and provide ideas for new product offerings. Such online communities are valuable as they provide innovative ideas for companies.
- **Swarms:** Swarms occur naturally and can contribute to finding solutions. When a large number of people with different expertise get together for a common purpose and follow simple rules of engagement, it is called a swarm. Benkler (2006) describes this as 'social production' in which groups take part in peer production. Swarms operate in high numbers, and companies can do well to make use of their collective intelligence. Bonabeau and Meyer (2001) write that rigorous mathematical models have been developed to understand and use 'swarm intelligence', and they are now being applied to business, helping companies solve diverse tasks.

Such communities develop by themselves. Companies can make use of them if they help users become part of culture to engage in communal creativity. At best, companies can create platforms or enable technologies within an ecosystem in which communities thrive. Fisher (2019) writes that companies can gain a distinct competitive advantage from engaging with online communities.

Online communities have three dimensions: *participants*, meaning who should join the online community; *platforms*, showing where they interact; and *purpose*, explaining why users should join the community. Companies need to address all three aspects. Online communities provide reviews and feedback, give suggestions for product development and engage in co-creation.

Another aspect of communities is that they build a check for companies if they are not acting ethically, responsibly or against the public interest. Communities form suddenly against such practices and are instrumental in spreading negative publicity. Companies therefore need to track community activities as they have the potential to harm the image of the brands. Social media and communities have thus emerged as powerful tools for PR.

■ LEVERAGING SOCIAL MEDIA FOR PUBLIC RELATIONS

Since it involves people, social media is effective in generating PR activities as well. Companies and their ad agencies exploit this new form of communication by involving the company's base of followers and associates. Brands use this method to project their human face. However, the old ways of PR—posting press releases—do not work. Companies have to learn to communicate with social media natives in an interesting and informal way; otherwise, they will not be noticed.

The Internet has made PR public again after years of almost exclusive focus on media. Scott (2015) writes, 'the old rules of marketing and PR are ineffective in an online world' and that most resources spent on advertising are waste. In the online world, people want to be connected through three strategies.

- **Entertain me:** PR and marketing efforts should entertain users in some way.
- **Help me:** Communication should provide some utility to the user.
- **Love me:** PR efforts should result in developing loyalty and advocacy.

To be successful, PR content must have the following qualities.

- **Inspirational:** Content that makes people think positively is always welcome. Companies use relevant quotes, beautiful images and pleasant influencers to be inspirational.
- **Educational:** Content that shares the expertise that people can use is a welcome problem-solver for many. Companies add tips and tricks, video trainings and answers to common questions so that users can find value in it.
- **Conversational:** Content should be conversational in style so that users are drawn towards it.
- **Connection:** Product reviews, travel photos, lifestyle, events and team description serve to establish connections with users.
- **Promotional:** Schemes encouraging trials or purchase are very effective on social media. Customers can be given coupons or be asked to participate in competitions. This works in getting new people into the community.

Above all, the content has to be authentic because marketing hype is easily recognized and rejected. Communications have to be genuine. Attempts must be made to involve users in communications. Companies have to listen, respond, help and converse, and draw users into the purchasing process with a content strategy built around online content. All methods, such as blogs, videos, e-books, multimedia and others, have a direct impact on users. Everything has to be used so that people share and connect.

Much can be achieved by short and brief interjections, just the way human conversations are conducted. Companies seek a multiplier effect: By using paid media in conjunction with PR activities, the WOM can spread far and wide.

▓ INTEGRATING SOCIAL MEDIA WITH PAID MARKETING

Companies have discovered that social media can be used effectively if it is supplemented with paid marketing to spark online conversations that can positively influence brands and sales revenue. De Vries, Gensler and Leeflang (2017) show that traditional advertising is still relevant and that it is most effective for both brand building and customer acquisition. Hewett et al. (2016) write that traditional media news stories, online WOM and firm communications all echo one another in an 'echoverse'. Firms must manage the echoverse to get the desired business outcomes.

A study by Kumar et al. (2016) found that the synergistic benefits of using TV advertising with social media are quite substantial. They find a strong synergy between firm-generated content with both TV advertising and email marketing. John et al. (2017) write, 'The mere act of liking a brand on Facebook does not affect a customer's behavior or increase purchasing, nor does it spur purchasing by friends.' They offer a method that can be used along with social media: They found that users who liked a page were more likely to take meaningful action if they were shown paid posts and advertisements as compared to those in a control group. Supporting likes with branded content, however, could prompt meaningful behaviour change. That is to say, pull marketing efforts via social media are quite ineffective and must be supported by push marketing.

Evans and McKee (2010) explain that social media can be used effectively if three elements are executed simultaneously.

- **Engagement:** Companies have to introduce initiatives that encourage customer engagement.
- **Integration:** The company must integrate operations, service and marketing functions to create experiences both online and offline. The Social Feedback Cycle (Figure 6.5), which shows the loop that connects the past CX with the consideration stage of the next one, shows that integration across departments is essential.
- **Collaboration:** Social media encourages collaboration between a company and all its stakeholders, including customers, employees and dealers. It is an active link that encourages everyone to participate in the business (see Closing Case on My Starbucks).

FIGURE 6.5 *The Social Feedback Cycle*

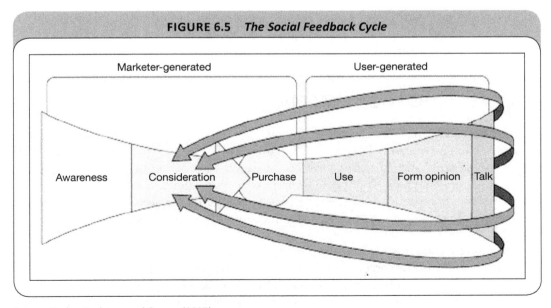

Source: Burby, Atchison and Sterne (2007).

A study by Stacey, Pauwels and Lackman (2013) found that marketing actions with small direct effects can have large total effects by stimulating social media conversations. Among the conversation topics, 'love for the brand' had larger long-term traffic effects, but neutral conversations on 'went there/purchased' drove traffic in the short run.

To encourage WOM, companies have to invest in SCRM, which yields long-term benefits for a company and goes beyond transactional or data-based CRM.

SOCIAL CRM

SCRM is the process of building long-term relationships with customers and engagement through social networking sites. SCRM integrates social media platforms with CRM systems to improve customer interactions with a brand. A detailed discussion on SCRM is included in Chapter 3.

Goldenberg (2015) describes several ways to incorporate SCRM in a company. It consists of:

1. Measuring traffic, brand mentions and conversions
2. Social listening and engagement
3. Establishing and managing private communities
4. Fostering collaboration between channels and partners
5. Enterprise collaboration, co-creation and customer suggestions
6. Dealing with negative comments and feedback

SCRM and other activities on social media must be backed with measuring their effectiveness. Companies must get adequate returns from it. In the next section, we describe the social media ROI measures for measurement of activity for its effectiveness.

MEASURING SOCIAL MEDIA ROI

Social media ROI must go beyond getting fans or views—what is of real value is in the quality of the engagement. Hoffman and Fodor (2010) suggest that returns from social media investments should not always be measured in revenue generated but also in changes in user behaviour. Changes in awareness levels or increase in WOM publicity are also beneficial for a company. Social media ROI can thus be measured by two approaches: measuring volume and reach, and second, measuring engagement and quality.

- **Measuring volume and reach:** This aspect measures the number of followers and penetration in the target market and includes the following.
  - **Number of fans and followers:** This measure gives a broad estimate of the number of people connected with the brand on social media sites, which shows how successful the brand of interest is for the target audience.

o **Brand volume:** This refers to the number of times the brand is mentioned by people. This is a broad indicator showing the engagement of people with the brand.

o **YouTube views:** This refers to the number of people viewing the company's YouTube channel or the videos posted by it.

However, volume and reach metrics are not enough because the number of fans and followers may or may not translate into company revenues. Deeper metrics are required.

- **Measuring engagement and quality:** This measurement shows the quality of interaction of the brand with potential customers. The typical engagement/quality metrics are as follows.
  o **Brand conversation:** The number of times a brand is being talked about as well as positive comments and replies on the main social profiles.
  o **Content dissemination:** A metric that shows the number of times that people have shared brand content and how brands have engaged with their audience. This includes retweets on Twitter, the number of brand posts or shares on Facebook and the number of shares of videos of the brand channel on YouTube.
  o **Overall sentiment:** Positive comments minus negative comments.

SOCIAL MEDIA METRICS

A social media dashboard shows engagement metrics from multiple platforms on a single screen. Data from Facebook, Twitter, LinkedIn, Instagram and other sites are collected and shown in real time. Tools such as Brandwatch, Facebook Insights and Google Analytics help provide insights, but the idea is to put it all together into one dashboard (Figure 6.6).

Once data are collected, companies can calculate the marketing ROI, which is a calculation of the revenues generated from an activity minus the marketing costs incurred. Raab (2011) writes that new metrics are needed, such as response tracking, quality of audience, content analysis, traffic analysis and influence measurement.

Kumar et al. (2010) suggest calculating the metric of *customer's engagement value* (CEV) which is the sum of four components: CLV, *customer referral value* (CRV), *customer influence value* (CIV) and *customer knowledge value* (CKV), expressed as follows:

$$CEV = CLV + CIV + CRV + CKV$$

- **CLV:** CLV shows the total financial revenues earned from a customer over his or her entire lifetime with the company minus costs. It is a measure of the lifetime profitability gained from a customer relationship.
- **CIV:** A measure of customers' influence on other customers and prospects. It reflects the value of WOM activity of a user which persuades and converts prospects

FIGURE 6.6 *An Example of Social Media Dashboard**

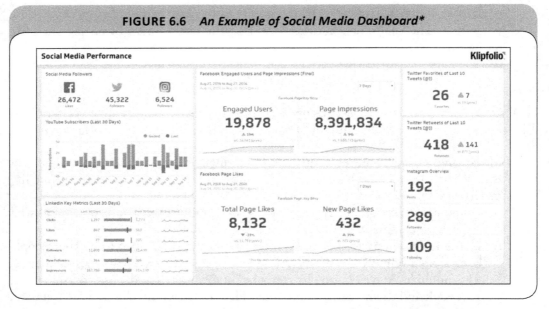

Source: https://www.klipfolio.com/resources/dashboard-examples/social-media (accessed on 16 February 2021).

Note: *It shows mentions and activity on social media in real time.

to customers. CIV is calculated by adding the influencer's own purchases plus the business attributable to him of the purchase value of his or her followers. Through CIV, influencers can be ranked on the basis of earnings influenced by them.

- **CRV:** CRV is the value of each customer's referrals of new customers. It includes the average number of successful referrals that the customer makes.
- **CKV:** Customers add value to the company by helping others to understand the product and answer their queries, and also participate in the knowledge development process by co-creation. This is represented by CKV, which adds value to a company's service creation and delivery.

To measure social media ROI, Kumar and Mirchandani (2012) suggest three metrics: *customer influence effect* (CIE), *stickiness index* (SI) and CIV.

These components are explained below.

- **CIE:** CIE represents the influence of an individual on another user/s regarding a particular product category.
- **SI:** The SI measures the activity of users who like to talk about the product or brand. It matches an influential individual to a particular category: for instance, a user who discusses desserts and milkshakes is likely to like ice cream also. SI helps to identify (a) the number of social media users in the region who actively discuss ice cream and (b) other categories that people who discussed ice cream frequently talked about.

TRACKING NEGATIVE STORIES

An invaluable role played by social media is the monitoring of negative and harmful comments posted by users. Since social media multiplies the reach of a customer sharing a bad experience, the impact on business can be great. Companies need to track the negative comments and, more importantly, respond to them to control the damage. There is also the issue of brand sabotage, which is deliberately launched to harm a brand by some disgruntled groups.

Kahr et al. (2016) write that social media monitoring and CRM systems can quickly detect the imminent outbreak of brand sabotage. Companies can use big data analysis to monitor sentiments in real time, which can track words containing hatred, frustration and hostile thoughts. Close monitoring of social media can alert companies about negative comments to imminent sabotage attacks so that they can take quick action to manage the crisis.

Many companies set up social media command centres that track consumer comments and sentiments in real time (see Marketing Insight 6.5). These centres track all social media sites, monitor all brand mentions wherever they occur and display them on giant screens. Teams can visually analyse comments from thousands of users at a glance. Negative comments, for instance, are shown as red dots and positive comments as green dots. When such dots accumulate on a particular area, a company immediately comes to know about a building trend.

The challenge is to respond to these comments in real time and not let the damage spread. Companies must answer queries and complaints as they occur; any delay will tend to increase the negative sentiment.

MARKETING INSIGHT 6.5 *Social Media Command Centres*

Growing numbers of global companies such as Gatorade, Dell and Nestle have built multi-million-dollar mission control centres for social media, writes Holmes (2012). These are dedicated hubs for monitoring and responding to social media comments and queries, displaying real-time statistics and indicators, tracking consumer sentiment and displaying social media market share.

Dell has a social media command centre in Texas that tracks comments made on different forums and answers complaints. Gatorade's social command centre tracks how products are received by consumers. The Red Cross has found a unique use of social media: to reach out to victims during natural disasters.

Nestle has a Digital Acceleration Team (DAT) at its headquarters in Vevey, Switzerland. It tracks online sentiment to show how people respond to its brands. Its employees manage communities and track the company's global brands. Hackathons and team projects are conducted to help them learn and to use 'digital vitamins' in marketing. The DAT uses four principles: *listen*, *engage*, *transform* and *inspire*. It has a social content management system

---

(Continued)

(Continued)

(CMS) with tools such as Buddy Media (Salesforce), Vitrue (Oracle) and Wildfire (Google) to monitor social media. DATs have been established in India, Italy, China and other countries.

Command centres monitor millions of social conversations from Facebook, Twitter, YouTube, LinkedIn, blogs and others.

What benefits do social media command centres generate for companies?

Source

Holmes, R. 2012. 'NASA-style Mission Control Centers for Social Media Are Taking Off.' *Fortune* (25 October). Available at: http://fortune.com/2012/10/25/nasa-style-mission-control-centers-for-social-media-are-taking-off/ (accessed on 20 January 2021).

CONCLUSION

There is little doubt that companies have to use social media in their marketing efforts. Although consumers reject commercial overtures as they engage with each other, a successful strategy consists of 'seeding' social endorsements.

Social media strategy can be gained by traditional advertising, which still remains an effective medium to build brand and customer acquisitions. Traditional advertising encourages C2C conversations and will stimulate preference. The volume of such conversations stimulates customer acquisitions. Social messages must complement traditional advertising. Thus, integrating traditional advertising and social messages must be a firm's strategy. Social media thus has a multiplier effect on the firm's marketing efforts. Companies must take care to not abandon traditional or other forms of advertising because these have substantial synergies between them.

SUMMARY

Social media is a powerful force of marketing in the digital era, but it is not just a broadcast channel or a sales and marketing tool. Social media not only allows companies to hear what people say but also enables them to respond. There is thus a paradigm shift in marketing. Companies have to understand how to get people involved with their brands on a platform that is essentially social, not commercial, and become social brands. Social media has been used for various purposes in marketing. It has been used as a supplement or a substitute to media spend, as a saviour by dying or niche brands, as a soft metric of effectiveness and sometimes as a sales driver.

To achieve marketing objectives, various social media tools are available from targeted ads and appvertising to building brand communities. The idea is to use paid, earned, shared and owned media. A social media strategy consists of engaging customers to influencer marketing. A successful strategy consists of supplementing social media marketing with paid marketing to spark online conversations that can positively influence brands and sales revenue. Three elements must be executed simultaneously: engagement, integration and collaboration, which lead to building SCRM.

It is also important to measure the effectiveness of marketing spends on social media through ROI calculations. This is shown by CEV which is the sum of four components: CLV, CRV, CIV and CKV.

Social media is also helpful in tracking and responding to negative stories and brand sabotage. For this, many companies set up social media command centres that track consumer comments and sentiments in real time. Data analytics help not only to know about consumers but also to predict what products and services people will need and when they will need them, which can lead to specific and targeted advertising.

KEY TERMS

Appvertising: Mobile application advertising that enables placing of ads inside phone applications through video ads, banners, surveys and so on.

Big data: Big data consist of the huge volumes of data that are being created by users as they use the Internet.

Crowdsourcing: The practice of obtaining information by enlisting the services of a large number of people via the Internet.

Influencer marketing: The use of people with a high number of followers on social media to drive a brand's message.

Predictive analytics: The practice of extracting information from existing data sets in order to determine patterns and predict future outcomes and trends.

Social brand: A brand or a company that is seen as a person on social media, creating content, connecting with its customers and having two-way conversations.

Social capital: The links, shared values and understandings in society that enable individuals and groups to trust each other and thus work together.

SCRM: SCRM is the process of building long-term relationships with customers and engagement through social networking sites.

Social media: The creation, sharing and exchanging of information and ideas on online social networks.

Targeted ads: Ads that are directed to specific and precise audiences.

WOM: An unpaid form of promotion in which satisfied customers tell other people how much they like a product or service.

CONCEPT REVIEW QUESTIONS

1. Explain the importance of social media in marketing. Why is it becoming an essential tool for marketing?

2. Describe the various social media platforms and explain how they could be used in marketing of products and services.
3. What is a social brand? Why is it necessary for brands to become social brands?
4. Describe social media strategies and explain how they have been used over the years for various functions.
5. What are the social media methods and tools available that companies can use in their marketing efforts?
6. What is influencer marketing? How does it work? Illustrate your answer with examples.
7. Explain the concept of SCRM. How does it help in marketing?
8. How can companies measure the benefits of using social media? What are the metrics available and how can the effectiveness of marketing campaigns be tracked?
9. Why is it necessary to integrate social media with paid marketing? Explain the synergy between the two.
10. Describe some of the social media metrics that are used to track effectiveness of social media marketing.

CRITICAL THINKING QUESTIONS

1. Most social media marketing ROI measure the number of likes, followers or shares of content that a brand is able to earn. Are these measures accurate? How can impact on sales revenue be measured? How can companies increase their social media ROI?
2. How should a social media marketing strategy be devised? What are the elements that should be included in this strategy?
3. Influencer marketing has gained huge traction in recent years. Should such posts be treated as conventional advertising? What kinds of disclosures or controls are needed? What should be the checks against influencers peddling wrong or harmful products?
4. What is SCRM? How is it different from traditional CRM? Do companies actually invest in SCRM? Give examples of companies doing SCRM and show how they are doing it.

PROJECTS AND ASSIGNMENTS

1. How can companies/brands transform themselves into social brands? How can they acquire human qualities? Take a brand that has successfully become a social brand and explain how it could change itself.
2. Conduct a research project on famous influencers in different categories of products. How did they gain influence and how are they using it for marketing? Also conduct

a survey in your class to find out how many of your classmates actually check for influencers' opinion.

3. Select a brand or company. Start following its social media pages. Write a paper to show what elements of social media marketing strategy they are using. Comment about their effectiveness in driving sales.

4. How is social media used by small businesses and non-profits in getting followers and supporters? Select a small business or a non-profit organization in your area and study how they use social media. Can you make any recommendations to them?

■ REFERENCES

Andzulis, J. M., N. G. Panagopoulos, and A. Rapp. 2012. 'A Review of Social Media and Implications for the Sales Process.' *Journal of Personal Selling & Sales Management* 32, no. 3 (Summer): 305–316.

Asano, E. 2017. 'How Much Time Do People Spend on Social Media?' *Social Media Today*, 4 January. Available at: http://www.socialmediatoday.com/marketing/how-much-time-do-people-spend-social-media-infographic (accessed on 21 January 2021).

Benkler, Y. 2006. *The Wealth of Networks—How Social Production Transforms Markets and Freedom.* London: Yale University Press. Available at: http://www.benkler.org (accessed on 21 January 2021).

Blasingame, J. 2017. 'The Power of Building Customer Communities.' *Forbes*, 7 May. Available at: https://www.forbes.com/sites/jimblasingame/2017/05/07/the-power-of-building-customer-communities/#1a4f3b64486c (accessed on 21 January 2021).

Bonabeau, E., and C. Meyer. 2001. 'Swarm Intelligence: A Whole New Way to Think about Business.' *Harvard Business Review* 79, no. 5 (June): 107–114.

Burby, J., S. Atchison, and J. Sterne. 2007. *The Changing Landscape of Marketing Online—Actionable Web Analytics.* Indianapolis, IN: John Wiley & Sons.

CMO Survey. 2017. 'Results: New and Archived Reports Containing CMO Survey Results and Insights.' Available at: https://cmosurvey.org/results/august-2017/ (accessed on 21 January 2021).

Davenport, T. H., L. D. Mule, and J. Lucker. 2011. 'Know What Your Customers Want before They Do.' *Harvard Business Review* 89, no. 12 (December). Available at: https://www.researchgate.net/publication/294366602_Know_what_your_customers_want_before_they_do (accessed on 21 January 2021).

DeMers, J. 2015. 'The 7 Most Important Qualities of Social Brands.' *Forbes*, 8 January. Available at: https://www.forbes.com/sites/jaysondemers/2015/01/08/the-7-most-important-qualities-of-social-brands/2/#65d6dc992f13 (accessed on 21 January 2021).

De Vries, L., S. Gensler, and P. S. H. Leeflang. 2017. 'Effects of Traditional Advertising and Social Messages on Brand-Building Metrics and Customer Acquisition.' *Journal of Marketing* 81 (September): 1–15. Available at: http://dx.doi.org/10.1509/jm.15.0178 (accessed on 21 January 2021).

Evans, D., and J. McKee. 2010. *Social Media Marketing.* Indianapolis, IN: John Wiley & Sons.

Fisher, G. 2019. 'Online Communities and Firm Advantages.' *Academy of Management Review* 44, no. 2. Available at: https://doi.org/10.5465/amr.2015.0290 (accessed on 21 January 2021).

Fulgoni, G. M. 2015. 'How Brands Using Social Media Ignite Marketing and Drive Growth.' *Journal of Advertising Research* 55, no. 3 (September): 232–236.

Goldenberg, B. J. 2015. *The Definitive Guide to Social CRM: Maximizing Customer Relationships with Social Media to Gain Market Insights, Customers, and Profits.* Pearson, NJ: Pearson FT Press.

Hewett, K., W. Rand, R. T. Rust, and H. J. van Heerde. 2016. 'Brand Buzz in the Echoverse.' *Journal of Marketing* 80, no. 3 (May): 1–24.

Hoffman, D. L., and M. Fodor. 2010. 'Can You Measure the ROI of Your Social Media Marketing?' *MIT Sloan Management Review* 52, no. 1 (Fall): 41–49.

Holt, D. 2016. 'Branding in the Age of Social Media.' *Harvard Business Review* 94, no. 3 (March): 40–50.

John, L. K., D. Mochon, O. Emrich, and J. Schwartz. 2017. 'What's the Value of a Like? Social Media Endorsements Don't Work the Way You Might Think.' *Harvard Business Review* 95, no. 2 (March–April): 108–115.

Kahr, A., B. Nyffenegger, H. Krohmer, and W. D. Hoyer. 2016. 'When Hostile Consumers Wreak Havoc on Your Brand: The Phenomenon of Consumer Brand Sabotage.' *Journal of Marketing* 80 (May): 25–41. doi:10.1509/jm.15.0006

Kozinets, R. V., A. Hemetsberger, and H. J. Schau. 2008. 'The Wisdom of Consumer Crowds: Collective Innovation in the Age of Networked Marketing.' *Journal of Macromarketing* 28, no. 4: 339. doi:10.1177/0276146708325382

Kumar, A., R. Bezawada, R. Rishika, R. Janakiraman, and P. K. Kannan. 2016. 'From Social to Sale: The Effects of Firm-generated Content in Social Media on Customer Behavior.' *Journal of Marketing* 80, no. 1 (January): 7–25.

Kumar, D. 2016. *The Connected Consumer*. New York, NY: Business Expert Press.

Kumar, V., and R. Mirchandani. 2012. 'Increasing the ROI of Social Media Marketing.' *MIT Sloan Management Review* 54, no. 1 (Fall).

Kumar, V., L. Aksoy, B. Donkers, R. Venkatesan, T. Wiesel, and S. Tillmanns. 2010. 'Undervalued or Overvalued Customers: Capturing Total Customer Engagement Value.' *Journal of Service Research* 13, no. 3: 297–310. doi:10.1177/1094670510375602

Kumar, V., R. Venkatesan, and W. Reinartz. 2006. 'Knowing What to Sell, When, and to Whom.' *Harvard Business Review* 84, no. 3 (March): 131–137.

Lee, B. 2013. 'Building Customer Communities Is the Key to Creating Value.' *Harvard Business Review* (1 February). Available at: https://hbr.org/2013/02/building-customer-communities (accessed on 21 January 2021).

Moorman, C., B. Ross, and H. Gorman. 2014. 'Integrating Social Media into Your Marketing Strategy.' *Forbes* (18 December). Available at: http://www.forbes.com/sites/christinemoorman/2014/12/16/12-tips-for-integratingsocialmedia-into-your-marketing-strategy/ (accessed on 21 January 2021).

Pikas, B., and G. Sorrentino. 2014. 'The Effectiveness of Online Advertising: Consumer's Perceptions of Ads on Facebook, Twitter and YouTube.' *Journal of Applied Business and Economics* 16, no. 4.

Piskorski, M. J. 2011. 'Social Strategies That Work.' *Harvard Business Review* 89, no. 11 (November): 116–122.

PriceWaterhouseCoopers. 2016. 'They Say They Want a Revolution: Total Retail 2016.' Available at: https://www.pwc.com/gx/en/retail-consumer/publications/assets/total-retail-global-report.pdf (accessed on 21 January 2021).

Raab, D. M. 2011. 'New Metrics for Social Media. *Information Management* 21, no. 6 (November–December): 24–25.

Safko, L., and D. K. Brake. 2009. *The Social Media Bible: Tactics, Tools, and Strategies for Business Success*. Hoboken, NJ: John Wiley & Sons.

Scott, D. M. 2015. *The New Rules of Marketing and PR*. 5th ed. Hoboken, NJ: John Wiley & Sons.

Shih, C. 2009. *The Facebook Era: Tapping Online Social Networks to Build Better Products, Reach New Audiences, and Sell More Stuff*. Upper Saddle River, NJ: Prentice Hall.

Stacey, E. C., K. H. Pauwels, and A. Lackman. 2013. *Beyond Likes and Tweets: How Conversation Content Drives Store and Site Traffic* (Marketing Science Institute Report). New York, NY: Marketing Science Institute.

Stauffer, J. 2012. 'Social Brand Planning.' *Journal of Brand Strategy* 1, no. 1 (April–June): 40–49.

Stokes, R. 2013. *eMarketing: The Essential Guide to Marketing in a Digital World*. 5th ed. Cape Town: Quirk eMarketing (Pty) Ltd.

Treacy, M., and F. Wiersema. 1995. *The Discipline of Market Leaders: Choose Your Customers, Narrow Your Focus, Dominate Your Market.* New York, NY: HarperCollins.

Van Bockel, H. 2014. *The Social Brand: Transform Your Brand to Win in the Social Era.* Powell, OH: Social Publishing House.

Vizard, S. 2017. 'Social Media Spend Failing to Live Up to Expectations.' *Marketing Week* (16 March). Available at: https://www.marketingweek.com/2017/03/16/social-media-spend-failing-live-expectations/ (accessed on 21 January 2021).

CLOSING CASE

USING SOCIAL MEDIA EFFECTIVELY

Using social media in marketing has two main challenges: (a) how to get people involved in corporate campaigns and (b) how to make users go beyond likes and sharing of content. After all, companies use tools to achieve marketing objectives. As a result, while content sharing is a great awareness tool, it also seeks to achieve higher sales and revenues. This case study describes some companies that have been able to use social media effectively.

Maersk: An unlikely success story is that of the world's largest container shipping company, a unit of the A.P. Moller-Maersk Group, a Danish business conglomerate. Although the company is not a consumer goods company, it has used social media most effectively. It used social media platforms to engage with customers, creating pages more popular than Disney and many other companies.

Maersk Line's entry into social media began in 2011 and was done in-house. There was scepticism about a container haulage company entering the social media space. In an interview to McKinsey and Co. (2013), the company admitted, 'At first, we didn't expect to sell shipping containers through social, though we're learning now that in fact we can.'

Katona and Sarvary (2014) describe Maersk's use of social media platforms. The company used social media in four areas: communications, customer service, sales and internal usage. Usually, social media posts are used to push products or news to followers. Instead, Maersk chose to have a spontaneous and flexible approach, drawing on its own culture. The factual content was chosen instead of manufacturing stories. The company used 10 different social media platforms. While Facebook was used to engage with followers in a visual and conversational way, Twitter was used as a news outlet and LinkedIn as a platform to reach its customers. The channels were segmented into four quadrants: fans, customers, employees and experts.

Maersk used pictures from its archives of 14,000 photos of ships, seascapes and ports, which no one was using. The company decided to add stories and share them to describe the company's rich history. Facebook audience loved it, leading people to take photos of Maersk ships themselves and posting them. The pictures often had a whimsical touch, such as one

(Continued)

(Continued)

post with a photo of a giraffe on a container ship. Pictures from the public and users encouraged others to take photos of Maersk ships around the world.

The company says that focusing on metrics such as followers and fans should not be the main focus, which were just vanity numbers. Instead, the value gained from employee engagement, customer insights and innovation was invaluable. Social media introduced pride among employees since their friends and family now knew about their work, improving their perception of the company. The efforts also saved the company money in terms of customer service since issues were resolved before the customer care team needed to intervene. Finally, social media has also had cultural effects on Maersk by adding transparency and empowering employees.

Coolatta: The Coolatta campaign went beyond content and not only encouraged purchase but also generated free advertising for a new product launched by Dunkin' Donuts in 2009. Users were encouraged to try out the new drink and take pictures with it. Facebook was used to motivate people to take their pictures with the new drink and make it their profile picture. This encouraged purchase and also generated publicity when people posted their pictures, thus getting into the feeds of friends. The campaign was called 'Turns Your Profile Pic into Prizes'. Combining it with Twitter, @dunkindonuts was used to generate traffic on the fan page. Thus, the company succeeded in getting the pictures of the drink in the feeds of friends and shared them further. The tagline was 'Grab It, Snap It, Post It and Win It' (Figure 6.7). The company's Twitter followers increased as a result of the campaign. Its 'Keep it Coolatta' campaign is considered as the best social media marketing campaigns of all time.

Several other companies have tried the same technique of getting customers to pose with products and post pictures online, with varying results.

The campaign showed that it is not necessary to engage on every social platform. A well-chosen strategy with just a platform or two can generate enough product publicity.

Always: This example shows how a company can get associated with a social issue. P&G's Always range of sanitary products decided to fight gender stereotypes with their #likeagirl campaign on social media. The company found that girls' self-confidence fell as they grew up. The words 'like a girl' are used to describe boys who are weak or emotional. The company turned this on its head and asked girls to do things that they wanted to. Girls were asked to tweet their pictures doing things with the hashtag #LikeAGirl. It created a #LikeAGirl page which featured all the pictures. Combining it with an ad aired during 2015 Super Bowl and the use of influencers, the company established a brand by boosting the confidence of young girls and acquiring a socially conscious image in the process. The campaign shows that brands can gain identity and consumer acceptance when they associate themselves with a social cause. Social media platforms provide ample opportunity to highlight the message.

Questions for Discussion

1. What are the lessons learnt from Maersk about using social media?
2. How can companies incorporate social media into their communication plans?

FIGURE 6.7   *Coolatta Campaign Encouraged People to Post Pictures on Social Media*

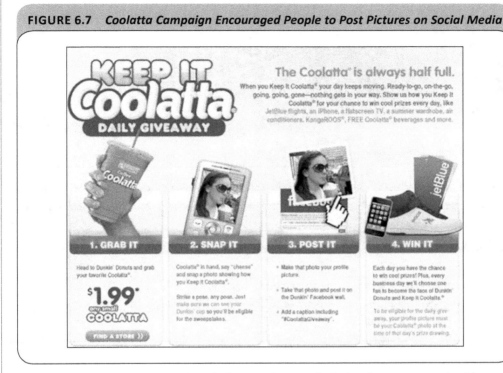

Source: http://blog.thoughtpick.com/2010/01/learn-sm-by-example-dunkin-donuts-campaign.html (accessed on 16 February 2021).

3. What are the elements of social media strategy that were used by Maersk, Coolatta and Always? How are different platforms used for different purposes?
4. How can companies create a compelling social media presence that involves both employees and customers?

Sources

Katona, Z., and M. Sarvary. 2014. 'Maersk Line: B2B Social Media—"It's Communication, Not Marketing".' *California Management Review* 56, no. 3: 142–156.

McKinsey and Co. 2013. 'Being B2B Social: A Conversation with Maersk Line's Head of Social Media.' May Available at: https://www.mckinsey.com/business-functions/marketing-and-sales/our-insights/being-b2b-social-a-conversation-with-maersk-lines-head-of-social-media (accessed on 20 January 2021).

http://blog.thoughtpick.com/2010/01/learn-sm-by-example-dunkin-donuts-campaign.html (accessed on 25 February 2021).

https://www.campaignlive.co.uk/article/case-study-always-likeagirl/1366870 (accessed on 25 February 2021).

CHAPTER 7

Brand Building in the Digital Age

Branding has been a major objective in traditional marketing. In this chapter, we discuss brand building in the digital age and find out what has changed since the advent of online technologies. After reading this chapter, you will be able to learn about the following:

☐ Brands in the physical and virtual worlds, and brand identity
☐ Building brands digitally through UX and CX
☐ Online brand experience, consumer intervention mapping
☐ Brand engagement and brand customer centricity
☐ Social curation and brands

OPENING CASE

ARE BRANDS DEAD?

Brands have traditionally led to recall and repeat buying. A strong brand image generates trust among consumers—it communicates the product's quality and is a guarantee for consumers. But the online world is notoriously fickle. What is today's darling may suddenly lose the users' fancy: think of Yahoo, Hotmail and Orkut. Today, customers are at freedom to visit any site and buy anything that suits their fancy. They live by the saying, 'You're only as good as your last product.' The moment that customers find a better site or app, they leave without giving second thoughts to their earlier custom. Leetaru (2019) questions whether brands matter in a world of infinite choice and availability.

Simonson and Rosen (2014) write that companies have to rethink about brand building. They write that brands lose their importance in a world where consumers can explore products at will. They have better sources of information, such as product recommendations, reviews and expert opinions. This makes brands less relevant today for the simple reason that consumers can make more rational decisions on the basis of information instead of brand images and logos. Indeed, consumers are trying out products from unknown manufacturers and niche brands more than ever before. The authors say that brands had become popular earlier because customers had little access to information in the past, so they responded to advertisements and their past experience while buying products. Brand loyalty resulted since customers felt confident of the product quality as opposed to that of unknown producers. In an article, The Twilight of Brands, Surowiecki (2014) writes that the Internet has weakened the power of brands.

Today, with more information, thanks to the Internet, consumers are exposed to alternate products, recommended by online friends or trusted online reviewers. E-commerce sites offer easy comparison between products, and customers can be influenced to buy a lesser known brand than spend on an expensive product supporting a bigger brand name. In the retail space analogy, big name brands do not control the retail spaces of the web and customers are free to choose products with better features and prices. This leads to the conclusion that brands will continue to lose their importance.

Another important reason for the decline of brands is that viral online posts can damage carefully built images instantly. Since consumers are influenced by messages and reviews posted online, brands face immense dangers.

The opposing view is that brands are becoming more important, not less. Skibsted and Hansen (2014) write that brands still have immense importance. Digital brands such as Apple, Google, Microsoft, IBM and Twitter are reputed names today, commanding immense loyalty. Those who mourn the death of brands make the mistake of missing out on the meaning and methods of branding in the digital economy. The methods used by Google, Facebook and other similar companies are simply different from the methods used traditionally. The brands are kept meaningful for users by offering services and staying relevant in their lives. UX has taken over the mass media advertising used in the past.

Further, even in times of excessive information, customers tend to stick to their habits rather than try out new and unknown brands and buy the ones that have strong emotional appeals. So instead of debating the death of brands, companies have to identify the methods of strengthening their brands when traditional tools are losing importance. Dooley (n.d.) writes, 'Branding isn't dead, but, now more than ever, it needs to be authentic!'

The methods and benefits of branding have indeed changed. Brands in the physical world command price premium, while many online brands thrive by using different business models that allow offering services free or at highly discounted prices.

Traditional brands have to learn how to use new tools such as UX, touch point influence, social media and other tools along with advertising and other media interventions. Brands do not rely on their names but offer value at every stage. They build emotional appeals by being honest and transparent, telling their stories and connecting to their customers.

While reading this chapter, try to answer the following questions:

1. Do you think that branding is still relevant in the virtual world? Give your reasons for your answer.
2. What can companies do to remain relevant in both physical and virtual worlds?

(Continued)

(Continued)

3. If indeed it is true that modern consumers are fickle and not concerned about brands, what is the role of marketing in the future?
4. Will the power of brands shift to powerful online brands? What are the consequences of high concentration of commercial power by these companies?

Sources

Dooley, R. n.d. 'Is Branding Dead? Our Brains Say No!' Available at: https://www.neurosciencemarketing.com/blog/articles/is-branding-dead.htm (accessed on 22 January 2021).

Leetaru, K. 2019. 'Will E-Commerce Be the Death of Brands?' *Forbes*. Available at: https://www.forbes.com/sites/kalevleetaru/2019/07/10/will-e-commerce-be-the-death-of-brands/#5b79936875af (accessed on 22 January 2021).

Simonson, I., and E. Rosen. 2014. *Absolute Value What Really Influences Customers in the Age of (Nearly) Perfect Information*. New York, NY: Harper Collins.

Skibsted, J. M., and R. B. Hansen. 2014. 'Brands Aren't Dead, but Traditional Branding Tools Are Dying.' *HBR*. Available at: https://hbr.org/2014/02/the-brand-is-dead-long-live-the-brand (accessed on 22 January 2021).

Surowiecki, J. 2014. 'Twilight of the Brands.' *The New Yorker*. Available at: https://www.newyorker.com/magazine/2014/02/17/twilight-brands (accessed on 22 January 2021).

▉ INTRODUCTION

Brands help consumers to recognize a company or product as distinct and different from those of other companies. While branding is generally understood in traditional marketing as a name, logo or design used to create a distinct image, branding actually implies the mind-space created among customers. It consists of reputation gained by a company and the positive feelings that customers feel for the name or symbol of the brand.

The power of branding is evident in the trust exhibited by consumers in the products. It is similar to the rush of positive feelings experienced by immigrants in a foreign country when they recognize something from their native country. Very often, products may not be very different from competitor offerings, but a perception of superiority is established in the consumers' minds. Effective branding creates a wall for competitors which they find difficult to breach.

We have seen that in the online context, branding a CDJ begins with an online search, called the FMOT. It is here that branding plays a part. Branding will make the customer go to his or her preferred site rather than searching online. For example, if a user needs to buy a mobile phone, he or she could do an online search, visit Amazon or the Samsung website. The strength of the brand will determine consumer preferences. Similarly, if one is looking for a yoga teacher, branding will make sure that one searches for a particular name or just 'yoga teacher near me'.

Online branding means that the brand is already present in the buyer's consideration set and he or she need not conduct a search for it. This is achieved not simply by building awareness but by a combination of consumer engagement, recommendations and positive reviews, offline advertising and customer value. This chapter looks at branding basics and online techniques that help build brands for the long term.

BRANDING BASICS

Keller (2013) gives four steps or fundamental questions that customers want to know about brands. These four questions are as follows:

4 dimensions of a brand.

1. Who are you? (core values)
2. What are you? (brand meaning)
3. What do I think or feel about you? (brand responses)
4. What kind of association should I have with you? (brand associations)

The answer to these questions gives us the basis to study brand management. The first question is answered by establishing a strong *brand identity*, the second is answered by establishing *brand meaning*, the third by *brand responses* and the last by building *brand relationships*. These questions are required to be addressed with both physical and online brands.

Brand building is a step-by-step process. Crucial to building brands are the core values that help build brand identity and meaning in consumers' minds, finally leading to brand relationships.

The same is true in the online world. The core values, meaning and trust are the reasons why people visit some websites more than others. These are the reasons that consumers buy from a particular online store, even though others have similar product offerings. In e-commerce, branding becomes important because customers cannot touch and feel products, but will order products on the sites they trust.

WHY BRANDING MATTERS

The brand is the main reason that customers buy from a company repeatedly. It builds loyalty and establishes familiarity among customers, leading to trust. Since companies look for e-loyalty, brand building has to be a major component of the online strategy. Branding helps in a number of benefits for a company as it:

1. Creates a great first impression
2. Makes the product memorable and recognizable
3. Builds an emotional connect
4. Differentiates from competitors

5. Allows companies to charge price premium
6. Creates customer loyalty and advocacy

To build on the aforementioned benefits, brands have to use and build online capabilities to engage proactively with customers, and that too with authenticity and transparency. People will interact with brands only if the content is authentic and entertaining, and allows them to express themselves through the following capabilities.

why Branding matters

- **Trust:** Users trust what the brand does in the social space more than they believe in its advertising.
- **Entertain:** Online users or millennials look for brands to entertain them.
- **Listen:** Users feel a responsibility to share feedback with companies after a good or bad experience.
- **Involve:** Customers want to be involved in a variety of co-creation activities.
- **Express:** Consumers want to use social media as the preferred platform for expressing an opinion on a brand.
- **Value:** Every online activity should be seen from the value that it adds to the brand; mere presence is not enough.
- **Enjoy:** Make brand interactions enjoyable and build CX on it.

If they can be involved by brands, users will welcome interacting with them online and want to know about the products, their origin, their manufacture, whether they have safe ingredients and so on. Thus, brands must spark their interest. When this is achieved, connected consumers are willing to tell their friends and spread the word on social media, sharing photos and videos with them (see Marketing Insight 7.1).

Branding must underlie all online activities, starting from the company's website, apps and social media interactions. But this is not enough, it must extend to the physical space as well. The next section describes branding in physical and virtual worlds.

MARKETING INSIGHT 7.1 *Digital Branding: Aldo Shoes*

Aldo is a Canadian brand of shoes and accessories that was launched in 1972 by Aldo Bensadoun with its mission, 'A journey to create a world of love, confidence, and belonging'. The brand values of Aldo consist of compassion and ethics, with the aim of influencing society in both fashion and social responsibility.

The company was among the first in its category to go for e-commerce, and its website is integrated with social media and 'lightening fast' interactions. According to its website (Aldoshoes.com), it offers:

a new responsive website and omnichannel strategy that raises the bar for retail online, in-store and on mobile. We are committed to offering our consumers a universal digital experience that is accessible, responsive, social, and human-centred, with the ability to easily evolve and scale over time.

The Aldo website (https://www.aldoshoes.in/) tells the story of the brand, along with the pro-files of its leaders. It has integrated marketing functions throughout its corporate departments.

Aldo gets about 20 per cent of its sales from e-commerce. It uses Instagram innovatively (Figure 7.1), setting itself apart from other brands. The company has invested in a new site design that builds on marketing engagement rather than on the transaction process. Its site, aldoshoes.com, succeeds in engaging customers by showcasing the latest collection, together with brand stories. The site provides positive experiences through pleasing visuals. Recognizing the omnichannel approach, it informs customers about the nearest stores or they can make a purchase on-site.

How does Aldo build a highly engaging brand presence?

Source

Aldoshoes.com

■ BRANDS IN PHYSICAL AND VIRTUAL WORLDS

Online branding can be defined as building an identity for a product or service, improving visibility and establishing credibility in the virtual world. Khan, Rahman and Fatima (2016) write that corporate visual identity, emotional experience and functionality are the strongest predictors of brand satisfaction and brand loyalty compared to lifestyle and corporate dimensions.

Online branding methods are quite different from traditional branding methods. In traditional marketing, the company creates an advertising message, adds attractive images and uses mass media to spread the message. This has remained a powerful method to build brands. Some of this advertising has shifted to online platforms, but its objective changes; instead of showing advertisements, the online advertisement must motivate users to click on the link or the ad that opens the brand's page for them.

Further, traditional advertisements are placed in newspapers or on TV channels where consumers see them while they are reading news or watching TV programmes. This is called *interruption marketing* because it interrupts what they are reading or watching. But this strategy does not work in the online environment because consumers search for whatever is in their minds and are least interested in being interrupted by advertisements that pop up on their computers or mobile screens. Online branding thus must find ways to promote brands and find a place in consumer-initiated communications (Table 7.1).

Although the online branding approach is quite different from traditional branding, many advertisers still follow the traditional approach in which advertisements are placed on sites just as they are placed in newspapers or TV channels. Others try to make sure their ads are seen and pop up when a user opens a website. These are mere irritants and do nothing for building any brand image. Further, given the efficacy of ad blockers, the viewing of ads does not work that way: People are quick to block ads or avoid sites that have pop-ups. Online branding must therefore find ways to get people interested in brands and share their stories and experiences with their friends and acquaintances online. This

TABLE 7.1 *Approach of Traditional and Online Branding Methods*

Traditional Branding	Online or Digital Branding
Advertising	Consumer engagement instead of advertising
Company-initiated communications	Consumer-initiated communications
Use of mass media	Individual targeting
One-to-many communication	One-to-one communication
Interruption marketing	Engaging customers through content and brand stories

is facilitated by creative approaches that include building brand stories and creating digital relationships.

Of course, companies have to find their own digital strategies since different strategies work for different companies and products. More than presenting product offerings through ads, companies must get consumers interested in their stories so that they post pictures or status updates with brands. Consumers also do not like being spoken down to, so companies have to understand the nuances of communication and the elements of brand identity in the virtual world.

ONLINE BRAND IDENTITY

Brand identity consists of the visible elements of a brand, such as colour, design and logo, which help to identify and distinguish the brand in consumers' minds. It includes what the brand says, its values and what people feel when they see it. It can also be summed up as the personality of the business with a trust and a promise to its customers. Jeff Bezos is widely attributed with the saying, 'Branding is what people say about you when you're not in the room.'

Brand identity can be seen as a set of brand associations for customers. Brands leave impressions on customers long after the sale has been accomplished. Companies use brand identity elements to shape that impression. For example, Unilever's brand identity consists of a distinctive logo that is recognized as 'U' which is used as an umbrella brand for all its sub-brands. The blue colour elicits confidence among consumers. The 'U' image conveys a highly diversified company. The website (hul.co.in) is dynamic and conveys its values. It opens with the hashtag #HULStandsWithTheNation and the image conveys washing, health and safety. This is the brand's face or personality. These elements communicate authenticity to customers.

Aaker and Joachimsthaler (2000) emphasize the importance of developing a plan to communicate the key features of brand identity and increase brand awareness. Table 7.2 lists the elements of online brand identity. Successful brands use all of these in an optimum combination (see Marketing Insight 7.2).

TABLE 7.2　*Elements of Online Brand Identity*

Element	Description	Examples
Brand values	What the business promises	Dependability, delivery, trust
Brand assets	Distinguishing characteristics of the online business	Trademarks, fonts, colours, style, design, app icon, logo
Brand associations	What people associate with the business	Ease of use, social connections, emotions
Brand awareness/loyalty	Recall, preference over similar apps or sites	Repeated use of app or site
Brand personality	Human personality traits associated with the brand	Friend, companion, advisor
Brand positioning	Perception with respect to other similar apps	Value or ease delivered
Brand voice	Social issues supported by the site	Vocal for local, Made in India

Brand identity is important because it is the reflection of everything it stands for. A brand is said to live in the 'minds and hearts of consumers', and this statement is more valid in the online world. Identity, therefore, is crucial for the long-term sustainability of the brand.

MARKETING INSIGHT 7.2　*Rebranding Uber*

Uber is a ride-sharing online brand. It has become popular the world over, registering phenomenal growth. The size of the company can be seen from the fact that it does over 15 million trips each day. Its popularity is reflected in the fact that the word 'Uber' is today used as a default verb and noun.

Bowman (2018) explains that the company had some bad years in which it got negative publicity concerning its business practices and work culture. Newspapers reported that Uber tracked users even after the ride had ended and also tracked devices even after the app was deleted by the users. Uber was breaking the rules and the brand was suffering. In China, Uber drivers used stolen iPhones to request rides so that demand went up artificially, increasing their rates.

Such negative publicity had left the brand wounded and people were turning against it. It went into a transition phase after its CEO Travis Kalanick was ousted and Dara Khosrowshahi took over.

The company had two logos, one for the Android app and the other for the Apple app. The letters in the UBER were widely spaced and were seen as awkward by some people. Besides, the company introduced extensions such as UberX, Uber Eats, Uber Commute, UberPool and other services. To show its changing culture and evolving company, Uber

(Continued)

(Continued)

needed a new brand identity. It decided to go back to its values and refresh the five pillars that the company Uber wanted to be known for: grounded, populist, inspiring, highly evolved and elevated. Further, it needed a logo that could be recognized easily whether seen on a vehicle or on mobile phones as an app icon.

As we have explained in this chapter, a brand is the perception of consumers. It is based on their experiences with the brand and the emotions they felt on coming into contact with it. A strong brand evokes memories and experiences among consumers and is based on trust and credibility. Brand design must reflect that it represents a living company showing not only what the company does but also acts as a connection and recognition with its customers.

Uber wanted to present its brand personality by redesigning itself. Hempel (2016) describes Uber's attempt to transform its purpose and reputation. The earlier logo was thought to represent an exclusive corporate club that had developed from its earlier objective of providing black car service to the elite in California. But now the company had changed and wanted an image that represented its ride-sharing business.

Uber's objective for redesign was that it had to communicate to customers that it had got over its earlier ways by getting a new CEO. It opted for a complete redesign. CEO Dara Khosrowshahi explained that the company was being reinvented with a fresh start. He wrote that the change represented 'new leaders, a better company culture, and improvements to our app'.

The new logo was launched in 2018. The company wanted to communicate a sense of mobility, accessibility and friendliness, and to project a cohesive brand system that was instantly recognizable globally. Since it operated in different markets and cultures, it should be efficient to manage and execute. The redesign included brand assets that included typeface, photography, illustration and composition system that could be used for advertising and printing promotional materials.

The redesign was accomplished by design studio Wolff Olins with guidance from the company's design team. Nine elements of brand identity were kept in focus while redesigning the brand: logo, colour, composition, iconography, illustration, motion, photography, tone of voice and typography. Wolff Olins explains that the design was kept simple and minimal because it had to be used in markets around the world. Hence, localized colour and patterns were not used but a simple design that could be used everywhere and localized with local cultures and content. The twin objectives of simplicity and global usage were thus achieved.

The new design represented a break from the previous work culture and CEO, and showed to customers that it was moving into a new era.

What can be communicated by brands through their design elements? Is the rebranding of Uber successful?

Sources

Bowman, A. 2018. 'Uber's Powerful Rebrand and What Your Business Can Learn from It.' *Crowdspring*. Available at: https://www.crowdspring.com/blog/uber-rebrand/ (accessed on 22 January 2021).

Hempel, J. 2016. 'The Inside Story of Uber's Radical Rebranding.' *Wired*. Available at: https://www.wired.com/2016/02/the-inside-story-behind-ubers-colorful-redesign/ (accessed on 22 January 2021).

ONLINE BRAND DIFFERENTIATION

Branding results in product differentiation. It distinguishes a company from other companies in the same space. Brand building is a painstaking effort over time, since reputation takes time to build. Customer loyalty has to be built solely on what is available online—the content, design and logos used—along with traditional advertising. For instance, an app will exist among many other apps on a user's mobile phone: What makes a person open a particular app or visit a website repeatedly is the subject matter of branding and the value it offers.

Mere online presence or smart designs for branding are not enough. Brands must articulate the following in both the online and offline worlds.

- **Mission:** Core values, sense of purpose and the vision of its founders.
- **The 'face' of the brand:** The brand's logo and app icon or the brand ambassador.
- **Credibility and trust:** Security, functioning of the website, delivery, payments and refunds.
- **Advertising:** Advertisements include all elements of brand identity, including colour schemes, logos, brand spokesperson, appearance and looks.
- **Brand personality, stories and heritage:** The brand as a living being helps to establish relationships. Online brands are often associated with their founders.
- **Online brand reflection:** How customers feel or perceive themselves as a result of engaging with a brand online.
- **Experience:** The frequency and depth of customer interactions that a brand builds online and offline.

Look closely, and you will find that all successful online brands build on the aforementioned elements. One distinct advantage of the online environment is that companies are not limited to fixed format advertising. They need not make their point in the 15-second TV commercial. They have great flexibility for building stories in an online environment because they get unlimited space and opportunities for talking to customers. In the physical world, they have to buy advertising space that is not conducive for lengthy interactions or stories, but online, they can post any content for any length of time. Thus, online branding goes beyond logos and short taglines. Today, brands have the means to build an online experience that can create space in the customers' minds. They can tell their stories, appeal emotionally, build perceptions and involve people with ideas that inspire and resonate with their core purpose.

BUILDING BRANDS DIGITALLY

Brands exercise a powerful pull effect on customers. Existing brands look to online activities to reinforce their power. Online businesses too have realized the importance of branding to get customers to their websites. The concepts of online-only and offline-only are vanishing because brands are built in both physical and virtual worlds (see our Closing case on Walmart and Amazon). While traditional businesses are using URLs and QR codes for their online presence on their marketing materials, online businesses use website design and online ambience along with their physical presence to build their brands.

Businesses need to establish logistical and technical networks to support their operations. Crossover from offline to online can extend a brand's reach to a wider audience. On the other hand, by establishing a physical presence, online companies build better delivery and customer service capabilities.

Digital marketspace is virtual and intangible, but offers increased interactivity and real-time brand experiences. The important thing is that brands should build value in both the offline and online worlds. That is why online companies are setting up physical shops. The Google store, for instance, allows people to touch and experience Chromebooks. When people tried the product and played with it, they could understand what the product was all about. Apple, Microsoft and Amazon have all set up physical stores so that people can experience their products.

Morgan-Thomas and Veloutsou (2013) write that the major difference is the context in which the customer experiences the brand. Online context tends to be:

1. Information rich
2. Dynamic
3. Characterized by excessive information flows
4. Technologically innovative

Businesses have to integrate these capabilities into their brand building efforts by using them creatively. The main building blocks of online branding are experience and interactivity. It must be emphasized that marketing and design are just tools to build brands, but the foundation of online brand building is the experience of customers which is described as UX and CX.

ONLINE BRANDING BASICS—UX AND CX

Online branding has two components: experience of customers with the brand and the online experience with brand properties and communications. These are called UX and CX.

UX design is the process of influencing users by their interaction with digital devices. It is an online function and consists of ease of using the website, navigation, discoverability, interacting with others, comparison, ease of payments and buying, that is, UX is associated with the quality of digital interactions of a user. Design elements are part of UX (see Marketing Insight 7.3).

CX is an interaction between a company and consumers when they experience a brand's products and services. It includes perceptions and feelings resulting from all the

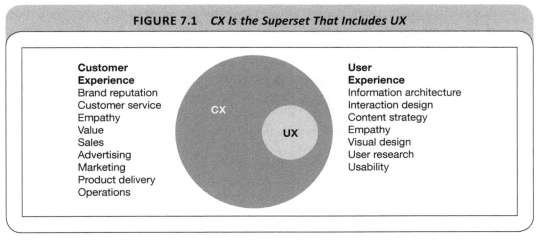

FIGURE 7.1 *CX Is the Superset That Includes UX*

Customer Experience
Brand reputation
Customer service
Empathy
Value
Sales
Advertising
Marketing
Product delivery
Operations

CX

UX

User Experience
Information architecture
Interaction design
Content strategy
Empathy
Visual design
User research
Usability

CDJ
customer
decision
journey

Source: https://usabilitygeek.com/ux-strategy-it-is-all-about-the-experience/ (accessed on 15 April 2021).

touch points that a person experiences with the brand. One requires online capabilities, the second calls for marketing capabilities.

UX and CX designers must work together. If they work separately, there will be a mismatch in CX. All the brand touch points across the CDJ, whether physical or online, must be integrated. Some brands have an excellent website and deliver excellent UX, but deliveries and offline experience are weak. On the other hand, customers may love certain brands but find their online presence boring or cumbersome. With time, customers will switch to other brands that offer both UX and CX positively. However, UX is not enough alone, even for online brands; the importance of UX and CX is shown in Figure 7.1.

The design elements used in UX are described in Marketing Insight 7.2. UX builds the following advantages.

- **Useful:** All content on a website must be useful for users. Irrelevant content and too many heavy files or auto-playing videos are useless and will lead to a user flight. A message match ensures that customers see the content on clicking a link that matches with what is offered in the link leading to it. Websites should provide easy navigation, that is, companies should visualize the sequence of navigation by users and make it easier for them by arranging pages as per their search paths.
- **Findable:** Consumers use search engines as a first step in the buying process. Hence, the brand's online presence must have high rank in search engines. All pages must be working; 'not found' error messages push users away.
- **Credible:** Credibility, honesty, transparency and objectivity are important. Testimonials and experts must be authentic and so must all other information. Detailed pictures help build credibility.
- **Desirable:** Products and online presence must be desirable. Quality, consumer interactions both before and after sales and design promote desire.

- **Accessible:** Products and online services must be accessible to the target audience. A fast-loading website is essential: ideally, a website should load in less than 2 seconds. Many users will turn away if the loading time is too long.
- **Valuable:** A professional design that is easy to navigate with the right ambience communicates trustworthiness to users. It will also contribute to CX.
- **Functional:** Once visitors come to the site, they must be retained and gently pushed ahead in their purchase decision. Websites should be functional and have dynamic, compelling content that encourages people to explore the products offered. The content should be short, easily readable and understandable. Visuals and multimedia help to keep users engaged. Unnecessary pop-ups and advertisements are best avoided.

CX is impacted by the following.

- **Product:** The main experience that a customer gets is by using a product or service. Products and deliveries define companies. So the starting point is to have a great product or service that is well liked by customers.
- **Response time:** The time taken by a company to respond to users' requests. This is often difficult for companies that have different departments. If the response time is excessive, customers will move to another brand.
- **Friendliness:** Kind, empowered and friendly employees contribute greatly to CX. This becomes a source of differentiation and customer loyalty.
- **Convenience:** Consumers look for convenience in their dealings. Hence, companies have to provide easy ways of doing business, both online and offline.
- **Atmosphere:** It consists of looks, sounds and smells that users experience when they interact with brands. That is why brands have to always present a clean space with good lighting and ambience.
- **Expectations:** Brands must meet customer expectations in all their touch points.

We next describe how brands build touch point influence by using elements of CX.

MARKETING INSIGHT 7.3 *Design Elements in UX*

To create strong brands, companies must find out first the profile of their audience. The questions to be answered are as follows: Why should anyone look for the brand? What is the value proposition? Who are our customers? What can our app offer consumers that others cannot? How is the service from a me-too competitor?

These questions are answered by researching customers, competitors and markets. For online brands, the first step is to find out what value is gained by users in using their app.

Once the value is articulated in a clear language, the attention shifts to appearance. Font type, colour and imagery are used. Luxury brands, for instance, use very clear and distinct fonts. The appearance is enhanced by matching visuals and language. The logo is the brand ambassador, as it will sit on people's phones as an app. It is the most recognizable part of the brand. It will help to create familiarity with consumers. While designing a logo, it is important to think small, suitable for to be seen as an app on the phone.

A colour palette adds to the identity. Once decided, the same colour, typeface and font is used throughout the business. Templates provide a unified, credible and professional look.

The brand should be consistent but flexible. This is important in the online world because people are always looking for the next best thing. Flexibility allows for adjustments in product offerings, campaigns and space to grow in related areas. Airbnb, for instance, grew into transportation and experiences business from its initial role of renting out rooms. BookMyShow went beyond offering movie tickets and now covers many kinds of events.

Online brands should create brand guidelines so that it is reflected across channels. This lays the guidelines for content. Every piece of content that is published reflects the brand. Great content conveys a great brand to its customers, while boring content conveys a boring brand.

The language should match the personality of your brand. For a high-end or B2B brand, professional language must be used. If the brand addresses young people, the language must be casual. The tone and language used should match the brand's personality. Finally, a strong brand identity establishes emotional bonds with consumers.

It is important that a unique identity is established. If a brand copies its competitors, it becomes a 'me-too' brand that will always be compared to others.

Companies must use Google Analytics and social media discussions to track how people are responding to the brand. The name should reflect the service being offered. Common names such as books.com, advertising.com and advice.com are avoided. Spotify, Reddit, Paytm and so on are names that convey the service being offered.

BUILDING TOUCH POINT INFLUENCE

Consumers interact with brands in numerous ways. These interactions occur as customers search for products and make up their minds. The process is called CDJ, which is described in Chapter 4. Every stage in the CDJ is a marketing touch point. Companies today have the means to map these interactions, and thereby to understand consumer behaviour.

A touch point is described as any point of contact between a brand and consumers as they decide about the products or brands they wish to buy. The interaction may be direct between a company and consumer when the company controls the experience. Or it could be indirect when consumers write reviews or post pictures on their own. Baxendale, Macdonald and Wilson (2015) write that the positivity of in-store communication is more influential than that of other touch points. They found that advertising, impact of retailers, social effects and third-party endorsements add touch point positivity. Consumer behaviour can be influenced more by positivity as compared with touch point frequency alone.

Touch point mapping allows companies to visualize and improve every touch point experience. These touch points can be offline or online.

- **Offline touch points:** Displays, ads in media, billboards, promotional schemes, interaction with sales personnel, stores and supermarkets, telemarketing, delivery and service
- **Digital touch points:** Website, online ads, search engines, social media, blogs, reviews, e-commerce and chatbots

Brands try to influence these touch points so that discreet interventions can be made to help in consumers' purchase journeys. Further, since customers move between online and offline touch points seamlessly, there is need to integrate experiences in both real and virtual worlds.

Analysing touch points helps in understanding customers and identifying their *pain points*. A pain point is a problem that users face and can be identified if users end their interactions with a company or brand abruptly. Pain points are diverse and may vary from small irritants such as not being able to save searches to larger problems like payment gateway malfunctioning. Removing these will ease customer interaction.

Touch points can be classified into three areas: (a) pre-purchase, (b) purchase and (c) post-purchase (Figure 7.2). These are described below.

1. **Pre-purchase:** Before buying, a customer interacts with the website, advertisements, social media sites and reviews. Of these, the website is the most important controllable variable in a company's marketing plan: The 'About Us' page on it is

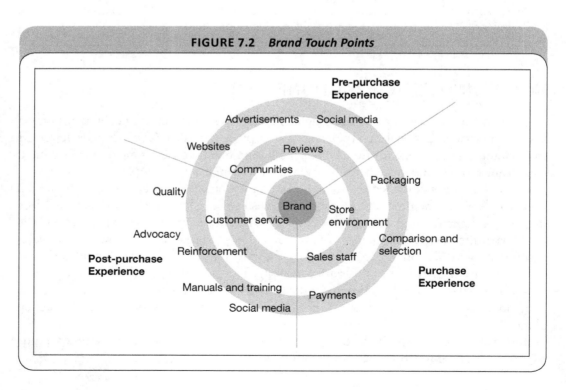

FIGURE 7.2   *Brand Touch Points*

an opportunity to describe the brand or company and tell stories associated with it. Many brands encourage interactions on their websites. The website of Maggi noodles, for instance, hosts a list of recipes that users can try. It also provides a link to how the company creates shared value. Print, outdoor and TV ads still remain powerful consumer touch points. Peer influence is sought on social media sites, while reviews and other interactions help consumers make up their minds. Customers can discover deals on their mobiles even while they are shopping in a store or take delivery from a store of a product they ordered online. Care must be taken to ensure that channels do not cannibalize their own sales by putting online and offline channels into competition with each other.

2. **Purchase:** While purchasing, consumers interact with the physical environment, friends and the website or e-commerce site. The physical environment consists of display, packaging, delivery, ambience and salesperson interaction. These interactions can be made information-rich by digital technologies. Salespersons equipped with hand-held devices can help customers compare with online offerings. The online purchase interaction consists of comparison, selection and payments. Immediate information must be generated about delivery once an online order is placed. In this way, purchase touch points can be influenced positively. Further, an offer to customize messages and products individually adds to the touch point influence. Customization means discovering at what stage of buying a customer is and making interventions accordingly. If customers are looking for information, the company can make reviews available and, if the customer is ready to buy, a push in the form of an offer can be provided. These interventions are data driven.

3. **Post-purchase:** Manuals, service and follow-up constitute post-purchase interactions. For example, Amazon is a pure e-commerce play but delivers in branded boxes. In an effort to influence post-purchase behaviour, customers are encouraged to use packaging for alternate uses, which spreads visibility and WOM publicity. Customer service and follow-up play a part in converting customers into advocates. Hence, integrating experiences across touch points is essential.

While companies try to add value at every stage of CDJ, this capability implies that new sources of value are added. For instance, companies use their data to offer services that consumers may require. For example, if a customer is travelling, a company can use weather data of the destination site to automatically offer cab services to customers so that they do not have to look for a cab at a rainy airport. Such innovation leads to offering better services or features continually.

Edelman and Singer (2015) write that understanding CDJs can be a source of competitive advantage since companies can capture customer insights better than their competitors. When these insights are fed back into their marketing programmes, they increase the company's ability to deliver value.

Brand touch points lead us to building a digital brand ecosystem, which is the overall experience designed by companies for their customers. This is described in the next section.

■ DIGITAL BRAND ECOSYSTEM

A digital brand ecosystem refers to the brand experience that companies design for their customers and the methods used to deliver it. UX and CX combine to deliver an overall brand experience, which is the reason that a *digital brand ecosystem* is built by companies using technologies, digital devices and apps to deliver a CX intended by a company. All devices and technologies work in a symbiotic way to form the ecosystem in which a brand functions with the objective of communicating and engaging customers. It consists of deciding how the brand message is delivered and tracked across all channels of communication.

A customer may use a taxi hailing service, a banking app, access audios and videos, and buy stuff from e-commerce sites. All these become a part of the digital ecosystem, a system connected across apps (Figure 7.3). Consumers find it convenient as they can accomplish most of their tasks using the digital ecosystem. It is in this ecosystem that brands must find their space and build customer relationships. For example, the Airtel app does not simply offer information on plans and schemes, but includes bill payments, money transfer, music, live TV and streaming content.

A digital brand ecosystem shows the following:

- Users of a product or service
- Customer needs and motivations, goals and objectives

FIGURE 7.3 *Digital Brand Ecosystem*

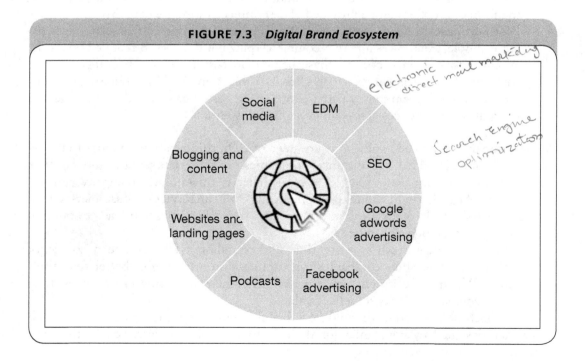

FIGURE 7.4   *Digital Brand Ecosystem*

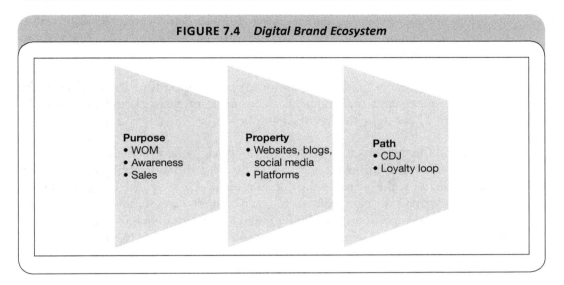

- The sources of information that they use
- Connected apps that allow them to accomplish tasks
- The digital devices or digital channels used by them
- Touch points of the brand with consumers
- People or technology that influence their decision-making

The digital brand ecosystem can be tracked by 3Ps: property, path and purpose (Figure 7.4).   3P

- **Property:** Property refers to digital properties that are visible to the public and serve to connect the company with its customers. These consist of a company's website, search engine links, apps, social media, blogs and third-party review sites. Each property adds to the brand experience in its own way, leaving impressions in the visitors' minds.
- **Path:** Path refers to the consumer journey that describes the purchase process. Path and property are interlinked since property is the means that determines the path. Companies must build a repeatable path for customers to engage with their digital properties and complete their purchase journeys. Customers follow the path to a company's most engaging property, which then directs them to other properties and finally to the buying and payment zone, followed by post-purchase interactions. The objective is to create a loyalty loop so that the customer feels loyal and makes repeated purchases.
- **Purpose:** At the outset, a company must determine its purpose and the type of experience it wants to impart online. For instance, some companies may want to sell online, while others may want to build positive WOM and lead customers to their physical stores. For the former, an e-commerce site is useful, for the latter,

an informational site is required. A clear purpose defines what kind of online properties a company must invest in and the paths taken by customers. It also shows what must be measured and tracked.

A digital brand ecosystem not only helps customers in accomplishing their tasks but also helps companies understand their audience, consumer interactions and influence the purchase decision. These steps are described as follows.

- **Understand the audience:** The company can track users, which channels they use and their offline and online interactions. A map can show a graphic representation of all interactions, the stages of the decision-making process, the triggers to buy as well as the potential 'pain points'. It also shows the points at which the users compare with competitors. The digital brand ecosystem helps companies to know how products are being used and what features are being most liked by consumers. These insights can help to discover hidden features that the company may not be aware of, thus building a competitive advantage.
- **Understand consumer interactions:** The digital brand ecosystem shows how and when customers are interacting with various pages and platforms on which the brand exists. It shows triggers of consumer behaviour, and the company can respond quickly to these triggers. The company can know which platforms are more effective than others and which encourage the desired interactions. The use of data, such as time spent on the site, types of comments posted and the number of shares, shows the quality of engagement with the brand. Companies can identify interactions that are disjointed or not working as expected, and can thus connect these different touch points to create an integrated experience that users expect.
- **Influence the purchase decision:** As the consumer moves among various touch points, companies can work out strategies to influence the touch point experience so that the purchase cycle becomes shorter. All points of the CDJ are influenced and companies build loyalty loops so that the consumer does not have to go through all steps of the CDJ every time.

It can be understood from the above that digital brand ecosystem helps to build brand experience by using sensory, cognitive, affective and relational dimensions.

■ BUILDING BRAND EXPERIENCE

We have seen that a powerful method of online branding is to deliver brand experiences through digital technologies. Online brand experience is defined as the quality of the experience that users get on the basis of marketing stimuli provided by the brand on the Internet. Experience is built through brand touch points, which are the points at which a consumer receives stimuli relating to the brand or interacts with it. In online environments, touch points are virtual and must be managed through websites, search engines, online promotions and social media. All such touch points must be integrated to provide a single and unique brand experience.

Simon, Brexendorf and Fassnacht (2013) write that online brand experience is built through the following four dimensions.

- **Sensory:** Appealing to the senses
- **Affective:** Consisting of feelings and emotions
- **Cognitive:** Appealing to intelligence, creativity and reasoning
- **Relational:** Developing social relationships

Hence, brands must use technologies to convey sensory and aesthetic appeal, cater to intellectual needs and invest in creating emotional and entertaining content.

- **Sensory:** Websites can deliver distinct visual and audible stimuli that deliver sensory experience. Since they cannot deliver the sense of touch, taste and smell, they must use the online media that they have available effectively. Hence, websites must be aesthetic besides being functional. The use of multimedia adds to the sensory experience with videos and animations. Interactive features further stimulate the user's senses. The lack of actual taste and smell is made up with luscious descriptions along with beautiful visuals. The experience is enhanced when customers can create avatars of themselves and 'try on' clothes or accessories by wearing them virtually. 3D images allow the users to zoom in and view the product from different angles. Companies create virtual showrooms, and users can walk through them and experience the environment complete with sounds and even a virtual assistant.
- **Affective:** Affective experience covers the emotions, feelings and moods of consumers when they come into contact with a brand touch point. The use of stories, heart-warming ads and social causes contribute to the affective experience. Online platforms allow longer ads than conventional TV, helping in storytelling. Indeed, many companies have shared emotion-arousing ads on social media sites. Some of these have been very effective and are shared widely. Feelings and moods can be influenced by engaging consumers through games. Such affective experiences not only deliver online brand experience but also build emotional bonds with consumers.
- **Cognitive:** Cognitive brand experience refers to stimulating the consumer on an intellectual level. Providing information, educating consumers and involving them in problem-solving activities leads to cognitive experience. The brand not only provides information but also lets consumers interact with others, gaining expert tips or advice, along with other engagement methods. The use of competitions, games and quizzes too engage customers on the cognitive level.
- **Relational:** The relational brand experience is built by introducing a social context. People like to belong to a group and interact with others having similar interests. Companies create brand communities to impart a sense of belongingness for

members. Brand communities create bonds and a sense of belongingness among members and also between consumers and the brand. Tools that encourage brand communities are discussion boards, 'ask an expert' and similar features. Companies can also invest in multiplayer online games to encourage a sense of community.

All this will add to the engagement and increase willingness of consumers to post comments or generate content, sharing content and writing reviews. Features such as chats with employees, review sections or ability to post pictures and text add to engagement. Companies have to integrate these methods and must use all of them in varying degrees. Different digital platforms must be used together with experiences in the real world. This is accomplished by an omnichannel approach.

■ OMNICHANNEL BRAND BUILDING

Omnichannel brand building refers to the integration of online and offline channels to deliver a consistent brand experience. All channels should speak the same language and deliver the same messages. The colour schemes of brands, the style and language must remain the same across the channels.

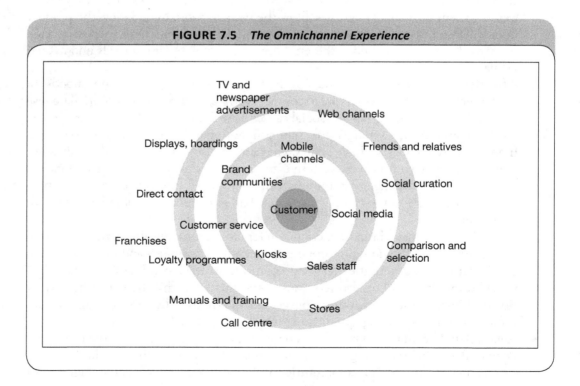

FIGURE 7.5 *The Omnichannel Experience*

Very often, brands make the mistake of using different channels to send different messages. For example, a company's message is very often diluted by what distributors and agents convey. Also, online and offline channels sometimes offer different discounts and schemes, so customers get confused. If a customer pays more for a brand and later discovers that it was available cheaply on a different channel, it creates cognitive dissonance and brand image is damaged.

Omnichannel brand experiences cover a host of channels (Figure 7.5). All physical channels along with digital channels combine to create a holistic brand experience. Companies have to learn to be consistent across all these diverse channels. Maslowska, Malthouse and Collinger (2016) sums up the four components of omnichannel customer engagement: (a) customer brand experience, (b) brand dialogue behaviours, (c) brand consumption and (d) shopping behaviours.

An omnichannel approach leads us to intervene in CDJs at the right time with the right message. Consumer intervention mapping thus becomes an important tool to influence consumers most effectively.

■ CONSUMER INTERVENTION MAPPING

Consumer intervention mapping is a tool for visualizing and enhancing customer touch points in the CDJ over three stages: pre-purchase, purchase and post-purchase. Sinclair et al. (2018) describe a tool that visualizes the points within a product's life cycle where stakeholders are able to intervene in the expected journey (Figure 7.6). It shows how consumers interact with marketing stimuli as they decide their purchase and later on after they have made the purchase. The points in the chart show the points of exposure or interaction with marketing stimuli and how companies can intervene to smoothen the CDJ.

All touch points are indicated by the dots on the chart. For instance, if the chart shows many dots in the pre-purchase section while the purchase area is empty, it shows that companies should intervene to nudge the consumer into the purchase and later, in the post-purchase section. Empty portions of the map will show gaps in brand communication. This will help improve sales and encourage recommendations from customers.

The map also shows the need to engage consumers across channels. It can be seen in the chart that consumers move seamlessly between the virtual and physical worlds, necessitating the management of omnichannel experiences. At each stage, brands have to devise ways of brand engagement.

■ BRAND ENGAGEMENT

Brand engagement refers to the interest generated among consumers about a brand's content and their willingness to interact with it. Customer engagement is delivered by

FIGURE 7.6   *Consumer Intervention Mapping Shows the Touch Points in Consumer Decision Journey*

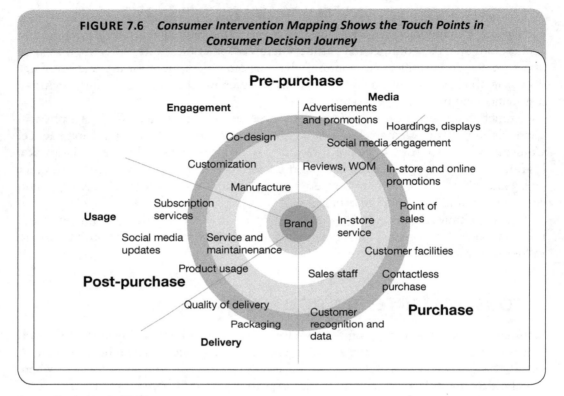

Source: Sinclair et al. (2018).

four actions: (a) Touch points experience; (b) Brand actions and brand experience; (c) Brand dialogue and content; and (d) Physical interaction with the brand. Customers move through these components in a dynamic and non-linear fashion.

1. **Touch points experience:** The experience of customers when they come into contact with a brand's touch point determines the quality and length of their engagement. Hence, tracking touch point experience becomes important. Many software providers offer touch point analysis tools that show the number of times consumers engage with a media platform and the time spent by them on it. This can be used to map how customers interact with brands. A touch point cockpit or a dashboard shows coverage of target markets.

2. **Brand actions:** What a brand does constitutes brand actions. These include all communications and online/offline activities of the company as well as its openness to outside activity, such as customer involvement with product development. It is not just what the company does and communicates but also the investment it makes to use and create platforms for stakeholder interaction. Done properly, such actions enthuse consumers to interact with brands. As mentioned elsewhere in the

book, consumers wish to interact with brands provided the activity interests them. All the media available, owned, paid or earned reflect brand actions. Modern marketing tries to stimulate engagement with brands, which is in contrast with traditional marketing, which was more focused on purchase.

3. **Brand dialogue and content:** Companies create content to encourage conversations. This has given rise to *dialogue marketing*, which means building audiences through compelling content and delightful experiences that encourage customers to enter into dialogues with the brand. Interacting with a company gives consumers a sense of importance and helps in building relationships. Each dialogue and interaction generates data and these data are used to customize messages and experience for individual consumers. Customers can be motivated to enter into dialogues and interactions by offering rewards.

4. **Physical interaction with the brand:** The emphasis on online activity often results in companies ignoring brand interactions in the physical world. Yet, consumers flit easily between online and offline worlds. That is why physical interaction adds to brand building. If a person orders a dress online, for example, it is the physical world that delivers it. Experiences across channels are therefore important and successful companies integrate them.

Underlying this activity is the philosophy of customer-centricity, which means always keeping the customer in central focus. This is explained in the next section.

■ BRAND CUSTOMER CENTRICITY

Customer centricity means that the brand has a sharp focus on providing a positive experience at all points in the CDJ. Brands with customer centricity focus on all interactions to build relationships and have powerful CRM programmes. They are designed to deliver positive product and service experience leading to building brand image. Brand centricity consists of various activities as shown in Figure 7.7.

- **Understand customers:** Companies use data mining to understand their customers. Detailed profiles are made and feedback is encouraged across channels.
- **Customer-focused leadership:** Customer-focused leadership means instituting best industry practices. Companies adopt methods used by others to make every CX effortless and seamless. CRM best practices can track the activities and conversations that consumers have online so that it can respond quickly to queries and comments. Some brands keep in touch with customers by using traditional methods such as interviews, surveys, focus groups and appointing customer advisory groups. But also important is tracking sales and CRM data, web data, blogs, reviews, social data and other data sets.
- **Design the experience:** Touch point tracking leads to better experience. Bottlenecks are removed by being customer centric. For example, if many users leave the website

FIGURE 7.7   *Brand Customer Centricity*

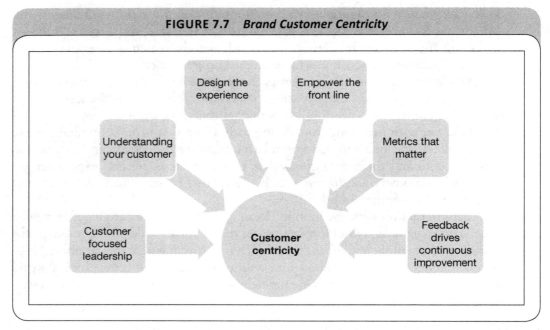

Source: https://2stallions.com/blog/5-customer-centric-approaches-that-makes-sense/ (accessed on 15 April 2021).

quickly, it means that the company was not able to hold their interest. It would have to redesign the website to make it more pleasing and interactive. Similarly, every touch point can be designed to provide opportunities for creating brand experience.

- **Empower the front line:** The most neglected area in marketing is the 'last mile' delivery or the point of sale. In e-commerce, delivery is usually entrusted to a third party. In traditional business, the salesperson who deals with the customer is usually the lowest paid employee in a company. So while companies spend a lot of resources building the brand experience, the last mile delivery is left to employees who may not be motivated enough to deliver a memorable brand experience. The efforts of brand building thus become jeopardized at the stage of the last mile delivery.

- **Metrics:** For companies to assess their customer centricity, they must have an objective measuring system to know whether their efforts are working or not. Some of the metrics that are used are customer retention score, contribution to profitability and customer referrals. Some other metrics used by companies are average response time, CSAT scores, net promoter score (NPS) and contribution by channel.

- **Feedback:** A customer-centric brand values feedback from customers. It institutes systems for getting feedback and also to track online customer conversations. Since many customers prefer to remain silent, brands have the task to find the views that are often not expressed.

Customer-centric organizations are able to build brands that stay in their customers' minds. However, it is important to remain proactive at all times. A customer-centric brand should be able to identify problems before they arise. Marketing Insight 7.4 shows how luxury brands use customer centricity to deliver an online feeling of exclusivity.

The next step is to make the brand widely visible over the Internet. One method of achieving this is social curation or sharing content on sites where it is seen by a large number of users.

MARKETING INSIGHT 7.4   *Luxury Experience Online*

Luxury brands face a dilemma of whether to go online or not. For years, these brands maintained their aura of exclusivity. Their stores are found on the high streets of fashion, their interiors, design, people and experience—all emit luxury at every step. Luxury brands spell class the world over and have a very high customer centricity.

The online environment poses a dilemma for them. Should they limit their presence to physical stores only and maintain their exclusivity or should they go online and risk rubbing shoulders with lower end brands and face the danger of losing their exclusive appeal? Moreover, the Internet is replete with sites selling imitation or fake luxury goods. Would customers trust anything purchased online? High-end companies also face the risk of losing control over their brand image and storytelling since customers yield more power online. Kapferer (2017) writes that the democratizing interactive nature of the Internet compels a change in traditional luxury communication strategies.

Another problem is exclusivity, which could be maintained in physical markets by having stores in high-end retail streets, airports and five-star hotels. There is no such distinction online—one website is as good as another. But online does offer an advantage: High-end customers can browse and shop from the privacy of their homes. By not going online, luxury brands realized that they would be losing out on their customers.

For years, luxury brands resisted going online but realized that new technologies could well be deployed to build their brands online. While it is true that search engines do not differentiate between luxury and common brands, they could still reap online benefits. For one thing, the very rich could customize and buy luxury products without leaving their homes. Brands could also deliver online experience by using exclusive design elements. Luxury brands realized that they could create their own space in the online world, and in the process expose the sites selling fake products.

A report by McKinsey and Co. (2015) shows that 'three out of four luxury purchases, even if they still take place in stores, are influenced by what consumers see, do and hear online. Digital, in other words, is now the engine of the luxury shopping experience.'

It was found that the customers of luxury brands are tech-savvy and usually have multiple digital devices. Their homes are digitally connected with the latest high-end devices, and rich customers engage with technology in the best possible way. They were also found to be active on social media.

This represented an untapped opportunity. Luxury brands could use their customers' homes to deliver a seamless multichannel experience, and brands have seized the opportunity after shedding their initial hesitation. Brands such as Rolex, BMW, Mercedes, Chanel,

---

(Continued)

(Continued)

Gucci, Prada and Hermès are now invested online to influence the complex CDJs. Indeed, the sales of luxury goods online have outperformed those of other brands. Sales are generated from two sources, the brands' own websites and from the sites of luxury department stores.

Luxury brands found that beauty products and ready-to-wear garments were the most popular categories online and have contributed to their growth. For example, if a customer could not find a particular size or variation in the store, it could be immediately ordered online and delivered personally to their homes. It was also noticed that the online touch points and recommendations exerted great influence, so stores were equipped with digital displays and mirrors. The online presence of high-end brands has therefore been quite a success. Contributing to the success have been the following factors.

- **Physical store:** Luxury customers like to see and experience products in physical stores that convey luxury much better than websites. Stores remain an important element in luxury branding: any online strategy cannot do without in-store experience. Well-trained salespersons can help deliver a memorable experience.
- **Peer influence:** The very rich are very conscious of their peers. Both traditional interactions and digital conversations are important influencers.
- **Online experience:** Luxury brands convey their exclusivity by online store design and experience (Figure 7.8). Investments were made for a customer online through the brand's site and other means. Luxury brands have rich brand assets and unique brand heritage. All these are effectively used online. The main challenge is to transfer the in-store luxury experience to the online environment and has been done quite well by brands.

Kluge et al. (2013) write that homepage design significantly affects consumers' perceptions. Thus, luxury brands have to communicate distinctiveness and uniqueness by their homepage design. They found that web page design must have the following characteristics:

FIGURE 7.8 *Luxury Brands Create Online Experience by Simplistic Design, Glamorous Models and Use of Light and Colours*

Source: https://www.ironpaper.com/luxury-fashion-website/ (accessed on 15 April 2021).

- The use of dark background colours
- Exclusive and glamorous models
- The use of a larger or full-screen space to present the content
- A horizontal navigation bar
- A substantial reduction of elements

Do you agree that luxury brands are able to deliver an exclusive experience online? How?

Sources

Kapferer, J.-N. 2017. 'The End of Luxury as We Knew It?' In *Advances in Luxury Brand Management*, edited by J. N. Kapferer, J. Kernstock, T. O. Brexendorf, and S. M. Powell, Part of the *Journal of Brand Management: Advanced Collections* book series. doi: 10.1007/978–3–319–51127–62

Kluge, P., J. Königsfeld, M. Fassnacht, and F. Mitschke. 2013. 'Luxury Web Atmospherics: An Examination of Homepage Design.' *International Journal of Retail & Distribution Management* 41, nos 11/12: 901–916. Available at: https://doi.org/10.110 (accessed on 22 January 2021).

McKinsey and Co. 2015. *Digital Inside: Get Wired for the Ultimate Luxury Experience.* Available at: https://www.mckinsey.com/business-functions/marketing-and-sales/our-insights/digital-inside-get-wired-for-the-ultimate-luxury-experience (accessed on 22 January 2021).

◼ SOCIAL CURATION AND BRANDS

Dialogue and interaction build relationships. Thus, companies have to build an ongoing dialogue with customers. Social curation, or sharing content on social channels, encourages such dialogue.

Social curation is the collaborative sharing of content. It can be built around particular themes and communities. If a brand gets associated with a social cause, it can curate content around that cause and attract users to interact with that content. This is called *humanizing a brand* since it gives brand meaning and personality. This is easy when companies are built around values. Brands can thus institute programmes to curate content related to their business and values, which is helpful in attracting customers. Kotler (2017) writes that increasingly brands are adopting human qualities, and hence must be physically attractive as well as socially and emotionally appealing.

For example, a company can curate content about its history, including past advertisements, achievements and customer feedback. This content will attract customers who can learn about brand values. For example, financial companies curate content about investment advice, while real estate companies write blogs and share content about advice on house hunting. Anyone who clicks for such advice thus gets connected to the brand.

Some popular sites of social curation sites are Digg, Delicious and Reddit, which allow users to share articles. Users, including brands, can submit a story to digg.com as a way for users to share web content and news articles on the Internet. Users can express their approval to the content by clicking a 'thumbs up' icon on Digg. Delicious is a social bookmarking service for storing, sharing and discovering web bookmarks, while Reddit is a network of communities based on people's interests. Brands use these for curating content, which also impacts the ranking of the content.

Another example of social curation website is pinterest.com, which allows users to pin and share images. The site allows users to 'like', 're-pin', comment on content shared by others and put it on their own boards. Hall and Zarro (2012) write that user comments offer valuable sources of understanding consumer likes and dislikes. Pinterest allows sharing opinions and personal histories, building narratives and so on. They write, 'Pinterest represents a sharing and curating experience that offers insight into information use, reuse and creation on the social web.'

Social curation is important as it helps spread online brand content. Content is increasingly a shared social experience, write Villi, Moisander and Joy (2012), as people like to interact with content that has been shared by their friends. A survey by Pew Research (Purcell et al. 2010) found that in the USA, three-fourths of the online users read news that is shared by their friends. Newman and Dutton (2011) write that this increases the importance of communities in distributing media content.

◼ CONCLUSION

Building brands remains to be an important activity in marketing. However, brand building is no longer online or offline; it must encompass methods in both domains. Brands must develop capabilities to deliver CX seamlessly across channels. When we realize this, we find that shops are not enemies of e-commerce. Both have specific roles, with the common objective of delivering experience and serving customers.

Building brands online follows traditional methods. Keller's model of customer-based brand equity described in his book, *Strategic Brand Management* (2013), is still relevant, and online methods enhance brand identity, impart brand meaning, elicit brand responses and build brand relationships.

Online branding exerts a pull element and means that users go to a particular site for the purchase transaction rather than use a search engine. In that sense, the FMOT need not be the search engine. The objective of marketing is to build brand equity that is achieved through emotional connect, trust, online experience, responsive service nature and fulfilment. Online brand equity is positively associated with brand experience, brand attitudes and brand attachment (Rezaei and Valaei 2017).

Online branding must combine the elements described in traditional marketing by having a consistent brand message across channels, adapting to social media and other platforms and methods, utilizing multiple channels to connect with customers, understanding them and involving them and building a system of engaging customers in diverse activities from design to experience.

SUMMARY

The methods for online branding, or building brand identities, are quite different from traditional branding. Instead of mass advertising, online branding depends on consumer engagement. Online branding has two components: CX with the brand and the experience with online brand properties and communications (UX).

Branding consists of defining the purpose and basic values of the brand, building on assets and heritage, and finally delivering brand experience across channels. The technologies and systems used to deliver brand experience constitute a digital brand ecosystem. The digital brand ecosystem is tracked by 3Ps. This helps in understanding consumers and their interactions, and also in influencing their purchase decisions.

Online brand experience is delivered through four dimensions: sensory, affective, cognitive and relational. However, the need of the hour is omnichannel brand building. The four components of omnichannel customer engagement are (a) customer brand experience, (b) brand dialogue behaviours, (c) brand consumption and (d) shopping behaviours. Customer engagement is delivered by four actions: (a) touch points experience, (b) brand actions and brand experience, (c) brand dialogue and content, and (d) physical interaction with the brand.

To achieve this, companies have to maintain customer centricity throughout the CDJ. This includes understanding customers, customer-focused leadership, CX, metrics, feedback and empowering frontline workers. Finally, social curation is described as a method of sharing content on social channels and encouraging dialogues with customers.

KEY TERMS

Brand customer centricity: It means the ability of the brand to keep sharp focus on providing a positive experience at all points in the CDJ.

Brand ecosystem: It refers to the brand experience that companies design for their customers.

Brand engagement: The interest generated among consumers about a brand's content and their willingness to interact with it.

Consumer intervention mapping: A tool for visualizing and enhancing customer touch points in the CDJ over three stages: pre-purchase, purchase and post-purchase.

CX: CX is an interaction between a company and consumers when they experience a brand's products and services.

Dialogue marketing: The process of building audiences through compelling content and delightful experiences that encourages customers to enter into dialogues with the brand.

Digital brand ecosystem: The overall brand experience that companies design for their customers and the methods used to deliver it. It can be tracked by 3Ps.

Omnichannel brand building: The integration of online and offline channels to deliver a consistent experience to customers.

Online branding: Building an identity for a product or service, improving visibility and establishing credibility in the virtual world.

Online brand experience: The quality of the experience that users get on the basis of marketing stimuli provided by the brand on the Internet.

Social curation: The collaborative sharing of content on social channels.

UX: UX design is the quality of digital interactions with a user. It is the process of influencing users by their interaction with digital devices.

CONCEPT REVIEW QUESTIONS

1. What is the importance of branding? Is it relevant for online brands?
2. Describe the difference in methods of branding in traditional and online worlds.
3. What are the elements of brand identity? How are they used for online branding?
4. Explain UX and CX and their interaction in branding.
5. What is digital brand ecosystem. What is its purpose?
6. Discuss the elements of online brand experience.
7. Describe the various channels that are used in delivering brand experiences.
8. What is a customer intervention map? What does it show?
9. Describe the components of brand engagement.
10. What is social curation? How do brands do this and what are its benefits?

CRITICAL THINKING QUESTIONS

1. With short attention spans of modern consumers and their capability to access information, it is said that brands will not be able to sustain in the future. Describe your viewpoint and support your answer with the help of examples.
2. Companies spend a lot of effort on their logos, colour schemes, fonts and design. How far are these relevant in the online environment? What role do they play?
3. Analyse some brands on the basis of their customer centricity. Rate them on a scale of 1–10 on this aspect. What more could they do on improving customer centricity? Are they doing it in excess so as to turn customers away?
4. Analyse the touch points of a customer in their pre-purchase, purchase and post-purchase stages in a customer buying process of a laptop or mobile phone. Which touch points are more influential than others?

PROJECTS AND ASSIGNMENTS

1. Select a company such as Uber, BookMyShow, Paytm or Amazon. Describe the elements in their UX and CX, and describe how they interact to deliver CX.

2. Explore a site like Pinterest or Diggit and see the content related to brands. How are the brands doing it? Are they successful? How can brands optimize social curation?

3. Make a project on the comparison of luxury brand sites. What brand elements do you see that are commonly used? Which ones are unique to particular sites?

4. Search the Internet for brands that have failed or lost their customers, such as Orkut and Myspace. Describe the mistakes committed by them. How far can these mistakes be attributed to business models or operational failures?

▇ REFERENCES

Aaker, D. A., and F. Joachimsthaler. 2000. *Brand Leadership Building Assets in the Information Society*. New York, NY: Free Press.

Baxendale, S., E. K. Macdonald, and H. N. Wilson. 2015. 'The Impact of Different Touchpoints on Brand Consideration.' *Journal of Retailing* 91, no. 2: 235–253. Available at: https://doi.org/10.1016/j.jretai.2014.12.008 (accessed on 22 January 2021).

Edelman, D., and M. Singer. 2015. 'Competing on Customer Journeys.' *Harvard Business Review*. Available at: https://hbr.org/2015/11/competing-on-customer-journeys (accessed on 22 January 2021).

Hall, C., and M. Zarro. 2012. 'Social Curation on the Website Pinterest.com.' *Proceedings of the American Society for Information Science and Technology* 49, no. 1 (January). doi:10.1002/meet.14504901189

Keller, K. L. 2013. *Strategic Brand Management*. 4th ed. Essex: Pearson Education.

Khan, I. Z. R., and M. Fatma. 2016. 'The Concept of Online Corporate Brand Experience: An Empirical Assessment.' *Marketing Intelligence & Planning*. Available at: https://www.emerald.com/insight/content/doi/10.1108/MIP–01–2016–0007/full/html (accessed on 22 January 2021).

Kotler, P. 2017. *Marketing 4.0: Moving from Traditional to Digital*. New Delhi: Wiley.

Maslowska, E., E. C. Malthouse, and T. Collinger. 2016. 'The Customer Engagement Ecosystem.' *Journal of Marketing Management* 32, nos 5–6: 469–501. doi:10.1080/0267257X.2015.1134628

Morgan-Thomas, A., and C. Veloutsou. 2013. 'Beyond Technology Acceptance: Brand Relationships and Online Brand Experience.' *Journal of Business Research*. doi:10.1016/j.jbusres.2011.07.019

Newman, N., and W. Dutton. 2011. 'Social Media in the Changing Ecology of News Production and Consumption: The Case in Britain.' Paper presented at the 2011 International Communication Association Conference, Boston, USA, 26–30 May.

Purcell, K., L. Rainie, A. Mitchell, T. Rosenstiel, and K. Olmstead. 2010. *Understanding the Participatory News Consumer: How Internet and Cell Phone Users Have Turned News into a Social Experience* (Pew Internet and American Life Project). Washington, DC: Pew Research Center.

Rezaei, S., and N. Valaei. 2017. 'Branding in a Multichannel Retail Environment: Online Stores vs App Stores and the Effect of Product Type.' *Information Technology & People* 30, no. 4. Available at: https://doi.org/10.1108/ITP–12–2015–0308 (accessed on 22 January 2021).

Simon, C., T. O. Brexendorf, and M. Fassnacht. (2013). 'Creating Online Brand Experience on Facebook.' *Marketing Review St. Gallen* 30, no. 6: 50–59.

Sinclair, M., L. Sheldrick, M. Moreno, and E. Dewberry. 2018. 'Consumer Intervention Mapping—A Tool for Designing Future Product Strategies within Circular Product Service Systems.' *Sustainability* 10, no. 6 (June): 1–21.

Villi, M., J. Moisander, and A. Joy. 2012. 'Social Curation in Consumer Communities: Consumers as Curators of Online Media Content.' In *NA—Advances in Consumer Research*, Vol. 40, edited by Zeynep Gürhan-Canli, Cele Otnes and Rui (Juliet) Zhu: 490–495. Duluth, MN: Association for Consumer Research.

CLOSING CASE

CHANGING WITH THE TIMES—WALMART AND AMAZON

Walmart is a traditional retailer. Amazon is an online retailer. Both are big brands. Both want to ensure their longevity: While one is trying to adjust to the world of online retailing, the other wants to extend its reach in the grocery business in the real world.

Although both behemoths compete for the same customers, this case study is not about their competition or strategy. It shows how brands must make serious efforts to remain relevant in the changing times and develop capabilities that they lack. Both brands are using innovation and technology to build on their strengths, realizing that the future is neither offline alone nor online alone, but omnichannel. Instead of responding to competition, they follow the advice mentioned in the book *The Everything Store* by Brad Stone (2013): '….don't be worried about our competitors because they're never going to send us any money anyway. Let's be worried about our customers and stay heads-down focused.'

This is the secret recipe for both stores. Although Walmart is the world's biggest retail chain, it has little influence online. Amazon has continued its march and over the years and claimed almost half of the US online shopping market but seeks physical presence for expansion and have low-cost fulfilment centres in towns. But both brands realized that to remain relevant to today's customers, they must switch to omnichannel marketing. While online branding helps traditional businesses, online brands must venture into the physical world to remain relevant in the connected world.

The story of change in the direction of a huge shop like Walmart makes an interesting story. Walmart is 'creating a seamless experience to let customers shop anytime and anywhere online, through mobile devices and in stores', says its website. Walmart's position as the largest retailer means that it must constantly invest in new and innovative ways to maintain its position. The company may not have ventured into online retail earlier, but it must be said that it is a tech-savvy company. It analyses consumer data for assessing demand and retail store data for inventory management. It knows its customers' buying habits. Technology is the backbone through which it offers 'everyday low prices' making it popular among shoppers. The work-from-home protocols provide a boost to its online strategy, writes Boyle (2020). Consumers are already familiar with the Walmart brand, and the switch to online has been easy. The retail store advantage is that it keeps meat and vegetables closer to consumers and is able to make local deliveries faster.

The same capabilities are being extended to its online business. Investments in back-end technology that Walmart has made over the years are now helping its push into the e-commerce business. For instance, Walmart now offers a grocery delivery service that puts items straight into the customer's refrigerator, even when the customer is not at home. The 'In Home Delivery' uses smart entry technology, which is monitored by customers through cameras worn by delivery associates. Service agents bring supplies, organize customers' refrigerators and take returns of products that customers leave on their kitchen counters. When the customer returns home, the supplies are all in place.

For its e-commerce push, it has acquired companies such as Jet.com, Hayneedle.com, Shoes.com, Moosejaw and Modcloth.com, and has developed its arsenal to become a key e-commerce player. Instead of viewing e-commerce and in-store retail as two competing revenue streams, Walmart views them as complementary. Customers can order online and have it delivered to their homes, or they can pick up the package from the store. In doing this, Walmart has leveraged technology to offer real differences in the services provided to customers and also draws more people to its stores.

During the coronavirus outbreak, Walmart made its parking lots available for drive-thru testing, leveraging its physical stores. It has also opened health centres in its stores that offer medical and mental health services for a flat fee.

The physical presence of Walmart helps to reduce investments in fulfilment centres. It uses its physical stores as supply hub for online sales. Since stores are already making profits from grocery sales, adding e-commerce supplies adds little to costs. Online companies, on the other hand, have to invest in warehouses or fulfilment centres since they have no stores. Amazon, for instance, spends heavily for same-day deliveries and investing in its warehouses. Walmart thus gains an advantage in reducing costs since deliveries are the biggest expense in online sales and offers next-day shipping on select items.

In India, it has acquired a majority stake in a big e-commerce company, Flipkart. Walmart has invested heavily in IT investments, posing a challenge to the online dominance of Amazon. In the stores, it uses AI to monitor the inventory of perishable goods. By doing so, Walmart has broadened its customer base, becoming a retailing company operating in both the physical and virtual worlds. Walmart is using its well-established traditional retail business to adapt to online retailing, leveraging on its physical presence. Its campaign is paying off, writes Mullaney (2019).

Amazon is doing the opposite: It is trying to get a foothold in the grocery business. It has a huge online presence but has to invest heavily to match the advantages of physical stores that Walmart has. It faces a moment of vulnerability, writes Dooley (2020). It has taken over a traditional retailer Whole Foods. Although it lags behind Walmart, its revenues from grocery sales are rising considerably. Its battle arsenal consists of Whole Foods, Amazon Fresh and Amazon Prime same-day delivery.

Amazon has realized that it must have a presence in the physical space as well. Its 'Amazon Go' stores have added innovation to the self-serve convenience store. Customers simply pick up the goods and walk out. The billing is done automatically and the amount is deducted from the customers' accounts without the help of a cashier. Amazon offers quick shipping to get over its shortcoming of not having many physical stores. It offers next-day delivery for Prime members. In India, it plans to tie up with traditional grocers and mom-and-pop stores to expand its business.

Amazon is using technology in its physical stores and streamlining its supply chain. It has its own fleet for one-day deliveries, with drone deliveries in some areas, becoming a top-notch logistics company. Walmart is using technology to expand into the online business. Both Amazon and Walmart are changing the retail landscape, keeping customer needs in focus.

(Continued)

(Continued)

The case shows that brands must keep innovating to survive and grow in the changing environment. Both online and offline brands have much to gain from each others' experience.

Questions for Discussion

1. What is the importance of branding in online environments?
2. How do brands use online capabilities to extend brand image and experience?
3. How does customer centricity and touch point analysis help in building brands?
4. What are the elements of brand identity and how do they interact in online and offline worlds?

Sources

Boyle, M. 2020. 'The U.S. Is Shutting Down. For Walmart, It's Time to Step Up.' Bloomberg. Available at: https://www.bloomberg.com/news/articles/2020–03–17/the-nation-is-shutting-down-for-walmart-it-s-time-to-step-up (accessed on 22 January 2021).

Dooley, R. 2020. 'Is Amazon Vulnerable?' *Forbes*. Available at: https://www.forbes.com/sites/rogerdooley/2020/05/08/is-amazon-vulnerable/#346c324a6d64 (accessed on 22 January 2021).

Mullaney, T. 2019. 'This Is What's behind Walmart's Staying Power That Could Outmaneuver Amazon.' CNBC. Available at: https://www.cnbc.com/2019/08/15/walmarts-secret-weapon-in-its-quest-to-outmaneuver-amazon.html (accessed on 22 January 2021).

Stone, B. 2013. *The Everything Store: Jeff Bezos and the Age of Amazon*. New York, NY: Little Brown and Co.

CHAPTER 8

Digital Marketing Strategy

Learning Objectives

This chapter explains that digital marketing strategy is much more than making online content popular. It describes the four pillars of digital strategy, consisting of customer engagement, value chain transformation, re-imagining the business and rebuilding the organization. It also describes the tactics of strategy implementation.

After reading this chapter, you will be able to learn about the following:

☐ Digital strategy and its components
☐ Characteristics of 'digital masters' or companies that use digital technology better than everyone else
☐ Tactics of strategy, going beyond branded content, influencer marketing and managing communities
☐ Measuring marketing outcomes through digital marketing metrics

OPENING CASE

DIGITAL MASTERS: ASIAN PAINTS

Digital masters are companies that use digital technology to drive significantly higher levels of profit, productivity and performance, writes Westerman (2018). These companies are better than their competitors at two key capabilities: (a) digital capability and (b) leadership capability. The first is about using social, mobile, analytics and cloud to engage with customers and constantly introducing innovations into the business. This is the domain of IT people. But leadership capability is much more important because it is leadership that gives direction to the digital strategy.

Leaders understand that digital is not just a technology challenge but a transformation opportunity. 'Digital masters' are not technology companies but those companies that are able to use digital technologies effectively to transform themselves to drive growth and profits.

(Continued)

(Continued)

This case study describes the digital transformation of Asian Paints, the leading paint manufacturer that has reinvented itself in the home décor and home improvement. It is one of India's most valued Indian brands. Asian Paints decided to 'Go Digital' in 2013 with the vision: 'To deliver delightful and engaging experiences across all interaction points thereby creating a positive bias towards our products & services, thus building lifetime loyalty.'

This was the driving principle for digitizing the organization's functions, from customer engagement and CRM to dealer management systems, including supply chain and manufacturing operations. As a result, the company transformed itself from a paint manufacturer to a provider of home improvement services. Jha (2017) describes how the company reinvented itself from being a product company to becoming a services company (Figure 8.1), providing Ezycolour Consultancy to guide customers about colour, décor and *vastu* (traditional Indian system of architecture).

Understanding the consumer: The transformation began with building understanding of the customer. The company mapped customer journeys, touch points and identified customer segments. It was found that customers looked for help about colours and styles when they decide to re-paint their homes. The company thus decided to offer consultancy services, thus establishing and differentiating itself from other companies. It was able to identify two different customer segments for its services: the upper middle-class businessmen or the nouveau riche who wanted to display their wealth through their homes. The company named this segment 'Rangeela'. The second segment was that of the educated, foreign returned, techie who wanted a high-end home in India. People in this segment were well aware of market options and information. The company called this segment 'Bermuda'.

ERP: The company upgraded its ERP system to the new S/4 HANA and was one of the first in India to do so. Call centres, analytics, ML and autonomous manufacturing were optimized for deliveries and tracking to ensure high order fill rates. The SAP HANA platform empowered its teams with information about stocks, inventory levels and possible shortages.

FIGURE 8.1   *Asian Paints Is a Company That Offers Integrated Home Improvement Services*

Source: https://www.asianpaints.com/ (accessed on 16 February 2021).

An improved demand forecasting system helped to improve supplies and also to reduce inventory costs. The company uses data mining to improve logistics, people analytics and material sourcing.

CRM: The company's CRM system connects with customers, analyses data for loyalty, calculates NPSs and measures CSAT. It is connected to Paint Total, a service model for dealers offering services using consumer information.

Omnichannel consistency: A seamless experience to customers, dealers and influencers is provided by connecting all channels—physical, digital and human. The customer journeys across channels were mapped using a data architecture based on SAP enterprise application software combined with Adobe's Experience Management platform. This helped the company to develop seamless omnichannel customer journeys, helping to generate unique offers to each customer. An integrated view provides data to the call centres, consultants and dealers for responding to customer needs and queries.

Culture: Culture plays an important role for any transformation. The leadership of the company was able to re-imagine the future of the company by leveraging new business opportunities. The company was founded in 1942; one major achievement was to be able to get over the resistance from employees and partners and to change its culture towards adopting digital technology across physical channels.

Social media: The company used social media initially to address customer complaints and later for campaigns to educate customers about home décor solutions. In this way, the company has transformed itself from being a bricks-and-mortar business into a 'click-and-mortar' business.

Physical transformation: Along with its digital initiatives, the company undertook a physical transformation as well. To meet the needs of the modern customers, the company launched large showrooms with an average area of 10,000 square feet in partnership with dealers. Equipped with 3D visualization and virtual reality, these stores provide customers with a visual experience, allowing them to experience different colours and textures. Consultants assist in the decision-making process. IoT, AI, chatbots and natural language translation capabilities are also used.

Web presence: The company has a strong web presence with sites such as asianpaints. com, sleekworld.com and beautifulhomes.com. These serve as platforms for consumers looking for advice on painting and decorating their homes. Asian Paints tracks customer interaction data and leverages the data with advanced web analytics and personalization technology to position content with customer offers.

Although Asian Paints is known as a paint manufacturer, it has acquired companies dealing in modular kitchen space and bathroom fittings that fit perfectly with its thrust on the home improvement business. It has integrated technology into its operations, with the IT head as part of the corporate advisory board, which has helped the company to use modern technology in its business operations, keeping it ahead of the curve.

In 2008, Asian Paints adopted automated storage and retrieval systems at a time when robotic warehousing was entirely new in India and aligned it with its ERP system. Gains in inventory management, operations and supply chains added to the company's bottom line. It uses the cloud in its business operations, gradually shifting processes such as employee life cycle, sales engagement and customer visualization processes.

(Continued)

(Continued)

Given that Asian Paints is an 'old economy' company, it has managed the transition to technology very well. It has invested in people, culture and technology, using its legacy to build its brand equity. The company uses 3D visualization for showing various home décor options to customers. Partners use this to create visual models for customers, speeding up their purchase decision cycles. Customers can also interact with bots that assist them in their choices. The company uses the 'Eureka' app for generating new product ideas, which has been very successful. For dealers, a virtual territory sales officer app helps them to connect with customers.

Using an omnichannel approach, Asian Paints uses digital technologies to engage customers, dealers and influencers by supporting CDJs in the physical world using Colour Ideas and Signature Stores, and in the virtual world using websites and mobile technologies. It adds a human touch by providing colour consultancy through partners and dealers. Pain points of customers are eased by various means. One is a colour visualizer app, and another is the Signature Stores where the whole family can experience their home upgradation. An ecosystem has been created for contractors who play a key role in delivering services. Today, a contractor can engage with customers and the company through the mobile app.

While reading this chapter, try to answer the following questions:

1. What does digital strategy consist of?
2. What sets digital masters apart?
3. How can companies build a gravitational pull by deploying digital technologies?
4. What are the pitfalls to avoid while designing and implementing a digital strategy?

Sources

Jha, S. 2017. 'Revealed: How Asian Paints Leveraged Digital Innovations to Become Customer Centric.' *The Economic Times.* Available at: https://cio.economictimes.indiatimes.com/news/strategy-and-management/revealed-how-asian-paints-leveraged-digital-innovations-to-become-customer-centric/60053105 (accessed on 25 January 2021).

Westerman, G. 2018. 'Your Company Doesn't Need a Digital Strategy.' *MIT Sloan Management Review.* Available at: https://sloanreview.mit.edu/article/your-company-doesnt-need-a-digital-strategy/ (accessed on 25 January 2021).

■ INTRODUCTION

Digital strategy is often thought of using modern Internet and communication technologies in a company's business operations. Companies have used such technologies to communicate with stakeholders, reduce costs, engage customers and so on. But a digital marketing strategy is more than that and is limited by how people understand it.

The thrust of most digital strategies for many companies is to popularize content or to collect vanity statistics such as likes and shares. Thus, a lot of effort goes into making popular content. While this works for entertainers and celebrities because their business rests on their reputation, for companies this can hardly be seen as a viable business strategy. Digital marketing experts are limited by their focus on vanity figures rather than their significance in a company's marketing effort.

A digital strategy has to combine UX and CX, as described in Chapter 7. The challenge before companies is to integrate two diverse objectives:

1. IT objectives of using the web and social media by 'digital marketing experts'
2. Meeting the marketing objectives of growth and profitability

The IT department cannot be seen as a separate department but must be part of top management, as our case study of Asian Paints illustrates. Digital technologies have the power to redefine business. This is important to understand because some companies make the mistake of trying to adopt digital marketing while the rest of the companies stick to old ways of operations. As a consequence, they are unable to add value to their digital value chain (Chapter 2) or adopt processes that help them grow.

A digital marketing strategy is therefore not simply a strategy to use modern Internet and communication technologies, nor a plan to achieve digital goals through online channels, but much more.

UNDERSTANDING STRATEGY

Many digital marketing courses focus on gathering views on brand content, gaining followers or making users click on links and advertisements. Likewise, many companies misunderstand that a digital marketing strategy is simply about using modern Internet and communication technologies in conducting business. Chaffey and Ellis-Chadwick (2016) define digital marketing strategy as 'the approach by which applying digital technology platforms will support marketing and business objectives'.

A report by Deloitte (Kane et al. 2015) stresses that it is the strategy, not the technology, that drives digital transformation. 'The ability to digitally reimagine the business is determined in large part by a clear digital strategy supported by leaders who foster a culture able to change and invent the new,' it states. This shows that a business strategy must drive the digital, not the other way round. Yet, the report found that only 15 per cent of managers felt that their companies had a coherent digital strategy or had achieved *digital maturity*, the stage at which digital transforms processes, talent engagement and business models. Companies that are not digitally mature focus on operational technologies, whereas those that are digitally mature look to transforming the business.

The starting point of digital strategy is an Internet marketing plan (see Marketing Insight 8.1). An important point is that digital strategy is not about technology. Individual digital technologies, such as social, mobile, analytics and cloud, cannot individually contribute meaningfully to a company strategy, but the real strength arises from their integration into the business. Benkler (2006) writes that new information and communications technologies do not simply introduce efficiency into traditional ways of doing business but also support fundamentally new ways of doing things. This is the basis of digital mastery.

MARKETING INSIGHT 8.1   *Internet Marketing Plan*

An e-marketing plan is a blueprint that describes how the marketing objectives of a company will be achieved by using digital techniques. A strategic Internet marketing plan provides a view of the objectives that are to be accomplished and how. A plan is essential as it helps the company and its managers to stay focused on the final outcomes. Without a plan, companies can easily fall into the trap of posting content across channels without achieving additional revenue. A detailed plan will consist of the following:

- What the company wants to accomplish through the Internet
- Timelines for the initiation of online interventions
- Who will be in charge of the Internet marketing plan?
- How will the company implement the plan?

The steps involved in the Internet marketing plan are as follows.

1. **Establish objectives:** At the outset, a company should decide what it wants to achieve by an online presence. This is an important first step since many companies simply try to follow others without clear and stated objectives. The objectives can vary from brand building, providing information, engaging customers, generating interest, targeting prospects or accomplishing sales. A company must establish what it wants to achieve on the Internet along with sub-objectives.
2. **Define the target market:** On the Internet, it is possible to define the users who will be exposed to a company's messages. By slicing and precise targeting, marketing spends can be made efficient. The audience can be defined according to demographics such as age, gender, location and other data. Companies can target their current customers or try to increase their market share by targeting new users or new market segments.
3. **Discover the gaps:** Competitor analysis helps to discover the gaps in the market. It gives clues about the segments that can be served with digital methods and solutions to the problems faced by customers. Competitor analysis also helps in benchmarking processes.
4. **Set budgets:** It is possible to spend a lot of money on the Internet without corresponding sales or revenue. Fake users and scams, based on the number of followers, often short-circuit the online efforts of advertisers, and many companies have fallen victim to such scams. Clear budgets based on outcomes must be established at the beginning of an online marketing plan. Since all efforts can be tracked in real time, flexibility is needed in the budgeting process so that the company can change channels as and when needed.

5. **Establish timelines:** To keep marketing efforts firmly in control, companies should establish timelines based on outcomes. Strategy performance must be tracked on a weekly or monthly basis against objectives. Many tools are available for this. The most commonly used is Google Analytics, which helps companies know how they are performing.

6. **Select the channels:** Companies have to decide the online channels that they wish to choose. Each must arise from the objectives. Companies may, for instance, decide to use any combination of their own website, social media, email, community platforms and review platforms, depending on what they want to achieve.

7. **Define responsibility:** Very often, companies create a separate team to handle online and social media activity. This creates problems. Since online activities must always result from marketing objectives, the marketing team must have the responsibility of online interventions. More than that, all departments must be integrated into the customer interface because the customer deals with a company, not a department. Departmental silos must be broken. So while marketing leads the online thrust, everyone in the company must be involved to provide one, integrated response to the customer.

While making the Internet marketing plan, companies should leave room for creativity of employees. People must look for new and better ways of accomplishing objectives. Examples in this book show how companies that use creativity tend to capture customer interest.

DIGITAL MASTERY

Although every company is using digital technology in one way or the other, companies that have achieved digital maturity—called digital masters—do so much better than everyone else. Hence, they remain ahead of their competitors. It is not a matter of which technology or software package they use, but how they make use of technology to implement business practices. Digital masters have two capabilities in which they excel.

1. **Digital capabilities:** Digital masters invest in digital capabilities that contribute directly in improving business processes and customer engagements that shorten CDJs. They are always looking for technologies that help in solving business problems.

2. **Leadership capabilities:** Digitally mature companies have the capability of leading change. They use data streams and combine them with technology solutions for future growth, make better decisions and build efficiency in their supply chains. They are better able to understand customers and use their leadership capabilities to drive transformation and modify their business models.

Companies that are able to do this most effectively are referred to as 'digital masters' by Westerman, Bonnet and McAfee (2014). Digital masters are not technology companies but those companies that are able to use digital technologies to improve their existing businesses. Our case study of Asian Paints in this chapter and Nike in Chapter 1 show how a paint manufacturer and a sports goods company reinvented their models and brought them closer to their customers by using technology. Such companies report better profits than others in the same industry. On the other hand, even a company like Microsoft (see Marketing Insight 8.2) can lose track of its customers and miss out on growth opportunities. It was only after the company reinvented itself that it could become a master again.

Digital masters can be distinguished from other companies in their use of technology. For example, many companies simply follow the latest trend and adopt it because everybody else is doing it. So they invest in blogs, creating branded content, engage on social media and so on without a clear strategy. Such companies are dubbed as *fashionistas* who flaunt technology, but it does not contribute to profits. Unfortunately, there are a large number of companies that fall in this category.

On the other extreme are *conservatives* who are very careful in deploying technology. They invest in a few functions, but an integrated approach or a leadership role is missing. Conservative companies stress on control and thereby miss opportunities in business. Usually, there are no digital leaders on their boards.

Digital masters get over the limitations of both fashionistas and conservatives. Digital masters drive their strategy from the boardroom rather than adding digital components to their functions. This is an important distinction. Not only does it help gain efficiency from new technologies but also shows the company a path to tap new markets and to reinvent itself.

Carr (2003) writes that companies fall into the trap of focusing on technology as an end in itself, whereas technology must be used as a means to achieve strategic objectives.

Apart from tracking customer behaviour and enhancing experience across channels, using digital technologies to increase reach and engagement, and building social media experiences, digital masters use data analytics to put CX at the centre of their strategy. Another point to note is that digital masters do not differentiate between physical and digital experiences and successfully integrate the two. This is the basis of digital strategy, as described in the next section.

MARKETING INSIGHT 8.2   *Microsoft's Digital Strategy*

Microsoft, the company founded by Bill Gates, is well known for the computer revolution it spawned by providing operating systems that made personal computers useful for millions of people around the world. It was the most valuable company for many years but lost out to other companies such as Google, Amazon and Apple. In 2007, a blog post 'Microsoft Is Dead' became highly popular. Having missed out on the mobile revolution, it seemed that the company that gave the world Windows would slowly vanish as other companies and technologies continued to gain favour.

It did not happen that way. In 2018, Microsoft briefly became the most valuable company in the world once again, pushing Apple to the second place. Naughton (2019) describes how

Microsoft came back. It is a great comeback story: Microsoft had not been in the reckoning for the first position since 2002. And behind the comeback is an excellent use of a strategy that encompasses using digital technologies, company culture and transformation. The company changed course when Satya Nadella took over as CEO, replacing Steve Ballmer in 2014.

Microsoft at one time had been dubbed an 'evil empire', and thereafter had let the mobile and social media revolution pass it by. It had not been able to capitalize on its OS capability, giving up the advantage to Google's Android system.

This case study describes how Microsoft has turned around to again (Novet 2018) be reckoned as the world's most valuable listed company, worth over $1 trillion. Some of the things it did are described below.

- **Open source:** Earlier, the company relied on its Windows domination. Bill Gates had articulated his dream of a computer on every desk, each running Microsoft software. The dream had been realized and, for many years, Windows became ubiquitous. However, the company could not capitalize on developments that came about later. The world changed perceptibly because of the rise of the Internet, cloud computing and the arrival of smartphones. Mobiles used Google's Android and the company could hardly make a dent with its late arrival of Nokia mobile phone running on the Windows operating system. Under Nadella, Microsoft gave up its obsession with Windows. Instead, it opted for open-source software projects using Linux in cloud technologies and even in Windows 10.
- **Cloud services:** Nadella was instrumental in changing the direction to cloud services. The company put sales emphasis on Microsoft's Azure cloud services. Today, it competes with Amazon Web Services, which is the market leader in the commercial cloud.
- **Partnering:** The digital world is all about partnering and networking. Microsoft moved away from pushing its Windows monopoly and instead focused on developing partners. This ensured the expansion of Azure's portfolio and also ensured the ability to work with companies' existing data centres. Instead of competing, Microsoft has formed partnerships with competitors such as Dropbox, Red Hat, Salesforce and even Amazon.
- **Culture:** For years, Microsoft remained centred around Windows. This prevented it from cashing in on other developments that were taking place. Satya Nadella can be credited with altering the culture of the company; rather than designing products and services around Windows, he steered the company towards a new way of doing business. Instead of focusing on vertical integration with Windows, Microsoft became a horizontally diversified company. It developed its cloud computing capabilities, and the open source helped target its services at iPhone, Android and Linux users. Developers were freed from building systems compatible with Windows only and instead Microsoft became a more customer-focused company, developing products for them rather than for Windows.

  In the process, the image of the company also changed: from being a monopolistic threat, it is now seen as a responsible corporation in the networked world. While Google and Facebook face heavy fines for data misuse and their use of monopoly power, Microsoft has not faced such controversies in recent years.

(Continued)

(Continued)

The rebound of Microsoft provides lessons for companies operating in the digital world, becoming important lessons in digital strategy. In becoming a digital master again, Microsoft came back to the following underlying principles to succeed in the digital world.

- **Focus on customers:** Very often, companies focus on their products and think of ways of making them exclusive. This was the mistake that Microsoft committed by focusing on Windows. Instead, companies should look for ways to serve customers, even if it means networking with competitors.
- **Find new ways of doing business:** By tracking trends, companies can discover new ways of doing business. Microsoft found new ways of doing business by developing cloud capabilities. Microsoft developed completely new capabilities in cloud computing and now competes with the market leader, Amazon Web Services.
- **Work with competition:** Rapaciousness does not work in today's world. Earlier, Microsoft squeezed and crushed rivals using its monopoly power. Today, software by rival companies runs on Azure as the company has adopted an inclusive way of doing business.
- **Data privacy:** Another important aspect of digital business is that of data privacy and taxation. Some large companies have been fined for breaches in data security or for avoiding tax in different countries. Companies collect a lot of information from customers and they must address data security and privacy laws, which is an essential requirement in digital strategy.

There's a lesson to be learnt from Microsoft—companies must change and adapt with digital capabilities (*The Economist* 2019). Long-term survival depends on how new opportunities are used.

How could Microsoft change its direction? Which elements of digital strategy did it use?

Sources

Naughton, J. 2019. 'How Microsoft Reinvented Itself.' *The Guardian*. Available at: https://www.theguardian.com/commentisfree/2019/may/12/how-microsoft-was-resurrected-as-the-third-most-valuable-tech-company—1-trillion-dollars (accessed on 25 January 2021).

Novet, J. 2018. 'How Microsoft Bounced Back.' *CNBC*. Available at: https://www.cnbc.com/2018/12/03/microsoft-recovery-how-satya-nadella-did-it.html (accessed on 25 January 2021).

The Economist. 2019. 'What Microsoft's Revival Can Teach Other Tech Companies.' Available at: https://www.economist.com/leaders/2019/07/25/what-microsofts-revival-can-teach-other-tech-companies (accessed on 25 January 2021).

FOUR PILLARS OF DIGITAL STRATEGY

The mistake that many companies commit is that they take up disparate digital initiatives. Digital marketing misinformation abounds on the Internet. Rather than following digital

TABLE 8.1 *Four Pillars of Digital Strategy*

Reimagine the Business	Value Chain	Customer Connect	Rebuild the Organization
Expand the scope	Open innovation	Engaging and acquiring customers	Managing digital transition
Reinvent the business model	Industry 4.0	Optimizing CDJs	Designing an organization for innovation
Use a pull strategy through platforms and ecosystems	Omnichannel strategy	Measuring marketing ROI for each intervention	Skills, capability and talent management

Source: Adapted from Gupta (2018).

fads, digital strategy consists of integrating online marketing activities and going beyond vanity to profitability metrics. Gupta (2018) explains that successful companies do not treat digital strategy as separate from their overall strategy, so it is important to integrate all aspects of business. He writes that companies must embed digital technologies into their operations and DNA. For example, companies may implement electronic payments because of ease of use, but rather than functioning as stand-alone systems, they can be integrated into the company's cash and credit management system and also into the sales and order system. The framework for digital strategy is shown in Table 8.1.

Digital strategy is a plan to achieve competitive advantage, growth and profit by making use of data assets and technology-based initiatives. It starts from the executive leadership by integrating marketing and adopting technologies that help it to achieve these objectives. It has four pillars, which consist of the following:

1. Engaging customers and helping them to move to the next stage of their decision journeys
2. Transforming the value chain in such a way so that value is added at each stage of operation, from manufacturing to marketing
3. Re-imagining the business
4. Rebuilding the organization

The transformation of the value chain has been discussed in Chapter 2. Open innovation is the norm as companies collaborate with their customers and other parties. Industry 4.0 represents smart factories, industrial Internet and predictive maintenance, 3D printing, virtual reality and a shift from centralized to decentralized production. At the same time, omnichannel strategy results in fusion of the physical and digital worlds. The elements of digital strategy are explained in the next section.

■ RE-IMAGINING THE BUSINESS

Competition is no longer defined or restricted by traditional boundaries. Companies become consumer-centric, customer-focused and not product-focused as in the past. Competition is also not limited to existing competitors but can come from unimagined sources. An app that solves customer problems on the basis of deep customer knowledge can threaten existing businesses. For example, in the digital world, the competition to a travel agency is not with other travel agencies but with a search engine that is able to provide information better than the agency. New data-based business models and new ways of creating value must be found.

Expand the Scope

Digital marketing is generally misunderstood as promoting and branding business through digital media. However, digital technologies allow the expansion of scope of business. Johnson, Christensen and Kagermann (2008) describe ways in which the scope of business can be expanded.

- **Accomplish tasks in better ways:** For example, companies need not invest in surveys to understand consumer behaviour but can get accurate insights by data analysis.
- **Solve a long-standing problem:** E-wallets and micropayments have helped the poor to have accounts and keep their money secure. Similarly, Netflix has solved the problem of delivering entertainment to people's homes. By solving problems, companies are able to expend their scope and tap new customers.
- **Expand markets and help to tap new market segments:** Newspapers and books now publish electronic versions, helping to expand their reach to areas where they are not available. Restaurants use home delivery apps to expand their business.

Reinvent the Business Model

Digital technologies lead to reinvention of business models in four ways (Johnson et al. 2008).

- **Changing the customer value proposition:** Digital technologies allow companies to anticipate customer needs. E-commerce companies, for instance, track purchase data and offer subscription services that save customers' time for reordering.
- **Changing the profit formula:** Companies can alter their revenue and cost structures by using new technologies. Digitizing supply chains changes the profit formula. For instance, companies can use AI and just-in-time methods to save inventory costs.
- **Key resources:** Key resources refer to elements that create value and differentiation. These are a combination of people, technology, facilities, equipment and channels.

- **Key processes:** Companies build specific processes that help them achieve a competitive advantage. A simple process like helping customers track shipments, for example, becomes a key process in achieving differentiation. Similarly, companies can use digital techniques to automate or improve recurrent tasks that are either efficient or help customers in some way.

Using a Pull Strategy

Companies use the web's capabilities to develop an ecosystem that exerts a pull on customers. In the digital age, the focus of marketing has shifted from *push to pull*. While push ads and notifications are increasingly blocked, consumers seek out products themselves. Bonchek (2017) explains that, in such an ecosystem, 'the new challenge is to have influence from a distance' and draw a parallel to how gravity exerts a force of pull. Like the solar system, the company's digital strategy is at the centre and customers are like planets. They are in orbit and feel the gravitational pull. This implies that the company's core—or digital strategy—must exert a strong enough influence to pull them in towards the company. To achieve this, new business models must have three essential qualities.

- **Attract:** The digital strategy must be a pull strategy, attracting customers and influencing them.
- **Observe:** Companies must not be too pesky and interfere in the lives of consumers. They should influence from a distance through data analysis and participate in the larger culture.
- **Be ubiquitous:** Just like gravity, companies must use technologies to be everywhere. They must develop the ability of reaching anyone at any time across the globe.

The gravity analogy sums up how companies must exert influence in the online space, that is, the focus of companies changes from products to purpose, so as to exert pull influence on people and get them into the brand's orbit just as gravity pulls an object closer. Influence is gained by going beyond products, encouraging interactions among people without controlling them. Companies must develop *gravity generators*, *experiential orbits* and *force multipliers* so that customers do not leave the orbit of the brand and the pull becomes stronger successively.

- **Gravity generators:** People feel attracted to a company if they feel a shared purpose with it. They may or may not be customers but people attracted to the company for some needs or reasons.
- **Experiential orbits:** Keeping customers in orbit means maintaining ongoing relationships with them. The company does not focus on individual transactions but on having long-term relationships with its customers.
- **Force multipliers:** When customers and stakeholders start exerting their own gravitational pull, they become force multipliers. The company can be visualized as

a solar system with the core of shared purpose and stakeholders orbiting around that purpose.

CUSTOMER CONNECT

Companies know which customers to acquire by analysing long-term profitability and CLV. Engaging customers by influencing MOTs and storytelling is possible in the digital era. Interactions at each stage can be measured through metrics, and marketing spends can be optimized. Customer connect must have the objective of moving consumers along their decision journeys to purchase and post-purchase recommendations.

- **Engaging and acquiring customers:** Customer engagement is the new rule of marketing. CRM systems are designed for this purpose (Chapter 3). Getting customers involved with companies and brands is the new challenge. Companies adopt various methods, such as encouraging two-way communication, providing platforms for reviews and comments and using social media. Emotional connections are established for long-term bonding with brands.
- **Optimizing CDJs:** The CDJ describes interactions with brands as the prospect moves towards deciding what to buy (Chapter 4). This means optimizing cross-channel experience. Technologies must be used to 'lead rather than follow customers on their digital journeys', write Edelman and Singer (2015). CDJs are a source of competitive advantage in the digital era. By optimizing CDJs and making them innovative, compelling and interesting, companies can earn their customers' loyalty. Hence, companies must invest in automation to personalize their interactions and journeys, and deliver content that customers appreciate.
- **Measuring marketing ROI for each intervention:** One major advantage of digital marketing is that companies can measure the effectiveness of each intervention, as explained in Chapter 6. Other metrics such as cost per lead (CPL), profitability per customer, loyalty scores and others are explained in Chapter 9.

REBUILDING THE ORGANIZATION

Companies have to restructure their internal operations and integrate all functions. Department silos are broken down with one objective: customer centricity. Employees are trained to encourage customer participation in all business functions. A new company emerges with capabilities of data analytics, ML and AI.

The formulation of digital strategy leads to developing new capabilities of both digital and traditional businesses. Favaro (2016) writes that digital technology can be used to

1. Expand companies' boundaries upstream or downstream
2. Add value to the business through information and delivery

3. Change target consumers and find new segments
4. Enhance value proposition to target customers through products or services
5. Differentiate from competition—use social media or big data to differentiate

Managing digital transition: Every company must therefore turn into a 'math house', writes Ram Charan (2016). 'Every winning company will be using algorithms, or mathematical rules for processing information, to shape end-to-end customer experience,' he writes. As the volume of data increases exponentially, companies must process streaming information from various sources: sensors, search engines, social media, retail stores and so on. Algorithms process these huge data to produce amazing results and help businesses with insights that would not be available otherwise.

Every company thus needs to transform itself into a data powerhouse. The first important change is that companies think beyond their products and build platforms that involve all partners, including customers and outsiders: Metcalfe's Law states that the more the people associated with the platform, the more will be its value. General Electric, for instance, which is a traditional company, has created a platform for the entire energy industry.

The second change required is to break the silos that the traditional industry is comfortable with. All departments must operate as one. Companies must therefore digitize all operations across channels: Customers may interact with product design or manufacturing, then move to partner channels for delivery and then to service. CX across all units and channels must be unified, which requires breaking of departmental silos. Very often, managers will have to overcome cultural resistance as well.

Designing an organization for innovation: Most organizations, both in the developed and developing worlds, are not designed for innovation. Rigid organizational structures are created to achieve functional efficiency. That is why they face difficulty in adapting to the digital revolution. Gürkan & Tükeltürk (2017) write that decentralization, autonomy and risk management are required. However, these are difficult to achieve in the present organizations that encourage departmental empires. Zacca and Dayan (2017) say that large organizations are focused on maintaining the status quo by making administrators out of managers and hence the resistance to change. But reinventing business models requires a redesign of traditional organizations. Managers have to be geared to new technologies, a certain amount of risk-taking and keeping track of marketing metrics. Further, what is required in today's world is 'enterprise agility' so as to respond quickly to changes, respond and adapt to customer needs, increase efficiency in operations, engage customers and empower employees.

Skills, capability and talent management: The digital era requires new skills and capabilities. The challenge before companies is to recruit people who act like venture capitalists rather than managers and who continuously look for areas of growth. Traditional hierarchies have to be dismantled and freedom has to be given to the teams. Performance indicators rest on agile practices that gain digital talent and leadership. To retain talent, career paths and growth avenues have to be designed. HR, which traditionally manages things such as recruitment, compensation and similar functions, has to acquire new capabilities. For example, we have seen that organizations have to be customer-centric, which can only be achieved if employees are happy, motivated and dedicated. HR thus has to move beyond its traditional functions and take part in the strategic objectives of an organization. Above all, a culture has to be established that achieves two things: first, it must empower people to deliver results; second, it must attract, retain and reward talent.

Digital strategy, thus, is an all-encompassing term that goes much beyond adopting technologies. It includes developing people and processes, organizational redesign and customer centricity.

To achieve the above objectives, digital strategy uses a number of tools and tactics. These tactics include going beyond branded content, site optimization and inbound links, investing in keywords and building communities (Blasingame 2017). Techniques like just-in-time marketing, AI and programmatic marketing are also a part of digital strategy. Finally, companies are able to achieve segment-of-one marketing by deploying data analytics.

The above discussion makes it clear that successful companies do not follow 'me-too' digital interventions. Using content marketing or social media marketing without a strategy has resulted in enormous waste of marketing resources. Strategy requires that companies think beyond these tools and deploy them to meet specific ends and long-term objectives. The next section discusses a strategy that goes beyond content marketing.

◼ DIGITAL STRATEGY: BEYOND BRANDED CONTENT

As we have explained earlier, branded content has a limited value on social media. People do not want to get brand messages but look for neutral and real reviews of products.

A plethora of digital marketing articles has led companies to believe that developing content is the way to engage audiences. Called 'content marketing', it led to a great push towards branded content. Content marketing is a marketing technique that involves the creation and sharing of online material, such as videos, blogs, infographics, podcasts, social media posts and other types of content, so that it drives interest in the company's products or services.

Companies thus invested a lot of time and money creating such content. But there were two problems with this: (a) how would people get people to this content, and (b) even if they saw the content, would it lead to a purchase?

Online content that is consumed widely contains stories, characters, entertainment or delivers value of some kind. A list of the 100 most popular YouTube channels based on subscriber count[1] shows that brand content is not popular; only TV channels, celebrities,

---

[1] https://socialblade.com/youtube/top/100/mostsubscribed (accessed on 25 January 2021).

entertainers and other types of content providers dominate the list. Similarly, Instagram's top rankings[2] are also dominated by entertainers, many of them unknown. As the list is updated based on the number of followers, it shows the popularity of young entertainers from all over the world who have gained viewers. There are no brands or companies on the top rankers' list, showing that brand content is nowhere in the reckoning on social media sites.

Since the most popular content is that of celebrities, film stars, singers and the like, brands now have to compete directly with high-quality entertainment created by professional entertainers. It is highly unlikely that a company's content has any chance to be seen by users in the face of such high competition. To get over this, companies buy advertising on YouTube, wherein their advertising video is shown before and during the video that the user is watching. Most viewers skip the advertising video or simply abandon the content. Platforms such as Netflix and Amazon offer advertising-free content and are thus gaining traction worldwide.

Another strategy is to create funny content or hire influencers to make content popular and viral. The resultant content does get views and shares, but the question remains: does it bring in business? After all, a company is not in the business of content but must sell products and services.

The main problem that branded content faces is that users can opt out of ads. Companies cannot buy fame on the Internet as they were able to do in traditional media. Now they have to compete directly with real entertainment. Brand content is seen as spam. Social media platforms charge companies if they want to push their 'sponsored' content into the feeds of people who are following them or are defined by the companies. This shows the need to use a combination of digital elements.

■ DIGITAL ELEMENTS IN STRATEGY

Digital marketing must use a combination of methods. Methods such as influencer marketing, site optimization, inbound links and keyword advertising are very useful for spreading the message. These are described in this section.

1. **Influencer marketing:** Since branded content does not work, companies use influencers to spread their message. Influencers are celebrities or experts in their field, or people who give genuine feedback to other users, and that is the reason that they command a huge following online. Companies are therefore engaging influencers beyond social media (see Marketing Insight 6.5 in Chapter 6). They can extend their influence through events, podcasts and other methods. Among the ways in which they are used are as follows.

---

[2] https://hypeauditor.com/en/top-instagram/ (accessed on 25 January 2021).

i.   **Podcasts and video series:** Influencers are included in video series or podcasts so as to reach the users who follow them. Such podcasts or videos become quite popular and result in customer engagement. Influencers can be used as creative leads: instead of using them to endorse a brand, they are often used as partners. Communication messages can be worked out with them since they know the people who follow them. They are seen as authorities in their fields and involving them at the concept-building stage makes the storytelling natural.

ii. **Events:** Events help build brand engagement. They can be brand-sponsored events that include product launches, promotions in a retail store or a mall or other sponsored events. If the event is of interest, consumers will share and post content about it, tagging the brand. It is a natural extension of influencer marketing. However, the impact of an influencer event cannot always be predicted. If they are centred around a mission or point of differentiation of the brand, it might help. They can also be used in trade events as influencers are helpful in attracting visitors to the brand stall. They can be used to give live advice or autographs, thereby involving customers. Storytelling in industry events also tends to get people involved. They add to their interest and create a buzz around the brand.

iii. **Product development:** Influencers can be involved in product development by offering suggestions and consumer insights. Some influencers have created their own beauty lines, their own apps or even their own influencer marketing platforms. The danger is that an influencer-founded brand could compete with the client brand.

iv. **Customization:** Influencer marketing also uses customization of products. Sometimes companies even launch co-branded collections with them. Co-branded products thus have a good chance of succeeding with the followers of the influencers.

However, influencer marketing must be used with caution. Influencer fraud is a huge problem. It occurs when influencers inflate the number of followers by adding fake accounts or using bots to generate comments. Influencers are known to 'buy' followers, thereby reducing the efficacy of advertising through them. Another method is the use of pods or groups of people who form alliances to write positive comments and click on 'likes' on each other's posts. Instagram pods can increase post-engagement levels without any marketing ROI. Influencers build their brand by making deals with these pods. A report in *CBS News* (Cerullo 2019) states that influencer fraud is resulting in a loss of $1.3 billion annually in the USA alone. Badshah, a popular rapper, admitted to having paid ₹75 lakh for fake social media followers, exposing the racket in influencer marketing (*The Week* 2020).

2. **Site optimization:** SEO or website optimization is the process of adding content on a website so that search engines track words and rank them higher in their results pages. Search engine algorithms track a website's relevance and readability based on

a number of factors and rank it on user searches. Higher ranking is extremely helpful since most Internet users tend to click on the first few results they see. That is why companies try to optimize their websites so that they are shown as high as possible in the search results. Site optimization depends on several factors such as the use of keywords, dynamic content, design and other technical issues that are friendly towards search engines. SEO is different from paid advertising as it refers to unpaid or 'organic' results. If a company's website is among the first few search results, it will tend to get more clicks from visitors from the search engine.

The SEO manager has to therefore know how search engines and their algorithms work, as well as identify the keywords used by people when they search for certain products. The SEO process involves modifying the content and coding of a website so that the search engines pick up specific keywords and rank the website higher. Another way of increasing traffic is by providing inbound links.

3. **Inbound links:** Inbound links are links from other sites that lead to a company's website. For example, for a company selling fitness equipment, getting a link in blogs or opinions expressed by fitness experts would be very important. This means that companies must collaborate with a wide variety of influencers. However, it is important to get high-quality links that are featured in authoritative, trustworthy and credible sites. Examples of high-authority sites are reputed newspapers or news channels, genuine influencers and experts in their domain. Anchor text is the text that contains the links. It is descriptive text that interests the user enough to click. Links should also come from diverse sources. Inbound marketing shows the importance of working and collaborating with others in the age of digital marketing. No digital strategy is complete without collaboration.

4. **Keyword advertising:** Keyword advertising is a form of online advertising in which words or phrases are linked to search engine advertisements. When a person uses a particular phrase or words to search the web through a search engine, certain ads appear right on top. These ads are paid by the company so that its advertisement appears right on top of the search results listing. The efficiency of such ads can be measured with methods such as PPC, cost per action or cost per mille.

Digital strategy is effective only if it contributes to revenue and profits. All the elements of digital strategy described in this chapter must serve a single purpose: increasing marketing ROI. The next part of the chapter describes the methods and metrics used to show whether digital marketing efforts are performing well.

◼ MARKETING ROI

Marketing ROI consists of calculating the profit generated and the revenue growth linking them to the marketing initiatives undertaken by a company. Through this metric, organizations get to know which marketing efforts are resulting in revenue growth. It measures the efficiency of a marketing spend and provides a means to compare spends on various digital channels. Marketing ROI can be measured by a simple formula:

$$\frac{\text{Incremental revenue}}{\text{Marketing spend}} \times 100$$

A better measure is that of attributing profit to a market spend. This considers customer acquisition cost per channel and gives an indication whether incremental profits are worth the marketing effort or not.

$$\frac{\text{Incremental profit} \left[\text{incremental revenue} - \text{cost of customer acquisition}\right]}{\text{Marketing spend on channel}} \times 100$$

These measures, however, do not take into account the intangible benefits obtained by marketing activities. Court et al. (2012) write that companies have to ask five basic questions so as to improve returns on marketing spending. These questions relate to the following:

- Finding the exact influences on consumers
- Financial efficiency in marketing plans—how accurately is it hitting a small, moving target with highly focused messages
- Monitoring how fast the organization is responding to customer comments
- Measuring the impact of multiple channels of communication and marketing

All metrics must ultimately measure the impact of marketing activities on consumer recall, the perceptions of people of the business and their impact on sales leads and revenue.

ANALYTICS IN A DIGITAL ECOSYSTEM

One major advantage of digital marketing over traditional marketing is that the results of initiatives can be measured in real time. Metrics help to measure aspects about marketing programmes so as to know their performance. The most important metrics are related to the key performance indicators (KPIs).

A KPI measures a company's performance related to targets and objectives that are critical to its operations. It shows how effectively a company is achieving its key business objectives. KPIs can be compared with past performance to know the efficiency of a company's marketing programme.

Metrics measure the activity, while analytics makes sense of that activity. The information leads us to know the trends that help managers to make decisions about their marketing efforts. A summary of the important digital marketing metrics is given in Table 8.2.

These metrics make it possible to measure—often in real time—the effects of marketing initiatives, giving marketing managers the power to know where to channel their advertising spends. Measures also go beyond the awareness metrics that are often touted

TABLE 8.2 *Digital Marketing Metrics*

Transactional data	What a customer is buying and at what time
	Shopping basket analysis
	Tracking buying history and habits
Location metrics	Age, income, social status, leading to better market segmentation
	Micro targeting consumers
Conversion metrics	Traffic sources, new visitor conversion rate
	Interactions per visit, value per visit
	Cost per conversion
	Bounce rate
Loyalty measures	Measuring recency, frequency and monetary value
	Patterns of purchase
	Customer acquisition, customer activity, customer win-back
	Share of the wallet, customer lifetime value
Digital data	Search engine data, browsing habits, email
Social metrics	Analyses of posts on social media, tracking likes, dislikes, comments, brand shares
	Personal data for micro targeting
	Customer referrals, influence, engagement value
	Sentiment analysis
Sensor data	Weather, volumes, sales forecasting, in-store behaviour of customers
	Geo-targeted advertising
	Product operating information from customer sites
Marketing data	Market share, sales growth, segment-wise sales analysis

as success of campaigns and provide information on conversion and loyalty as well. The metrics can be better understood by breaking the marketing funnel.

■ BREAKING THE FUNNEL

We can capture marketing metrics with respect to the traditional marketing funnel. This is shown in Table 8.3, which shows the metrics that are needed at each stage of the marketing funnel.

The marketing funnel can be divided into two stages: upper funnel and lower funnel (Figure 8.2). The first two stages—awareness and consideration—contribute to upper funnel metrics and the next stages consisting of purchase and advocacy represent lower funnel metrics. The upper funnel involves building reach and the second stage is about

TABLE 8.3   *Metrics and What They Achieve*

Stages in the CDJ	Objective	Activity	Key Performance Indicators Measurement
Awareness	Top-of-the-mind recall	Posts, content, promotions	No. of impressions, reach
Consideration	Customer engagement	Posts, collaboration, responses	Visitors, engaged customers, traffic
Purchase decision	Conversion	Offers, promotions, comparison, reviews	Sales, conversions
Advocacy	Customer recommendations	Influencers, co-creation, community	No. of referrals, influencer activity, WOM

FIGURE 8.2   *Digital Marketing Must Influence Both Stages of the Marketing Funnel*

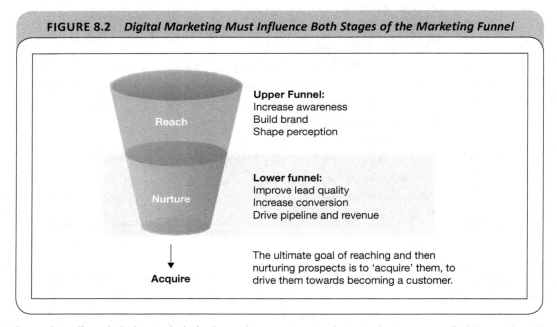

Upper Funnel:
Increase awareness
Build brand
Shape perception

Lower funnel:
Improve lead quality
Increase conversion
Drive pipeline and revenue

The ultimate goal of reaching and then nurturing prospects is to 'acquire' them, to drive them towards becoming a customer.

Source: https://www.linkedin.com/pulse/understanding-metrics-vs-analytics-marketing-steve-miller/ (accessed on 15 April 2021).

nurturing and engaging the contacts to convert them into customers. The third aspect is that of consumer loyalty.

Businesses realize that they must have the capabilities to influence the full funnel and not just the upper funnel. They have to develop engagement tactics that reach and nurture prospects and drive them towards the second half of the funnel and thereafter to loyalty.

The upper and lower funnel metrics that are used in the two stages of the marketing funnel are summarized in Figure 8.3.

FIGURE 8.3   *Commonly Used Metrics in the Two Stages of the Marketing Funnel*

Upper funnel metrics	Lower funnel metrics
Awareness: Mentions + shares + links + impressions **Average Engagement Rate:** No. of likes + shares + comments of a post divided by total number of followers, multiplied by 100.	**Conversion Rate:** No. of visitors who take action on a page (subscribes, downloads, register, etc) divided by total visitors.
Audience Growth Rate: Net new followers divided by total audience on each platform, multiplied by 100	**Click-through Rate (CTR):** No. of times that people click on a call-to-action link in a post.
Post Reach: No. of people who saw a post divide by total number of followers, multiplied by 100	**Bounce Rate:** No. of page visitors who click on a link in a post but leave immediately without taking an action. Tracked by Google Analytics
Social Share of Voice (SSoV): No. of people who mentioned a brand on social media compared to competitors.	**Usage Index:** Category purchases by customers of a brand, compared with purchases in that category by average customers in the category.
Applause Rate: No. of approval actions (e,g. likes) divided by total number of followers, multiplied by 100	**Cost-per-Click (CPC):** Amount paid per individual click on a sponsored post or ad.
Virality Rate: No. of people who shared a post divided by number of unique views or impressions	**Cost per Thousand impressions or Cost per Mille or (CPM):** Amount that a company pays for one thousand views or clicks of an advertisement
Amplification Rate: Ratio of shares per post to the number of overall followers.	**Social Media Conversion Rate:** Total number of conversions from social media divided by the total number of conversions and multiplied by 100

UPPER FUNNEL METRICS

Running targeted digital campaigns involves time, money and effort. Companies want to know if their campaigns are effective in meeting their objectives. One common metric is sales. But before a campaign drives sales, other metrics of effectiveness of marketing efforts are tracked. Companies need to know how customers are getting engaged with their online efforts. The idea is that if people interact with a company and its campaigns, they will probably buy its products when the requirement arises, and the customer will have the brand in his or her consideration set.

Upper funnel metrics consist of traffic data and social media engagement. These are discussed here. The traffic data are measured by the following metrics.

- **Awareness/engagement:** Awareness can be measured through website traffic, open rate in emails and the number of users who opt in mailing lists of the company. On social media, the number of shares, likes and comments provide an indication of awareness. Branded search, or the number of search engine queries that includes the name of the company or brand, also shows awareness levels. Another metric is brand recall and lift, in which companies find out how many users remember their brand within two days of the marketing initiative.
- **Website traffic:** The number of users who visit a website is a measure of website popularity. It gives an idea about the website's performance and the content hosted on it. This is a broad metric of traffic, but it does not show whether the traffic has any value for the company or not. Website traffic is a good starting point, but companies have to go beyond this metric.
- **Click rates:** If users click on the links that a company sends them, it means that people are interested in its products or services and they find the links worthy of spending their time, that is, people are motivated enough to read the mail and follow through by getting more information through the link.
- **Dwell time and bounce rate:** This metric shows how long users stay with the brand pages. If they leave immediately, it is called 'bounce'. Bounce rate and dwell time are an indication of UX. If it is not satisfactory, users will leave quickly. Companies try to increase dwell rates and decrease bounce rates.
- **Cost per visitor:** Traffic can be built by spending on online advertising and promotion. Cost per visitor tells us how much money a brand is spending to get users to its site.
- **Targeted page views:** Page views occur when a page is loaded on a browser. It shows how many users are going through the content. Pages per visit and time spent on them are important metrics about awareness.
- **Subscribers:** The number of subscribers to email lists, white papers, opt-in and so on also shows the number of people involved.

- **Email open rates:** If users exhibit high open rates of email, it means that the emails are relevant to them. On the other hand, if open rates are low, it means that the customers find no interest with emails.
- **Unsubscribes:** If people find messages useless, they tend to 'unsubscribe' to messages. This means that the company is either sending too many emails or that the emails are useless and uninspiring.

Apart from the above, engagement on social media is also part of upper funnel metrics. A major chunk of useful data is generated by users on social media sites. This is shared willingly by people and reveals a lot about them. It is highly useful in building consumer engagement. Automated social content measuring systems are available for companies to track this vast amount of data. Some common methods to monitor social media include tracking engagement, reach and consumptions, as described below.

- **Engagement metrics:** Engagement refers to the number of people who are actively involved with a brand's online presence. Engagement metrics show the effectiveness of a brand's posts and how they connect with fans and followers. It is a measure of the brand's ability to capture users' attention and shows the effectiveness and relevance of the content when users share it on their pages. The average engagement rate shows how many users are actively sharing and commenting on brand posts.

    Engagement rate is calculated by adding the number of people who liked, commented, tweeted, shared or clicked on a brand post as a percentage of the total number of fans or followers. It helps to measure a company's effectiveness at engaging the audience, showing the types of posts that are most likely to be shared or commented upon and the quality of the content created. Engagement and engagement rate can be calculated as follows:

$$\text{Engagement} = \text{Likes} + \text{Website registrations} + \text{Comments} + \text{Shares}$$

$$\text{Average engagement rate} = \frac{\substack{\text{The number of engagement actions} \\ \text{(likes} + \text{shares} + \text{comments of a post)}}}{\text{Total number of followers}} \times 100$$

    Engagement is a metric of brand awareness. When posts are shared or liked, they become visible in other people's feeds. Through engagement metrics, companies learn about the types of content that the audience is interested in, which in turn helps them in creating content that is liked by their customers.
- **Reach:** Reach refers to the number of people who are exposed to an advertisement or content. In digital marketing, reach is the number of unique users that saw the content. There are three types of reach—organic, paid and viral.
  - o *Organic reach:* Organic reach refers to the number of unique people who see the content on their own, without a paid effort. When people share content on their own, they increase organic reach.

o *Paid reach:* Paid reach consists of the number of unique people who saw a company's content as a result of paid promotion, advertisements or paid content.

o *Viral reach:* Viral reach refers to the number of unique people who saw a post as a result of someone else's actions. It gains quick growth in terms of views or interactions since the content is found so interesting by users that it is shared repeatedly.

These three metrics can help companies to know which type of content is liked widely. To be effective, companies try a mix of the three types of reach for maximum exposure. They try to increase the number of followers or fans through organic reach. They make interesting content so that it is shared widely and achieves viral reach. They may also place paid ads on popular sites to increase the number of exposures.

- **Impressions:** Impressions consist of the number of times that the brand content is seen by consumers. When the content is displayed on a user's page and it is seen by users on their own, it is *organic*, when it is a result of online advertisements, it is *paid* and *viral impressions* means the number of times the content is shared or commented. The difference between impressions and reach is that impressions measure the number of times the content is displayed, while reach measures the number of unique people who saw the content.

- **Consumptions:** Whenever a user clicks anywhere in a post, it is called consumption. Companies encourage clicks on links, photos, videos and content, which shows how users are engaged with the content. The people who click are called consumers. They can be segmented by the type of engagement action taken.

LOWER FUNNEL METRICS

Lower funnel activities relate to encouraging user conversion. Everything that results in users taking action that helps them move faster along their customer journeys relates to the lower funnel. It shows the conversion from visitors to customers. It also sends a positive signal to Google and results in better ranking positions in Google search. User conversions and loyalty metrics are important measures in lower funnel metrics.

The important metrics about user conversions are described here.

- **Click-through rate:** The percentage of people who click on a company's link from search result listing, ads, links on another website and so on. This rate shows the number of interested users who are most likely to get converted.
- **Time on site:** The average amount of time a visitor spends on the website also shows the level of engagement.
- **Page views per session:** The average number of pages a visitor sees per visit, which shows the level of interest of the visitor.

- **Return visits:** The percentage of returning visitors in a given time period. Returning visitors show the number of people who are actively evaluating the product and actually thinking of making a purchase.
- **Action taken:** The percentage of visitors who took action, such as making a purchase, subscribing to a newsletter, requesting a demo, leaving a comment or sharing content.
- **Bounce rate:** The percentage of visitors who leave the website after viewing only one page is an indication of disinterested users. If the marketing spend is resulting in high bounce rates, it means that it is focused on the upper funnel.
- **Conversion rate:** Conversion rate refers to the number of website visitors who convert into paying customers. This is an important metric that shows whether the brand is getting the right kind of traffic as against generating random traffic that is of no value to the company.
- **CPL:** CPL is a measure of the cost incurred by the company in acquiring organic and paid leads.
- **Marketing qualified lead (MQL):** A lead that is more likely to become a customer than others is called a marketing qualified lead. Users who have shown interest by going through a number of web pages, downloading material and participating in engagement on other can be said to be MQL.
- **Sales qualified opportunities (SQOs):** Qualified leads who show potential for a deal are SQOs. Such leads have a high probability of closing. Prospects at the middle of the funnel, which are now ready to move to the next stage in the sales process are sales qualified leads as they have met certain conditions in the sales process.
- **Lead velocity rate (LVR):** The LVR is a measure of the real-time growth of qualified leads month over month. By identifying the growth rate, it can predict future growth in qualified leads. It is calculated as follows:

$$\text{LVR} = \frac{\text{No. of qualified leads (current month} - \text{last month)}}{\text{No. of qualified leads last month}} \times 100$$

- **Pipeline contribution:** Pipeline contribution measures the average number of days required to move prospects from one stage to the next. This progression works faster when marketing campaigns are involved. Mostly used in B2B sales, pipelines can be accelerated by improved targeting, qualification and conversion. Identifying better MQLs and more qualified leads lead to better conversions.
- **Revenue contribution:** Contribution margin is the selling price per unit minus the variable cost per unit. In the digital context, it is a calculation of revenue per click calculated after deducting the cost per click and other variable cost.
- **Retention rate:** Customer retention rate is a calculation of the percentage of customers that the company has been able to retain over a given period of time. The formula for calculating retention rate is as follows:

$$\frac{\text{No. of customers who remained with the company during the measurement period}}{\text{No. of customers at the start of measurement period}} \times 100$$

- **Churn rate:** The rate at which customers stop doing business with a company is called the churn rate or the attrition rate. It is calculated as follows:

$$\frac{\text{No. of customers or subscribers who discontinue their subscriptions in a given time period}}{\text{No. of customers or subscribers at the beginning of the time period}} \times 100$$

- **CLV:** CLV is a measure of the total revenue generated from customers by a company over their lifetime.
- **Upsell/cross-sell value:** The value of additional products or higher versions of products sold to customers as a result of product recommendations increases the profitability of a company. This can be calculated by adding up the value of extra or higher value products sold to customers who searched for a basic product.

LOYALTY METRICS

Customer loyalty is the driver of profitability. It is based on the fact that the cost of acquiring new customers is much higher than serving and nurturing existing ones. This is important in digital marketing, as the cost of customer acquisition is sometimes much higher than in traditional marketing.

- **Customer testimonials:** The number of positive customer reviews, comments and endorsements relating to a brand. This can be increased by asking customers to leave a review. Customers are encouraged to create written, video or online testimonials about the products they have bought.
- **CSAT score:** The number of people who express satisfaction or happiness with a brand or company. It is achieved by creating a small survey by asking a question in which customers are asked to rate their experience on a linear scale or to tick a box with options of poor, fair, good, great and excellent. The scores are added up and divided by the total number of respondents and multiplied by 10.
- **NPS:** Only one question is asked: How likely is it that you would recommend a company or a product to someone else? Customers are asked to answer on a scale of 0 to 10. Those who rate highly, giving a score of 9–10, are called *promoters*, while those who give a low score of 0–6 are called *detractors*. The NPS is the number of promoters minus the number of detractors, divided by the total number of respondents and multiplied by 100. Those who rate the company 7 or 8 are called passives. Companies can follow up with detractors and passives to understand why their experience was not excellent. This can provide actionable insights that can convert detractors into promoters.
- **Repurchase ratio:** The repurchase ratio is the number of customers who return to a business or brand repeatedly, divided by one-time purchasers. While most search

and display advertising is focused on acquiring new visitors, repeat customers contribute to revenues without extra expenditure. Companies realize that, instead of investing heavily in generating traffic, it is much more profitable to focus on repeat customers. Repurchase ratio is calculated by dividing the number of customers who renew their subscriptions by the number of people who cancel after their first or trial period. The repurchase ratio is the number of repeat customers divided by the number of non-repeat customers. Digital technologies make it possible to target every customer individually and to personalize customer engagement in such a way that repeat customers are targeted individually with loyalty programmes.

- **Upsell ratio:** Upsell ratio is the ratio of customers who buy an expensive version of a product divided by the number of customers who buy the basic version only. Through this ratio, companies can convert their customers into buying more expensive versions by highlighting their features.
- **CLV:** The CLV is a calculation of the total revenue earned from customers during their lifetime. This metric helps to identify highly valuable customer segments and provides a long-term focus to companies. The CLV of a customer is calculated by multiplying the average purchase value per customer by the number of customers to get the customer value. Then the customer value is multiplied by the average customer lifespan to get the CLV. Predictive models can determine how a customer's value changes over time, which can be influenced by marketing strategies to optimize CLV.
- **Customer loyalty index (CLI):** The CLI takes into consideration multiple factors such as NPS, upselling and repurchasing. It is based on three questions asked from customers:
  1. How likely are our customers to recommend us to your friends and family?
  2. How likely are they to buy from the company again in the future?
  3. How likely are they to try other products of the company?

The answers are evaluated on a scale of 1 to 6 as follows:

100	80	60	40	20	0
1	2	3	4	5	6

The score of 1 is assigned to a response of definite yes (100%), and a score of 6 is assigned to a definite no (0%). The CLI for a customer is the average score of their three responses.

The idea is that customers are moved to lower scores through engagement methods. It helps companies build loyalty profiles of customers.

Apart from upper and lower funnel metrics, some qualitative methods are also used. They are described in the next section.

■ QUALITATIVE MEASURES

Qualitative methods measure the intangible benefits of marketing efforts. These include the following.

- **Target audience:** Companies want to have a profile of their ideal visitors, their motivations and their needs. This will help in knowing what type of content to produce, which platforms to buy advertisements on and how best to influence them. Data analysis helps to discover five qualitative components of customers:
  - o Type of customers
  - o Source of information they use
  - o Demographic information such as age, gender, marital status, location, job title, income and education
  - o Triggers and pain points that show what compels them to take action
  - o Queries and objections in the purchase process
- **Keywords and topics:** By identifying with the most profitable keywords and topics, companies can know which keywords contribute the most to conversions. Content marketing is used to generate new leads, as it motivates users to click on links. It is effective cost-wise too, as it delivers long-term benefits since no extra expenses are involved. Paid search, on the other hand, needs a continual cash flow to maintain results. Content marketing has the advantage of being less expensive and more persuasive without being intrusive.
- **Stories:** Digital storytelling is a powerful tool to get users' attention, since people associate themselves with experiences of others. Effective stories help build trust and connect emotionally. Hence, they have a better chance of conversion. Stories associated with a brand show how posts are effective in driving awareness for brand content. Brands post stories of their origin and interesting titbits from their history to build stories and encourage users to post their own stories. Stories that are shared or retold contribute to the qualitative benefits of marketing efforts.
- **Title tags:** A title tag is a piece of code that is an accurate and concise description of the content on a page. Title tags are a major factor in helping search engines understand what website pages are about, and they are the first piece of information people will see when they use a search engine. Title tags show up in three important places: search engine result pages (SERPs), web browsers and social networks. By measuring title tags and finding out which ones are effective, the company knows which ones should be promoted. The first step is to write a copy that gets the click. Once the visitor does that, the tags should reinforce that he or she has come to the right place. Tags include important keywords but, at the same time, they have to be different so that the tags stand convey the competitive differentiation.
- **Meta description:** A meta description is another piece of HTML code meant to provide a summary of a web page. It is not a ranking factor in Google but an important element of the SEO strategy. Meta descriptions appear underneath the

blue clickable links in the SERPs. Therefore, they impact users, specifically, whether the user clicks on a result or not. High-performing meta descriptions are what companies aim for, which help in getting more clicks from the same ranking position.

CONCLUSION

Digital strategy is thought to be about using online methods for marketing. However, digitization is changing the nature of competition. According to McKinsey's director Paul Willmott (McKinsey and Co. 2014), it is 'blurring the lines between sectors, placing fresh demands on both leadership and organizational strategy'. This calls for a radical change in approach. The danger is that companies either adopt an incremental approach or get trapped in the 'shiny object' syndrome, that is, investing in cool digital technologies that do little to generate value in the company's business models.

This chapter shows that companies must lead with strategy and then deploy technologies to meet the objectives of that strategy. Very often, it is not about digital only. Companies have to integrate both physical and digital capabilities to become leaders in their fields. It also leads to a complete business transformation.

Digital strategy is a road map of redefining companies for the changed era. Porter and Millar (1985) had described how information gives companies the competitive advantage. They had written that IT changes every value proposition at every point, changing the nature of the competition, changes industry structure and creates a competitive advantage. Digital strategy strides across all the three developments.

SUMMARY

A digital marketing strategy is about strategy, not technology. Yet, many companies focus on adopting digital technology as part of their marketing efforts, which prevents them from making full use of the opportunities offered by the digital revolution. Digital strategy has the power to redefine the business, and this is illustrated in the chapter by two case studies on digital transformation, Asian Paints and Microsoft.

Today, every company is using digital technology in one way or the other, but digital masters or companies that have achieved digital maturity are able to do so much better than everyone else. Digital strategy must combine the digital capabilities through which companies solve their business operations by deploying technology and the leadership capabilities that lead the companies' thrust for change.

Digital strategy rests on four pillars: (a) re-imagining the business, (b) value chain optimization, (c) customer connect and (d) rebuilding the organization. Successful companies are able to develop an ecosystem that exerts a pull on customers. The digital elements in strategy are influencer marketing, site optimization, inbound links and keyword advertising.

All activities must contribute to increasing marketing ROI. This is measured by metrics and analytics that are described in this chapter. A number of digital marketing metrics are described in this chapter. An important method is to break the marketing funnel: The upper funnel metrics consist of awareness and consideration, and the next stages consisting of purchase and advocacy represent lower funnel metrics. Another set of metrics is those measuring loyalty. Finally, qualitative methods measure the intangible benefits of marketing efforts.

KEY TERMS

Click-through rate: The percentage of people who click on a company's link from search result listing, ads, links on another website and so on.

Content marketing: A marketing technique that involves the creation and sharing of online content so that it drives interest in the company's products or services.

Digital maturity: The stage at which digital transforms processes, talent engagement and business models. Companies that achieve digital maturity are called digital masters.

Digital strategy: Digital strategy is a plan to achieve competitive advantage, growth and profit by making use of data assets and technology-based initiatives. It consists of customer engagement initiatives, transforming the value chain, re-imagining the business and rebuilding the organization.

Inbound links: Links from other sites that lead to a company's website.

Influencers: People who command huge following online; they are celebrities or experts in their field or they give genuine feedback to other users and are able to influence others.

Influencer fraud: Influencer fraud occurs when influencers inflate the number of their followers by adding fake accounts or using bots to generate comments.

Keyword advertising: Form of online advertising in which words or phrases are linked to search engine advertisements.

Marketing ROI: The practice of calculating profit generated and revenue growth and linking them to the marketing initiatives undertaken by a company.

Reach: The number of people who are exposed to an advertisement or content.

SEO: The process of adding content on a website so that search engines track words and rank them higher in their results pages.

CONCEPT REVIEW QUESTIONS

1. Define digital marketing strategy. What are its components?
2. Which companies are dubbed 'digital masters'? What are their characteristics?
3. What is meant by customer connect? How is it achieved?
4. What are the characteristics of an organization to meet the challenges of digital transformation?
5. What is meant by pull strategy? How do companies build 'pull' in their digital strategy?

6. Why do companies need to look beyond branded content?
7. Describe influencer marketing. How are they helpful in marketing? What are the shortcomings of this method?
8. What is marketing ROI? How is it measured?
9. Explain the various digital marketing metrics. What are upper and lower funnel metrics?
10. How is loyalty measured? Describe certain methods to measure loyalty.

CRITICAL THINKING QUESTIONS

1. Critically examine the statement that 'digital marketing strategy is an approach that will support marketing and business objectives through the application of digital technology platforms'. Does that have a larger purpose?
2. What is implied by the statement that digital strategy is not about technology? What are its implications, both from the point of view of a company's top management and from the point of view of functional areas?
3. In what ways does a digital strategy lead to re-imagining a business? Compare the case studies of Microsoft and Asian Paints in this chapter to show how digital drives new business models.
4. It is said that digital strategy leads to transforming an organization. How far is this statement true? Many companies simply use digital technologies in functional departments with success. Compare such an organization with a digital master and see whether there are any differences.

PROJECTS AND ASSIGNMENTS

1. Digital marketing strategy is often understood as gathering views on brand content, gaining followers or making users click on links and advertisements. Conduct a survey of a few companies to see how far this statement is true. Ask the managers the objective of their digital marketing strategy. How many companies see it as an integrated approach?
2. Interview the manager of a company in your town. Ask him or her about the digitization of the company. What challenges were faced by the company? How were they overcome?
3. Check out the most famous influencers in digital marketing. Examine their social media pages. On this basis, list the characteristics of successful influencers and describe their activities.
4. Select a brand and check out its social media channels. Describe what the brand does on its social media channels. Is the content geared towards generating likes and shares or does it do something else?

REFERENCES

Benkler, Y. 2006. *The Wealth of Networks—How Social Production Transforms Markets and Freedom.* New Haven, CT: Yale University Press.

Blasingame, J. 2017. 'The Power of Building Customer Communities.' *Forbes.* Available at: https://www.forbes.com/sites/jimblasingame/2017/05/07/the-power-of-building-customer-communities/#740520da486c (accessed on 25 January 2021).

Bonchek, M. 2017. 'A Good Digital Strategy Creates a Gravitational Pull.' *Harvard Business Review.* Available at: https://hbr.org/2017/01/a-good-digital-strategy-creates-a-gravitational-pull (accessed on 25 January 2021).

Carr, N. G. 2003. 'IT Doesn't Matter.' *Harvard Business Review.* Available at: https://hbr.org/2003/05/it-doesnt-matter (accessed on 25 January 2021).

Cerullo, M. 2019. 'Influencer Marketing Fraud Will Cost Brands $1.3 Billion in 2019.' *CBS News.* Available at: https://www.cbsnews.com/news/influencer-marketing-fraud-costs-companies–1–3-billion/ (accessed on 25 January 2021).

Chaffey, D., and F. Ellis-Chadwick. 2016. *Digital Marketing: Strategy, Implementation and Practice.* 6th ed. Harlow: Pearson Education.

Charan, R. 2016. 'How to Transform a Traditional Giant into a Digital One.' *Harvard Business Review.* Available at: https://hbr.org/2016/02/how-to-transform-a-traditional-giant-into-a-digital-one (accessed on 25 January 2021).

Court, David, Jonathan Gordon, and Jesko Perrey. 2012. 'Measuring Marketing's Worth.' *McKinsey Quarterly*, 1 May. Available at: https://www.mckinsey.com/business-functions/marketing-and-sales/our-insights/measuring-marketings-worth# (accessed on 15 April 2021).

Edelman, D. C., and M. Singer. 2015. 'Competing on Customer Journeys.' *Harvard Business Review.* Available at: https://hbr.org/2015/11/competing-on-customer-journeys (accessed on 25 January 2021).

Favaro, K. 2016. 'Don't Draft a Digital Strategy Just Because Everyone Else Is.' *Harvard Business Review.* Available at: https://hbr.org/2016/03/dont-draft-a-digital-strategy-just-because-everyone-else-is (accessed on 25 January 2021).

Gupta, S. 2018. *Driving Digital Strategy: A Guide to Reimagining Your Business.* Boston, MA: Harvard Business Review Press.

Gürkan, G. C., and S. A. Tükeltürk. 2017. 'Strategies for Innovative Organization Structure: Innovative Culture and Open Innovation.' In *Global Business Strategies in Crisis: Strategic Thinking and Development*, edited by Ü. Hacioğlu, H. Dinçer, and N. Alayoğlu, 185–199. New York, NY: Springer.

Johnson, M. W., C. M. Christensen, and H. Kagermann. 2008. 'Reinventing Your Business Model through Disruptive Innovation.' *Harvard Business Review*, December. Available at: https://hbr.org/2008/12/reinventing-your-business-model (accessed on 15 April 2021).

Kane, G. C., D. Palmer, A. N. Phillips, D. Kiron, and N. Buckley. 2015. 'Strategy, Not Technology, Drives Digital Transformation.' *MIT Sloan Management Review.* Available at: https://sloanreview.mit.edu/projects/strategy-drives-digital-transformation/ (accessed on 25 January 2021).

McKinsey and Co. 2014. 'Digital Strategy: An Interview with Paul Willmott.' Available at: https://www.mckinsey.com/business-functions/mckinsey-digital/our-insights/digital-strategy (accessed on 25 January 2021).

Porter, M. E., and V. E. Millar. 1985. 'How Information Gives You Competitive Advantage.' *Harvard Business Review.* Available at: https://hbr.org/1985/07/how-information-gives-you-competitive-advantage (accessed on 25 January 2021).

The Week. 2020. 'Rapper Badshah Admits to Paying ₹75 Lakh for Fake Social Media Likes, Followers.' Available at: https://www.theweek.in/news/entertainment/2020/08/08/rapper-badshah-admits-to-paying-rs-75-lakh-for-fake-social-media-likes-followers.html (accessed on 25 January 2021).

Westerman, G., D. Bonnet, and A. McAfee. 2014. *Leading Digital: Turning Technology into Business Transformation.* Boston, MA: Harvard Business Review Press.

Zacca, R., and M. Dayan. 2017. 'Entrepreneurship: An Evolving Conceptual Framework.' *International Journal of Entrepreneurship and Innovation Management* 21, no. 1/2: 2–26.

CLOSING CASE

SUCCESSFUL DIGITAL TRANSFORMATIONS

Some companies have succeeded in their digital transformations. These companies have invested in omnichannel approach, IoT sensors and data analytics. Consider the following companies that have gone through digital transformation (Albanese 2018).

- **The New York Times:** The newspaper industry has been struggling for many years. Their content is easily searchable online, and many newspapers provide e-papers or their entire editions on the Internet. As a result, the newspaper reading habit has been declining. Both circulation of papers and their advertising revenues has been falling for many years, and some have folded up. *The New York Times* did not fall into this trap. It implemented a subscription model so that users pay for its online content. It reported more than $800 million in digital revenue in 2019, with over 500 million digital subscribers, which is far greater than any other newspaper group. Thus, it does not depend on advertising for its revenue.

- **Fidelity:** Fidelity is another company that has gone against the tide. The financial industry has faced disruption from digital, but its mobile app has been able to garner users and revenue. The app provides a desktop trading experience so that users can trade and invest even when they are mobile.

- **Disney:** Disney has been one of the great successes in digital transformation. In 2015, it started investing in digital technologies. It has installed IoT sensors in their parks. A RFID band called MagicBand wristband is provided to its guests. These bands are connected to the sensors and act as payment, hotel room keys and even ride tickets. In this way, Disney is able to collect data about its customers that are used to improve UX.

- **Walmart:** Walmart has been making things easier for consumers. It has bought online businesses such as Jet and ModCloth. The Walmart mobile app can be used by customers to calculate the costs of their shopping lists. At the store, the app's 'store assistant' guides them to items on their list via a map.

These companies have used different strategies for their digital transformation. At the heart of their transformation is a strong focus on the customer. They borrow wisdom from the physical world: companies that keep the customer firmly in their focus will always remain one step ahead of the competition or changing technology.

Questions for Discussion

1. How have these companies transformed themselves digitally?
2. What are the common elements of their digital transformation?
3. Comment on the digital strategy followed by these companies.
4. What are the steps for reinventing organizations?

(Continued)

(Continued)

Source

Albanese, J. 2018. 'These Four Companies Have Been Saved by Digital Transformation.' *Inc.* Available at: https://www.inc.com/jason-albanese/these–4-companies-have-been-saved-by-digital-transformation.html (accessed on 25 January 2021).

CHAPTER 9

Digital Marketing Tools and Technologies

Learning Objectives

In this chapter, we describe the tools and technologies that are a part of the digital marketing ecosystem. Since the objective of digital interventions is to enhance CX across decision journeys, a comprehensive view has to be taken.

After reading this chapter, you will be able to learn about the following:

❑ Using online communication with integrated marketing communications tools
❑ Understanding customers and consumer engagement technologies
❑ Deploying AI for enhancing CDJs
❑ Technological advances in retail and how they shape consumer response

OPENING CASE

IBM WATSON AND MARKETING

Every minute, thousands of comments are written on social media platforms. Marketing companies require the capability of processing these comments to figure out what customers are saying about their brands. IBM Watson does just that: It allows NLP and analytics, and transforms a host of operations across industries.

Watson supercomputer mimics the human thought process to analyse information, which represents a major development in big data analytics. It can answer questions posed in natural language quickly, becoming an aid to marketing managers. Lotze (2018) explains how it is transforming industries: It goes through social media along with other easily available data with proprietary data and continuously learns from that information using ML.

Its predictive analytics ability makes it popular in a variety of applications, including predictive healthcare, customer service, investment advice and CRM. It allows customers to use 'Watson as a service' which makes it flexible for clients to extend its applications.

(Continued)

(Continued)

IBM Watson is being used in marketing as it is helpful in understanding customer behaviour and thereby influencing it. Its predictive ability can pinpoint the exact time when a customer is most likely to buy products. IBM Watson Marketing Insights track customers across omnichannels and are able to predict user behaviour. Some of the marketing applications of IBM Watson are described below.

- **Predict consumption patterns:** Watson collects data from credit cards, sales records, social networks, locations, web pages and many other sources and makes high probability predictions about consumption patterns. It is able to spot trends and fashions, informing companies about shifting tastes.
- **Track sentiments:** Sentiment analysis means tracking people's feelings and emotions. Very often, people say something and mean something else. Watson can recognize irony and sarcasm in text and decipher the true meaning of the posts. It goes over the immense data being posted on the Internet—which is impossible to do manually—and finds out its real meaning. Hence, it tracks the comments of products, movie trailers or advertisements and can work out whether people like them.
- **Generate leads:** By using social listening, Watson is able to track signals that may lead to sales. Industry reports, competitor analysis and information about current customers is analysed to predict sales, thereby generating leads. For example, if it finds questions being raised about a product's performance or discussion about its efficacy, it can automatically notify the sales team to contact and follow up.
- **Predict product success:** Watson analyses reactions from a company's customer base to predict how people are going to react to new product offerings.
- **Customer service:** Data from various sources, along with previous experience of customer cases and issues, are used by Watson to create a cloud-based bank of solutions that is available to customer service representatives. They are able to get answers to questions on the basis of this bank of customer service intelligence. That is why Watson is called an 'insight engine' rather than a search engine. Customer interactions are thus made more enriching and efficient.
- **Advertising:** Using data streams of weather, time of day, location and consumers, Watson delivers personalized ads to customers. Ads are changed based on the location or the weather in real time. For instance, if a heat wave is expected in an area, customers in that area are warned to stock up on products that are generally consumed in hot weather.
- **Retail:** Using data analytics, Watson is able to present products to customers that are linked to the customers' purchase cycle and their customized preferences. This makes retail more efficient and customers reduce their search time.
- **Efficiency:** Watson tests, measures and optimizes digital content, such as ads and website pages, to identify areas where marketing efforts would be best directed. Watson can thus suggest ways to eliminate ineffective marketing and make the marketing effort more efficient by deploying spends where they are most effective. Innovative A/B testing techniques are used to maximize conversions through digital media such as emails, websites, social media, online content and more.
- **Supply chain:** Supply chains are dependent on a number of uncontrollable factors, such as weather, logistics and unstable partners. Watson creates supply chain

transparency, highlighting disruptions and even potential disruptions. As a result, inventory and freight costs are reduced significantly.

- **Marketing HR:** Watson can scan resumes and create an ability-based personnel database. A side-by-side comparison metric gives insights to managers who can then make informed decisions about salesperson recruitment. It also helps to increase retention rates.

While reading this chapter, try to answer the following questions:

1. What are the tools and technologies that are being used in marketing?
2. What are the tools and methods for increasing traffic to a company's content?
3. How can technology help in enhancing customer engagement?
4. How can technologies make CDJs smooth?

Sources

Lotze, K. 2018. 'How IBM Watson Is Revolutionizing 10 Industries.' *Tech Republic*. Available at: https://www.techrepublic.com/article/how-ibm-watson-is-revolutionizing–10-industries/ (accessed on 28 January 2021).

http://www.forbes.com/sites/markfidelman/2013/09/04/ibms-watson-set-to-revolutionize-marketing/ (accessed on 26 February 2021).

■ INTRODUCTION

The Internet offers many tools and technologies for marketing: from communication at one end of the scale to complete marketing automation on the other. The challenge for companies is to integrate these tools into their marketing programmes. This depends on their understanding and vision: While some companies integrate online communications with its integrated marketing communications (IMC) process, others are able to integrate business processes to offer convenience to customers (Keller 2016). Businesses that understand the complete range of services leading to CSAT are able to build great business models.

For instance, Uber could well be a taxi-hailing service, but it does not stop at that. Starting from providing a taxi within a short period of time, it provides a way to track the ride along with easy payments as well as entertainment during the rides. All this is done by using various tools and technologies that the Internet provides. Several technologies are being developed that have a promise to automate marketing functions (see Opening Case: IBM Watson).

E-media includes any digital, interactive or online communications. The use of e-media for marketing and marketing communications purposes is frequently referred to as cybermarketing, which takes advantage of direct communications with customers and exploits direct marketing opportunities. It offers many opportunities, not just advertising, for marketing communicators. The digitization of telecommunication transmissions is resulting in interactivity. These developments have a substantial effect on marketing communications.

We discuss tools and technologies that help various marketing areas, including the following:

- Integrating online communication methods into the IMC process
- Understanding customers and improving engagement
- Traffic building: Internet traffic plan
- Search engine marketing and optimization
- Deploying AI
- Sentiment mining
- Retail technological advances

◼ INTEGRATING ONLINE COMMUNICATION INTO IMC PROCESS

At the outset, it must be understood that the Internet is not another communication channel that has to be integrated into the marketing communication programme of a company. Unfortunately, many companies still think of it as an additional communication channel. They add on a social marketing channel or a website to their offline communication efforts, and hence are not able to reap the full benefits offered by new technology.

The Internet allows companies to enter into two-way dialogues. They now have the means to influence each touch point in the CDJ. This is a great leap in the field of marketing. But this calls for new skills and methods. Above all, it requires an integrated approach because piecemeal interventions will only confuse users.

IMC is the process of integrating a company's messages so that they work together and deliver a coherent message to prospects and customers across varied channels. It is usually understood as integrating all the elements in the marketing communications mix so that messages are not disjointed. For instance, very often, there is a price or discount mismatch across offline and online channels, causing consumer dissatisfaction. IMC ensures that one, coherent and integrated message is sent across channels.

With online capabilities, the role of IMC assumes to be much bigger than communicating: It becomes a means of influencing the various stages of the marketing funnel or the CDJ. In that sense, its role is to bring a company's 'marketing communications to life'.

Online communications are a means to achieve the following synergies:

- **Segmentation:** Companies now have the capability to collect information about users who show similar buying habits and thus build accurate segments that are not limited to the broad demographic and social characteristics as was done in the past.

- **Influencing CDJs:** The Internet allows for many different communication modes, from one-to-one communication methods to discussion and review forums, to social media interaction and much more. This is both an opportunity and a challenge. The opportunity is that a company's communications can be flexible, but the challenge is to influence each touch point.
- **Tailor the communications:** Online IMC allows for the integration of offline mass communications into one-to-one, tailor-made messages for individual customers. These offline messages can result into building synergy with individualized communications.
- **Integrating complex information:** Companies now get vast amounts of information from multiple sources and must harness different data sets in their marketing efforts and build accurate consumer profiles.
- **Powerful CRM:** Customer data and feedback are automatically captured. Together with other data streams, companies can build powerful CRM systems that can help consumers move up the loyalty ladder. They also have access to many databases that help them communicate with precisely targeted communications.

Gurău (2008) writes that companies have to adopt a proactive–reactive approach in online communication since the Internet is a transparent and interactive medium. Such communication has to be flexible and customized to individual consumers, but this is not an easy task. Bruhn and Schnebelen (2017) write that the strategic components of customer-centric IMC are relationship orientation, content orientation and process orientation. Peltier, Schibrowsky and Schultz (2003) say that this is the time of 'interactive IMC' that is flexible, current and quick. A successful IMC includes all of these elements.

Companies have to build their IMC interventions keeping the above objectives in focus. The following methods have to be used optimally.

ONLINE IMC TOOLS AND METHODS

Marketing communication is done through different digital media channels. These channels and their characteristics are summarized in Table 9.1.

- **Display advertising:** Online advertising consists of placing advertisements on popular sites and platforms that people like to visit. Ads are placed in the form of banners, text or image ads. The idea is that visitors to the site will see and click on the ads. Communication has to be compelling so that consumers do not see it as intrusive.
- **PPC advertising:** PPC is an advertising model in which companies do not pay for advertising space on a website, but on the basis of the number of times that users click on the ad or link. It can also refer to the links that are placed in the sponsored links of a search engine. These links are shown right at the top of the search results, and payment is based on the number of times that users click on the links. A good

TABLE 9.1 *Digital Channels and Their Characteristics*

Method	Objective	Technique
Search engine marketing	Improving rank in search engines	SEO, PPC
Affiliate marketing	Traffic from collaborations and partnerships	Links on third-party websites, co-marketing, link building, sponsorship, editorial, commission based
Display advertising	Advertising space on high-traffic sites and earning clicks	Banner ads, pop-ups, ad networks, targeted placement of ads, programmatic advertising
Content marketing	Engaging content that leads to brand interest and clicks	Text, blogs, pictures and videos that are liked and shared
Email marketing	Targeted messages and newsletters to users	Email messages based on customer needs, CRM-initiated messages
Social media	Earning customer advocacy and WOM recommendations, PR	Brand pages, blogs, reviews, advertising on social media sites, communities and influencer activity, interactive content
Viral marketing	Content that is shared widely across platforms so that it spreads exponentially	Involving users to spread content
Online communities	Groups consisting of passionate consumers connected voluntarily	Brand communities

PPC campaign consists of choosing the right keywords and then using them to lead users to websites that are optimized for conversions. It is tricky for advertisers since the cost per click may appear less but, when linked to actual conversions or revenues, it may work out extremely high. There is also a problem of artificial traffic, where agents hire people or employ bots to click on links. Users have no intention of buying, but traffic is generated. Companies pay more and agents collect a commission.

- **Content marketing:** Content marketing is the process of creating and sharing content online that is relevant and of interest to a defined audience with the objective of driving profitable customer action. It does not explicitly promote a brand that is aimed at stimulating interest in a company's products or services. Figure 9.1 shows the types of content that fulfil four functions: educate, entertain, inspire and convince. Educate and entertain represent awareness, while convince and inspire represent purchase. The vertical scale is shown to be rational at one end and to be emotional as one goes up.

Content marketing is aided by a CMS software that is used to manage the creation, modification and optimization of digital content that enhances the digital experience of

FIGURE 9.1 *Content Marketing Fulfils Four Functions: Educate, Entertain, Inspire and Convince*

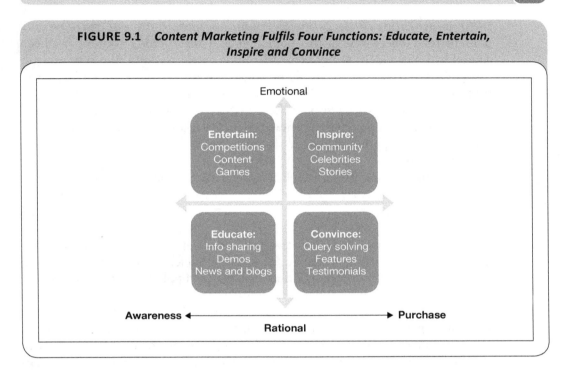

customers. The CMS software allows users to collaborate for producing and editing digital content. Successful companies use it as a system for managing the customers' digital experience across channels. It integrates email, mobile apps, social media, websites and any content that is posted anywhere on the Internet. The CMS consists of two parts:

1. A content management application that allows a user to add, modify and remove content from a website
2. A content delivery application that automatically compiles the content and updates the website

   - **Email marketing:** Email marketing involves sending advertising and commercial messages to people via email. The idea is that people will see the messages when they open their mail, read them and get influenced. However, very often, it is untargeted advertising; companies purchase email lists and send messages indiscriminately to them. This usually annoys users who mark unwanted mail to trash or spam folder. As a consequence, the response rates of email marketing are dismally low.
   - **Viral marketing:** When users spread the message of a company—usually voluntarily—by sharing it on various platforms, it is called viral marketing. It is tricky because it is not easy to make consumers spread commercial messages— they do so only if they are involved with the content. The technique is very

useful in marketing of videos and electronic content. In the past, three types of content have become viral: (a) humorous and entertaining content has been shared by users widely, (b) content involving celebrities and film stars and (c) complaints and negative posts. However, while its efficacy in spreading ideas, messages and videos is established, the spread of product messages and the resultant effect on sales are doubtful. Furthermore, since messages are spread voluntarily, how companies can make their messages viral is also in question. Most users are quite unlikely to forward brand messages as required by a marketing company.

- **Affiliate marketing:** When a seller ties up with other websites that direct customers to its site, it is called affiliate marketing. Directing sites are called affiliates and they earn a commission for each visitor directed by them to the seller.

- **Participatory communication networks:** Participatory communication means involving people who are connected with a product in the decision-making process. The Internet enables connecting experts, suppliers, customers, channel partners and others on a communications platform.

- **Social media communities:** Social media communities are groups of people who voluntarily participate on online platforms for sharing common experiences and interests. Such communities are formed by people having common interests who contribute information and experiences on the platforms. There are three main types of social media communities.

  o **Communities of interest:** Very often, people with common interests come together on platforms to discuss and share information on shared interests. Since messages and discussions are of interest to the group, such platforms become popular among the community. Companies try to develop 'stickiness' around their products and brands so that users stay with the communities.

  o **Communities of task:** Communities of task focus on helping people who want things to be done, such as home search or product reviews. Information is shared on these platforms regarding common tasks that are of interest to people who want information. Such communities exist for products and services as well. A person seeking a home, for instance, will seek out information online about localities and community services.

  o **Communities of vocation:** Professional connections or communities are referred to as 'communities of vocation'.

- **Social media advertising:** Some companies place ads on social media sites to reach target audiences. They can select the characteristics of their target audience and the ad is shown in the feed pages of the selected audience only. Users can therefore be targeted precisely for the best results. The two-way communication afforded by social media makes it ideal for below-the-line (BTL) campaigns (see Marketing Insight 9.1). Companies have to learn to create content so that users do not feel spammed. Instead, they should lead users to engage in activities so that they visit the site and make purchases. Some social media sites have inserted a 'buy button' with ads so that users can make a purchase without leaving their social media accounts. Several social media management tools are available to optimize spending on such platforms. Major social media platforms include Facebook, Instagram, Twitter, LinkedIn, Pinterest, YouTube and Snapchat.

o **Facebook:** Facebook is a very popular social media platform. In terms of numbers, it surpasses other platforms. It offers detailed demographic data of users for specific targeting. Facebook ads can help in building awareness, reach, user engagement, website traffic, generate leads and so on. Users can immediately communicate with companies through Facebook Messenger. The 'shop now' button is designed to increase conversions. Companies can also post photos and videos of their activities. They post 'stories' that show the video for six seconds and remain for 24 hours, an ideal way to inform about new launches or changes. Messenger ads are also becoming popular.

o **Instagram:** Instagram is very popular with millennials and Generation X, so it is a platform to reach this demographic. Pictures and videos can be used on an Instagram post, along with a 'call for action' button. Instagram stories ads display photos or videos up to 120 seconds long.

o **Twitter:** Companies use their Twitter accounts to gain followers and make them aware of their offerings. Tweets can also be promoted to users based on their characteristics. Tweets with website cards encourage people to visit a website. Tweets can be used to start conversations about a brand.

o **Snapchat:** Snapchat is used to increase awareness of a brand and to drive traffic to a company's website or app. Companies use it to increase user engagement and encourage app installs. Snapchat is popular with younger users: most of its users are 18–24 years old.

MARKETING INSIGHT 9.1   *ATL, BTL and TTL Marketing*

While advertising, companies make a choice between using mass media or personal one-to-one experience-based marketing. These are classified as above-the-line (ATL) and below-the-line (BTL) techniques.

- **ATL marketing:** Any intervention in mass media is referred to as ATL marketing. Use of TV, newspapers, radio and other mass market advertising falls in this category. Such messages are aimed at large audiences and are useful in brand building. ATL consists of using TV, radio, press, display advertising, outdoor media and the like.
- **BTL marketing:** When companies use direct messages or experience for customers, it is called BTL marketing. Targeted messaging, demos, see-and-touch campaigns such as setting up kiosks in malls, sampling, direct selling and other similar techniques that

(Continued)

(Continued)

are aimed at individuals are all part of BTL campaigns. The Internet encourages BTL methods. Techniques such as SEO, direct mail, paid search, email marketing and direct customer engagement on social media are all part of the BTL universe.

It is generally felt that BTL campaigns are more effective than ATL campaigns because messages in mass media are easily forgotten, but a personal experience with a product or brand is not. However, the point of divergence between the two is reach. Whereas mass media campaigns help reach millions of people in a short period time, personal marketing reaches only a limited number of people. BTL also calls for different capabilities, such as recruiting a large sales force and setting up stalls in high-traffic areas. ATL techniques entail huge media costs, while BTL methods require investments in frontline personnel and high rentals that must be paid for popular sites.

The Internet encourages BTL methods since customers can interact with companies individually on common platforms, building consumer engagement. Companies try to create content so that consumers feel motivated to engage with them. Computer-based systems that respond to the user's actions, called interactive media, work with the user's participation. This encourages customer-led marketing campaigns: when customers are sufficiently engaged and satisfied with a company or a brand, they start recommending it online. Such recommendations transform into customer advocacy.

- Of course, it is up to the companies to choose the marketing methods they would like to utilize on the basis of their marketing objectives. Some great brands have been built by using mass media, while others use BTL techniques only. Still others mix the two: They advertise in mass media but push sales through personalized marketing.
- **Through-the-line (TTL) marketing:** When companies use both techniques as a blend or use an integrated approach or ATL and BTL, it is called TTL.
  Online marketing consisting of ads is ATL but, when targeted at engagement, falls in the BTL category. How the company uses these in its communications mix will vary from company to company.

Which method of marketing should be used under which circumstances?

UNDERSTANDING CUSTOMERS AND IMPROVING ENGAGEMENT

Students of marketing usually use concepts of segmentation, targeting and positioning (STP). The concept, briefly, is that consumers can be clubbed together on the basis of common characteristics so that marketing programmes can be specifically devised for these groups.

STP is sharpened considerably in the online environment because modern technologies provide a lot of data relating to the consumer. Payne et al. (2017) write that firms must collect data and use it to create information-intensive customer communication strategies.

Apart from socio-economic profiles of consumers, companies can access purchase habits, credit card records, health records, physical locations and even their state of mind. Modern systems track consumer activities on a real-time basis. Geographic information systems and beacons in shops track the physical location of the consumer, helping in targeted marketing. All these data are used to build precise segments, drive traffic to brand pages and devise targeted social media campaigns.

Consumer Engagement

Customer engagement is the process of building ongoing interactions with customers and involving them through online channels with the objective of building a relationship with them. Data analytics let companies optimize and improve customer engagement at each stage of the customer life cycle.

Consumer engagement has three components: customer acquisition, CSAT and customer retention.

1. **Customer acquisition:** Large pools of suspects are tracked to find out which of them might convert into customers. Behavioural and social media tracking can generate leads that can be followed up. Another aspect is that companies can choose which suspects to target: Rather than messaging blindly to a large number of people, only those who show promise are targeted. Triggers are highlighted by automatic interaction detection)technologies. Clickstream data are used to develop a probability-based optimization approach for the customization of information and sending specific messages to individuals.

2. **CSAT:** Companies track different channels to track how customers feel about brands. Even if a customer does not complain, online conversations show whether a customer is happy about a brand or company. It could be a small matter that the company could solve just by sending a message. This kind of intervention is generated by constant customer tracking and is part of the customer engagement programme. The system is also used to predict which customers are most likely to leave through dynamic churn modelling, so that they can be retained by company intervention.

3. **Customer retention and loyalty:** Sophisticated CRM programmes are aimed at customer retention and loyalty. Companies can identify the customers who are most profitable or who bring in the most revenue. This leads to creating loyalty programmes to retain the most valued customers. Through CRM, companies build a proactive relationship with profitable customers, leading to their retention and loyalty.

Companies engage with customers on social media or through email, websites, forums or other platforms on which they are in contact with each other. The idea is to build an emotional connect and a deep bonding with customers at all levels: WOM recommendations, co-creation and sharing of content, complaints and loyalty. Since these behaviours occur at different stages of the CDJ, all stages must be managed through automation. Some of the ways that consumers can be engaged by companies are as follows.

- **Content marketing:** Customers are attracted through interesting content. This builds awareness of the brand, leading to evaluation and conversion.
- **Events and webinars:** Events and webinars are held to engage customers. They are successful if customers find them interesting or useful.
- **Video marketing:** Videos have emerged as tools for storytelling and gaining customer interest.
- **Participatory communication networks:** Participatory communication is the process of dialogue which involves consumers in the sharing of information, building perceptions and opinions and also involving them in decision-making. It facilitates their empowerment.
- **Co-created content:** Involved consumers like to collaborate with companies to co-create content. They participate in advertising research or post content that is favourable to the company on their social media pages.
- **Interactive digital networks:** Interactive digital networks are computer-based systems that respond to the user's actions by presenting content such as text, images, videos, audio or video games. They are powerful automated tools for engaging customers.
- **Online communities:** Virtual communities can be of great help to companies as they consist of passionate customers. They help with diverse activities from content creation to marketing intelligence.
- **Gamification:** Gamification involves applying game dynamics to mobile apps to encourage users to return to the app. Gamifying the app uses psychology to hook customers, resulting in increased traffic and users' engagement with the company.
- **Mobile apps and automation:** A mobile app is a programme designed to run on a smartphone and offers quick access to a company's services.
- **Personalization through mass customization:** Through mass customization, a company can make individualized products using mass production techniques. It allows flexibility and personalization of products.
- **Personalized messaging:** Instead of sending one message to all consumers, the company delivers a specific, individualized and valuable message to users.
- **Direct customer interaction:** Direct interaction with customers is the key to get them engaged, as customers like the attention they get and feel valued.

TRAFFIC BUILDING: INTERNET TRAFFIC PLAN

The purpose of all online advertising is to generate traffic on the company's pages. Advertising, search engine promotion and affiliate marketing are used to get users to visit the brands' pages. Search methods for traffic building are very common in digital marketing. Companies want to know the people who are visiting the website, what pages they visit, how long they stay and where they have come from. There are eight default marketing channels that build traffic.

1. **Organic search traffic:** When people search for something in a browser and click on a result that is not a paid ad, it is called organic traffic. Such traffic is generated by its own.

2. **Paid search traffic:** Paid search refers to the efforts of advertising on search engines. It is generated when users click on a company's link shown by the search engine, usually above other results. Since these advertisements are paid for, it is called paid search traffic.

3. **Display traffic:** Traffic generated through display advertising such as Google AdWords, banner advertising and contextual ads.

4. **Referral traffic:** When users click on a link provided on another website, it is called referral traffic.

5. **Affiliate traffic:** Visitors who click on links to other sites to reach a company's site is called affiliate traffic.

6. **Direct traffic:** Direct traffic refers to visitors who come to the site by typing its address into their browser. It may also include traffic from unrecognized sources as well.

7. **Social traffic:** Users who are directed from links on social media sites, but it does not include ads placed on them.

8. **Email traffic:** Traffic generated from clicks on links sent in email messages.

TRAFFIC VOLUME AND QUALITY

Apart from volume, website traffic has to be measured in terms of its quality. Two issues arise here: getting traffic from automated bots and the use of deceptive tactics to build traffic. Both give the impression of high popularity but actually means nothing for a business.

1. **Humans versus bots:** Website traffic includes both human visitors and automated bots, which are automated computer programs that roam websites. Human visitors generate business. Some bots serve an important purpose: an example is Googlebot, used by Google to crawl websites and using the information for indexing in Google Search. Search engines use such bots to rank sites, and it is important to get featured in their results. This is where using the right words in website content becomes important. Unfortunately, there are also malicious bots that can cause harm. Website security helps to keep these malicious bots away.

2. **Deceptive tactics to build traffic:** Many sites use deception to build traffic. Misleading names and descriptions tend to lure visitors, or pop-up ads open automatically when users visit a site. Some websites also use deceptive buttons that

users tend to click, leading to unwanted ads or visits to an unwanted site. Other example is automatic pop-ups or pop-unders, where the advertiser's website gets loaded in a separate window. Such tactics do not generate conversions and are actually quite useless. They tend to annoy visitors and may be blocked by search engines. However, they show artificial traffic on websites. Sometimes, malicious software may get installed by clicking on these pop-ups.

■ SEARCH ENGINE MARKETING

There has been a great change in the way marketing takes place in the Internet age. In the digital economy, the purchase process starts when a person searches for the product online. A study found that for 88 per cent of consumers, a search engine was the first step in the buying process.

Since the first stage of the purchase process is the ZMOT, the challenge for companies is to get a high rank in the search engine so that when a customer looks for a product, a link to the company's website is displayed higher than others. This is the basis of search engine marketing (SEM), defined as promoting sites to increase their visibility and position in search engine results by placing ads in search engines.

SEM is done through paid advertising and SEO.

- **Paid advertising:** A company pays search engines to show the company's name when consumers use certain keywords to search for products. This type of advertising is called PPC, that is, the company pays according to the number of click-throughs obtained through the search engine. Google Adwords is commonly used as paid advertising. It is a form of inorganic growth as it is paid for.
- **SEO:** SEO is a practice of optimizing content on a website so that it is ranked high on a search engine. It is an unpaid method; hence, it generates organic traffic. The higher the rank, the more impact it has on the traffic to a website. A company uses keywords in its content that are picked up by search engines, helping it to achieve a higher ranking in search engine results. This method generates traffic to the site for free. Search engines rank sites on the basis of relevance so that an attempt is made to use such content that helps the site to get a high rank in search results. This is also called site optimization.

Keyword advertising: Keyword advertising helps companies to associate themselves with certain keywords that assist SEM. For instance, by adding 'refrigerator' as its keyword in advertising, the search engine will display the name of the company dealing in the product every time a customer searches for a refrigerator. Keyword searches are thus the most relevant to a company's business. Once they know which keyword is generating the most traffic, companies place a bid on the keyword. All search marketing revolves around keywords.

Keyword value: This is the average value that an advertiser pays to advertise on Google. Whenever a user clicks on a sponsored search result, the company pays the search engine. This is called PPC. It helps to assess how much is the value of the keyword. Popular keywords attract a higher rate. Advertisers can bid on certain words of their choice. When visitors click on the ads in the SERP, the company pays the amount that it has bid on the keyword. This is the basis of PPC advertising.

Keyword portfolio evaluation: Keywords can be analysed using two key parameters: (a) the frequency of the use of the keywords as a search query on the Internet, and (b) the level of competition or the number of sites ranked in search results for a particular keyword. Choosing the right keywords is an essential part of SEO strategy. Correctly selected keywords determine the success of the Internet marketing campaign. Companies can evaluate keywords based on the traffic that each one generates. The right keywords relating to their business are chosen and ranked thorough analysis and evaluation with the help of a keyword suggestion tool. A number of programs are available for keyword analysis, including Google's Keyword tool.

Site optimization: Website optimization implies the use of tools to generate traffic and conversions. It involves improving the website elements that contribute to traffic and conversions. Traffic comes from various sources, such as SEO, paid search, social media, affiliates and other sources.

A/B testing and website optimization: A/B testing is a method of comparing two versions of a web page or app to determine which one is preferred by users. It consists of showing two or more versions to users at random who have to click on the one that they prefer. Another way is to show different versions to different groups. The company shows the existing page alongside the one with changes, such as adding a headline or a button, or even a complete redesign of the page. The original version is showed to a select audience known as the control group, and the changed version is shown to another group to see which one performs better. By doing this, a company can come to know which version will perform better for conversions. Changes in websites or apps can be compared before launching them for best results. Such testing provides decisions based on data and removes guesswork from website optimization. The impact of every change can be measured by tracking metrics, so that companies can take best decisions about design.

Conversion rate optimization: It is the practice of improving the conversion rate of advertising and marketing activities. It is aimed at getting a person to take an action.

Conversions are a consequence of good marketing. Hence, websites must be optimized for SEO through adding meta tags, relevant keywords and H tags so that search engines can do their job. Some of the factors that contribute to site optimization are as follows.

- **Speed:** The time taken to load the web page impacts the rankings on both desktop and mobile. Pages that load slowly result in high bounce rates because people simply go to other sites. Several tools are available to analyse the speed performance of a web page, showing whether a site is 'heavy' and takes time to load, which will directly impact the performance.

- **Google Search Console:** Google Search Console analyses the website and helps improve its ranking and boost conversions. It shows the volume and the source of traffic. It can be used to find the bounce rate, efficacy of referral sites and so on.
- **User behaviour:** User behaviour is tracked through reports on where people click on a site, when they scroll, where users come from and so on. A heat map shows where the most clicking activity occurs.
- **Readability score:** Every time a new post or page is created, a tool can calculate its SEO score and readability score. The keyword explorer tool can tell what people are searching for when they find a site, and the rankings with competitors show how efficient the website is. It can also show any issues that will prevent search engines from crawling the site.
- **Backlinks:** A backlink is a link from another site that leads to a page on the site. The more the backlinks, the more is the site value. Tools are available to analyse backlinks and compare with competitors' backlinks. Broken or irrelevant links can thus be repaired.

These and other tools help optimize web pages. New tools are being developed all the time. The objective remains the same—make it easy for visitors to navigate websites. Website optimization tools make attracting and converting traffic easier.

Social media campaigns: Social media campaigns are increasingly becoming popular. Such campaigns are coordinated marketing efforts across social media platforms and can be precisely focused and targeted. Social media campaigns are extremely helpful in

- Getting feedback from users
- Engaging customers
- Increasing website traffic
- Improving overall brand engagement
- Driving sales

A social media campaign usually has only one of these objectives. It involves a combination of platforms such as Facebook, Twitter, Instagram or blogs. Different social media platforms provide different types of user engagement, such as shares, comments or retweets. Social media marketing is part of a broader customer engagement strategy that includes customer acquisition, conversion and retention strategies.

These interventions are helped by AI. Since data flows are so large, it is not possible to track them or make use of them by humans. AI automates many marketing interventions, as described next.

DEPLOYING ARTIFICIAL INTELLIGENCE

AI, or the use of intelligent machines, has applications in a variety of functions in marketing, but its primary motive is to improve the customer journey and to increase the effectiveness of marketing campaigns. Since companies deal with large streams of data that cannot be analysed by humans, AI helps to gain insights into the target audience, thereby helping companies to track and manage customer touch points efficiently. AI helps companies to quantify interactions at all points so that companies know where to direct their efforts. It also helps in the automation of marketing functions. Companies use it for content generation, targeted ads, content development and design applications. Netflix uses AI effectively in a variety of ways (see Marketing Insight 9.2). It helps boost campaign performance and ROI. AI applications in business and marketing are expanding by the day. Some of the common applications are described below.

- **Sales forecasting:** Companies now have the methods to track how and what customers are buying. Predictive analytics show what customers are likely to buy in the future with reasonably accurate probabilities. This leads to accurate sales forecasting and inventory management, saving excess inventory costs and avoiding stock-outs.
- **Targeting and segmenting:** Based on customer data from every single interaction from decision journeys, accurate user profiles are made. Precise segmenting based on consumer behaviour is possible. Companies use AI solutions to refine customer profiles and thereby fine-tune marketing campaigns and create content for individual users.
- **Content curation and generation:** AI is used to curate and generate content for defined audiences and schedule sending of messages based on the customer state of mind. It helps to optimize search results based on the most appropriate search words.
- **Digital advertising:** AI helps in optimizing digital advertising campaigns based on deep customer insights and analysis. AI tools are able to analyse the huge consumer data that are sourced from online searches to social profiles. This leads to more effective digital ads. AI helps to deliver messages to customers on their devices or electronic billboards. These systems are based on complex algorithms and big data analytics. They can select the ads to be sent to highly targeted individuals. This is the basis of 'programmatic advertising', which is a technique for delivering the right message at the right time. It helps in increasing efficiency of advertising spends.
- **Programmatic marketing:** Programmatic marketing uses automated and real-time bidding for advertisements that purchase ad inventory that is used for targeting specific users in real-time specific contexts. For example, it allows placing of an ad in the split second that it takes for a user to open his or her email. This results in hyper-targeted ads, which are based on the assessment of every single ad impression

of users as their device loads a web page or app, and then decide in a split second whether to show the ad or not.

   o   The website or the specific web page
   o   The context of the article or video
   o   The location of the person looking at it
   o   The time of the day or day of the week
   o   The user's device and operating system
   o   Previous rate of viewing of the ad
   o   The neighbourhood of the ad

- **Chatbots:** Chatbots are AI programs that mimic human speech and can converse with a user giving the impression that one is chatting with a human. Chatbots operate in natural language and are quite helpful in answering common customer queries or service queries. Since experience is like talking to a person, customers feel like they are chatting with company representatives. The advantage is that chatbots are available at all times, which is not possible for human agents. They allow customers to help themselves and get answers to their queries quickly. As chatbots develop, they are being powered by AI to communicate using real-time, originally generated responses. This will make them more natural. It is possible that, in future, they are used in sales prospecting and in the lead generation as well. However, companies should not rely on chatbots for all customer service, and they should make contacting a human agent easy.

- **Customer engagement:** AI-enabled CRM systems help in building interaction with consumers, encouraging engagement in real time. Social conversations are monitored, which is very helpful in identifying consumer state of mind. Companies acquire the ability to communicate with consumers precise 'decision-making moments', thus reducing advertising spends and directly influence purchase.

- **Behaviour analysis and predictive analytics:** AI helps companies to know what consumers are thinking, saying and feeling about brands in real time. By analysing social media posts with AI tools, they know the feelings of customers. This analysis can be used to quickly market interventions. There are so much data about customers now that a company can easily track consumer behaviour. These enormous data are analysed by analytical tools and AI helps in providing real-time insights about customers and their state of mind. This leads to individual targeting as well as predictions about future customer needs.

■ SENTIMENT MINING

A very important use of AI in social media is that companies can track the emotions and sentiments of consumers. Sentiment analysis, also called 'opinion mining', involves analysing the text for finding the hidden emotions behind it. It uses NLP, computational linguistics, data mining, ML and AI to mine the text to determine the feelings and emotions of the person posting it.

The unstructured text of millions of online posts, comments, emails, blog posts, complaints, chats, discussion forums and social media is tracked using algorithms. Computer systems like IBM Watson (see Opening Case) are able to detect feelings such as happiness, sarcasm and sadness. In this way, companies can track the real feelings of consumers even if they are not expressed clearly. Sentiment analysis is of great use to track and understand the VOC including opinions, reviews and comments posted online. It helps to understand the emotional state of the users hidden in the text. This helps in determining the opinions about products and brands. Sentiment mining relies heavily on data mining, ML and AI, which are able to analyse unorganized and unstructured text contained in emails, blog posts, complaints and comments, chats, social media platforms, discussion forums and other sources.

There are four types of sentiment analysis.

- **Fine-grained sentiment analysis:** This type of sentiment analysis provides opinion analysis on a 5-point scale, ranging from very positive to very negative.
- **Emotion detection:** An analysis of social media sites can identify specific emotions such as happiness, frustration, shock, anger and sadness of users. AI systems can detect emotions behind the posts, which are then used for marketing purposes.
- **Intent-based analysis:** When analysis helps to recognize intent of the user in a text post, it is called intent-based analysis. Purchase intentions can thus be recognized and tracked, while complaints about products can be promptly attended to.
- **Aspect-based analysis:** Aspect-based analysis discovers the specific aspects about which users feel strongly about. For example, a customer may make a complaint about a product and the system will try to uncover which aspect of the product has been troublesome for the user.

Technology is not only advancing in the virtual sphere: it is also transforming retail in a big way. The spread of a global pandemic has pushed developments in contactless retail. The technologies used in retail are described in the next section.

MARKETING INSIGHT 9.2   *AI Application at Netflix*

ML and AI are now being used in a variety of businesses. Companies with very large customer bases rely on algorithms to sort customer data. Automation is the logical extension for them, since managing huge data streams is manually impossible. In this case study, we describe the use of AI and ML for the popular streaming company, Netflix. The company is using AI-related solutions to interact with customers and also to provide a better CX by providing solutions. Since ML improves with time, the company is able to provide better solutions, thereby increasing its business. The areas in which Netflix deploys AI technology are as follows.

(Continued)

(Continued)

- **Movie recommendations:** Movie recommendations are personalized based on the simple logic of 'users who watch A are likely to watch B'. These recommendations are calculated by analysing the watching history of other users, improving engagement rates and subscription renewals. Netflix has a huge collection and this feature helps users choose the best titles for consumption without going through the entire catalogue, which would be very tedious. AI leads each user to consume movies and also maximizes subscription loyalty.
- **Thumbnails and artwork:** Netflix scans video frames and images from a movie to generate a starting point or thumbnail that is shown to customers. Each image is ranked to figure out which thumbnails will have the highest probability of getting a click. The images of the actors or scenes from the film are used for the best results. Netflix found that users spent an average of 1.8 seconds considering whether to watch a movie on Netflix. This is where a thumbnail could have a great impact on clicking on the content. A small change in the thumbnail could result in more viewings.
- **Movie production:** Another area for data optimization is to find the best location for filming a movie scene. Predictions are based on past data, which use not only the location but the best times to do so. Constraints are built into the algorithm, such as the availability of actors and crew, the budget and costs and the requirements of the scene.
- **Post-production:** ML comes in useful for identifying quality checks based on historical data. Problems such as subtitles synchronization and integration of sound and movement are identified for a manual check.
- **Streaming quality:** Bandwidth usage and streaming quality are calculated using past usage data. With this help, the company can decide when to cache regional servers for better CX.

Each of these applications of ML has arisen from a business problem or a need. For instance, the need for better thumbnails and clicks leads to continuous A/B tests for each movie. They combine to deliver a CX that is valued across the world.

In what other areas can AI be deployed?

■ RETAIL TECHNOLOGICAL ADVANCES

Technological developments are fast changing the shape of retail. Digital signage, robotics, buy online pick-up stores, drone deliveries, interactive mirror displays and AR— these are part of the rapidly changing technologies that promise to revolutionize businesses. We will discuss these developments in Chapter 10.

- **Internet-enabled retailing—turning experience goods into search goods:** The success of e-commerce and the vast variety of products that are being sold shows that the Internet can transform experience goods into search goods. *Experience goods* are products that consumers touch and feel to assess their quality. *Search goods* are products whose quality is known before purchase and hence can be ordered without inspection. Klein (1998) had written that experience goods turn into search goods in three ways:

o The Internet lowers the search costs of product attributes.

o The Internet alters how consumers evaluate product attributes.

o The Internet makes it possible to experience products virtually without physically inspecting them.

The Internet removes informational bottlenecks and makes products and brands more transparent than ever before. Sometimes more information creates confusion in the customer's mind, but on the whole it makes it easy to search products online. Technology like 3D imaging helps experience products virtually. Sellers ensure that the information provided is what they see as 'best' for consumers.

- **Digital signage:** Digital signage consists of displays showing ads or messages in physical environments for a targeted audience. Such digital signage offers ease in changing content. It is more flexible than fixed signage, such as posters and signs, and can be changed according to need. For instance, a restaurant may display its breakfast menu in the mornings and lunch menu in the afternoons on digital screens without much effort. The digital signage ecosystem consists of digital displays or panels which are controlled by back-end software called content management software. A back-end computer and media player is all that is required. Digital signage provides an opportunity for brands to create a centralized network of messages that can be displayed according to the need. Digital displays use technologies such as LCD, LED, projection and e-paper to display digital images, video, web pages, weather data, restaurant menus or text.

- **Shops become showrooms:** Some online retailers have physical stores that stock all designs and sizes that consumers can try. When they like a particular style, colour and size, they order on the store app or at an in-store computer station or with a QR code. Bonobos has tried this concept in New York. Its 'guideshop' stocks every size, and customers are helped to find the style and fit that they want. Once selected, the order is placed and the product is delivered to customers' homes or it can be collected from a convenient location. Many online companies are now using this model, which results in providing the 'touch and feel' factor given to their products. Such showrooms require less retail space than traditional stores, which saves on rent.

- **Smart mirrors:** Fitting rooms are no longer in fashion because of the coronavirus scare. Customers are wary of trying clothes that have been tried by somebody else. So how do retailers get over this problem? A solution that has been tried is the memory mirror. One such has been created by MemoMi, a platform using AR and AI. Memory mirror enables customers to try products virtually and get recommendations. At Neiman Marcus stores, the mirror records an eight-second video to show how a dress would look on a person. It is also used to visualize a side-by-side comparison of two different dresses. The mirror is connected to the Internet so that customers can send their pictures to friends and seek their opinions.

- **Augmented and virtual realities:** AR is the practice of displaying information over people's real-time view of objects, people or spaces in the physical world. AR can play a valuable role in marketing programmes. It can help companies to enhance consumer engagement between users and brands, C2C among users and users with suspects. An interesting application of AR is that of Ikea, which provides an app to show the placement of furniture in the customer's home. The app takes the measurement of the room and suggests the furniture that would fit in the room most aptly. AR is also used as an alternative to smart mirrors; consumers can 'try' clothes and accessories virtually by superimposing 2D images of clothing on the user's body. Similarly, customers can view different frames of glasses by virtually getting their image superimposed on their eyes. Sophisticated models use a large number of cameras to show how users would look like in different dresses when they are in motion. Applications are endless. Home improvement can be visualized through AR to see how their renovated homes would look like. Virtual reality is also used to teach skills to customers.

- **Unattended retail:** Unattended retail provides convenience for shoppers as it is quick and impersonal. Vending machines, interactive kiosks and self-service applications like ATMs have constituted unattended retail so far. Now it has gone several steps ahead, incorporating AI, robotics and IoT. The spread of the global pandemic of coronavirus has led many companies to switch to contactless or unattended retail. The term 'phigipay' has been coined to describe the combination of physical, digital and payments universe. This is leading to the development of frictionless retail, in which customers simply walk into a store, take products from the shelf and leave. Products are recognized, counted, billed and payment is collected automatically, thereby saving time for the users. Unattended retail is enabled by self-service and AI technology and is expected to grow tremendously in the future.

- **Synergies with offline stores:** Perhaps the most important development in retail has been the integration with offline stores. Since customers flit from online to offline effortlessly, companies today must build synergies across channels. They must offer the touch and feel factor in offline channels and combine it with order and delivery efficiencies in online channels to offer a unique experience to customers. Many companies are already doing so. The future of business lies in such integration, called phygital (see Marketing Insight 9.3).

Such developments promise to change retail experience forever, but they are only a tip of what may be developed in the future. As technology advances, newer and innovative methods will be developed to help business. Moore's Law and Guilder's laws show the rapid development of online technologies.

MARKETING INSIGHT 9.3   *Phygital Experiences*

Retail is going through a tough time. Due to the coronavirus pandemic, retail stores look for new ways of doing business. Suddenly, they face the limits about what can be offered in the physical space. Integration with digital will help them survive in an increasingly difficult market.

Phygital (physical + digital) is a term used to describe the creation of CX by integrating digital experiences with physical ones, bringing together the sensory and human connection of visiting a store with a personalized digital layer. The intent behind combining physical and digital experience is to draw from the best of both worlds, and the ultimate goal is to give customers unique, highly personalized experiences that leave a lasting impression. It is also a way for brands to get more opportunities to sell their products.

Phygital enhances the experience to consumers—instead of clicking on a site or reading an email, phygital involves all of their five senses. This requires collaboration among front-end and back-end operations with the aim of improving engagement and product experience.

A phygital experience depends on engaging content and the use of digital innovation to deliver it. Both online and offline interactions are important: customers may decide to visit physical stores if they see funny messages on their phones, but then conversion depends on the physical experience they get. Content helps brands tell their stories, which are told both in the online and offline worlds.

But more important is how the channels are modified to meet new challenges. Warby Parker offers prescription eyeglasses which customers can 'try on at home'. It allows customers to pick 5 frames. These are sent for people to try them out and select the ones they like. Stores are also using AR apps that allow customers to try products in the comfort of their homes before purchasing.

Phygital is likely to see an exponential increase in the coming years. Real-time data will be matched with a user's in-store journey. Retail stores will be equipped with robots or humanoids that would recognize customers using face recognition technology and would learn about their purchase. Tracking purchase histories will make routine orders and deliveries quick.

For example, speaker manufacturer Sonos invested in stores with acoustically isolated sound chambers. Users were given an iPad in which they could play their choice of music, providing a unique and personalized experience. Sonos collected the data generated and came to know of every user's musical preference and could deliver a unique experience every time.

With a large Instagram following, Reformation is a lust-worthy clothing retailer loved by many professional women. But with a price tag on the higher end of the spectrum, many females want to really understand what they are getting before they invest. And they seek hands-on attention during the purchasing process. To meet this unique audience, Reformation had to find a way to blend digital and physical effectively, according to Liu.

Apparel maker Reformation offers an interactive experience through touchscreens on which customers can pick and choose the products they like. The stores have minimal goods, freeing salespersons to answer questions and cater to their customers.

At Glossier showrooms, customers can enjoy themselves by playing with make-up, taking selfies and digital mirrors.

MOORE'S LAW AND GILDER'S LAW

As technology continues to develop further, it will be adapted in more and more innovative ways. Aiding it are developments in hardware. More powerful chips will help deliver multimedia and 3D experiences. Moore's law describes how microchips are becoming more powerful by the day.

Moore's law is not a law in the actual sense of the word but an observation made by Gordon Moore in 1965 that technology was advancing so fast that the number of transistors[1] that could be put onto a microchip doubled every two years. This came to be known as Moore's law and has held true for almost 50 years. The first microchip made by Intel in 1971, which was co-founded by Moore, had 2,300 transistors, but today, a microchip of the same size contains some 5 billion transistors. This leads to an increase in speed and a decrease in price, which the industry has witnessed over the years. Although growth has slowed down in recent years, data density continues to grow exponentially. New transistors continue to be invented and the industry keeps reducing their size, and it is expected that Moore's law would continue to operate till 2025.

Gilder's law, given by George Gilder, states that the bandwidth of communication systems triples every 12 months. The law has held true, and it is expected that the bandwidth will continue to grow in the future too.

Both Moore's law and Gilder's law explain why the cost of computing and communications has fallen over the years. They also explain how computing and communications power increases exponentially with time.

CONCLUSION

Digital marketing tools help to achieve efficiencies in the marketing efforts of companies. They lead to getting traffic, optimizing conversion rates, better leads and engage customers with minimum cost. Optimized digital marketing tends to lead to more conversions and generates better revenue while also reducing cost. It also facilitates engagement with the target audience and helps in conversions. Digital marketing can help any business, regardless of size, to achieve its marketing objectives.

At the same time, technologies are developing and evolving. So it is important for marketing people to keep track of the trends and to adapt when new tools become available. However, it is easy to fall into the technology trap in which technology takes precedence over marketing objectives. When companies follow the latest trends simply because others are doing it, they are in real danger of falling into this trap.

---

[1] https://www.webopedia.com/TERM/T/transistor.html (accessed on 28 January 2021).

SUMMARY

Digital marketing is all about using tools and technologies to reach and influence customers. Technologies are now being used widely in a variety of marketing applications. The chapter discusses four sets of such technologies that revolutionize (a) the IMC of a company, (b) consumer engagement, (c) CDJs through AI and (d) modern retail.

The role of IMC is much bigger than merely communicating: It becomes a means of influencing various stages of the CDJ and to build powerful CRM systems. Various online methods, such as SEM, affiliate and display advertising, email and social media, are discussed.

Consumer engagement is facilitated through online technologies. Sharper strategies for STP are possible because companies have access to real-time customer data. It has three components: customer acquisition, CSAT and customer retention.

Tools and methods for increasing traffic to websites are discussed, such as SEM, paid advertising, SEO, keyword advertising and social media campaigns.

AI has found applications in a variety of functions in marketing, such as sales forecasting, targeting and segmenting, content curation and generation, digital advertising and chatbots. It helps in behaviour analysis and predictive analytics. A very important use of AI in social media is that companies can track the sentiments of people.

Finally, we discuss retail technological advances. Several innovations are being used that have made retail more responsive to consumers. Such developments promise to revolutionize the way that companies do business in the future.

KEY TERMS

ATL marketing: Any intervention in mass media is referred to as ATL marketing.

AI: The intelligence exhibited by machines.

AR: The practice of displaying information over people's real-time view of objects, people or spaces in the physical world.

BTL marketing: When companies use direct messages or experience for customers, it is called BTL marketing.

Chatbots: Chatbots are AI programs that mimic human speech and can converse with a user giving the impression that one is chatting with a human.

Consumer engagement: Customer engagement is the process of building ongoing interactions with customers and involving them through online channels with the objective of building a relationship with them.

Digital signage: Digital signage consists of displays showing ads or messages in physical environments for a targeted audience.

Email marketing: Email marketing involves sending advertising and commercial messages to people via email.

Gilder's law: The bandwidth of communication systems triples every 12 months.

IMC: The process of integrating a company's messages across channels so that they work together and deliver one, coherent message to prospects and customers.

Keyword advertising: The process in which companies associate themselves to certain keywords, which helps SEM.

Moore's law: The number of transistors that could be put onto a microchip doubled every two years.

PPC advertising: PPC is an advertising model in which companies pay on the basis of the number of times the users click on the ad or link.

Phigipay: The combination of physical, digital and payments universe.

Phygital (physical + digital): The creation of CX by integrating digital experiences with physical ones, bringing together the sensory and human connection of visiting a store with a personalized digital layer.

Programmatic marketing: Automated and real-time ad bidding that purchases an ad inventory that is used for targeting specific users in real-time specific contexts.

SEM: The process of increasing website traffic by placing ads on search engines in order to increase their visibility on search results of users.

SEO: SEO is the practice of optimizing content on a website so that it is ranked high on a search engine. It is an unpaid method and is hence known as organic traffic.

Sentiment analysis: Also called 'opinion mining', it involves analysing the text for finding the hidden emotions behind it.

Social media communities: Social media communities are groups of people who voluntarily participate on online platforms for sharing common experiences and interests.

■ CONCEPT REVIEW QUESTIONS

1. Describe the process of integrating online communication technology in the IMC process. How can it help in achieving synergies?
2. What are the various online IMC tools and what do they achieve?
3. What is the difference between traditional advertising and PPC advertising?
4. What is viral marketing? How is it done?
5. Describe the process of social media advertising. What are the advantages and drawbacks of this method?
6. Define consumer engagement. What are the methods of improving consumer engagement?
7. Describe some methods of improving website traffic. Which one is the most effective and why?
8. What is AI? Describe some AI applications in marketing.
9. How does sentiment mining help in marketing? Give some examples.
10. What is meant by turning experience goods into search goods? How does the Internet achieve this?

■ CRITICAL THINKING QUESTIONS

1. IMC is the process of integrating communication messages to deliver a coherent image. What is meant by an 'interactive IMC' that is flexible, current and quick? How is it achieved?

2. Social media is used for people to connect with each other. Yet, companies want to use this media for advertising purposes. When users are quick to deploy ad blockers, how can companies interrupt social media conversations and place their ads effectively?

3. All methods of digital marketing encourage people to click on a link. Do you think it is overdone? Will shopping be reduced to clicking on links in the future?

4. AI promises to automate many marketing functions. How are companies using AI? Will it lead to unemployment as jobs get taken over by AI? What are the safeguards that can be deployed?

PROJECTS AND ASSIGNMENTS

1. Visit a social media site such as Facebook, Snapchat or Twitter. Set up your advertiser account. Explore how ads can be placed on the site and on what basis can you select the target audience. Comment on the characteristics of audiences on these sites.

2. Set up your account with Google Ads. Find out how you can bid for keywords as well as the prices for certain keywords. Work out the campaign cost of an imaginary campaign that you can plan for a company.

3. Visit retail stores in your area and talk to store managers about the technology they are using in their business activities. Comment about the efficacy of using these technologies.

4. Interview some marketing managers and find out the state of AI applications they are using in marketing. Assess on what level are their companies operating. Do you think that AI implementation is above or below your expectations?

REFERENCES

Bruhn, M., and S. Schnebelen. 2017. 'Integrated Marketing Communication—From an Instrumental to a Customer-centric Perspective.' *European Journal of Marketing* 51, no. 3: 464–489. Available at: https://doi.org/10.1108/EJM–08–2015–0591 (accessed on 28 January 2021).

Gurău, C. 2008. 'Integrated Online Marketing Communication: Implementation and Management.' *Journal of Communication Management* 12, no. 2: 169–184. Available at: https://doi.org/10.1108/13632540810881974 (accessed on 28 January 2021).

Keller, K. L. 2016. 'Unlocking the Power of Integrated Marketing Communications: How Integrated Is Your IMC Program?' *Journal of Advertising* 45, no. 3: 286–301. doi:10.1080/00913367.2016.1204967.

Klein, L. R. 1998. 'Evaluating the Potential of Interactive Media through a New Lens: Search versus Experience Goods.' *Journal of Business Research* 41, no. 3: 195–203.

Payne, E. M., J. W. Peltier, and V. A. Barger. 2017. 'Omnichannel Marketing, Integrated Marketing Communications, and Consumer Engagement: A Research Agenda.' *Journal of Research in Interactive Marketing* 11, no. 2: 185–197.

Peltier, J. W., J. Schibrowsky, and D. E. Schultz. 2003. 'Interactive Integrated Marketing Communication: Combining the Power of IMC, the New Media and Database Marketing.' *International Journal of Advertising* 22, no. 1: 93–115. doi:10.1080/02650487.2003.11072841.

CLOSING CASE

XIAOMI

Xiaomi is a Chinese smartphone brand. Founded in 2010 by Lei Jun, it has become a brand to be reckoned with in just 7 years. The company's philosophy is to sell phones with high-end features at affordable prices. Xiaomi is now ranked among the top five smartphone brands in the world. It has gained a presence in India too and has expanded into many other products apart from the smartphone. It now sells wearable technology to smart home systems. What is remarkable is that Xiaomi has used digital engagement to establish its brand. Although it later added the traditional retail store format for sales, Xiaomi still conducts most of its sales on its e-commerce platform. Its flash sales became highly popular, through which it sells a limited quantity of phones online every week.

Xiaomi has become popular in recent years and commands the following of fans across many countries, witnessed by the huge crowds that attend its events. Hong (2014) shows how Xiaomi builds loyalty through social media: Its fans, or 'Mi Fen' in Chinese, add to the 'cult of Xiaomi' and exhibit loyalty and passion. Its online sales are a huge success, selling out within hours. Its strategy of selling smartphones with high-end features at lower prices compared to the competition, together with the optimum use of social media, has made it a brand to reckon with.

Xiaomi keeps its marketing costs down in its efforts to achieve cost leadership. It uses social media to connect with customers, saving on marketing spends on mass media, and passing on the savings to customers in the form of lower prices. Social media is used to engage with users creatively, launching products and organizing flash sales. The company is an example of effective use of social media to achieve customer engagement and fans. The method has helped it to expand outside of China and become a global brand.

Instead of focusing on the company and its brand, Xiaomi has effectively shifted its focus to its Mi fans. So the company launches new products online, offering new models and asking users to participate, learning about them in the process. Social media remains the main source of promotion for the brand. Daily posts and communications, promotions and contests help to maintain customer interest and interaction. 'Mi fans' discuss the company's latest products and activities online. They provide valuable feedback to the company. A loyalty programme offers points leading to product discounts. The company also rewards users by offering them a chance to become beta testers.

Xiaomi uses social media to organize Mi Fan Festivals and to build up excitement prior to its flash sale, contributing to customer engagement and taking Xiaomi-mania international. The brand has a huge following on Weibo, with over 8 million followers. Xiaomi's digitally focused, earned-media strategy therefore not only keeps its advertising costs down but also creates a sense of authenticity and high levels of user engagement.

Xiaomi's use of social media consists of interacting with its fans directly, listening to them, getting feedback and responding to online comments and queries quickly. Daily updates and events, with a game 'Kings of Knockout' for its Mi Fan Festival, which users could play and win discount coupons, generated huge interest. It promoted the events and its games on Weibo, Twitter, Facebook as well as Google+. Xiaomi adopts a tone on its social media profiles that makes its fans feel closer to the company, talking to them just the way their friends would, being super informal and playful, using words that one normally would not see in company communications, such as 'crazy sale' and *shiok* (local slang).

Xiaomi's methods of building friendships have been very effective. For instance, it asked fans, through a Facebook post, to share their orders. Over 2,400 comments were received, which was a record of sorts. Fans of Xiaomi in Singapore create Xiaomi-related creative projects, such as a Mi Rabbit origami and a Mi Rabbit comic, which is Xiaomi's mascot. In its Mi Fan Festival, Xiaomi sold large numbers of mobile phones but also more than 170,000 Mi Rabbits, showing that people actually like buying into its brand.

In 2013, Xiaomi started investing in IoT. Instead of building connected products in-house, Xiaomi decided to invest in tech companies that were making IoT products. These were integrated into Xiaomi's ecosystem and connected through Xiaomi's Mi Home app. The company now has over 400 hardware partners on its dedicated IoT platform, which is one of the largest IoT hardware platforms in the world. It has invested in new system capabilities that lead to the next generation of IoT devices and platforms.

The company's strategy is to connect smartphones and IoT devices. It has created its own Android-based operating system, called MIUI, pronounced 'Me You I', for use in its smartphones and tablets. The operating system has its own cloud services, security, apps, music, video player, browser and more. The MIUI Smart Living system includes many features such as Mi Work for office work, Mi Health for health and fitness, Mi Go for travel, Mi Home for home products and Mi Game for gaming activities.

Questions for Discussion

1. Discuss the digital marketing methods of Xiaomi. What do you learn from the case?
2. How was Xiaomi able to make an effective use of social media?
3. Describe the digital ecosystem of Xiaomi.
4. How was the company able to engage its customers? What are the lessons that can be learnt by other companies?

Sources

Hong, K. 2014. 'Xiaomi's Social Media Strategy Drives Fan Loyalty, Books It $242m in Sales in 12 Hours.' TNW. Available at: https://thenextweb.com/asia/2014/04/09/xiaomis-social-media-strategy-drives-fan-loyalty-books-it-242m-in-sales-in-12-hours/ (accessed on 28 January 2021).

CHAPTER 10

Trends in Digital Marketing

Learning Objectives

The use of digital methods in marketing has gained rapid acceptance. AI and other trends will only increase in the future and bring great convenience to users. But at the same time, we also identify trends that might curtail digital marketing. This chapter describes the trends and future of digital marketing.

After reading this chapter, you will be able to learn about the following:

☐ Understanding the evolving e-marketing landscape
☐ Identifying the trends shaping e-marketing
☐ Analysing the opportunities and threats brought forth by new technologies
☐ Appreciating the ethical considerations of data-based marketing

OPENING CASE

BEAUTY MEETS TECHNOLOGY

Beauty is big business. Now it is being married to data science; today, apps can identify skin conditions of users and suggest solutions. Selfies can be analysed to help customers choose the right hair colour or the appropriate cosmetics. Companies are combining tech with customer needs and are trying to customize products based on data recommendations.

One such company is PROVEN, which goes a step further. It combines AI and the latest research to provide a service of customized skincare for each individual. It calls itself 'the most well-researched skincare on earth' and has built a formidable database and combines it with AI, big data and academic research to offer customized skincare products made for each individual user (Figure 10.1). *Forbes* (DeAcetis 2020) calls it 'the Tesla of Skincare'.

The company has been founded on the belief that 'one-size-fits-all' skincare products are not suitable, as people have different skin types. The beauty industry usually has products for four skin types: dry, oily, sensitive and normal, but individual skincare goes beyond this classification.

FIGURE 10.1 *Skincare Company PROVEN Combines AI and Latest Research with Beauty Products*

Source: https://theeverygirl.com/proven-skincare-routine/ (accessed on 20 April 2021).

The company is founded by Ming Zhao and computational physicist Amy Yuan. They decided to use data and AI to build 'the Skin Genome Project' which went on to become the winner of MIT's 2018 Artificial Intelligence Award. It is a comprehensive analytical database of 20,000 skincare ingredients, thousands of products and millions of consumer reviews. It also combines scientific journal articles to add the latest research in skincare. Using ML and AI algorithms, the founders built correlations between people's skin and the ingredients required for each individual. In other words, this huge data is used to match specific ingredients to an individual's skin.

Customers are required to take a skin assessment on its website, answering a series of questions to understand their skin needs. The data combines the customers' environment and can make recommendations depending on where they live. For instance, people living in the hills get hard water and people living in plains or the coast usually get varying qualities of water. Similarly, people living in a cold climate have to use heating, which dries up the skin. The commercially available skincare products do not have the ingredients to cater to their special needs. PROVEN offers personalized and effective skincare for each individual's skin type and needs based on scientific research. The system takes into account pollution levels

(Continued)

(Continued)

in their place of stay, water hardness levels and whether they travel by air. After that, a personalized skin regimen is offered by using a combination of the most appropriate ingredients. Using its database of different skin profiles, a personalized skincare regimen is worked out based on 47 factors about an individual based on city environment, lifestyle, and skin concerns.

The system gets better with use as it uses ML techniques. The difference is that it uses its database of scientific findings and consumer reviews enhanced by dermatology and cosmetic formulation experts.

Based on this, PROVEN provides a skincare regimen for two months at a time so that it can be changed according to season and UV ratings of the city of residence of the individual customer.

PROVEN is one of the first steps of using AI in the beauty industry, but such initiatives will only increase in future. Another company that does this is Beauty Matching Engine, which uses AI personalization to predict and optimize customer journeys. In future, it is expected that AI will use a person's genetic information to formulate individual skincare regimens. It is only a matter of time before a company sharpens this further and comes up with beauty products based on an individual's genes.

The company has combined technology and beauty to offer customized products. Such initiatives of customizing products based on individual needs show how digital marketing of the future will evolve in the beauty products industry.

While reading this chapter, try to answer the following questions:

1. How can industries use new technologies and AI capabilities to enhance product offerings?
2. While customers look for convenience in getting personalized products, are they aware of the misuse or hacking of personal data? Is there a limit to the use of personal data? What dangers does it carry?
3. What are the trends that may give a boost to digital marketing, and what trends may work against it?
4. What is the future of digital marketing? What are the trends that may enhance it?

Sources

DeAcetis, J. 2020. 'The Tesla of Skincare Where Beauty Meets Technology.' *Forbes* (23 June). Available at: https://www.forbes.com/sites/josephdeacetis/2020/06/23/the-tesla-of-skincare-where-beauty-meets-technology/#5cd102546abd (accessed on 10 February 2021).

PROVEN website: https://www.provenskincare.com/ (accessed on 10 February 2021).

Taylor, M. 2018. 'PROVEN: This Female-led Tech Start-up Is Using AI to Customize Skincare.' *Forbes* (7 November). Available at: https://www.forbes.com/sites/meggen-taylor/2018/11/07/proven-this-female-led-tech-start-up-is-using-ai-to-customize-skincare/#1110fe8e744f (accessed on 10 February 2021).

INTRODUCTION

In this book, we have explored how marketing benefits from digital methods. Digital technologies help do things faster and more efficiently than manual processes, and big data changes the very premise of customer relationships. So great has been the euphoria about new technological advances that it is now commonly believed that they will disrupt old business models.

In fact, in recent years, there has been a lot of discussion about the death of traditional marketing. Lee (2012) writes that traditional marketing is dead as there is a paradigm shift in consumer behaviour. Thanks to smartphones and easy-to-carry tablets, consumer habits have changed. Today, consumers need not go to shops, but search products online and quickly place their orders for almost instant delivery. The coronavirus pandemic has pushed the applications of digital methods.

But even though digital marketing is the current mantra for companies looking for customers, it is fraught with dangers. 'There is an awful lot of mistrust and misinformation from so-called and often self-proclaimed gurus in the digital media industries,' writes Buehler (2014) in his book, *The Digital Delusion: How to Overcome the Misguidance & Misinformation Online*. Internet giants flood us with information about the efficacy of digital methods, and companies have been deluded into thinking that the online world is the next gold rush, writes Buehler.

This chapter discusses both sides of the question. It identifies trends that will contribute to the growth of digital marketing, and it also analyses issues which threaten its growth. It is a fast-evolving landscape. New technologies are contributing to the evolving e-marketing landscape. We begin our discussion with the changing marketing landscape in the next section.

EVOLVING E-MARKETING LANDSCAPE

Digital marketing is growing in India. As the access to the Internet increases and smartphones become cheap, more and more people are becoming digital savvy. The Internet is fast becoming a crucial part of people's lives and as COVID-19 forces people to avoid social contact, spending on digital platforms is expected to increase.

A major difference that has impacted marketing is the way that potential customers are reached. The ability to micro target and precisely track leads is of great advantage in marketing. Along with analysing customers' actions, companies know exactly how their marketing programmes are performing. They can make smart spending decisions and optimize their marketing campaigns and thus optimize their marketing ROI.

Digital marketing gives a lease of life to small businesses. For instance, traditional crafts of India are now being sold by e-commerce portals. Owners of small businesses use social media to spread their message. Since digital marketing can target consumers precisely, businesses concentrate on prospects that are most likely to buy, thereby reducing marketing costs. Some of the trends that are already commonly visible are as follows:

- **Mobile first:** Companies have to move on to mobile-first indexing. The number of users in India who access the Internet through mobile phones is close to 80 per cent. This means that advertisers should focus more on optimizing online content and campaigns for mobiles. Mobile first means that while content is optimized for mobile phones, it should perform seamlessly across all devices. When a company is focused only on mobile, it will backfire. For example, the Myntra's app moved on to mobile-only, resulting in loss of business. Advertisers should, thus, focus on mobile first and not mobile only.

- **Beyond keywords:** The strategy of stuffing content with keywords to get better search engine rankings is also evolving. The Penguin and Panda algorithms bypass keyword density and backlinks but focus on site quality. As a result, the use of keywords and SEO do not hold as much importance as they did earlier. The search engine has further evolved with the Hummingbird and RankBrain algorithms, which give higher ranking to sites that offer more human value; natural and conversational content has become more important than keyword density in Google.

- **Latent semantic indexing (LSI):** Google also uses LSI to understand a website more deeply. It is a technique that helps classify and retrieve information on key terms by scanning through unstructured data and identifying relationships between terms and their context to better index these records. It goes beyond keywords and uses related words to understand the content on a web page.

- **Social media:** The way that social platforms are being used is shifting. For instance, people use it to watch more videos and consume media as compared to its earlier objective of connecting with friends. Social media platforms are now being used as entertainment providers with new capabilities like virtual reality adding to the experience. Advertisers will have to understand the shift in how social media platforms will be used in the future and modify their strategy accordingly.

  Social media is evolving, and it remains to be seen what shape it takes in the future. While hordes of people use it, its click-through rates remain extremely low. Moreover, many companies have started feeling that it has become a hateful and violent place to advertise their products (see Marketing Insight 10.1). This was evident in 2020 when advertisers stopped advertising on Facebook for 'allowing racist, violent and verifiably false content to run rampant on its platform' (Thorbecke 2020). And though social media platforms let advertisers target very precise segments based on their likes, interests and opinions, the low conversion rates push the cost of customer acquisition much higher than expected. It remains to be seen how the social media space evolves to address the concerns of advertisers.

MARKETING INSIGHT 10.1   *Readjusting to Social Media*

Companies are discovering that social media is not just a space for engaging customers. It has unfortunately turned into a place where anything is posted, true or not. Hate speech and fake news are used to target brands and companies; posts and ads of companies can easily be turned into targets. Gupta (2019) reports that HUL ads are being regularly targeted on social media by a competitor such as Baba Ramdev and an army of right-wing trolls.

A very successful ad for Surf Excel, for instance, with more than 24 million views on YouTube, projects Hindu–Muslim unity during the Holi festival. The ad is harmless; it has the theme of 'rang laaye sang' or 'colours bring people together'. It shows a young Hindu girl protecting a Muslim boy from getting splashed in Holi colours. It is a pleasing ad and shows religious unity, but trolls on Twitter wrote that their religious sentiments were hurt and brought in religion to criticize the ad and the company.

Another ad for Red Label tea also got criticized in a similar way. Its 'ApnoKoApnao' ad shows a man who finds his father after abandoning him at Kumbh Mela, and then they share an emotional moment with two cups of Red Label tea. The video has more than 2.5 million views on YouTube. Baba Ramdev, who owns the Patanjali brand, attacked HUL along with others whose sentiments were supposedly hurt.

While it is possible that the company did not anticipate the backlash for these ads, it cannot be denied that social media is full of people who spew hate speech on anything and everything. While the ads connected with audiences emotionally, others feel that using social issues is a way to buy emotional equity for the brand. At the same time, it shows how competitors use social media to trash others' ads and hope to gain popularity. Patanjali, for instance, had huge plans to become a major fast-moving consumer goods company, but its sales have since faltered. 'The attack on HUL by Baba Ramdev is seen as a desperate move to play the swadeshi card again and drive the sales of Patanjali,' says a report.

When a large number of trolls make the post viral, brands cannot avoid the damage. The hashtag #boycottHUL trended on Twitter for a few days. However, no long-term harm was reported to HUL brands or the company. Both brands have earned the trust of consumers over the years, and such trolling does not have much effect. In any case, brands have to realize that trolling is a disease of social media, and they have to be careful about what they portray.

In 2020, the world saw protests against racism across the world. Once again, the hate spewed on social media came into focus. The concern for racism became so strong that many companies, including Unilever and Coca-Cola, decided to pause its advertising on social media platforms. Dockers and Levi's, too, said that they would pause advertising on Facebook and Instagram. Hershey's decided to cut spending on social platforms by almost one-third. More than 400 companies, including Verizon, Patagonia, REI, Lending Club and The North Face decided to follow suit and joined the #stophateforprofit campaign. Coca-Cola CEO and Chairman, James Quincey, said, 'There is no place for racism in the world, and there is no place for racism on social media.' He also announced the company's decision to reassess its advertising policies.

Facebook's shares fell sharply as a result. There was a widespread feeling that it should stop misinformation and hate speech on its platforms. Companies felt that Facebook had not

(Continued)

(Continued)

done enough to remove violent and divisive speech. There were calls to make social media platforms a safe space for consumers to communicate and engage.

For quite some time now, companies have been concerned that their ads do not appear alongside hateful or objectionable content. P&G announced that it wanted to ensure that the content and commentary is respectful to all people, and that the company is 'not advertising on or near content we determine to be hateful, discriminatory, denigrating or derogatory'.

How can companies deal with trolling of their brands online? Should they ban social media advertisements permanently?

Sources

CNBC. 2020. 'Coca-Cola Pauses Advertising on All Social Media Platforms.' 26 June. Available at: https://www.cnbc.com/2020/06/26/coca-cola-pauses-advertising-on-all-social-media-platforms-globally.html (accessed on 10 February 2021).

Gupta, P. 2019. 'Did Surf Excel Deserve Hoopla?' *Financial Express*, 12 March. Available at: https://www.financialexpress.com/industry/did-huls-surf-excel-deserve-hoopla-hul-breaks-silence-over-controversial-ad-experts-divided/1513329/ (accessed on 1 March 2020).

Kalra, N. 2019. 'How Right Wing Is Turning out to Be HUL's Biggest Nightmare on Social Media.' Bestmediainfo (11 March). Available at: https://bestmediainfo.com/2019/03/how-right-wing-is-turning-out-to-be-hul-s-biggest-nightmare-on-social-media/ (accessed on 10 February 2021).

- **Beyond content marketing:** Another important trend that is becoming evident is that companies have to move beyond content marketing. Advertisers have to get rid of their fascination for vanity statistics, which consist of comments and shares on social media but contribute little to sales. John et al. (2017) find that acquiring 'likes' on social media has no effect on consumers' attitudes or behaviours. Unfortunately, many content marketing campaigns still focus on vanity statistics. Advertisers now understand that the success of online content does not necessarily result in revenue growth.

- **Quality link building:** Link-building strategy is also evolving. Many companies make the mistake of building as many links as they can, but mass directory or article submission does not improve search engine ranking. The focus is shifting on getting links from relevant sites. Advertisers need to build quality links that make a difference to the rankings. If the content is very good that it cannot be ignored, people link to it naturally. This is the secret to building quality links.

- **Voice search through personal digital assistants (PDAs):** AI-driven PDAs such as Alexa and Google Assistant remain connected to people on a personal level in their daily lives, and the devices learn from their interactions. They are increasingly becoming popular and have the capability of listening and collaborating. These are expected to acquire new capabilities in the future and may well take over the shopping functions of owners independently. In the future, PDAs may well become e-commerce platforms because the share of voice search is increasing and may well dominate in the future. Amazon's Alexa, Microsoft's Cortana or Google's Assistant are all voice-based search engines that quickly provide results to users. For an advertiser, it means optimizing content with different questions on the same topic that users are expected to ask.

- **AI:** In the context of digital marketing, AI performs a meta-analysis of broad-spectrum data sets and then uses the analysis to make its own decisions. It is being used in a number of marketing applications, such as content creation, voice and face recognition, chatbots, digital assistants and delivering highly targeted marketing strategies. It is used in targeting, CX, service and other applications. For example, Amazon and Netflix already have AI features that offer buying recommendations and help with transactions. Another example of AI is in self-driving cars. It is expected that AI applications will only increase in the future. They will be used in marketing strategy because of their accurate ability to track consumer behaviour and will be able to take decisions to create an interactive and highly personalized experience.

- **Blockchain technology:** Blockchain is a decentralized digital ledger that is the basis for highly secure applications. In business, blockchain technology serves as a basis for preventing fraud and secures customer transactions.

- **Chatbots:** AI-based chatbots will be able to have 'real' conversations, thus increasing UX in a big way. They are being used in brand-focused social messaging platforms.

- **Micro-moment marketing:** Micro-moments are those moments when people use their smartphone to find something. They show the user's intention or need. In these tiny moments, companies can influence consumers. It is not about sending ads but to be able to 'catch' the user in the small window that the micro-moment offers. Thus, companies have to keep themselves visible and encourage engagement at this moment. The concept rests on highly customized content created by AI that reaches the user at that micro-moment.

- **Just-in-time (JIT) marketing:** JIT marketing describes the process of creating and delivering marketing content as and when it is needed, at a time when the customer is ready to buy. Hence, the marketing content matches with what consumers are looking for at a particular time and are in the perfect mood to buy. This is quite different from traditional marketing in which content is broadcast so that it reaches mass markets. In the digital era, broadcasting content to disinterested consumers works negatively, but JIT content will be welcomed. A JIT marketing model is a dynamic model that tailor makes campaigns for relevance and timely delivery. It consists of the following:

  o **Analytical buyer model:** JIT marketing is an analytical or predictive buyer model in which the company tracks users on multiple platforms and comes to know when a person is actively considering buying something. Both the message and the time of delivery is determined through data analysis.

o **Time element:** The time element is important because messages sent at the wrong time will be rejected. Companies, thus, have to look for real-time behavioural signals from users which are deciphered as customers interact with apps and their social media activity. The Opening Case in Chapter 3 shows how a retail chain can predict their customers' pregnancy stage by data analysis.

o **Dynamic content:** Dynamic content means that every customer is shown different content more tuned with his/her personal characteristics. It changes as the customer moves across stages in buying behaviour. Companies, thus, invest in digital asset management infrastructure that delivers responsive content placement.

o **Programmatic marketing:** Programmatic advertising is the process of automating the buying and selling of advertisements in real-time through an automated bidding system. Programmatic advertising enables brands or agencies to purchase ad impressions on publisher sites or apps within milliseconds through a sophisticated ecosystem (see Chapter 9). However, while programmatic ads are shown to interested individuals, there is a concern that they may appear next to extremist or violent content. Advertisers, thus, seek greater control on their programmatic efforts.

These developments help us understand what the future of e-marketing will look like. In the next section, we will discuss trends that will impact the short-term and long-term future of digital marketing.

▮ TRENDS AFFECTING DIGITAL MARKETING

The e-marketing landscape shows us that it is changing rapidly. Companies have to be aware of the trends that will affect digital marketing positively and those which will limit its growth. Advertisers have to keep track of these as they may become strong enough to impact their actions. The trends that have emerged over the years are summarized in Table 10.1 and explained in this section.

Rising Trends

Certain developments have the promise to increase the scope of digital marketing greatly. In this section, we will describe such trends.

Contactless Retail

The global COVID-19 pandemic has infused urgency into contactless retail. Although some retailers are using automated checkouts, robots and other methods and technologies for contactless retail have suddenly gained importance. Now, safety protocols demand

TABLE 10.1 *Trends Affecting Digital Marketing*

Rising	Declining
Contactless retail	Concerns for privacy
Location-based targeting	Distrust of social media
Individual segmentation	Data misuse
Predicting consumer needs	Hacking of personal data, surveillance and stalking
Personalization and precise marketing	Price discrimination

that shoppers should avoid crowded stores and that they are able to do their transactions with minimum or no human assistance. This has given a boost to online shopping and transactions worldwide.

Retailers, restaurants, apparel stores, grocers and so on are fast becoming contactless, writes Walton (2020). Combining online methods and emerging technologies, they are reinventing themselves to meet safety requirements. Many customers prefer ordering online than going to physical stores. For their part, physical stores will limit customers from touching objects they are not buying. 'Try and Buy' facilities will be discontinued, and consumers will be offered virtual experiences of products. Online shopping and e-commerce will grow and evolve to the changing times in many ways.

- **E-commerce:** People order goods via their desktops, mobile devices, voice assistants and text messaging platforms, without ever having to leave their homes or interacting with retail employees face to face. People who are not comfortable with online methods or those who do not have online access will also like to switch to e-commerce. Contactless delivery systems make e-commerce more acceptable today. The potential of e-commerce has, thus, increased a great deal.
- **Buy online, pick up in store:** This alternative allows customers to order online through an app and collect the order from a nearby store or locker. The advantage is that delivery charges are saved. This method allows an integration of both the online and in-store experience and is a safe method in which human contact is minimized. Sometimes, the facility of curbside pickup is offered, in which the customer collects the order from a conveniently placed locker. Curbside pickup will become more popular because of safety concerns after coronavirus.
- **Concierge shopping:** Concierge shopping provides a service of performing errands for clients who do not wish to visit retail shops, such as picking up a cake or dry cleaning and other similar jobs. The service is popular with working people and two-income families. It saves users from the effort of going to different shops and has the products delivered at home for a fee.
- **Mobile payments:** Mobile payments facilitate contactless shopping. A number of apps and e-wallets have become popular in recent years, and their popularity is

expected to increase further. A number of stores have devised their own payment systems by which customers can make payments without touching anything. Combined with automated checkouts, the system makes shopping much easier and safer.

- **Checkout-free retail:** Two technologies are already helping checkout-free retail:
  - **Scan and go:** This method allows customers to scan products by their mobile phones with the help of a retailer's mobile app. They walk out with the products, paying by means of a QR code as they exit.
  - **AI computer vision:** AI-enabled computer vision helps automatic billing and payments. It is also completely contactless. Customers scan an app on their phones as they enter a store; then, they pick up products from the shelves into their baskets and walk out. Cameras and sensors in the shelves identify products and charge customers accordingly. Many stores are already switching to scan-and-go concept stores, and they are expected to increase in the future. Amazon Go stores in the USA are enabled by AI-enabled computer vision.

These developments are helping in ushering in the era of contactless shopping. More innovations will no doubt emerge in the future. Businesses are trying to make their physical stores safe to reassure their customers. Scan-and-go mobile apps are expected to become more popular in the future.

Location-based Targeting

Location-based targeting takes advantage of the GPS in the mobile phones of customers to precisely pinpoint their location at any given time and send personalized messages related to the place they are at.

- **Hyperlocal marketing:** Hyperlocal marketing consists of targeting prospects in a very specific and geographically restricted area, such as a shopping area or a street. The method helps in delivering 'near me' offers on mobile phones. It is used to create extremely relevant and specifically targeted messages for customers in that area. Although it can lead to spam and poor UX, companies have to devise ways to make the messages relevant and useful. Hyperlocal marketing helps in community-based marketing and makes use of local influencers to drive sales.

  The technology uses techniques such as geo-fencing, geo-targeting, geo-conquesting and geo-exclusion. An example of location-based targeting is given in the case study on Colgate and Hindustan Unilever in Chapter 1, which explains how visitors at the Kumbh Mela were targeted using these methods. Data about user behaviour is combined with location to create timely and customized user engagement. This helps to create a precise message for the customer, delivered at a precise moment. Two methods that are part of geo-targeting are beacons and hyperlocal marketing. Kumar and Bruner (2007) compare location-based targeting to billboard advertising in traditional marketing, which guides customers to nearby restaurants or petrol pumps.

- **Beacon technology:** Beacons are small, low-energy wireless transmitters that use Bluetooth technology to send signals to smart devices nearby. They are installed at strategic places to send out signals to mobile devices within a range of a few metres. Whenever a user comes within that range, a message is triggered. Beacons enable companies to lure customers to products. For example, when a customer comes near the appliances section in a store, a beacon will send a message guiding the customer towards a special display. Beacons help in location targeting, customer mapping, visit tracking and cross-selling by sending messages for related products.

- **Individual segmentation and personalization:** Traditionally, customer segmentation has been done on demographic and lifestyle data, a standard technique that is taught in consumer behaviour courses. Characteristics such as age, income, education and lifestyle have served as the basis of segmentation. However, these are not very accurate predictors of behaviour but serve as clustering techniques. Today, segmentation is done on the basis of customer data, helping companies to target every single customer separately and deliver tailor-made experiences. So accurate are data-driven techniques that they can predict when a customer may buy a product. This is called 'segment-of-one' marketing, which is the ability to track and understand individual customers.

  Individual segmentation means that companies have the ability to track individual customers and understand their needs. It combines the data of individual customer behaviour with precisely targeted service delivery. Digital technologies allow personalization and customization. One aspect is personal messaging. The second aspect is personalizing products and services. Today, companies are allowing users to choose their own colours and styles in products ranging from apparel to cars.

  The method helps to deliver a personalized experience to every individual customer. It is achieved by creating a digital ecosystem based on data analytics and unique interface design. Segment-of-one marketing results in insight-driven personalization and customer attribution.

- **Predictive analytics:** Thanks to a very large amount of data, companies are becoming better at predicting consumer needs. With technological advancement, phones will be able to track their owners' context and need states. Through ML, they will be able to predict what their owners want, then deliver it before asking. Soon, devices will fully understand the mindsets of owners, which will result in content and experiences delivery based on that understanding. It is like having a microchip inside one's brain, tracking people at all times.

- **AI:** AI is enhancing marketing in many ways. Some of the applications that are being used are forecasting, visual search capabilities, customer insights, predictive analytics, chatbots and so on (see Marketing Insight 10.2).

MARKETING INSIGHT 10.2 *Using AI in the Fashion Industry*

As technology frontiers expand, diverse industries are using AI capabilities to assist in various functions such as purchasing, managing inventories, customer assistance and management. This case study describes AI in the fashion industry, which has embraced technology that helps in various ways, from design, operations to customer management. Several companies are using AI applications in a big way.

In the future, AI will be used in a variety of ways and applications: predicting fashion trends, enhancing customer engagement and CRM, getting accurate customer insights, dynamic pricing and co-creation with customers and personalization. AI can serve as virtual assistants to customers and provide specific recommendations to them based on their personal preferences. Fashion design of the future will, thus, combine creativity with technology.

- **Predicting trends:** Amazon's AI fashion designer system scans images to learn about fashion and trends and use that learning to generate designs. IBM Watson is being used to predict fashion in Indian movies through an analysis of images of celebrities, fashion shows and Indian clothing.
- **Inventory management:** A crucial area of control in the fashion industry is how much stock to keep. Excess stock means huge cash investment and unsold stocks in an industry where tastes change quickly. AI systems can help in demand forecasting, and ML algorithms can help make better manufacturing and inventory decisions. By generating predictions and designs, AI helps designers to track trending colours, patterns and styles and manufacture only those designs that are likely to be sold quickly. It can help manufacturers and retailers with predictive forecasting, capacity planning and merchandising and reducing lead times between manufacturing and display. The trend is catching up in India as well. In the process, it will free up designers to invest time for their creative work.
- **Customer connect:** AI helps in building customer connection. For example, IBM collaborated with Tommy Hilfiger and other technology firms to develop AI systems to provide CX and better functionality for designers. AI chatbots help in interacting with customers. Companies thus save money by hiring less staff even though the customers can get advice whenever they need it. Tommy Hilfiger's Facebook Messenger chatbot offers a shopping experience personalized for each customer. These chatbots help users to browse the designs based on their personal style preferences and make product recommendations as they go along. They become better and better as they use ML technology to learn about customer tastes. An example of a customer interface is that of Levi's 'Virtual Stylist', through which customers interact with the company just the way that they would with a shop assistant. The added advantage is that the system collects the wisdom of style experts and therefore is a wise assistant, so to speak. Customers can access the virtual assistant through Facebook Messenger anytime they want. Such a system enhances customer access and experience, and AI is able to provide company expertise as and when required. Customers feel as if they are in conversation with a real person. The Virtual Stylist, thus, becomes a highly learned and efficient personal shopping assistant who is available at all times. The Levi's website says that its chatbot gets real-life training that is available to its store stylists.

Customers can interact with it and clear doubts about their preferred design and fit, and the chatbot combines their choices with the availability of products.

- **Personalized recommendations:** AI-based systems track purchase data and learn about the styles that customers want to buy. This knowledge is used to make precise and personalized recommendations to customers, who save time as they do not have to browse the entire catalogue. An example of this is Stitch Fix, which offers 'personal styling for everybody'. Customers are asked to make a profile which is analysed by AI to offer clothing combinations to customers. The company delivers a personalized selection of clothes to customers, who pay for the clothes they keep and return the rest.
- **Returns reduction:** Returns add considerable cost for retailers. AI systems help in reducing returns by providing clear details and pictures, answering queries and all the information for customers to make good decisions, which helps reducing returns. Many fashion retailers use AI to recommend styles and sizes to customers based on their past purchases for returns reduction.
- **Product discovery:** AI helps in another way—by using visual search and product discovery. Customers post pictures of what they want, and the AI tool searches for it across sites and retailers. An example of this is Google Lens, through which users take pictures of a product, and search for similar styles through Google Shopping even if the customer cannot describe the style in words.

AI has many applications in the field of business. Many other applications will no doubt come in the future.

What other AI applications have a great role to play in the functional aspects of the industry?

Sources

Bhushan, K. 2018. 'How Artificial Intelligence Is Empowering Designers in India.' *Mint*, 14 August. Available at: https://www.livemint.com/AI/tdxtlGYRklB16h8rWj7A2H/How-Artificial-Intelligence-is-empowering-designers-in-India.html (accessed on 10 February 2021).

Levi Strauss & Co. 2017. 'Levi's Launches New "Virtual Stylist" Online Feature.' Available at: https://www.levistrauss.com/2017/08/31/levis-launches-new-virtual-stylist-online-feature/ (accessed on 10 February 2021).

■ DECLINING TRENDS

Despite its growth, there are several threats to digital marketing which may well derail how it works. How these trends play out in the future will impact digital marketing in a big way.

- **Concerns for privacy:** Today, immense individual data is used and manipulated by both companies and governments. As a consequence, concerns for privacy may well cause people to limit their digital gadgets. Governments are also enacting data privacy laws which may restrict the use of data from personal devices. For example, residents of Hong Kong have been deleting content from their social media accounts or getting rid of their accounts altogether after China passed its security law (*The Economic Times* 2020). Other governments, too, have been using social media content to crackdown on dissent. If this trend amplifies, digital marketing and data analytics methods may well be stymied, at least in such countries.

- **Digital detox:** Fake news, hateful posts and calls to violence are evidence of manipulating and brainwashing users. People are also realizing that heavy dependence on digital devices is leading to stress and anxiety. Work follows executives even to their homes and bedrooms. The need to detox digitally is now being expressed widely. Some people are switching digital devices off for varying periods of time. There are also reports of people deleting their social media accounts and limiting the use of digital devices.

- **Digital addiction:** Many people are realizing that apps are causing dangerous addiction to them. Companies use neuroscience to get people addicted to their apps. Haynes (2018) writes, 'Platforms like Facebook, Snapchat, and Instagram leverage the very same neural circuitry used by slot machines and cocaine to keep us using their products as much as possible.' The addiction is fast turning into a disease. The World Health Organization has included 'gaming disorder' as a disease, which refers to the inability of a person to stop gaming (World Health Organization 2018). Google (n.d.), too, has recognized the problem and says, 'We believe technology should improve life, not distract from it.' Its 'Digital Well-being' app has been downloaded almost 2 million times, and its well-being website encourages people to focus tech-time, unplug more often, minimize distractions and find balance as a family. There is clearly a concern among health and digital corporations that addiction could well blow out of proportion and cause public health disruptions that could derail spread of the digital in the future.

- **Stalker ads:** Hyper-targeted online ads are becoming increasingly common. Such ads follow the users persistently, whether they are visiting websites or using their social media sites. Following the online activities of users, advertisers know what they are looking for and start sending advertisements for those things. Every search becomes the basis of sending ads on whatever one subsequently does online. This may help consumers, but they can well be quite annoying. This is illustrated by the example of a user who reported that he searched for a coffin when his wife died. Later, whenever he was online, he would see advertisements for funeral services!

Ads may often be mistargeted, for instance, if one orders something for a friend, algorithms will keep sending ads for related products to the user. Irritating pop-ups, autoplay videos and the like further irritate users.

For these reasons, stalker ads are disliked by many users. A report by Pew Research (Heimlich 2012) shows that 68 per cent of Internet users do not like search engines and websites tracking their online behaviour to show them targeted ads. John, Kim and Barasz (2018) write that people do not like targeted ads in the same way that they do not like to be gossiped about. Companies getting information from other sites visited by a user are, in a way, indulging in collecting and spreading digital gossip. Hyper-targeting may well be seen as creepy by users, they write, which may reduce users' digital dependence.

- **Surveillance:** Increased surveillance by employers and governments is causing users to be careful about using digital media. There have been reports that people have lost their jobs for their social media posts. Worse, governments are using social media posts to jail people for holding political views. While dictatorships have traditionally censored free speech, *The Guardian* (Ingram 2019) reports that countries across the free world are formulating laws to imprison people who either post harmful content or those who disagree with governments. In India, too, social media posts have landed a large number of people in jail. To avoid such consequences, many users are using social media less or avoiding it altogether. This trend could well derail data analytics of the future.

- **Distrust of social media:** Although social media is widely used, distrust is building up against it. The misuse of social platforms in influencing voters has dented the credibility of social media and even of celebrity influencers. Erskine (2019) writes that instead, companies are opting to communicate with customers on messaging apps instead of social media. If this trend continues, we may well see a different digital landscape in the future.

- **Data misuse:** Data misuse occurs when personal data acquired for a particular purpose is used for other purposes for which it was never intended. Data misuse is the main reason for the loss of consumer trust. One way that users reduce their online footprint is by installing ad blocker software.

- **Hacking of personal data:** Hackers who steal personal data from sites and sell it or put details of users on the dark web further erode trust in digital methods. Data breaches are common and widespread. When credit card numbers and passwords are stolen it creates problems for users worldwide. With the emergence of IoT, home appliances, too, pose a threat to personal data (see Marketing Insight 10.3).

- **Price discrimination:** Data analytics and AI pose another problem for shoppers—their ability to extract higher prices from customers. Online companies not only have the data but are also able to conduct price experiments by showing different prices to different customers to see how they can increase prices and profit more from customers. The ability to change prices by the day or even by the hour gives immense power in the hands of companies. For example, the price of soft drink in a vending machine can now vary with the temperature: On warm days, customers pay a little more. Similarly, the price of the headphones may depend on how budget conscious a user is, as evidenced by his web history. Useem (2017) writes that companies are trying to regain some of the pricing power that they had lost through dynamic pricing methods. Using geographical location, for instance, an online business can figure out whether a consumer lives near a supermarket. If not, prices in those locations are adjusted on the higher side.

Using customers' data trail, companies use sophisticated algorithms and insights from economists and behavioural scientists for making price strategies. Which raises a bigger question: Could the Internet, whose transparency was supposed to empower consumers, be doing the opposite?

Online retailers now have the ability to exploit customers' varying willingness to pay. They conduct experiments that can generate demand curves for each individual so as to offer prices for the best profits. They also know how to present the best prices to customers; they are shown heavy discounts against a list price, tempting a purchase. An item costing ₹449, for instance, is shown as being offered at a 50 per cent discount on a list price of ₹899, even though its actual price was ₹399. This has been applied in non-standard items that do not have a list price. Prices are not fixed in the online world but change as per several variable factors.

The Amazon Selling Coach, for example, is a system that helps third-party vendors optimize their inventory and prices and is built to manage consumers' perception of price. The software identifies some goods for which prices are kept in line with competitors' prices, but everything else is priced higher. Using simulations on Netflix, Shiller (2014) found that using demographics alone to modify prices could increase profits by 0.14 per cent. But if users' web-browsing history was added to the analytics, it could result in an increase in profits by 14.6 per cent. Such pricing techniques work against the interest of the consumer.

- **IoT:** IoT allows users to control the environment and appliances of their homes, even remotely. Combined with AI, it can be used to place automated orders. But hacking and cyberattacks make this technology danger prone (see Marketing Insight 10.3). Consumers may become wary of using it if high profile hacking attempts succeed in the future.

MARKETING INSIGHT 10.3   *IoT Threats: Causing Disruption in Homes and Countries*

In the movie, *Live Free or Die Hard*, terrorists hack into computers across the USA causing havoc on the streets. Another movie, *Eagle Eye*, depicts how personal data is used by a computer to play with the lives of people.

Reality has caught up with science fiction. In 2020, it was reported that an Israeli cyberattack had caused a fire and explosion at Iran's heavily fortified and underground Natanz nuclear enrichment plant (*Outlook* 2020). The blast was triggered by a virus that attacked crucial components in the facility. It was similar to the Stuxnet, a virus used as a cyberweapon, which targeted Siemens centrifuges, triggered when it came across a particular number that matched the Natanz plant.

The IoT makes cyber warfare possible but threatens to move it right inside your home, and that threat is becoming real. The Google Home app, for example, allows users to control Google Nest, Google Home and Chromecast devices, which connect lights, cameras, appliances, speakers and practically everything inside a home. One can imagine the havoc that can be created if these controls fell in wrong hands.

People have gradually been giving up control of their personal data in exchange for convenience. Few users actually read the terms and conditions before giving permission to apps to access their personal data. IoT takes data from gadgets and appliances in people's homes. But there is a fear that users do not quite understand the repercussion of these powerful technologies in our everyday lives. Today, data feeds a global system which stores information about the places where we shop, bank, socialize, borrow books and vote. How this data is used is opaque and is not open to investigation and regulation.

One danger was illustrated by Samsung's smart refrigerator, launched in 2015. It allowed users to order groceries right from the kitchen. It also integrated Google's calendar to schedule supplies. But later, it was shown that hackers could gain access to the refrigerator and steal their owner's Gmail passwords. Another experiment in Germany showed that malicious code could be inserted into Philips's Wi-Fi-enabled light bulbs, which could spread throughout a building or even a city and play havoc with the lighting system. The worst fears envisaged in science fiction movies and novels are fast coming true by the IoT.

Data of users can be easily captured by governments, inimical countries and corporations. It is already happening; It was revealed, for instance, that Cambridge Analytica had used Facebook data of millions of people to help the Trump campaign in the USA in 2016. It also showed Russian meddling in US elections. Apart from the misuse of personal data, the incident showed how data can be misused for political ends. Another manifestation of this is the fact that the rise of social media has been accompanied by the rise of right-wing politicians, inequality, violence, populism and fundamentalism across the world. Yakowicz (2015) writes, 'Distributing more information ever more widely has not led us to greater understanding and growing peace but instead seems to be fostering social divisions, distrust, conspiracy theories and post-factual politics.' These reasons are enough to make people wary of digital methods.

Can these threats translate into large scale movement against digital tracking? Can you find other trends that may turn people away from the digital world?

Sources

Olenick, D. 2020. 'Philips WiFi Light Bulb Vulnerable to Attack.' *SC Magazine* (5 February). Available at: https://www.scmagazine.com/home/security-news/iot/philips-wifi-light-bulb-vulnerable-to-attack/ (accessed on 10 February 2021).

Outlook. 2020. 'Israeli Cyberattack Caused Iran Nuclear Site Fire: Report.' 4 July. Available at: https://www.outlookindia.com/newsscroll/israeli-cyberattack-caused-iran-nuclear-site-fire-report/1885682 (accessed on 10 February 2021).

Yakowicz, W. 2015. 'Why Hackers Are Trying to Get into Your Refrigerator.' Inc., 5 February. Available at: https://www.inc.com/will-yakowicz/a-smart-refrigerator-can-take-down-your-business.html (accessed on 10 February 2021).

■ FUTURE OF E-MARKETING

It is not easy to look into the future, especially because the e-marketing landscape is changing rapidly. In the past, predictions have failed, and bubbles have burst. There is

TABLE 10.2 *Future of E-marketing*		
Immediate Future	**Near Future**	**Far Future**
Omni-social presence	Loneliness and isolation	Increased sensory richness
Rise of influencers	Integrated customer care	Online/offline integration and complete convergence
Privacy concerns on social media	Reducing polarization in social media	Social media by non-humans

Source: Appel et al. (2020).

always the desire to try out new methods and technologies, and some work better than others, but companies have to safeguard against following fads.

Appel et al. (2020) have analysed the future of social media in marketing on three levels: immediate, near and far future. Their expectations are summarized in Table 10.2 and explained in this section.

Immediate Future

- **Omni-social presence:** For most consumers, social media increasingly intersects with most aspects of their lives, whether it is entertainment, paying bills, ordering food, booking tickets and so on. Social media platforms also keep adding features to remain relevant. Today, consumers live in an 'omni-social' world, which implies that almost all buying decisions are open to social media influence. That is, social interactivity directly influences consumer behaviour. Companies must explore how they can influence the CDJs which are affected directly by social media.
- **Rise of influencers:** Influencers and opinion leaders have become part of social media marketing. The idea is to use people who have high influence or high online following to plug products explicitly and implicitly. It is an easy way to reach the captive audience of the influencer and is used in both B2B and B2C situations. Celebrities have a huge following and charge heavily for their posts. Smaller brands tend to use micro-influencers who have fewer followers than celebrities. Companies use influencers with other elements of the marketing mix for optimum results. However, there is a downside to influencer marketing; the danger is that many influencers inflate their following by fake accounts, so the actual influence of some followers may be quite less than what they claim. *Scroll* (Ghosh 2019) reports that social media influencers often resort to inflating their following by buying fake followers. The report says that for ₹1,500, people can buy 20,000 followers. The efficacy of using influencers, thus, comes under a cloud and advertisers could turn their back on this method as well.

- **Privacy concerns on social media:** Increasing concerns about data privacy of consumers and their ability to trust brands threaten to derail social media marketing. So far, consumers have not shown much concern for privacy, but with increasing frauds and hacking of personal data, this is a rising threat.

Near Future

- **Meaningful connections:** Social media was supposed to increase friends and connections, but increasingly, it has resulted in cases of loneliness and isolation among users. For companies, the ability to build meaningful connections through brand communities will help in getting them interested users. This ability is not easy to acquire.
- **Integrated customer care:** Companies are already using social media platforms to provide customer care and service. They are using such platforms to answer customers' queries and communicating solutions to them. Social media-based customer care is expected to increase in the future, becoming more customized and personalized. Although companies provide apps for the purpose, direct messaging on social media is easier and faster.
- **Reducing polarization in social media:** Social media has turned out to be a place used by politicians and governments to polarize the public. Edelman (2018) found that nearly half of the consumers surveyed believed brands to be complicit in negative aspects of content on social media such as hate speech, inappropriate content, or fake news. To remain relevant, social media platforms will have to make sincere efforts to reduce polarization.

Far Future

Certain developments will affect the future of social media for the long term. These trends are already visible and are expected to increase in the future.

- **Increased sensory richness:** The Internet allows for a rich sensory presence. From pictures and text, users can post videos and multimedia. This trend is expected to increase further. Hashtags, calls-to-action and payments systems have already been incorporated in social media. In the future, there will be a further blurring of lines between offline and online worlds. Augmented reality (AR) will be used in a big way. For example, Ikea has an AR app that allows users to take photos of a space which is measured exactly, to show what a piece of furniture would look like in that space. L'Oréal has a mobile app called Makeup Genius that allows consumers to virtually try on makeup. It has also developed AR apps for hair colour and nail polish, as well as integrating AR into mobile e-commerce web pages for the luxury beauty brand Lancôme.

- **Online and offline convergence:** Since consumers shift from online to offline worlds easily, companies have to take an integrated view of the business. In the future, there will be even further blurring of lines between offline and online, changing how customers and companies interact with one another. Companies cannot take the view of online being separate from offline but will have to develop systems so that online and offline activities complement each other.

- **Social media by non-humans:** AI techniques have already made their presence felt in online marketing. Social bots, which are automated computer algorithms that automatically produce content and interact with social media users, are now part of social media platforms. Varol et al. (2017) write that an estimated 15 per cent of active Twitter accounts are bots. Having human names, they interact like human beings, and very often, users think they are interacting with humans. Stocking and Sumida (2018) write that most people cannot recognize that they are interacting with bots instead of human agents on social media. Some of these bots are benign when they act as information aggregators, but others spread misinformation and steal personal information. Given the mischief done by fake news and fake followers, social media platforms will have to regulate their use.

- **Insight-driven personalization:** One-to-one marketing helps a company to deliver individualized content to recipients. Personalization is achieved through data collection and analytics, creating contextual content and communicating with each customer individually. E-commerce sites, for instance, track what a customer is viewing online, and they dynamically change the page so that other relevant products are also displayed, easing the individual's search process.

- **Customer attribution:** Customer attribution means linking of sales and conversions to consumer touch points. This helps identify the points where marketing interventions would yield the best results. As a next step, companies can create customized journeys which can result in better customer acquisition and delivering better CX.

- **Data management platforms:** Data management platforms are required to manage data from a variety of sources with which a user interacts. Data sets from the users' browsing, social media activity, third party data and data from IoT streams are stored and analysed to learn about customers and their behaviour. Since the data tracks users on every intimate detail, it is very accurate and helps in precisely targeting individual customers. This can lead to micro-segmentation, a technique that groups small numbers of customers exhibiting similar behaviour to predict their precise needs. Customers in each micro-segment behave in predictable patterns. Hence, companies can direct specific marketing actions to each micro-segment for improved conversions at a considerably less marketing cost.

The large amounts of data give rise to machine analytics. Companies are investing in big data analytics capabilities, described in the next section.

BIG DATA ANALYTICS

Big data analysis consists of tracking data from diverse sources using advanced tools. Data is generated by users every minute, such as:

- Data left behind as people use browsers to do anything
- Data shared voluntarily by users on e-commerce and social media sites
- Blogs, posts, comments and reviews
- Data generated from gadgets in users' homes
- Data generated by the use of assistants such as Alexa and Google
- Data from stores and supermarkets such as purchase history, credit card usage and personal preferences
- Location and GPS data

All this data is collected and analysed for consumer behaviour insights.

With so much hyper-targeting, websites seem to have acquired the right to follow anyone who visits them. The ability of companies to track and individuals and target them brings forth a new dimension in digital marketing methods: that of ethics. Future online marketing methods must deal with questions about the ethical use of personal data.

ETHICS IN DIGITAL MARKETING

Consumers, today, give up their personal data to corporations in exchange for convenience in their shopping experience. The question of ethics arises because personal data is used for a variety of purposes without users' knowledge or consent. For instance, face recognition technology may be used to recognize customers and assist in automatic purchase and payments, but it can also be used by governments to track a person.

AI pushes the applications even more. It is rapidly evolving and is used in new ways every day. Both the volume of data and its personal nature have a major impact on the lives of people. Since AI combines personal and public data, emails, business transactions, surveys, financial data, and many other types, it has become imperative that it does not lead to harm to people or society.

IBM Solution Architect Jain (2019) defines ethics as 'Following the moral principles that prevent misuse of personal, public or corporate data that otherwise can result in discrimination or harm to the people.' There are several main aspects of ethics related to data:

- Data security, to prevent unauthorized access
- Unauthorized buying, selling or sharing of personal data with others
- Inflating number of followers of influencers
- Using followers or bots to attack competitors
- Inflating number of clicks on advertisements
- Targeting vulnerable sections of society

Data Security

Data privacy issues have been discussed for several years in several global forums, and various laws and regulations have got implemented in many countries. The use of data must ensure that algorithms are used or devised, which are fair and justifiable to all sections of society. So far, strong regulations governing AI-based processes do not exist, and organizations have their own guidelines that they may or may not follow.

However, AI-based decisions impact people's lives in many different ways. As more and more companies and governments adopt AI, these will have direct, indirect and long-term impacts on people and society. The European Union has enacted a law, the General Data Protection Regulation, which requires that people know, understand and consent to the data collected about them.

Public data is used to make decisions that can impact people directly or indirectly. A person's personal data can also impact others as algorithms make decisions based on common behaviour patterns. Very often, decisions are made using public or private data without taking consent.

The use of data by AI can impact society as follows:

- **Targeted campaigns:** When consumers are targeted specifically by AI predictions, it may cause a minor inconvenience to a major embarrassment if incorrect targeting is done.
- **Social and political influence:** An AI model could start targeting people to influence their social, political or ethical beliefs. The Facebook–Cambridge Analytica scandal in US 2016 election is an example of how personal data of millions of people was utilized for political gains. The information collected was detailed enough to create a profile which suggested what kind of advertisement would be most effective to persuade a particular person in a particular location for political events.
- **Financial decisions:** AI decisions can hurt consumers if they are grouped in high-risk categories. A post on Facebook about users' drunken parties or a penchant for outdoor risky sports, for instance, can put them in high-risk category and rates on loans and insurance policies will be increased as a result.
- **Legal and justice:** Theoretically, AI reduces the possibility of bias, but if an algorithm predicts the possibility of the crime being committed in the future, it introduces the worst kind of bias among judges. Criminal risk assessment algorithms are designed to analyse a person's profile and calculate a recidivism score that gives the probability of his/her committing a crime again. This impacts the judge's perception—a high score of recidivism will earn a higher sentence. Since risk assessment tools are based on historical data, consumers suffering because of something in their past is very high. Statistical correlations, such as relating low income with a high risk of crime, would actually cause low-income people to suffer. The algorithm could actually amplify such biases because it feeds on a vicious cycle of data.

Society stands at the crossroads of using data for shopping convenience, but it also raises important questions about using it to the detriment of the individual. How society tackles these issues remains to be seen.

Personal Data Misuse

It is said that data is the new oil. This leaves plenty of room to misuse this resource. Companies are tempted to misuse data or sell it to others. Users have no control on how their data is collected or used by companies. Their most intimate details about consumers are tracked, and unethical companies or employees use these unethically. Uber, for instance, has been accused of 'troubling disregard for privacy' and suffers loss of brand reputation. Other companies also have to guard against these unethical practices, which will cause both the company and its customers immense harm.

Inflating Number of Followers of Influencers

Since numbers count in digital marketing, individuals and companies are tempted to increase their followers or post-engagement through unethical methods. Automated bots increase the number of views, causing pay-per-click advertisers to pay for non-existent visitors. Influencers who plug products in their posts also charge on the number of followers and often inflate these figures by unethical methods.

Using Followers or Bots to Attack Competitors

Another unethical practice is to unleash hate speech and unsubstantiated rumours against competitors. Using anonymous means, companies encourage people to post bad experiences or harmfulness of competing products.

Inflating Number of Clicks on Advertisements

Agencies are also known to increase the number of clicks on advertisements to show their heightened efficacy. Many 'work from home' schemes recruit people to click on advertisements for small amounts, causing companies to pay out higher amounts for advertisements.

Targeting Vulnerable Sections of Society

Another unethical—and dangerous—practice is to use profiles to target vulnerable sections of society. E-commerce sites can increase prices for certain classes of customers. Other individuals are charged higher insurance premium based on tracking their personal habits or health history. Too much slicing and dicing data reveals vulnerabilities of people who are at a disadvantage as they can be targeted unfairly.

■ CONCLUSION

Many followers of digital marketing are focused on collecting a large number of likes, followers and shares. The logic is that once a large user base is built up, funds will flow from venture capitalists. However, marketing—whether digital or otherwise—must be based on a sustainable business model. Digital marketing has, therefore, to go beyond measuring likes or shares or the number of app downloads. The ROI on online spends has been found to be quite dismal, which is proved by the closure of early online players; even today, many online businesses struggle to make profits. Companies have to be aware of the evolving e-marketing landscape and be careful of the pitfalls in digital marketing.

More important than the new e-marketing tools that may be developed now and in the future is the traditional wisdom of marketing that will hold good in times to come because the basic laws of economics remain the same. For all their efforts to make their content viral, companies ultimately have to sell a product or deliver a service that generates some revenue. Ignoring these principles leads to digital marketing myopia where digital activities of liking and sharing gain importance over the real task of marketing. Shapiro and Varian (1999) write in their book, *Information Rules,* 'Ignore basic economic principles at your own risk. Technology changes. Economic laws do not.'

The old rules of marketing, therefore, cannot be ignored even as newer technologies are being developed:

1. Companies should have business models that add value for the customer.
2. Product and service offerings should always fulfil stated or latent needs or solve a problem for customers.
3. Companies must have clear revenue streams and not be dependent on capital infusions.
4. Businesses must adjust to change and be agile to respond to unexpected events.
5. Digital methods must assist in developing business in some way; they should not be treated as an end itself.

Digital leadership consists of creating the necessary digital ecosystem that assists in building brands and businesses. This can only be done by a sustained, painstaking effort. It is time that companies learnt to use technology for serving customers in the many ways that are possible today.

SUMMARY

This chapter discusses the benefits and dangers of widespread use of data. It identifies trends that will contribute to the growth of digital marketing, and it also analyses issues which may threaten its growth. It discusses the evolving e-marketing landscape. Some of the trends clearly visible today are the mobile-first strategy, the need to build quality sites, the rise of social media and voice search, and the need to go beyond vanity statistics.

The chapter identifies trends that contribute to the growth of digital marketing, such as the demand for contactless retail, individual segmentation, predictive analytics and customization. It also describes trends that threaten it, such as concerns for privacy, increasing distrust of social media, data misuse and fears of hacking and misuse of personal data.

The future of e-marketing is discussed in the context of e-marketing not being distinct from traditional marketing and that basic economic principles cannot be ignored. The future is attempted to be analysed on three levels: immediate, near and far future. The use of AI, chatbots and virtual reality could well transform CX altogether in the future.

Finally, ethics in digital marketing is discussed related to data security, sharing personal data, inflating the number of users or clicks, using bots to attack competitors and targeting vulnerable sections of society. Future marketing methods will have to deal with these ethical questions if they are to maintain the trust of consumers.

KEY TERMS

Blockchain technology: Blockchain is a decentralized digital ledger that is the basis for highly secure applications. In business, blockchain technology serves as a basis for preventing fraud and secures customer transactions.

Buy online, pick up in store: It is a business alternative that allows customers to order online through an app and collect the order from a nearby store or locker.

Concierge shopping: Concierge shopping provides a service of performing errands for clients who do not wish to visit retail shops.

Contactless retail: Contactless retail uses minimal or no human interaction. It consists of automated checkouts, robots and other methods and technologies.

Ethics in digital marketing: The following of moral principles that prevent misuse of personal, public or corporate data that can otherwise result in discrimination or harm to the people.

Hyperlocal marketing: Hyperlocal marketing consists of targeting prospects in a very specific and geographically restricted area, like a shopping area or a street.

JIT: JIT marketing describes the process of creating and delivering marketing content only when it is needed, at a time when the customer is ready to buy.

LSI: A technique that helps classify and retrieve information on key terms by scanning through unstructured data and identifying relationships between terms and their context to better index these records.

Location-based targeting: Using the GPS in the mobile phones of customers, their location is precisely pinpointed to send personalized messages related to the place they are at.

Micro-moments: Micro-moments are those moments when people use their smartphone to find something.

Mobile first: While content is optimized for mobile phones, it should perform seamlessly across all devices.

Predictive analytics: It is a branch of data analytics that helps in predicting what their owners want and help deliver it.

Programmatic marketing: Programmatic advertising is the process of automating the buying and selling of advertisements in real-time through an automated bidding system.

■ CONCEPT REVIEW QUESTIONS

1. Comment on the present and evolving landscape of e-marketing. How do you see it changing?
2. Why are companies becoming wary of using social media for advertising?
3. What are micro-moments? How can they be used in marketing?
4. Describe JIT marketing. How does it work? What are its advantages?
5. Describe the trends that are affecting digital marketing and may have an impact on its future.
6. What is contactless retail? What are its various methods?
7. Describe the process of location-based targeting. What are the technologies that help location-based targeting?
8. Discuss some applications of AI in business and marketing applications.
9. Discuss the future of social media in marketing in the immediate, near and far future.
10. What are the ethical issues in digital marketing?

■ CRITICAL THINKING QUESTIONS

1. People are increasingly giving up control of their personal data for the convenience of shopping. Most do not even read the terms and conditions required for the subscription to online services. What are the dangers of this? Can it lead to harms to society?
2. At a time when governments are increasingly using AI and surveillance techniques to track dissidents, do you think it will impact the spread of digital marketing? Is it possible that people get rid of their devices to avoid persecution?
3. Digital addiction is becoming a real threat. Companies use neuroscience to get addicted to their apps. Is it ethical? To what extent is it justifiable to get people addicted? Will it impact the digital marketing of the future?

4. What is your assessment of digital marketing of the future? Which of the trends mentioned in this chapter do you agree with and which ones do not appeal to you? Justify your answer.

PROJECTS AND ASSIGNMENTS

1. Undertake a survey among your friends to find out how they use social media to interact with companies and brands. Ask them about (a) the companies they follow on their social media accounts, (b) frequency of their clicking on ads on social media and (c) frequency of purchase or motivation for purchase obtained from their social media accounts.
2. Conduct a survey among your friends regarding their concern for digital well-being. Ask them how much time they spend online, whether they spend too much time on particular sites, and whether they are losing sleep because of their digital activity. What can you say about digital addiction?
3. Conduct a conversation with a chatbot on the website of a company. Make a complaint and see how it responds. Were you satisfied with the response? Did it provide adequate customer service?
4. Talk to the marketing manager of a company. Ask him how digital marketing is evolving in the company and how the future looks like. Make a report about digital marketing of the future based on your interview.

REFERENCES

Appel, G., L. Grewal, R. Hadi, and A. T. Stephen. 2020. 'The Future of Social Media in Marketing.' *Journal of the Academy of Marketing Science* 48, no. 1 (January): 79–95. Available at: https://doi.org/10.1007/s11747–019–00695–1 (accessed on 10 February 2021).

Bruner G. C., and A. Kumar. 2007. 'Attitude toward Location-based Advertising.' *Journal of Interactive Advertising* 7, no. 2 (March): 3–15. Available at: https://doi.org/10.1080/15252019.2007.10722127 (accessed on 10 February 2021).

Buehler, D. R. 2014. *The Digital Delusion: How to Overcome the Misguidance and Misinformation Online to Become the Leader in Your Industry*. Sydney: Digital Delusion.

Edelman, K. 2018. 'Trust Barometer Brands Social Media.' Available at: https://www.edelman.com/research/trust-barometer-brands-social-media (accessed on 10 February 2021).

Erskine, R. 2019. 'In an Era of Social Media Distrust, Some Brands Are Finding Ways to Get Intimate.' *Forbes* (31 January). Available at: https://www.forbes.com/sites/ryanerskine/2019/01/31/in-an-era-of-social-media-distrust-some-brands-are-finding-ways-to-get-intimate/#2ef9fb3d153c (accessed on 10 February 2021).

Ghosh, D. 2019. 'Beware Indian Social Media Influencers Promoting Brands.' 7 April. Available at: https://scroll.in/article/918579/beware-indian-social-media-influencers-promoting-brands-they-may-be-restoring-to-fakery (accessed on 10 February 2021).

Google, n.d. 'Find a Balance with Technology That Feels Right for You.' Available at: https://wellbeing.google/ (accessed on 11 February 2021).

Haynes, T. 2018. 'Dopamine, Smartphones & You: A Battle for Your Time.' Harvard University, 1 May. Available at: http://sitn.hms.harvard.edu/flash/2018/dopamine-smartphones-battle-time/ (accessed on 10 February 2021).

Heimlich, R. 2012. 'Internet Users Don't Like Targeted Ads.' Pew Research, 13 March. Available at: https://www.pewresearch.org/fact-tank/2012/03/13/internet-users-dont-like-targeted-ads/ (accessed on 10 February 2021).

Ingram, D. 2019. 'Foreign Governments Are Fed up With Social Media—and Threatening Prison for Tech Employees.' *The Guardian*, 12 April. Available at: https://www.nbcnews.com/tech/tech-news/foreign-governments-are-fed-social-media-threatening-prison-tech-employees-n993841 (accessed on 10 February 2021).

Jain, A. 2019. 'Ethics in AI—Responsibilities for Data Analysts.' Medium, 11 December. Available at: https://medium.com/ibm-watson/ethics-in-ai-responsibilities-for-data-analysts-part-1–80f113fb5e57 (accessed on 11 February 2021).

John, L. K., O. Emrich, S. Gupta, and M. I. Norton. 2017. 'Does "Liking" Lead to Loving? The Impact of Joining a Brand's Social Network on Marketing Outcomes.' *Journal of Marketing Research* 54, no. 1 (February): 144–155.

John, L. K., T. Kim, and K. Barasz. 2018. 'Ads That Don't Overstep.' *Harvard Business Review* (February). Available at: https://store.hbr.org/product/ads-that-don-t-overstep/r1801c?sku=R1801C-PDF-ENG (accessed on 10 February 2021).

Lee, B. 2012. 'Marketing Is Dead.' HBR Blogs, 9 August. Available at: https://hbr.org/2012/08/marketing-is-dead (accessed on 10 February 2021).

Shapiro, C., and H. R. Varian. 1999. *Information Rules: A Strategic Guide to the Network Economy*. Boston, MA: Harvard Business School Press.

Shiller, B. 2014. 'First Degree Price Discrimination Using Big Data.' Working Paper No. 58, Brandeis University, Department of Economics and International Business School. Available at: https://EconPapers.repec.org/RePEc:brd:wpaper:58 (accessed on 10 February 2021).

Stocking, G., and N. Sumida. 2018. 'Social Media Bots Draw Public's Attention and Concern.' Pew Research, 15 October. Available at: https://www.journalism.org/2018/10/15/social-media-bots-draw-publics-attention-and-concern/ (accessed on 11 February 2021).

The Economic Times. 2020. 'Hong Kongers Scrub Social Media History in Face of Security Law.' 3 July. Available at: https://economictimes.indiatimes.com/news/international/world-news/hong-kongers-scrub-social-media-history-in-face-of-security-law/articleshow/76777320.cms (accessed on 10 February 2021).

Thorbecke, C. 2020. 'Starbucks, Coca-Cola Latest to Join Facebook Ad Boycott.' ABC News, 29 June. Available at: https://abcnews.go.com/Business/starbucks-coca-cola-latest-join-facebook-ad-boycott/story?id=71510778 (accessed on 10 February 2021).

Useem, J. 2017. 'How Online Shopping Makes Suckers of Us All.' *The Atlantic* (May). Available at: https://www.theatlantic.com/magazine/archive/2017/05/how-online-shopping-makes-suckers-of-us-all/521448/ (accessed on 10 February 2021).

Varol. O., E. Ferrara, C. A. Davis, F. Menczer, and A. Flammini. 2017. 'Online Human-Bot Interactions: Detection, Estimation and Characterization.' Available at: https://arxiv.org/abs/1703.03107 (accessed on 11 February 2021).

Walton, C. 2020. 'Contactless Is Retail's New Must-Have Safe Word, but Executing It Is Easier Said Than Done.' *Forbes* (15 May). Available at: https://www.forbes.com/sites/christopherwalton/2020/05/15/contactless-is-retails-new-must-have-safe-word-but-knowing-how-best-to-use-it-is-easier-said-than-done/#1a7e34384758 (accessed on 10 February 2021).

World Health Organization. 2018. 'Gaming Disorder.' 14 September. Available at: https://www.who.int/news-room/q-a-detail/gaming-disorder#:~:text=Gaming%20disorder%20is%20defined%20in,the%20extent%20that%20gaming%20takes (accessed on 10 February 2021).

CLOSING CASE

CONVENIENCE OR SURVEILLANCE?

The futuristic movie, *Minority Report*, describes a time in the future when society is able to predict when crimes would be committed by a person. The world is full of cameras which use face recognition technology. Anyone walking into a retail store is recognized by an eye scan. Tom Cruise, playing the character of John Anderton, walks into a Gap store, his eyes are scanned automatically, and an AI voice greets him by name and asks him about past purchases. His purchase history and preferences are shown on screens.

Companies are using similar technologies today. Smartphones constantly transmit information about the location and habits of users. GPS, Bluetooth, Near-field Communication, cameras and Beacons are all used for hyper-location targeting. Companies build profiles of users based on their online and in-store actions. For example, the amount of time a person spends in a certain area and the items he/she picks up gives an accurate picture of the interests of the person. Technology is being developed through which visitors' photos function as cookies that help in identification and storage of user settings, making loyalty cards obsolete. As soon as a person walks into a store, his/her purchasing history based on camera footage and technology is available to the store staff.

It is not science fiction anymore. Casinos and theme parks click pictures of tourists and display them as they leave, encouraging purchase. Free Internet is provided in tourist places so that people can share their pictures on social media instantaneously, thereby helping the marketing efforts of such attractions.

Indee, a company in Bengaluru, has developed a product FaceTrack, which helps movie producers and TV channels get real-time feedback about consumer reaction of their programmes. The software performs facial analytics on the live feed, and changes in emotions are tracked. FaceTrack employs ML to track facial expressions of viewers and analyses their emotions continuously through a webcam, which helps producers know which scenes work and which ones do not. For instance, the system was able to track the displeasure of the audience when expletives were used in a funny scene. Based on that, the producers decided to drop the scene. The method is much faster than traditional market research, which involved bringing a select audience to theatres to watch a film and have them fill questionnaires.

Scanning technology is used by retailers in a variety of ways. Walgreens uses cameras, sensors and digital screens which immediately create smart displays for individual customers on store refrigerators. Using face-detection technology, it knows the customer's age and gender. Combined with other data such as outside temperature and how long the customer stands there, it presents an advertisement most likely to appeal to the viewer. The refrigerator doors change displays depending on the individual; for instance, if it looks as if the visitor is feeling hot, a display of water or ice cream is shown.

(Continued)

(Continued)

Digital marketing, thus, goes much beyond advertisements and uses technology in various ways, from gauging consumer interest and sentiments to actually assisting sales. It provides consumers exactly what they are looking for, thus enabling sales.

But there is a downside to this as well. The technology can well be used by government agencies to know the political leanings of people and put them in jail. This is happening in countries all over the world. The software could well make a mistake and identify the wrong person as committing a crime. Governments across the world track their citizens and jail them for holding opposing views. This is a real danger in present times.

Customers are today giving up their privacy for the convenience of being recognized by companies. But it may well go beyond simply selling of goods; companies often misuse the data to link a person's health records or medicine purchase history and get to know more about people than they bargained for. They can also make predictions about people.

Technology provides convenience to people. But it also has an ugly downside that is revealing itself now. In the future, companies will have to balance their need to analyse data with society's need to prevent its misuse.

Questions for Discussion

1. In what ways can face recognition technology be used to assist companies in their marketing efforts?
2. What are the dangers of face recognition technology?
3. Will the future of digital marketing be impacted if surveillance technology is used to track the political leanings of consumers?
4. What is the next frontier in digital marketing?

Sources

Christopher, N. 2017. 'Your Expression Is Cue for Movie Makers to Create a Blockbuster.' *The Economic Times*, 11 December.

Louis, M. S. 2017. 'How Facial Recognition Is Shaping the Future of Marketing Innovation.' Inc., 16 February. Available at: https://www.inc.com/molly-reynolds/how-facial-recognition-is-shaping-the-future-of-marketing-innovation.html (accessed on 11 February 2021).

Index

CPSIA information can be obtained
at www.ICGtesting.com
Printed in the USA
BVHW091926250721
612237BV00003B/22